犬夜叉

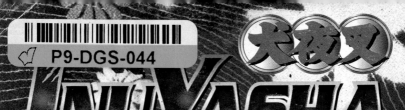

# InuYasha™

## Ani-Manga™ Vol. 5

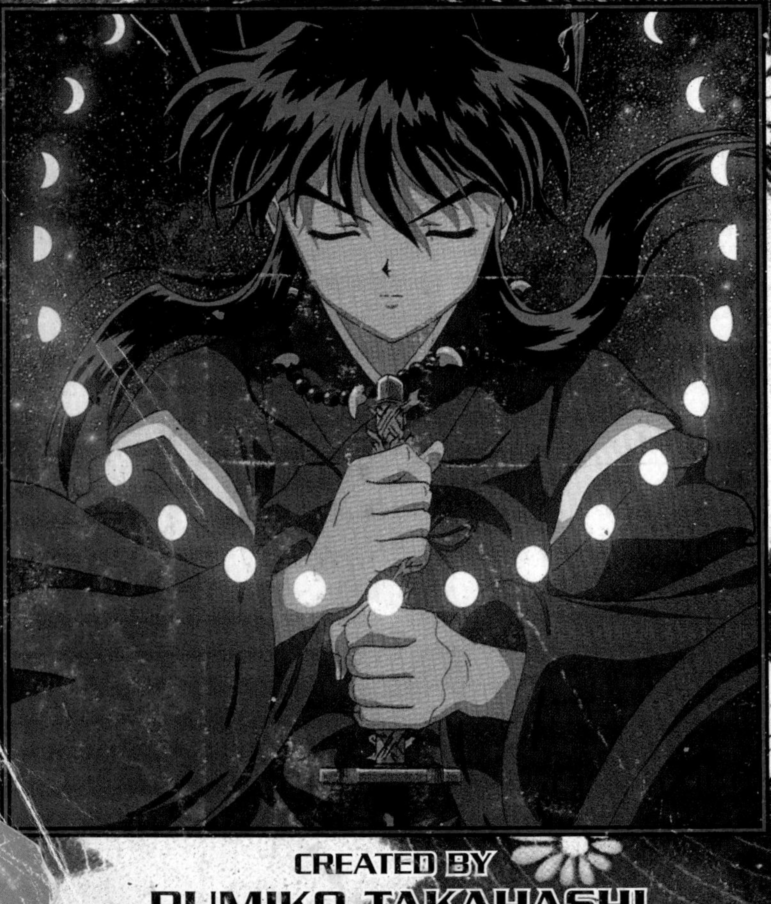

CREATED BY
RUMIKO TAKAHASHI

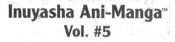

# Inuyasha Ani-Manga™
## Vol. #5

### Created by
### Rumiko Takahashi

Translation based on the VIZ anime TV series
Translation Assistance/Katy Bridges
Lettering/John Clark
Cover Design/Hidemi Sahara
Graphic Design/Andrea Rice
Editor/Frances E. Wall

Managing Editor/Annette Roman
Editorial Director/Alvin Lu
Director of Production/Noboru Watanabe
Sr. Director of Licensing & Acquisitions/Rika Inouye
Vice President of Sales & Marketing/Liza Coppola
Executive Vice President/Hyoe Narita
Publisher/Seiji Horibuchi

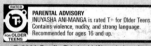

© 2001 Rumiko Takahashi/Shogakukan, Inc.
© Rumiko Takahashi/Shogakukan, Yomiuri TV, Sunrise 2000. First published by Shogakukan, Inc. in Japan as "TV Anime-ban Inuyasha"

"Ani-Manga" is a trademark of VIZ, LLC. New and adapted artwork and text © 2004 VIZ, LLC. All rights reserved. The stories, characters, and incidents mentioned in this publication are entirely fictional. No portion of this book may be transmitted in any form or by any means without written permission from the copyright holders.

Printed in U.S.A.

Published by VIZ, LLC
P.O. Box 77010
San Francisco, CA 94107

10 9 8 7 6 5 4 3 2
First printing, August 2004
Second printing, October 2004

www.viz.com

store.viz.com

# Story thus far

Kagome, a typical high school girl, has been transported into a mythical version of Japan's medieval past, a place filled with incredible magic and terrifying demons. Who would have guessed that the stories and legends Kagome's superstitious grandfather told her could really be true!?

It turns out that Kagome is the reincarnation of Lady Kikyo, a great warrior and the defender of the Shikon Jewel, or the Jewel of Four Souls. In fact, the sacred jewel mysteriously emerges from Kagome's body during a battle with a horrible centipede-like monster. In her desperation to defeat the monster, Kagome frees Inuyasha, a dog-like half-demon who lusts for the power imparted by the jewel, and unwittingly releases him from the binding spell that was placed 50 years earlier by Lady Kikyo. To prevent Inuyasha from stealing the jewel, Kikyo's sister, Lady Kaede, puts a magical necklace around Inuyasha's neck that allows Kagome to make him "sit" on command.

In another skirmish for possession of the jewel, it accidentally shatters and is strewn across the land. Only Kagome has the power to find the jewel shards, and only Inuyasha has the strength to defeat the demons who now hold them, so the two unlikely partners are bound together in the quest to reclaim all the pieces of the Shikon Jewel.

Inuyasha's greatest tool in the fight to recover the shards of the jewel is his father's sacred sword, the Tetsusaiga. The Tetsusaiga's power is only unleashed when it is being used to protect and defend humans... which is pretty frequently, considering the jams that Kagome gets herself into! In addition to troubles of the demon variety, Kagome is struggling to keep up in school. Her frequent trips into the past interfere with her academic studies... and her social life!

犬夜叉

# INUYASHA™

## ANI-MANGA™ Vol. 5

Contents

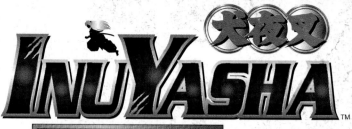

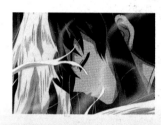

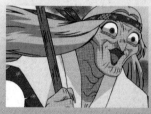

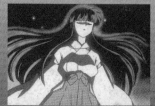

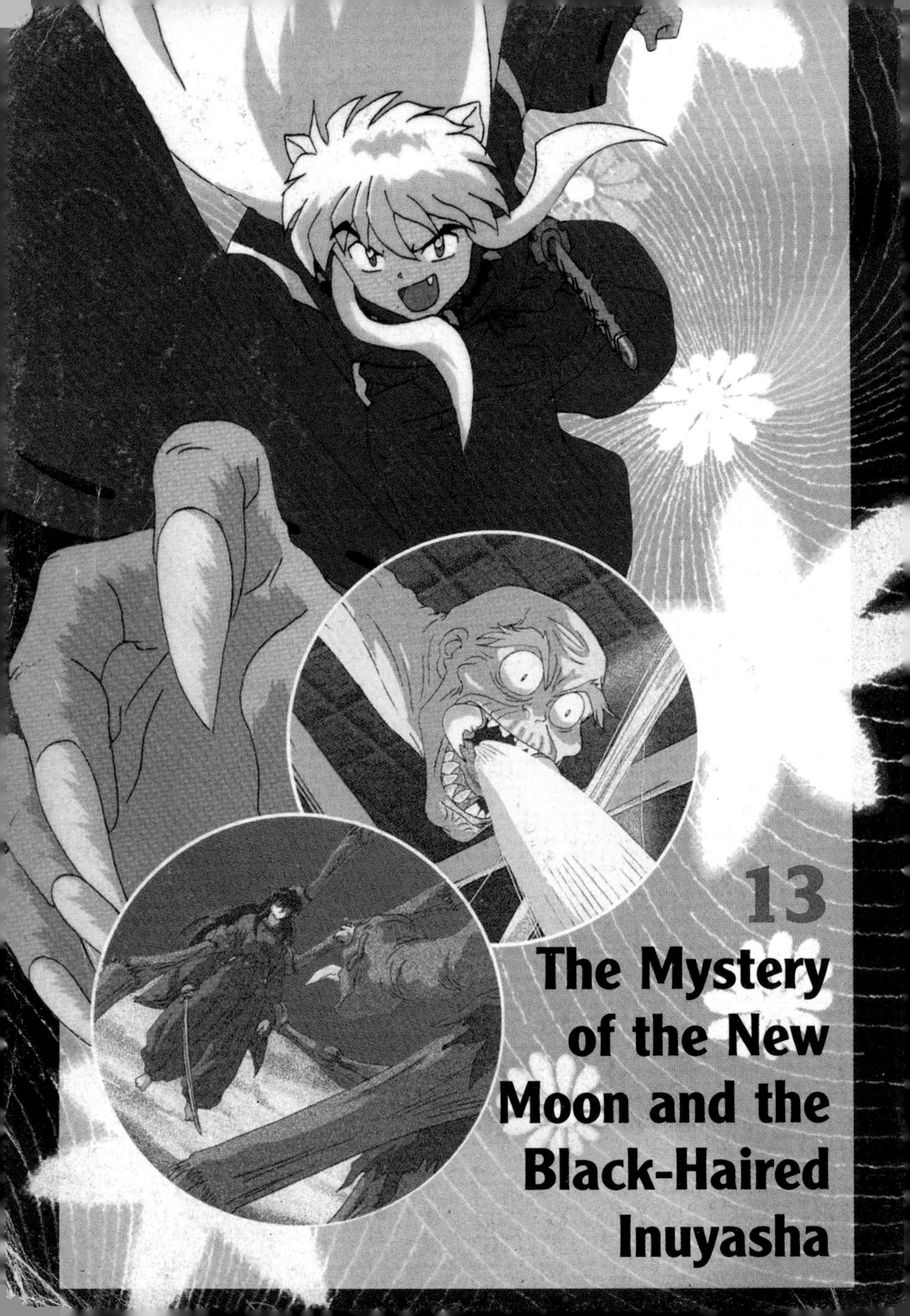

# 13
# The Mystery of the New Moon and the Black-Haired Inuyasha

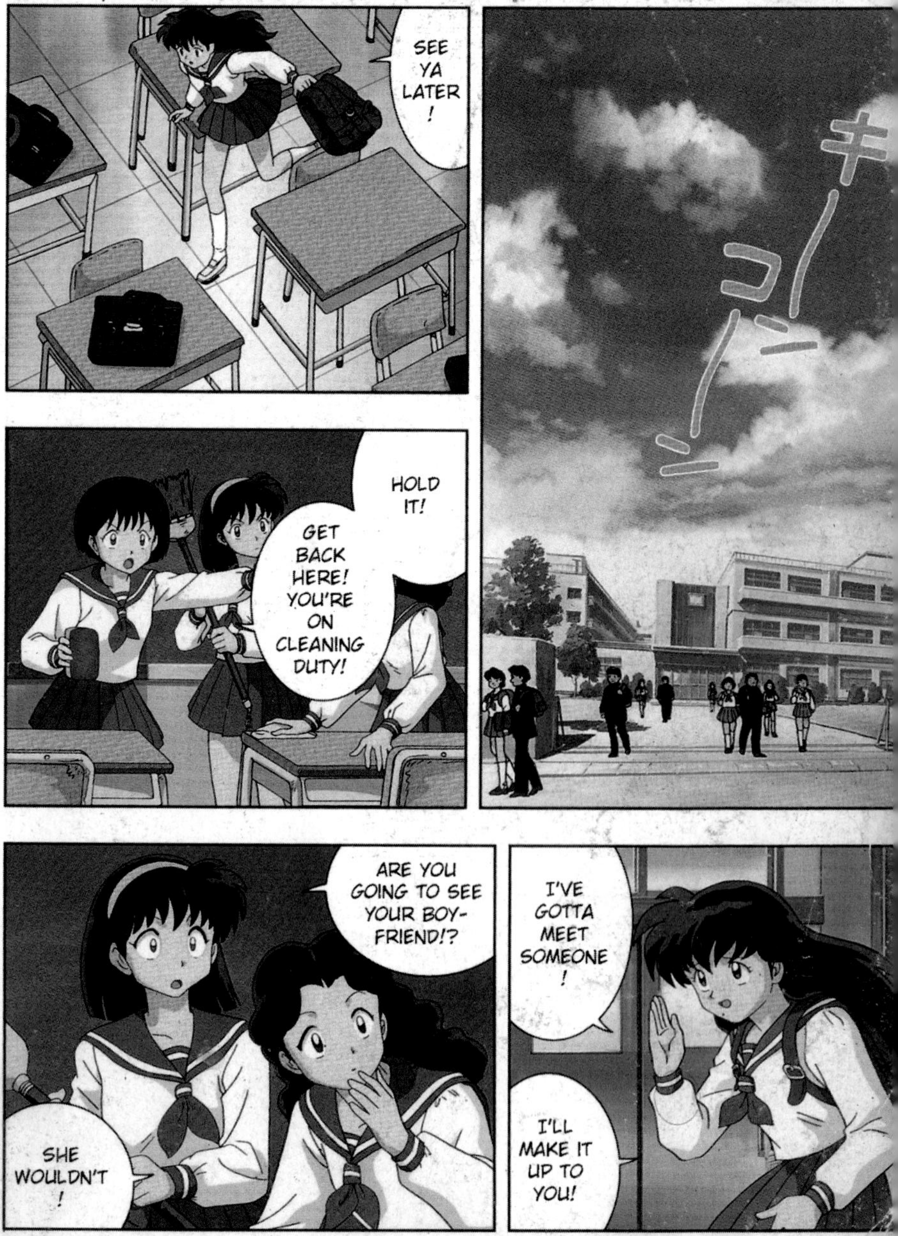

キーンコーン
SEE YA LATER!
HOLD IT!
GET BACK HERE! YOU'RE ON CLEANING DUTY!
I'VE GOTTA MEET SOMEONE!
I'LL MAKE IT UP TO YOU!
ARE YOU GOING TO SEE YOUR BOY-FRIEND!?
SHE WOULDN'T!

I TOLD YOU BEFORE!

I DO **NOT** HAVE A BOY-FRIEND!

BYE! I PROMISE, I'LL MAKE IT UP TO YOU!

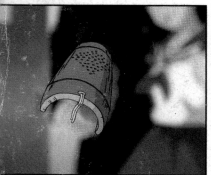

OOF!

OH...

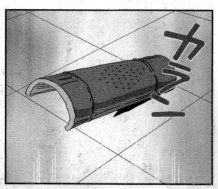

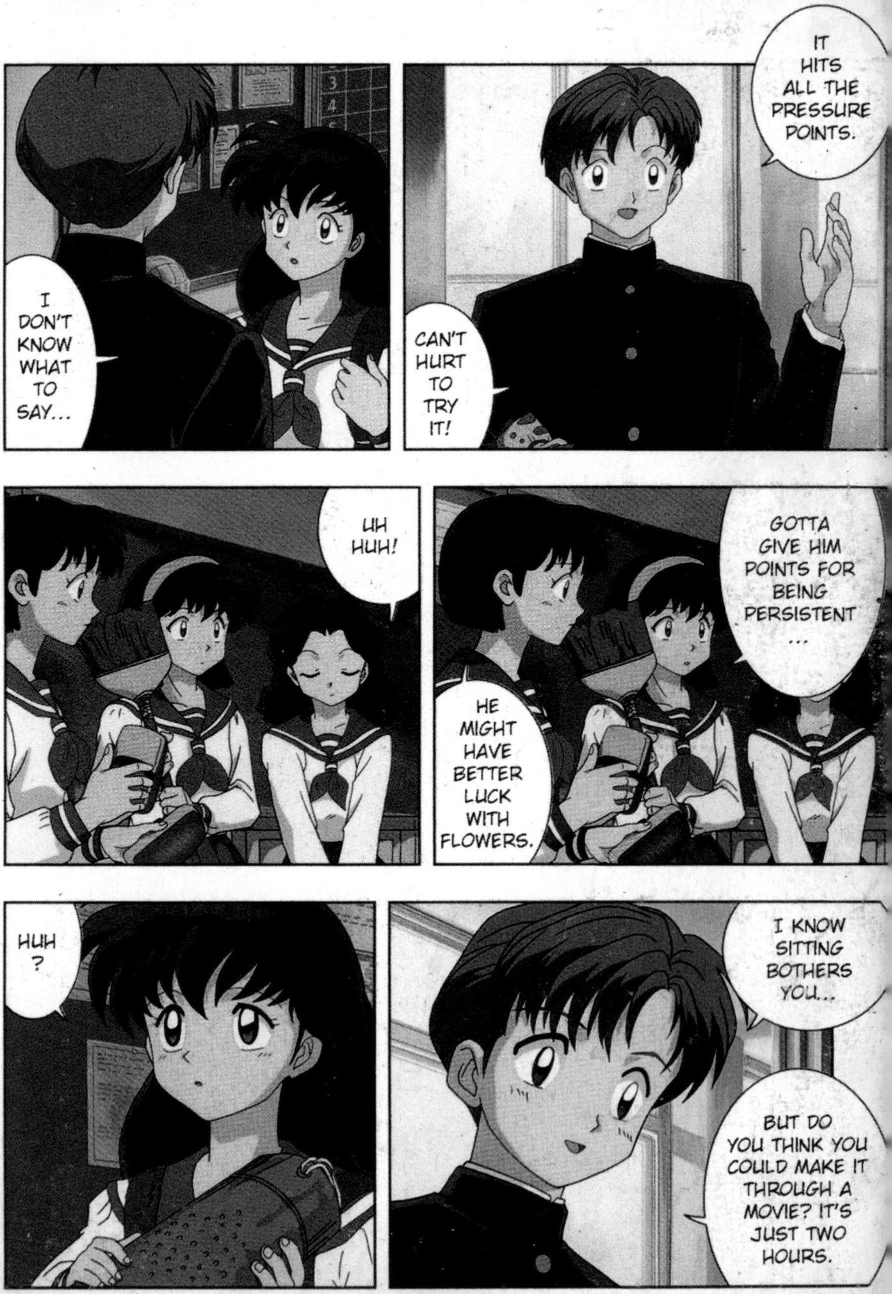
IT HITS ALL THE PRESSURE POINTS.
CAN'T HURT TO TRY IT!
I DON'T KNOW WHAT TO SAY...
GOTTA GIVE HIM POINTS FOR BEING PERSISTENT ...
HE MIGHT HAVE BETTER LUCK WITH FLOWERS.
UH HUH!
I KNOW SITTING BOTHERS YOU...
BUT DO YOU THINK YOU COULD MAKE IT THROUGH A MOVIE? IT'S JUST TWO HOURS.
HUH ?

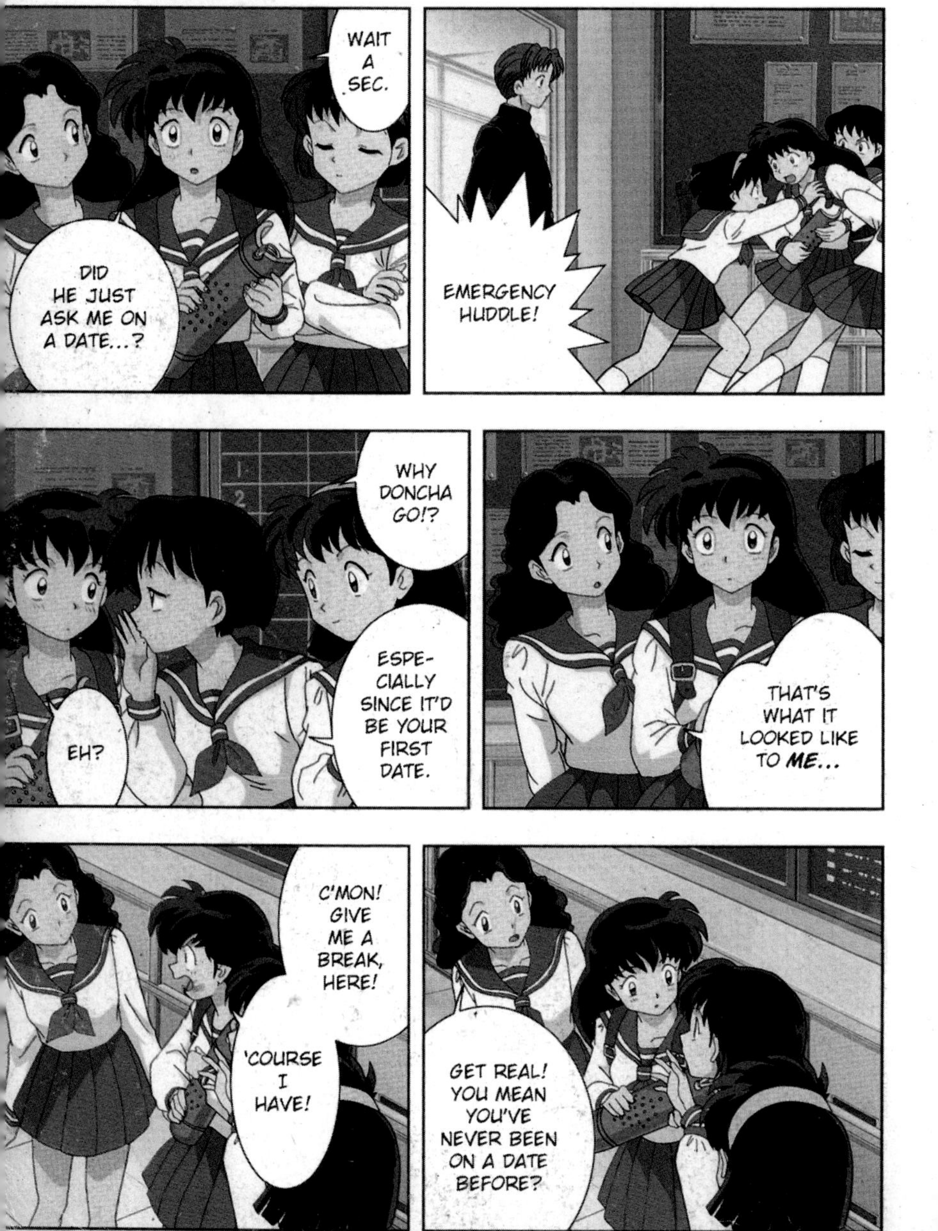
EMERGENCY HUDDLE!
WAIT A SEC.
DID HE JUST ASK ME ON A DATE...?
THAT'S WHAT IT LOOKED LIKE TO **ME**...
WHY DONCHA GO!?
ESPE-CIALLY SINCE IT'D BE YOUR FIRST DATE.
EH?
GET REAL! YOU MEAN YOU'VE NEVER BEEN ON A DATE BEFORE?
C'MON! GIVE ME A BREAK, HERE!
'COURSE I HAVE!

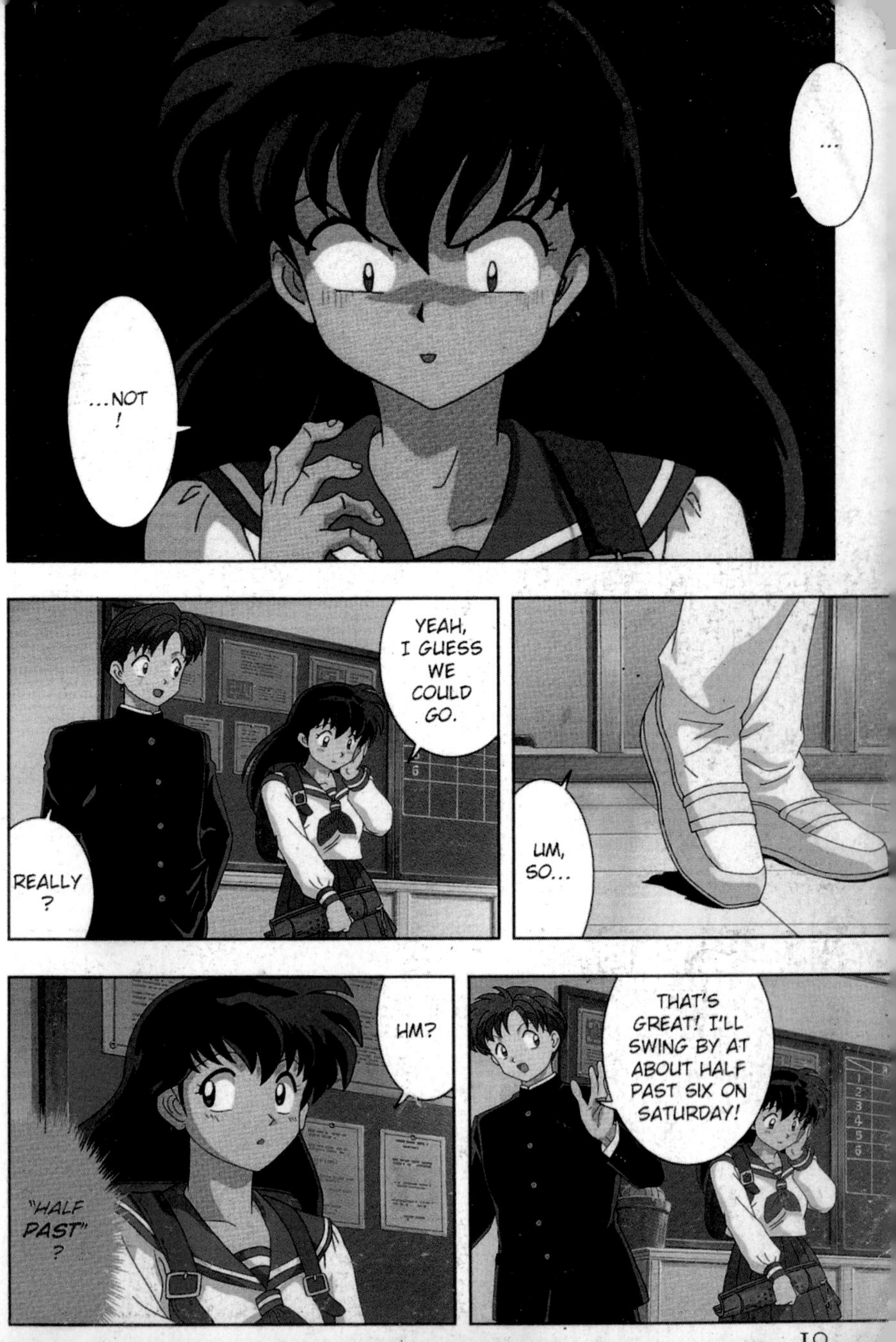
...
...NOT!
UM, SO...
YEAH, I GUESS WE COULD GO.
REALLY?
THAT'S GREAT! I'LL SWING BY AT ABOUT HALF PAST SIX ON SATURDAY!
HM?
"HALF PAST"?

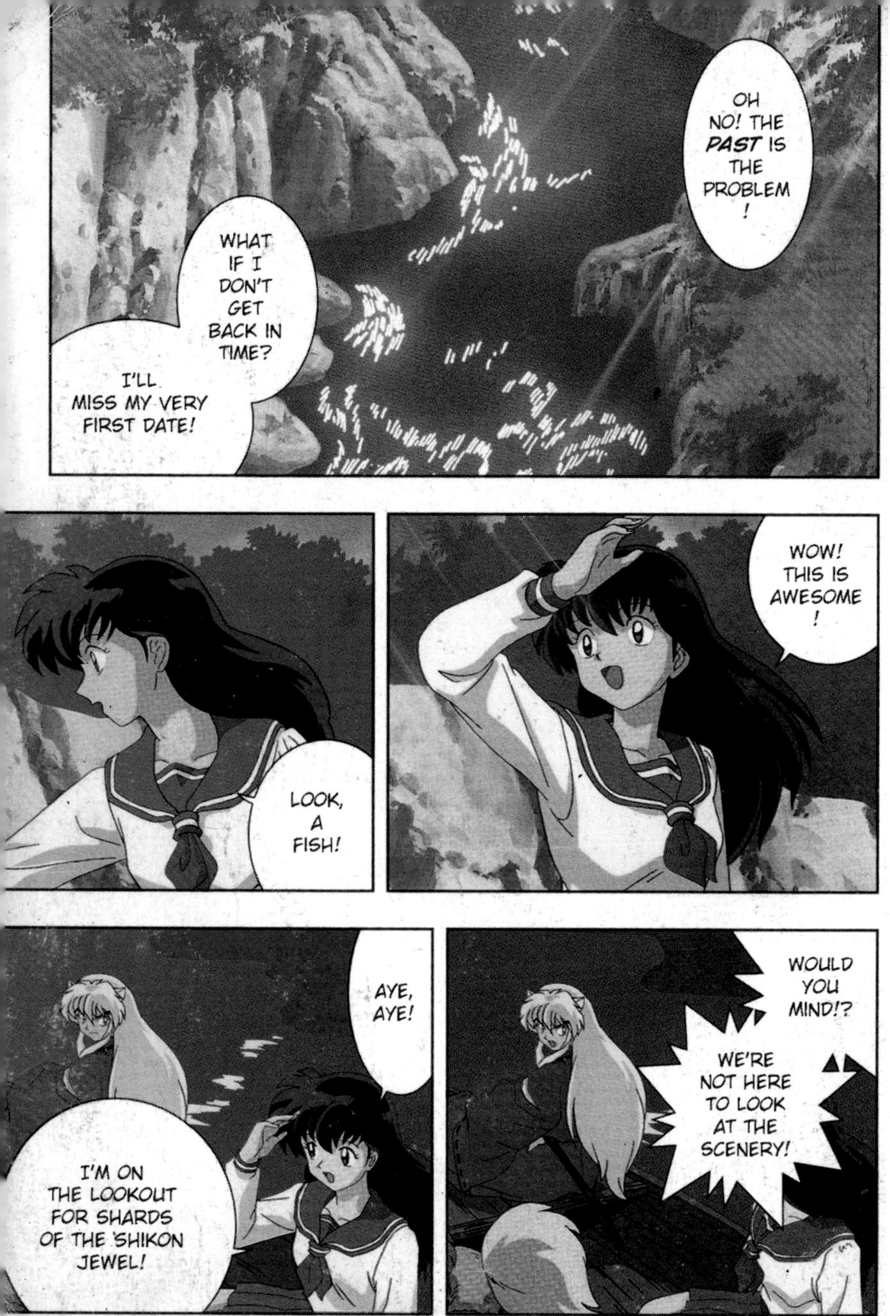
OH NO! THE PAST IS THE PROBLEM!
WHAT IF I DON'T GET BACK IN TIME?
I'LL MISS MY VERY FIRST DATE!
WOW! THIS IS AWESOME!
LOOK, A FISH!
WOULD YOU MIND!?
WE'RE NOT HERE TO LOOK AT THE SCENERY!
AYE, AYE!
I'M ON THE LOOKOUT FOR SHARDS OF THE SHIKON JEWEL!

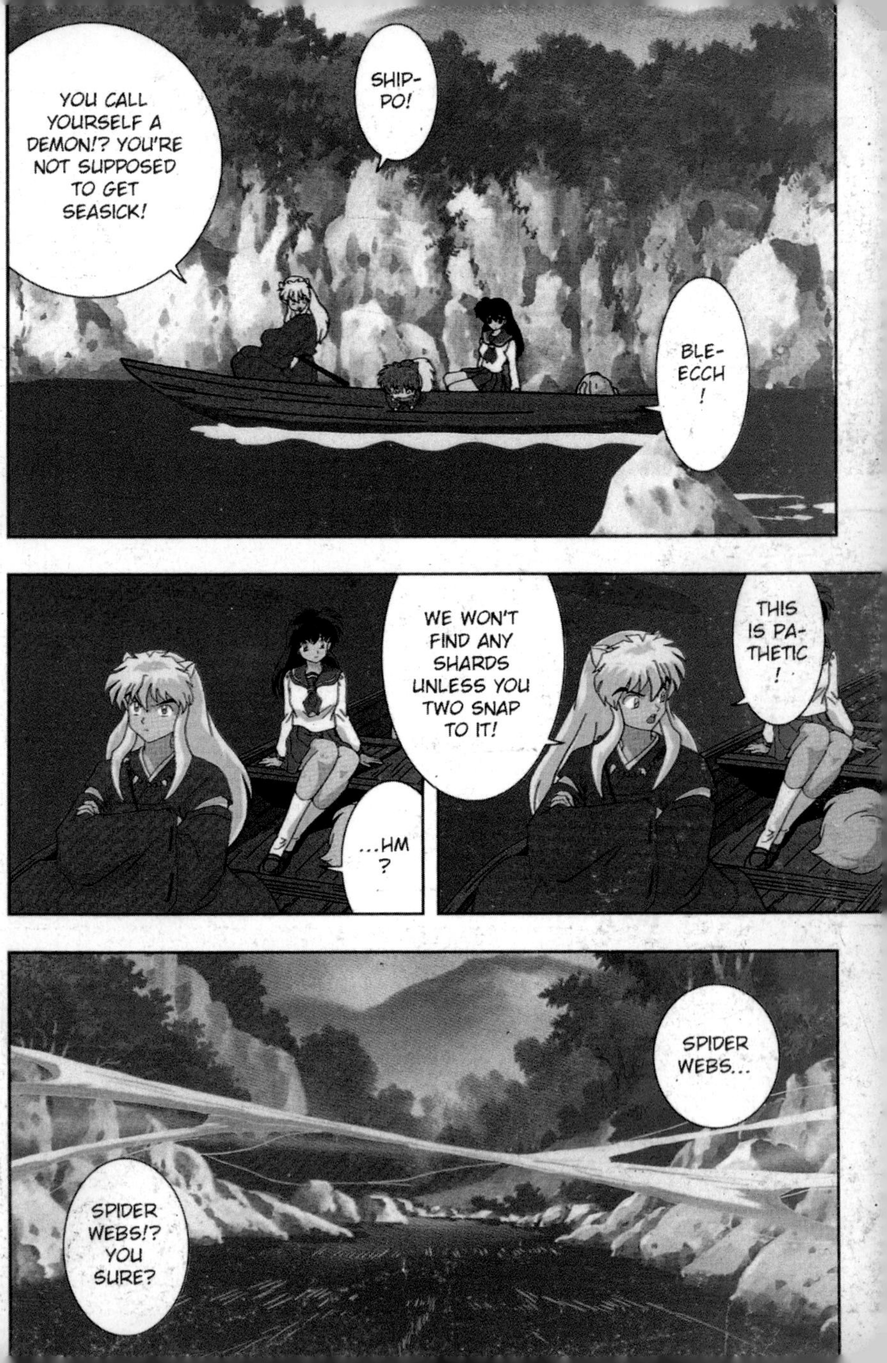
SHIP-PO!
YOU CALL YOURSELF A DEMON!? YOU'RE NOT SUPPOSED TO GET SEASICK!
BLE-ECCH!
THIS IS PA-THETIC!
WE WON'T FIND ANY SHARDS UNLESS YOU TWO SNAP TO IT!
...HM?
SPIDER WEBS...
SPIDER WEBS!? YOU SURE?

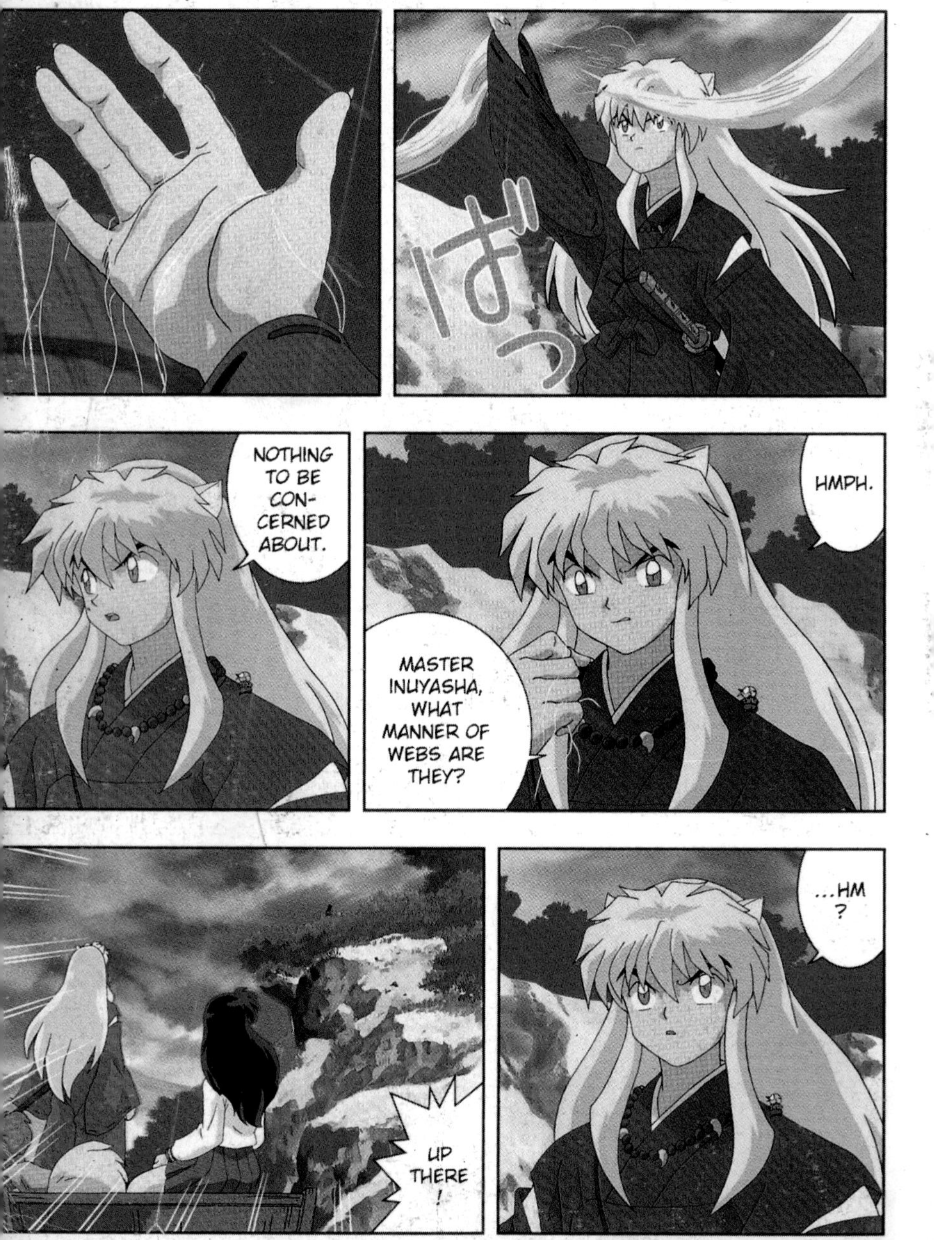
ぼっ
HMPH.
MASTER INUYASHA, WHAT MANNER OF WEBS ARE THEY?
NOTHING TO BE CON-CERNED ABOUT.
...HM ?
UP THERE !

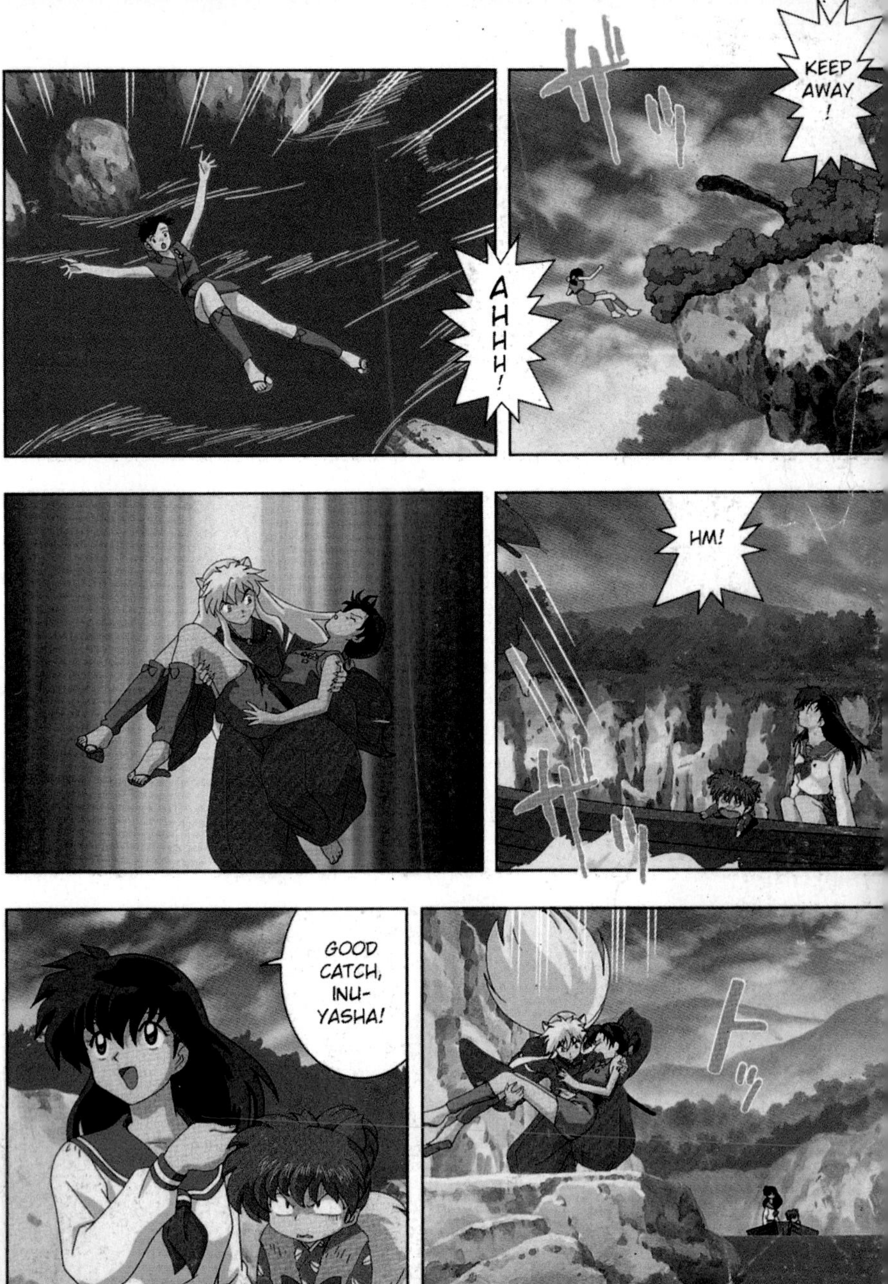
KEEP AWAY!
AHHH!
HM!
GOOD CATCH, INU-YASHA!

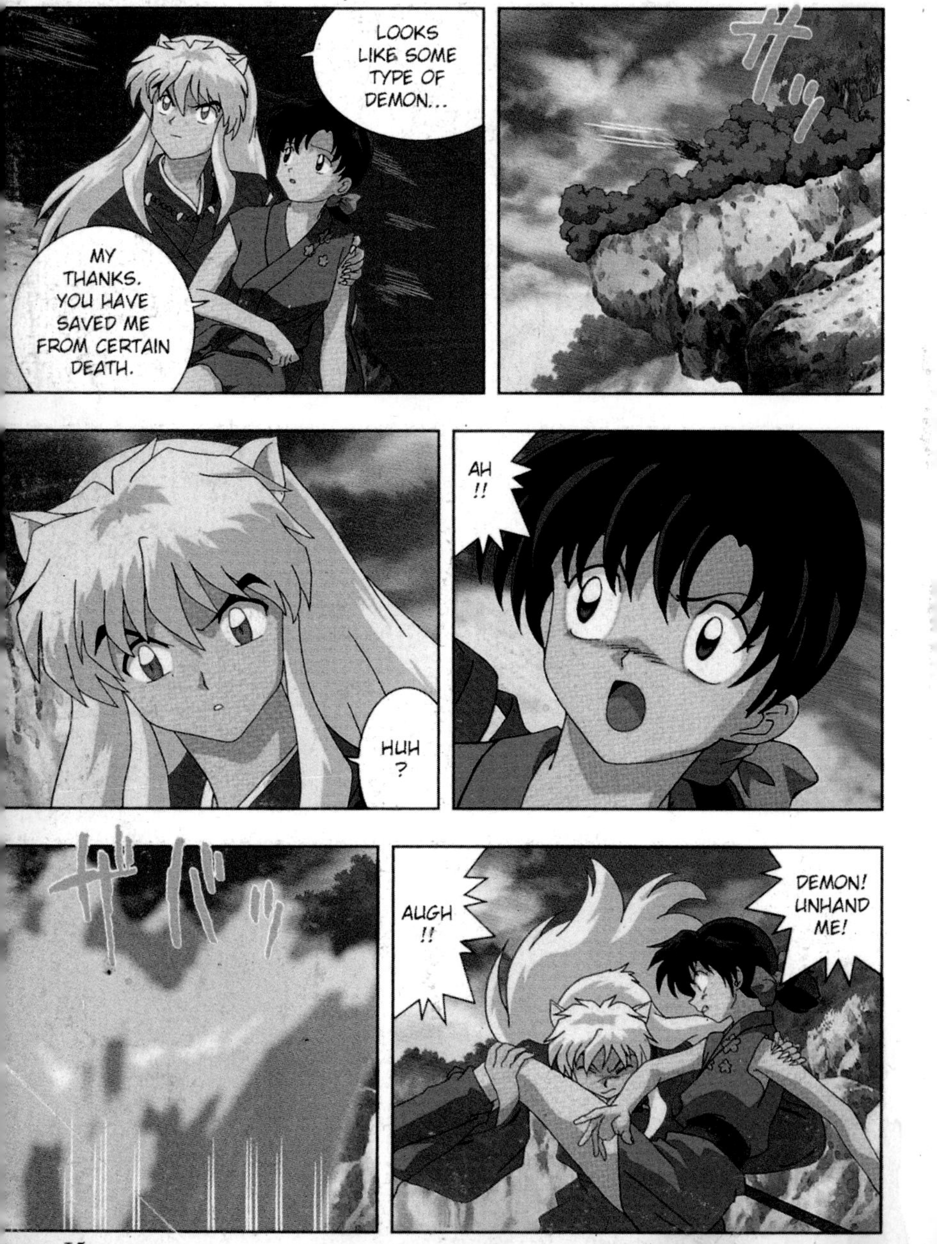
ザッ
LOOKS LIKE SOME TYPE OF DEMON...
MY THANKS. YOU HAVE SAVED ME FROM CERTAIN DEATH.
AH !!
HUH ?
DEMON! UNHAND ME!
AUGH !!
ザバッ

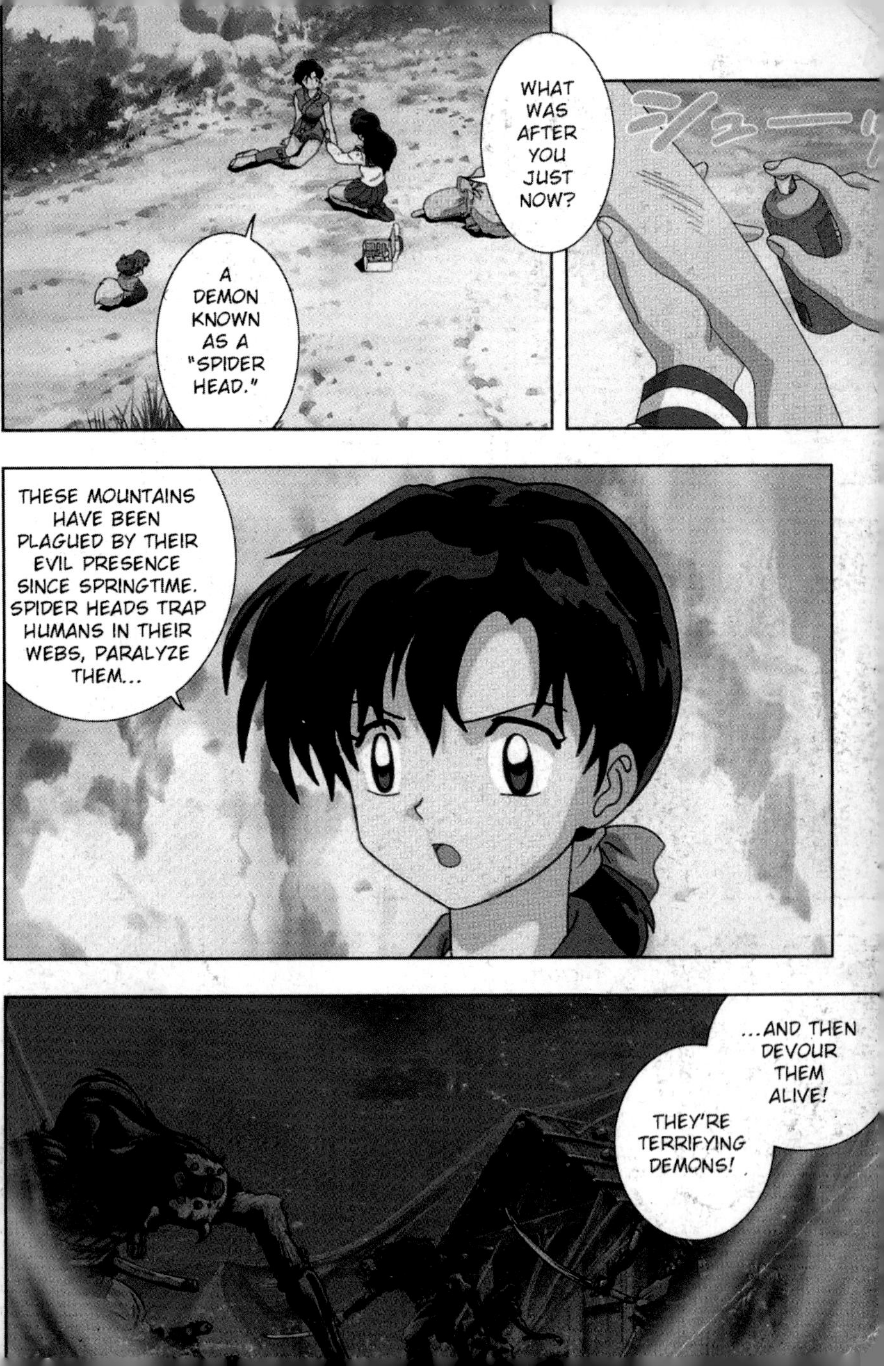
WHAT WAS AFTER YOU JUST NOW?
A DEMON KNOWN AS A "SPIDER HEAD."
THESE MOUNTAINS HAVE BEEN PLAGUED BY THEIR EVIL PRESENCE SINCE SPRINGTIME. SPIDER HEADS TRAP HUMANS IN THEIR WEBS, PARALYZE THEM...
...AND THEN DEVOUR THEM ALIVE!
THEY'RE TERRIFYING DEMONS!

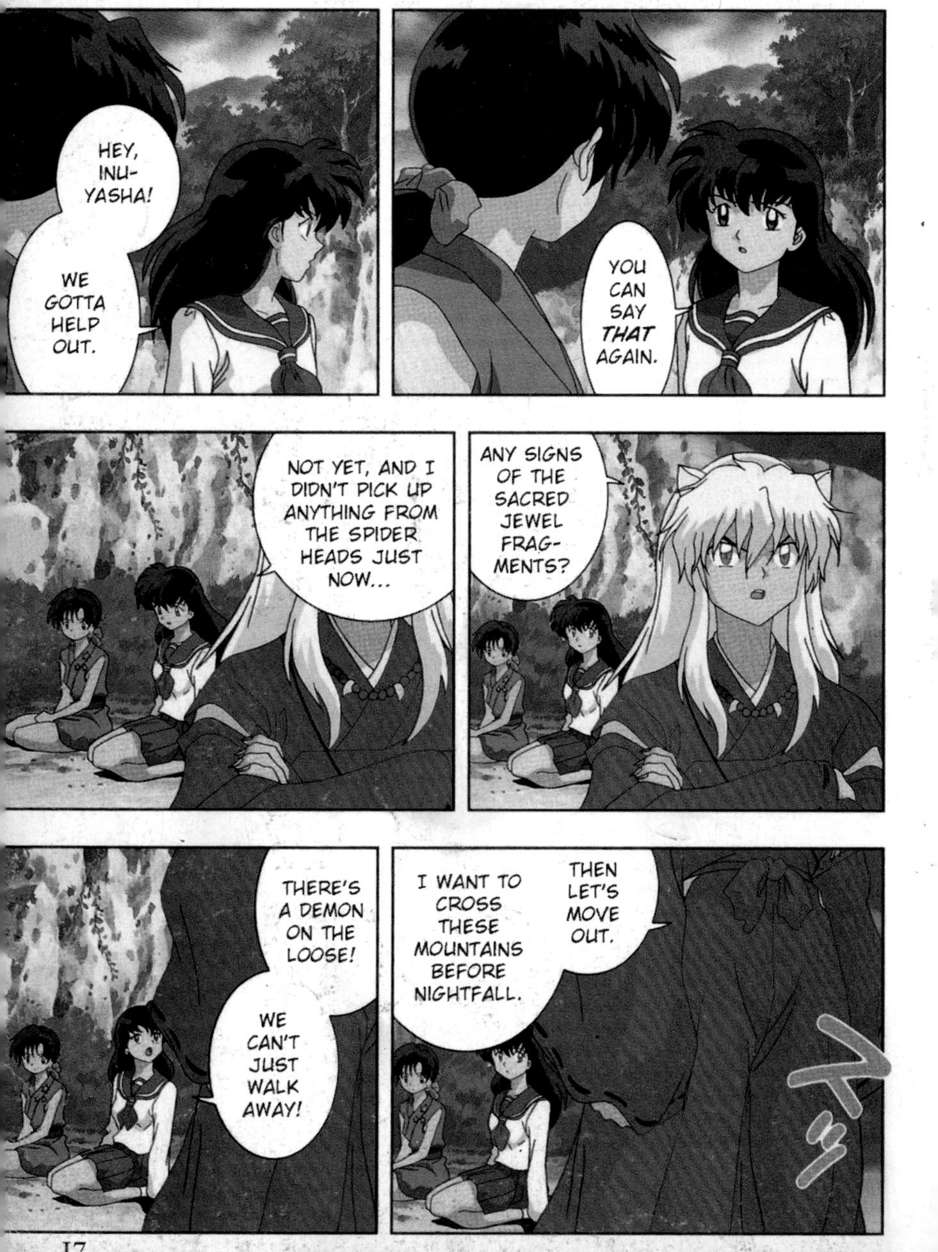
YOU CAN SAY *THAT* AGAIN.
HEY, INU-YASHA!
WE GOTTA HELP OUT.
ANY SIGNS OF THE SACRED JEWEL FRAG-MENTS?
NOT YET, AND I DIDN'T PICK UP ANYTHING FROM THE SPIDER HEADS JUST NOW...
THEN LET'S MOVE OUT.
I WANT TO CROSS THESE MOUNTAINS BEFORE NIGHTFALL.
THERE'S A DEMON ON THE LOOSE!
WE CAN'T JUST WALK AWAY!

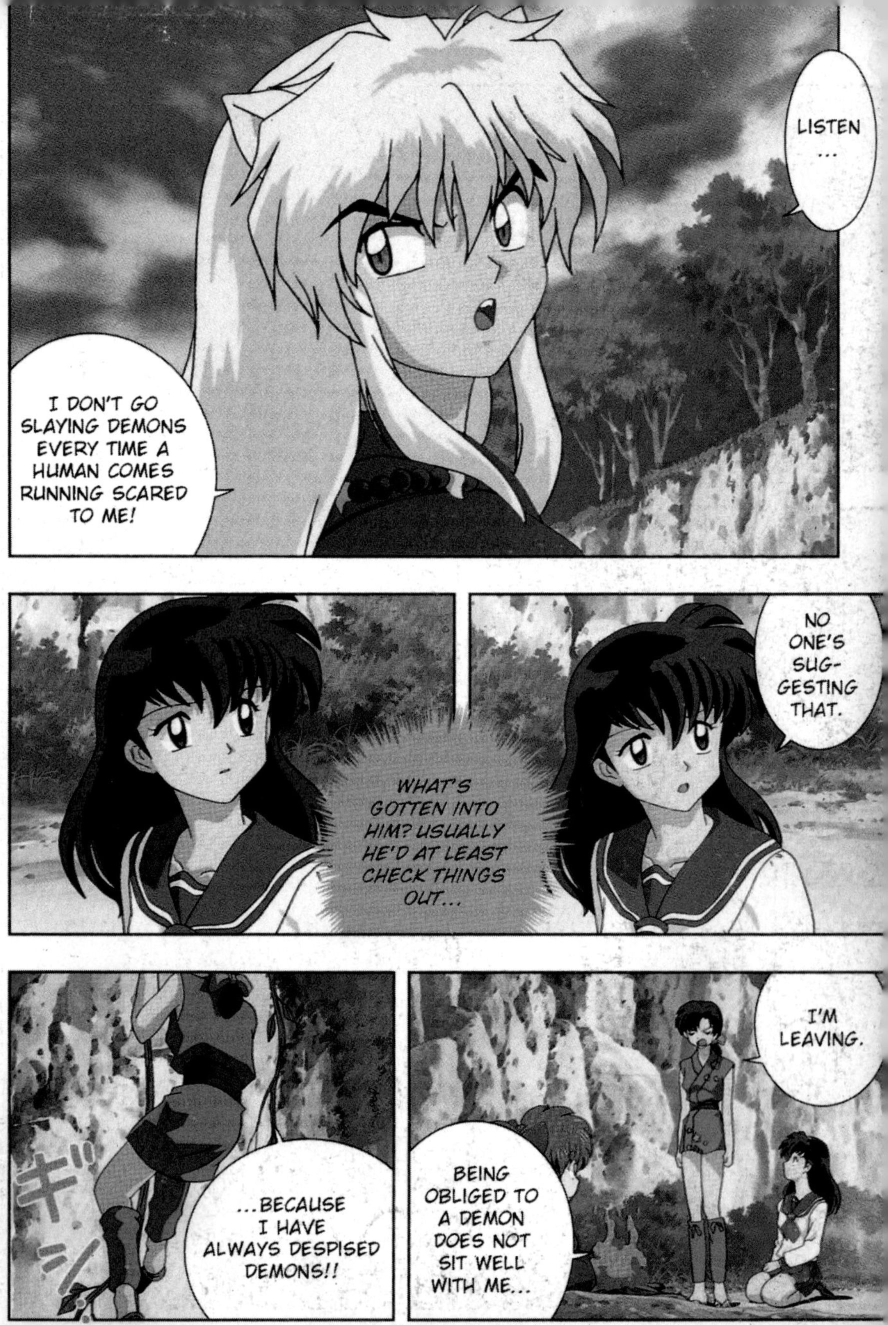
LISTEN ...
I DON'T GO SLAYING DEMONS EVERY TIME A HUMAN COMES RUNNING SCARED TO ME!
NO ONE'S SUG- GESTING THAT.
WHAT'S GOTTEN INTO HIM? USUALLY HE'D AT LEAST CHECK THINGS OUT...
I'M LEAVING.
BEING OBLIGED TO A DEMON DOES NOT SIT WELL WITH ME...
...BECAUSE I HAVE ALWAYS DESPISED DEMONS!!
ギシッ

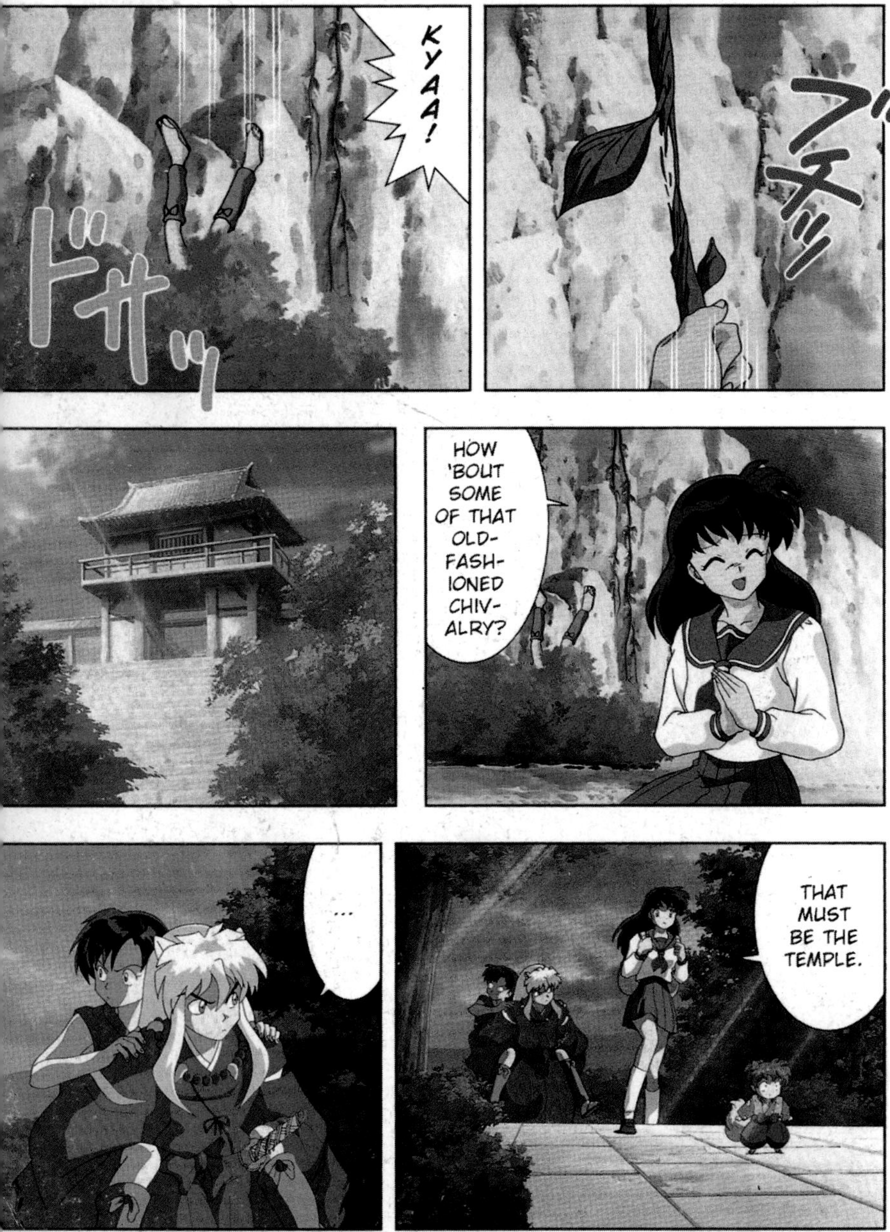
ブチッ
KYAA!
ドサッ
HOW 'BOUT SOME OF THAT OLD-FASHIONED CHIVALRY?
THAT MUST BE THE TEMPLE.
...

NA-ZUNA?

ARE YOU INJURED?

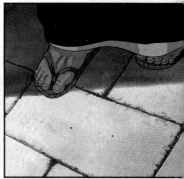

OH!

MASTER!

I HAD NO CHOICE BUT TO RELY ON THESE DEMONS TO BRING ME HOME.

IT SPIED ME WHILE I ATTENDED TO THE GRAVE-SITES.

I FEARED THAT A SPIDER HEAD MAY HAVE ATTACKED YOU...!

I'M SORRY, MASTER!

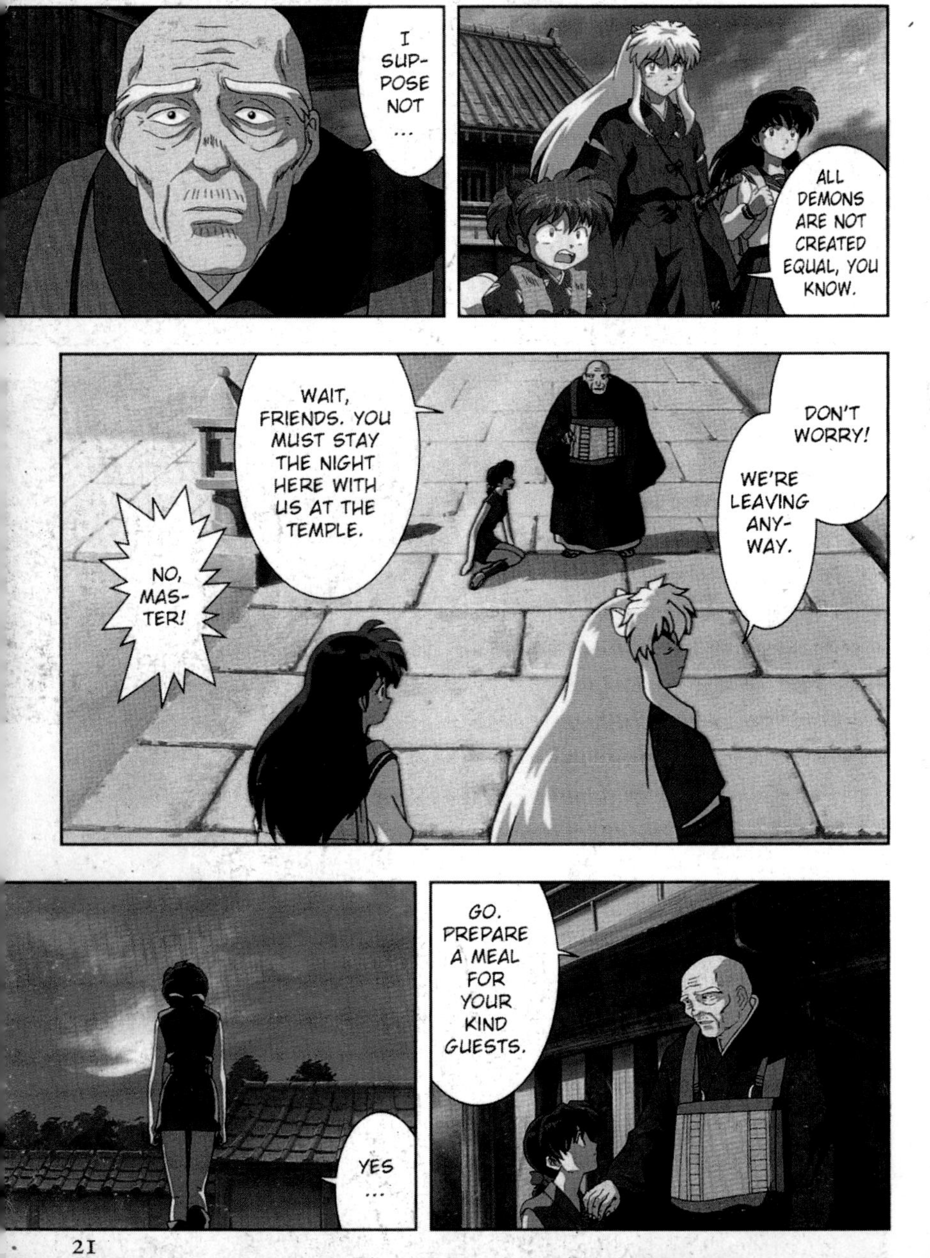
ALL DEMONS ARE NOT CREATED EQUAL, YOU KNOW.
I SUPPOSE NOT ...
DON'T WORRY!
WE'RE LEAVING ANYWAY.
WAIT, FRIENDS. YOU MUST STAY THE NIGHT HERE WITH US AT THE TEMPLE.
NO, MASTER!
GO. PREPARE A MEAL FOR YOUR KIND GUESTS.
YES ...

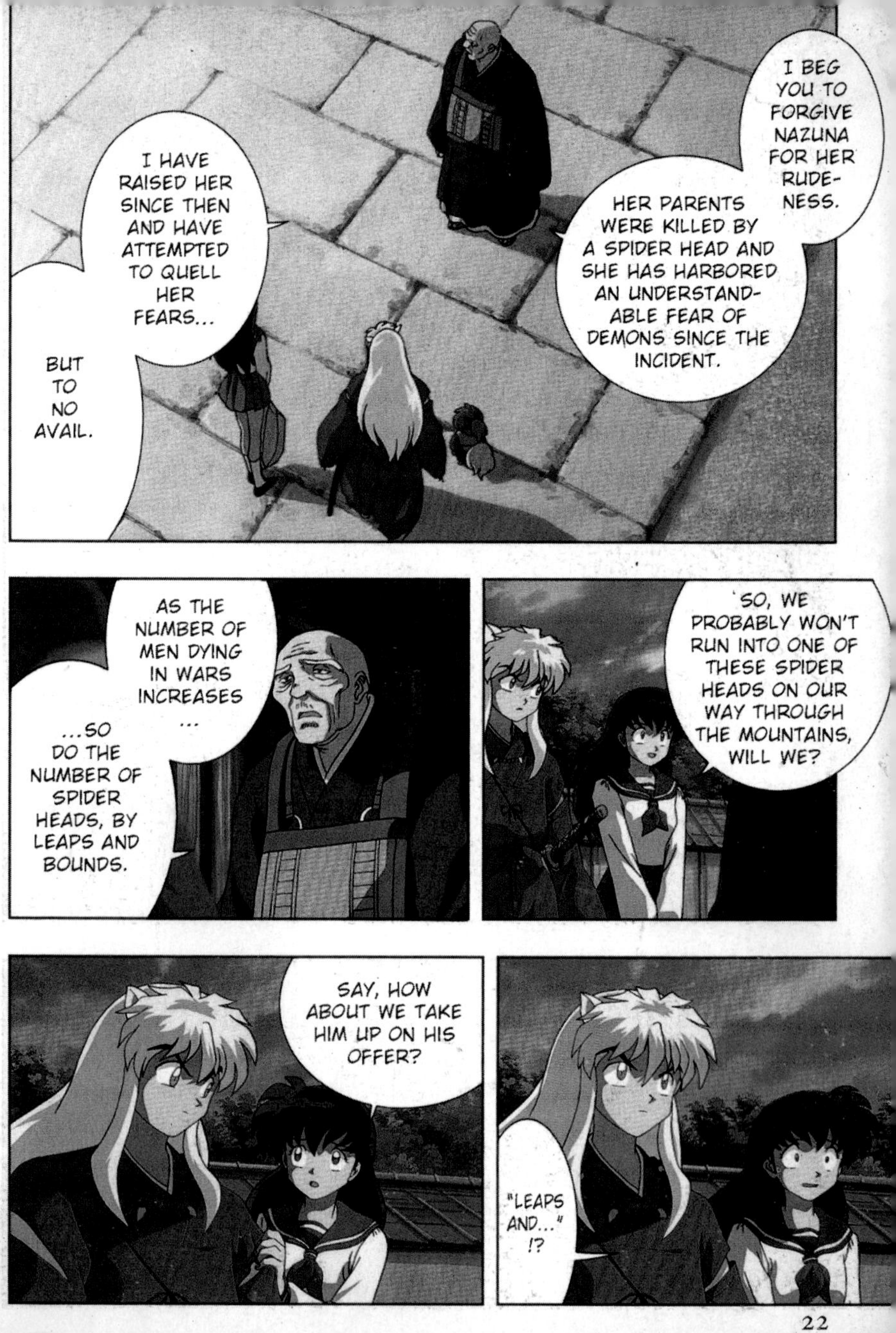
I BEG YOU TO FORGIVE NAZUNA FOR HER RUDENESS.
HER PARENTS WERE KILLED BY A SPIDER HEAD AND SHE HAS HARBORED AN UNDERSTANDABLE FEAR OF DEMONS SINCE THE INCIDENT.
I HAVE RAISED HER SINCE THEN AND HAVE ATTEMPTED TO QUELL HER FEARS...
BUT TO NO AVAIL.
SO, WE PROBABLY WON'T RUN INTO ONE OF THESE SPIDER HEADS ON OUR WAY THROUGH THE MOUNTAINS, WILL WE?
AS THE NUMBER OF MEN DYING IN WARS INCREASES ...
...SO DO THE NUMBER OF SPIDER HEADS, BY LEAPS AND BOUNDS.
"LEAPS AND..." !?
SAY, HOW ABOUT WE TAKE HIM UP ON HIS OFFER?

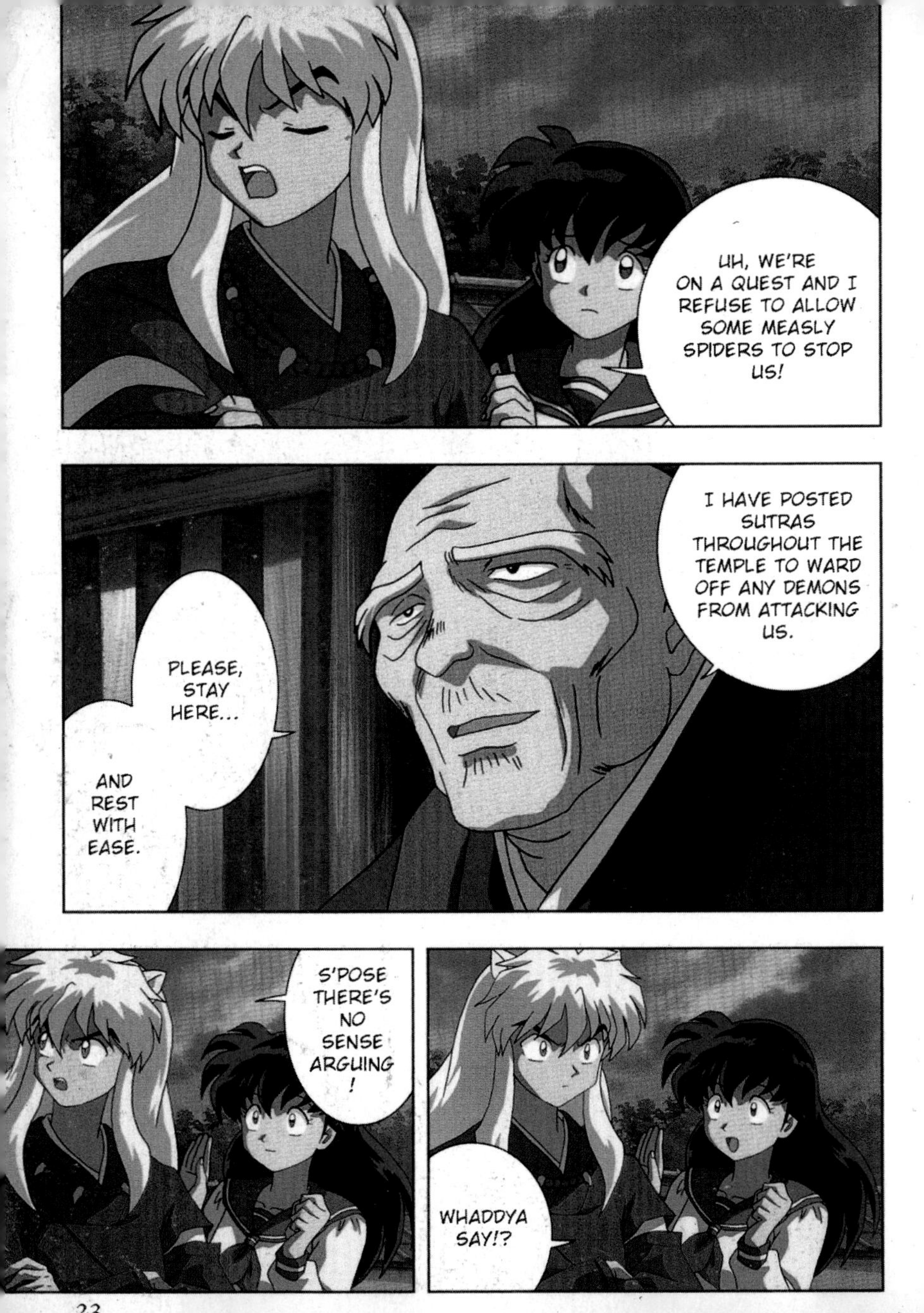
UH, WE'RE ON A QUEST AND I REFUSE TO ALLOW SOME MEASLY SPIDERS TO STOP US!
I HAVE POSTED SUTRAS THROUGHOUT THE TEMPLE TO WARD OFF ANY DEMONS FROM ATTACKING US.
PLEASE, STAY HERE...
AND REST WITH EASE.
WHADDYA SAY!?
S'POSE THERE'S NO SENSE ARGUING!

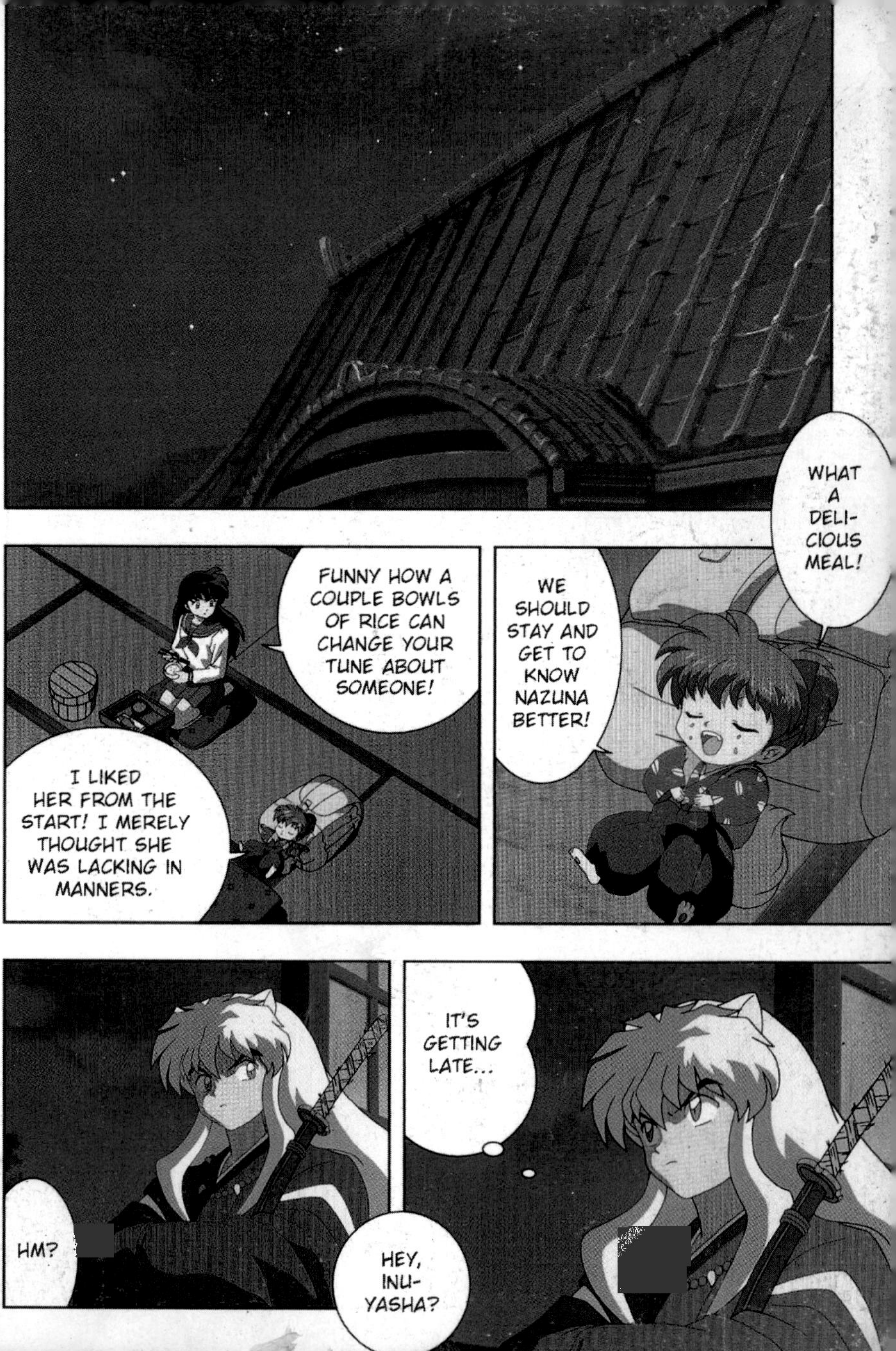
WHAT A DELI-CIOUS MEAL!
WE SHOULD STAY AND GET TO KNOW NAZUNA BETTER!
FUNNY HOW A COUPLE BOWLS OF RICE CAN CHANGE YOUR TUNE ABOUT SOMEONE!
I LIKED HER FROM THE START! I MERELY THOUGHT SHE WAS LACKING IN MANNERS.
IT'S GETTING LATE...
HEY, INU-YASHA?
HM?

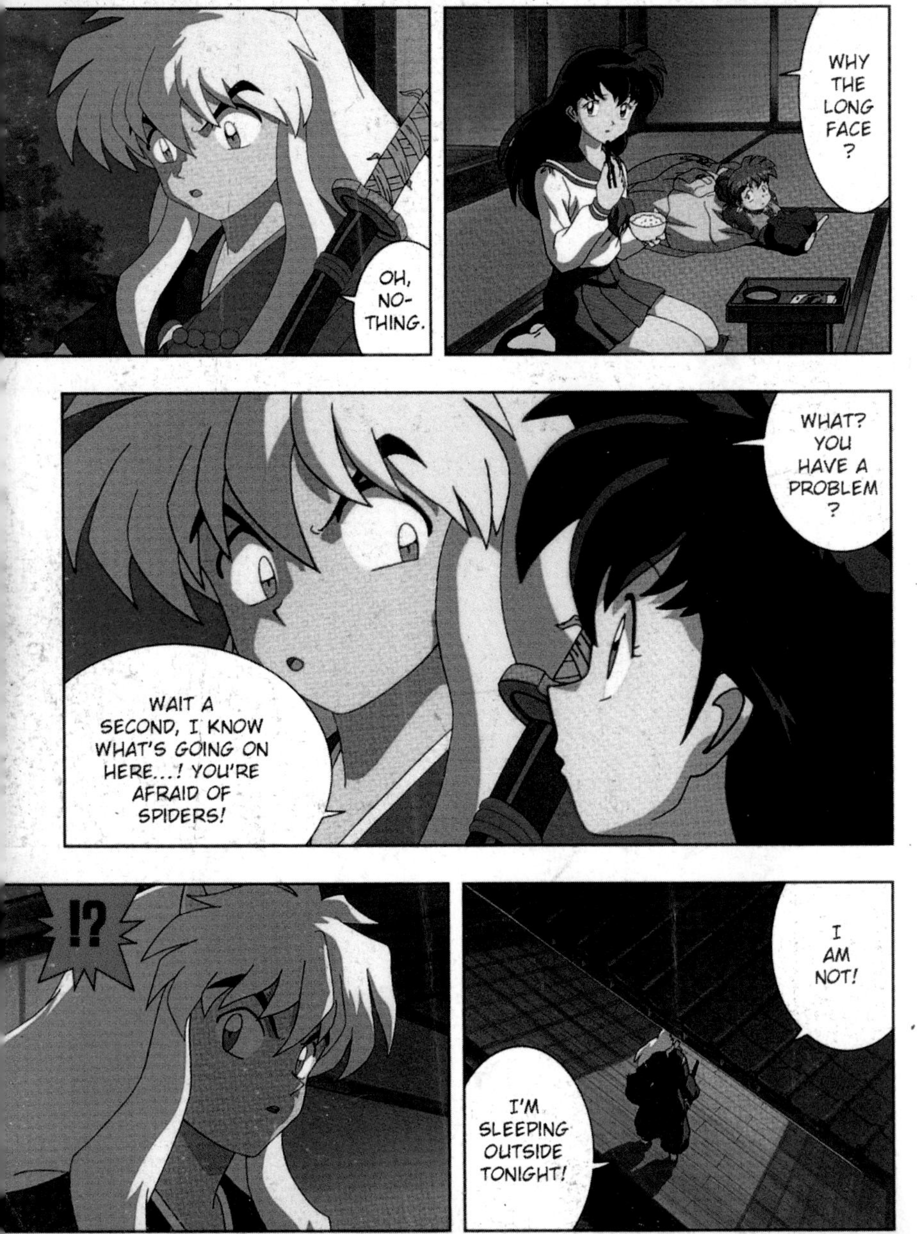
WHY THE LONG FACE?
OH, NO-THING.
WHAT? YOU HAVE A PROBLEM?
WAIT A SECOND, I KNOW WHAT'S GOING ON HERE...! YOU'RE AFRAID OF SPIDERS!
I AM NOT!
I'M SLEEPING OUTSIDE TONIGHT!
!?

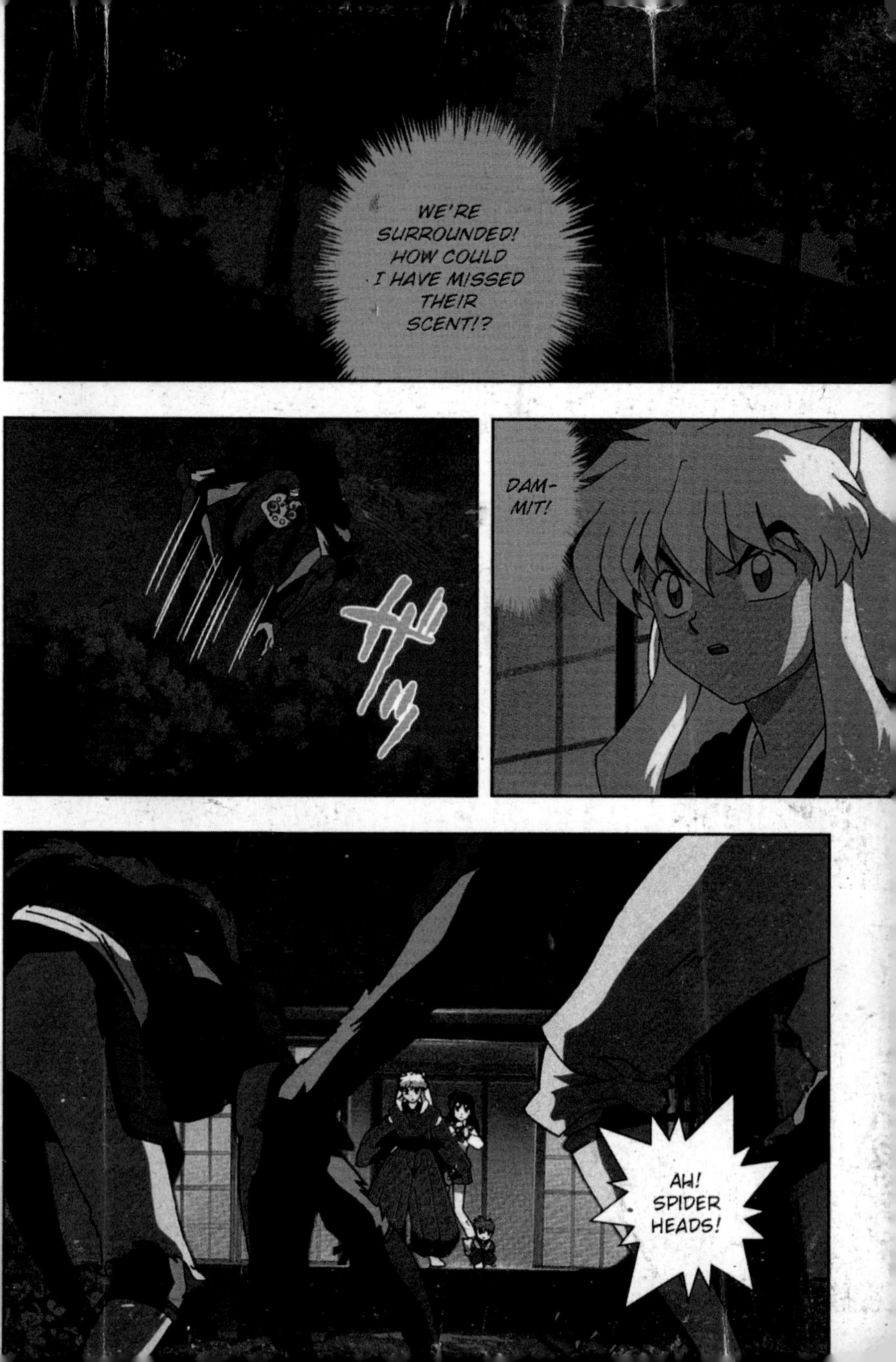
WE'RE SURROUNDED! HOW COULD I HAVE MISSED THEIR SCENT!?
DAM-MIT!
AH! SPIDER HEADS!

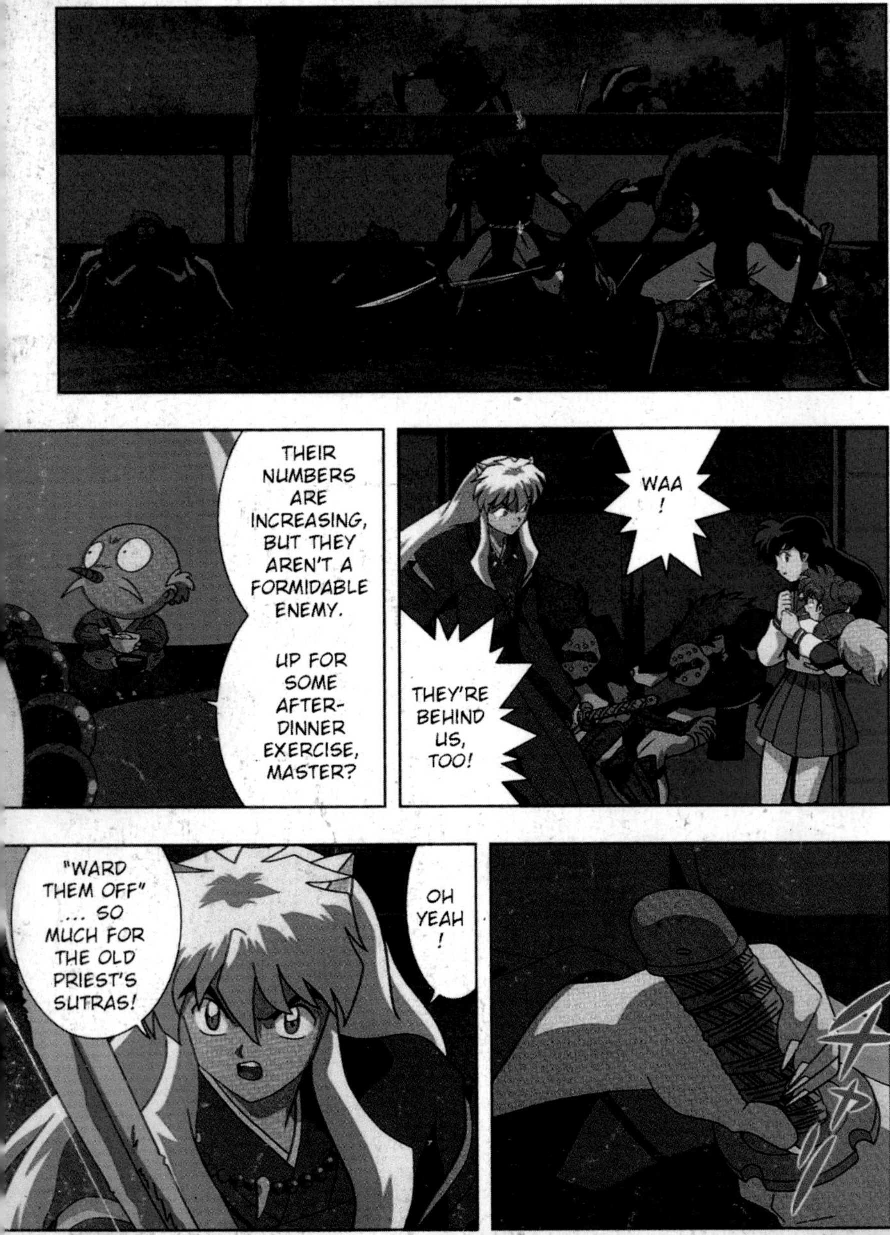
WAA!
THEY'RE BEHIND US, TOO!
THEIR NUMBERS ARE INCREASING, BUT THEY AREN'T A FORMIDABLE ENEMY.
UP FOR SOME AFTER-DINNER EXERCISE, MASTER?
OH YEAH!
"WARD THEM OFF" ... SO MUCH FOR THE OLD PRIEST'S SUTRAS!

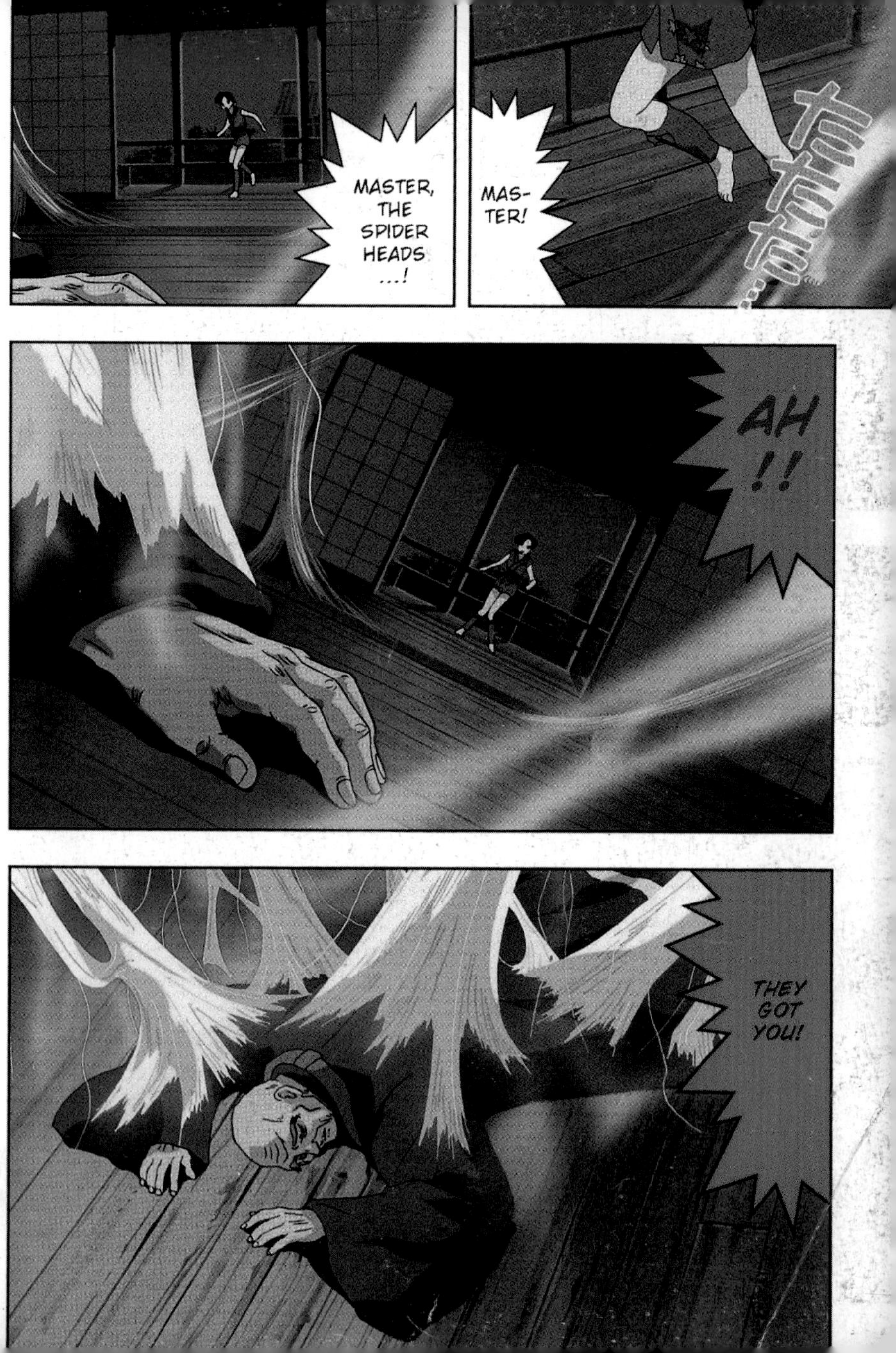
たたた…
MAS-TER!
MASTER, THE SPIDER HEADS ...!
AH !!
THEY GOT YOU!

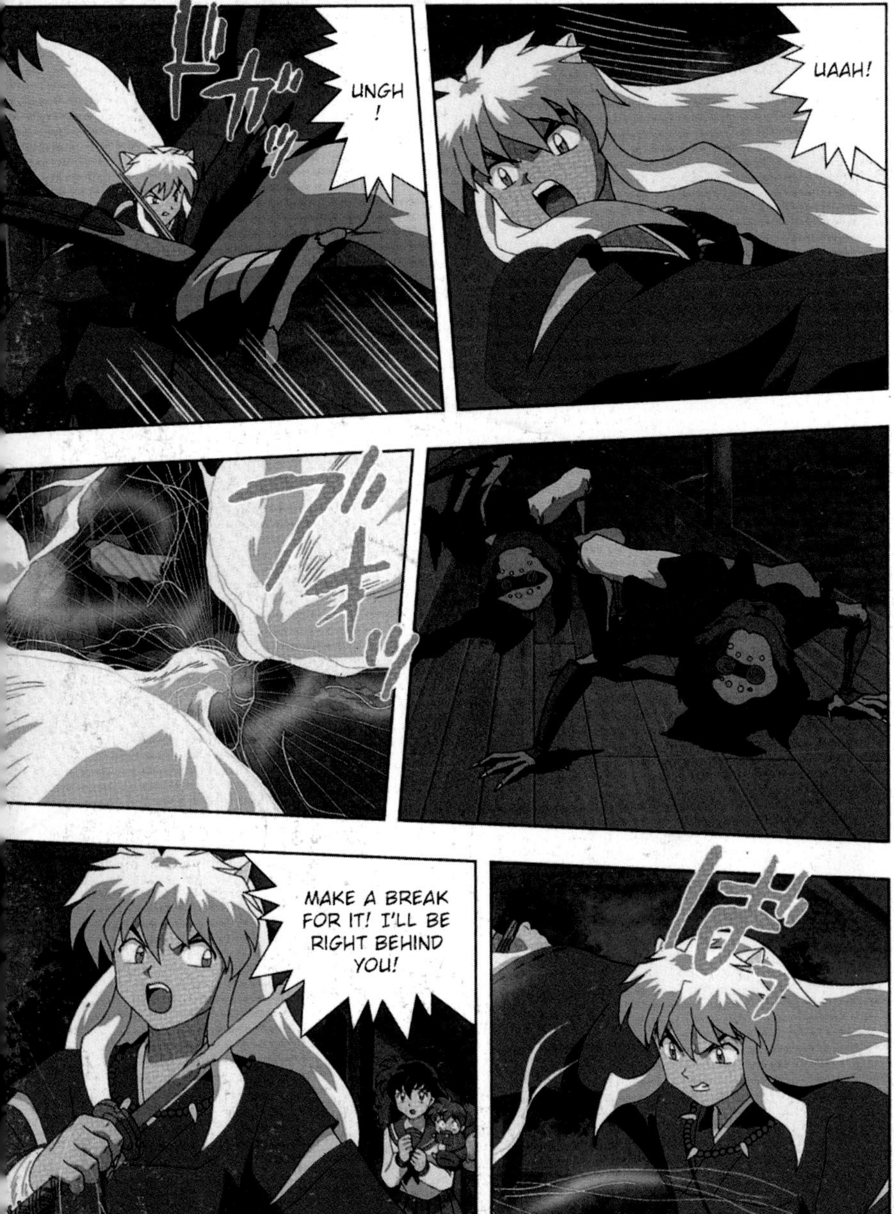
UAAH!
UNGH !
MAKE A BREAK FOR IT! I'LL BE RIGHT BEHIND YOU!

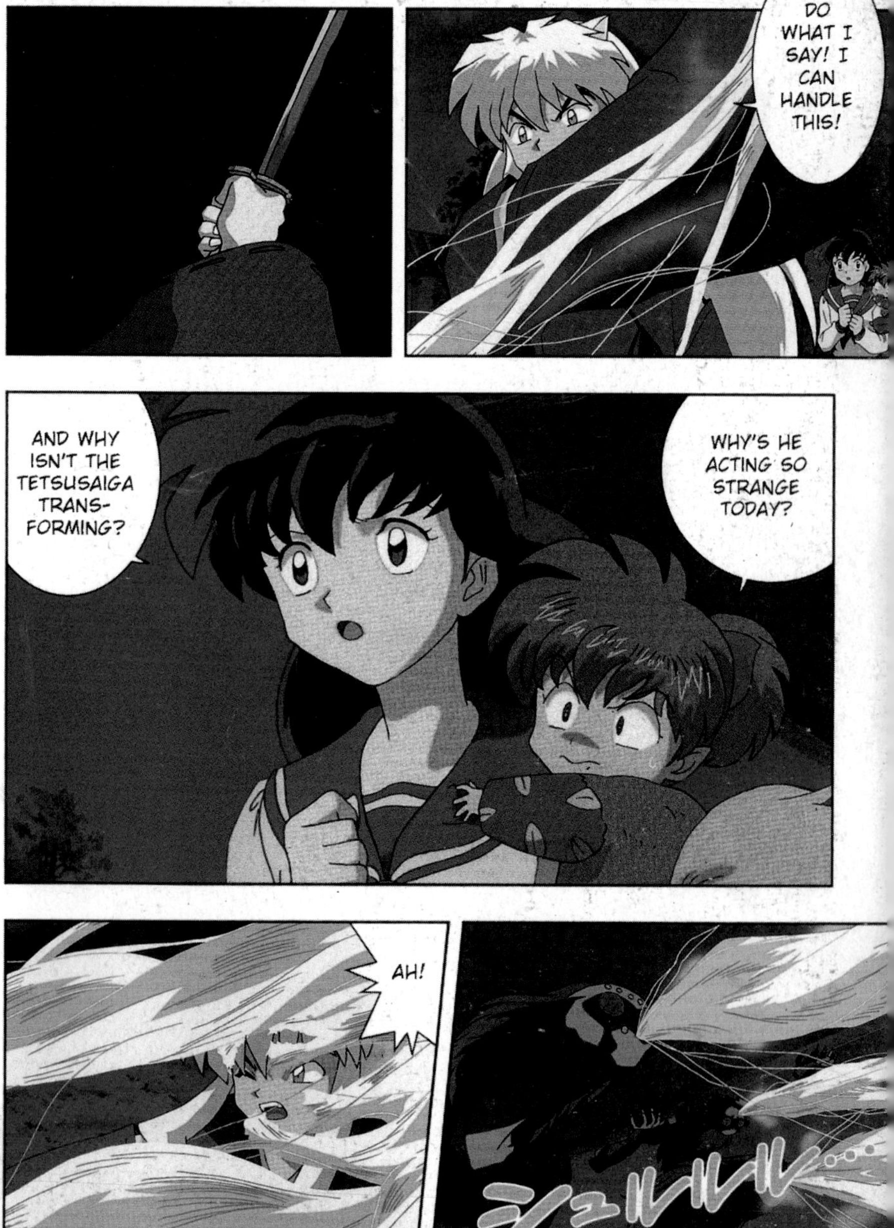
DO WHAT I SAY! I CAN HANDLE THIS!
WHY'S HE ACTING SO STRANGE TODAY?
AND WHY ISN'T THE TETSUSAIGA TRANS-FORMING?
シュルルル…
AH!

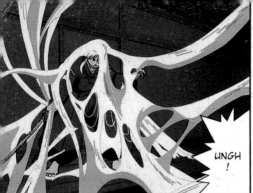

UNGH
!

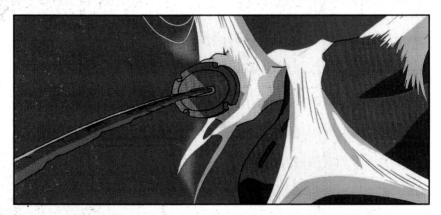

I'VE GOT YA!

WE GOTTA ES- CAPE !

UGH ...

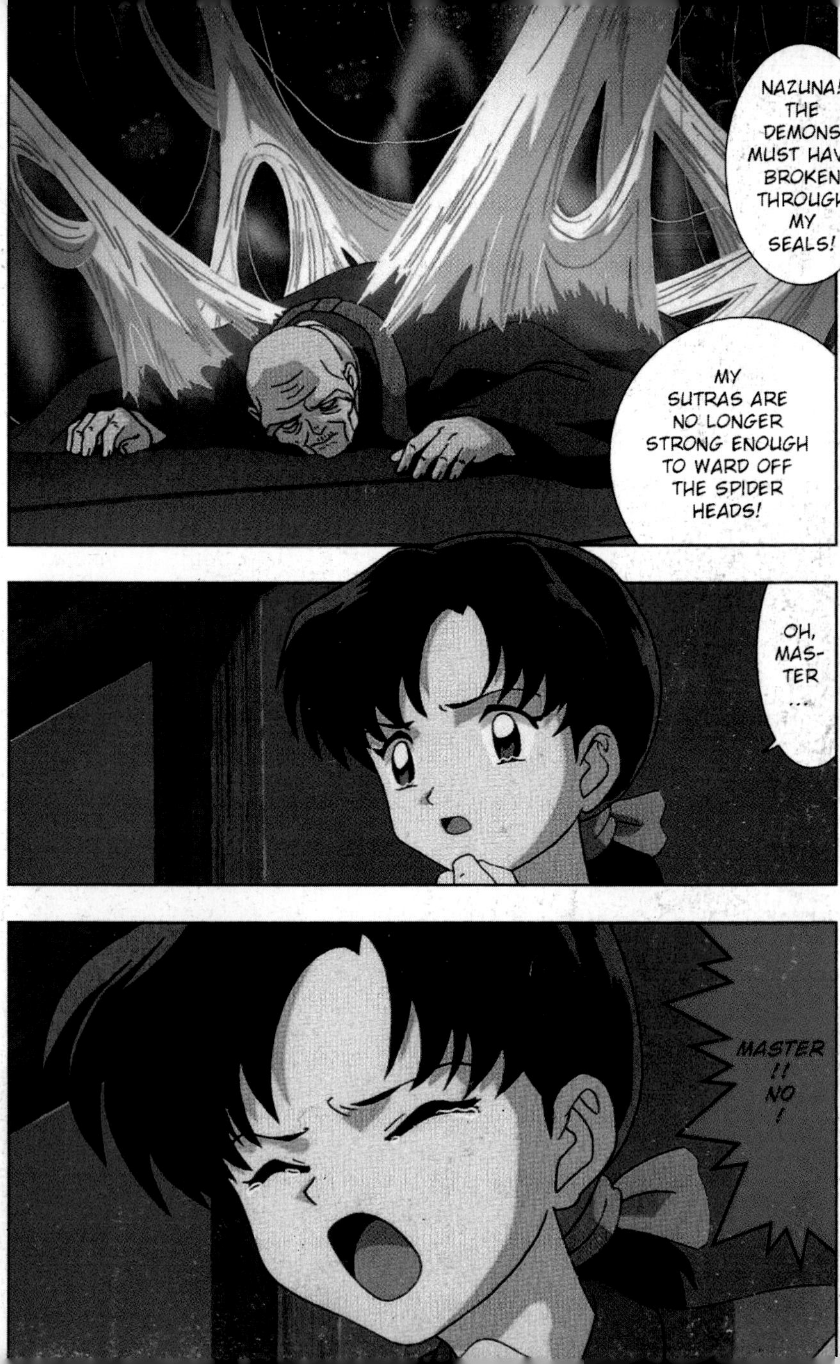
NAZUNA! THE DEMONS MUST HAVE BROKEN THROUGH MY SEALS!
MY SUTRAS ARE NO LONGER STRONG ENOUGH TO WARD OFF THE SPIDER HEADS!
OH, MAS-TER ...
MASTER!! NO!

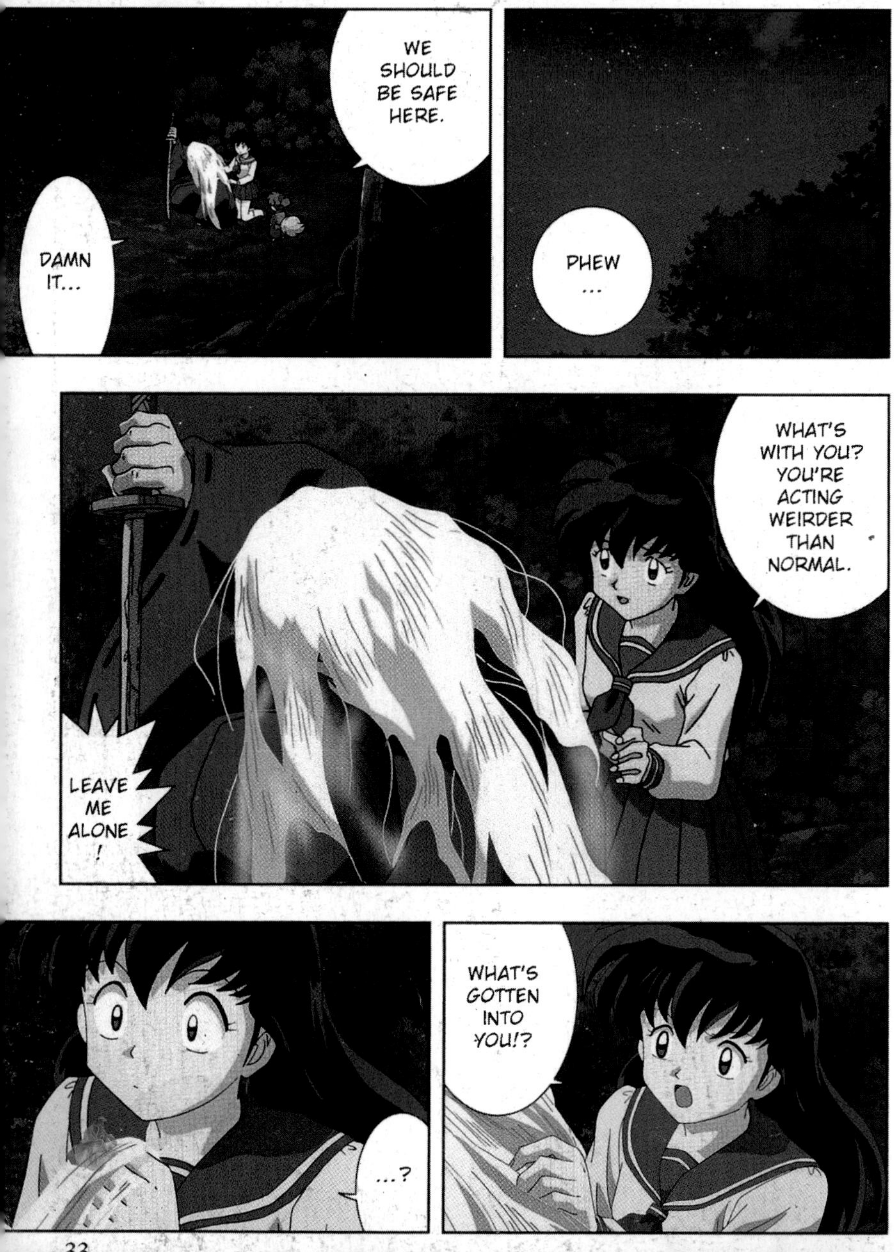
PHEW ...
WE SHOULD BE SAFE HERE.
DAMN IT...
WHAT'S WITH YOU? YOU'RE ACTING WEIRDER THAN NORMAL.
LEAVE ME ALONE!
WHAT'S GOTTEN INTO YOU!?
...?

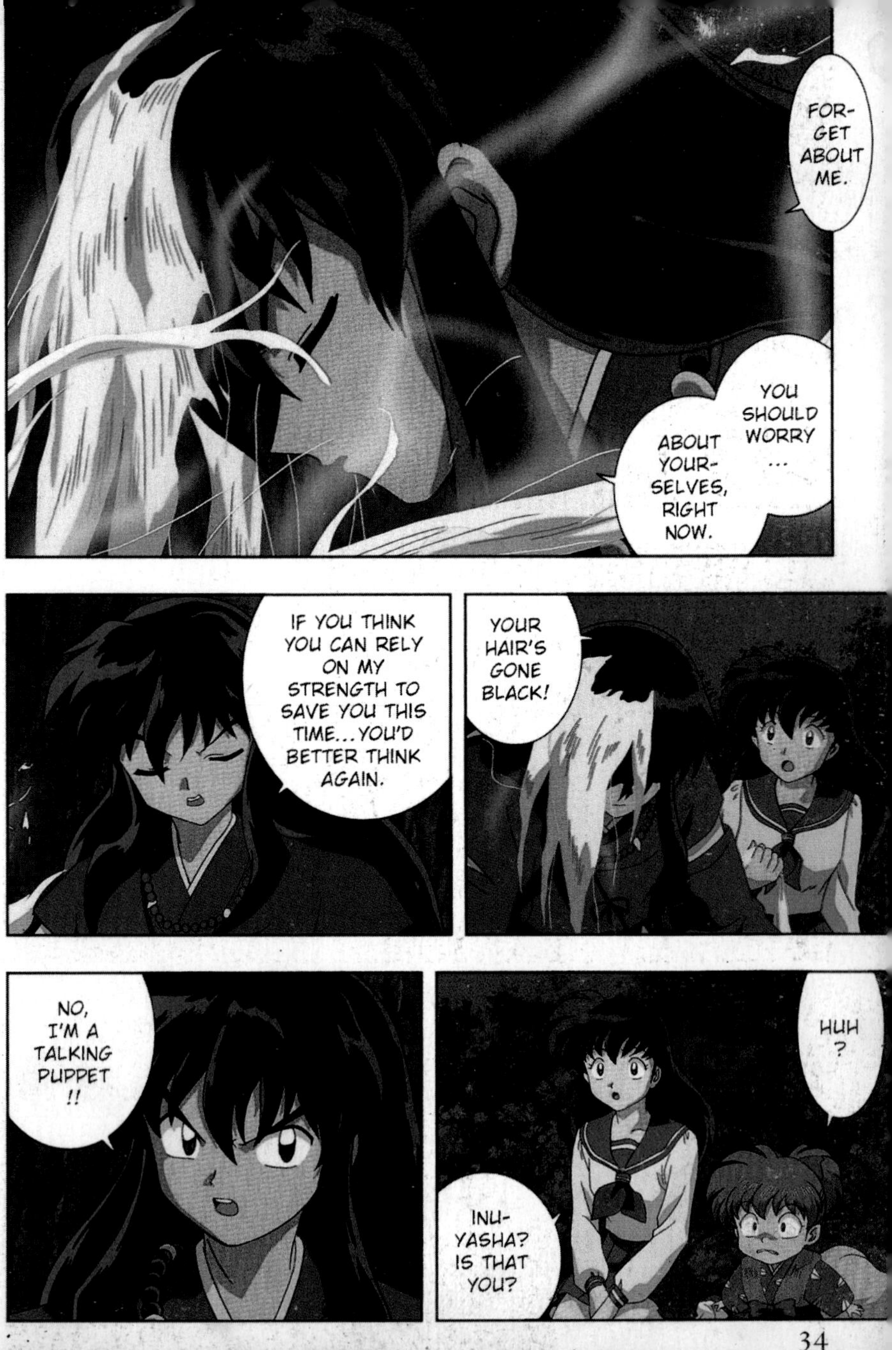
FOR-GET ABOUT ME.
YOU SHOULD WORRY...
ABOUT YOUR-SELVES, RIGHT NOW.
YOUR HAIR'S GONE BLACK!
IF YOU THINK YOU CAN RELY ON MY STRENGTH TO SAVE YOU THIS TIME...YOU'D BETTER THINK AGAIN.
HUH?
INU-YASHA? IS THAT YOU?
NO, I'M A TALKING PUPPET!!

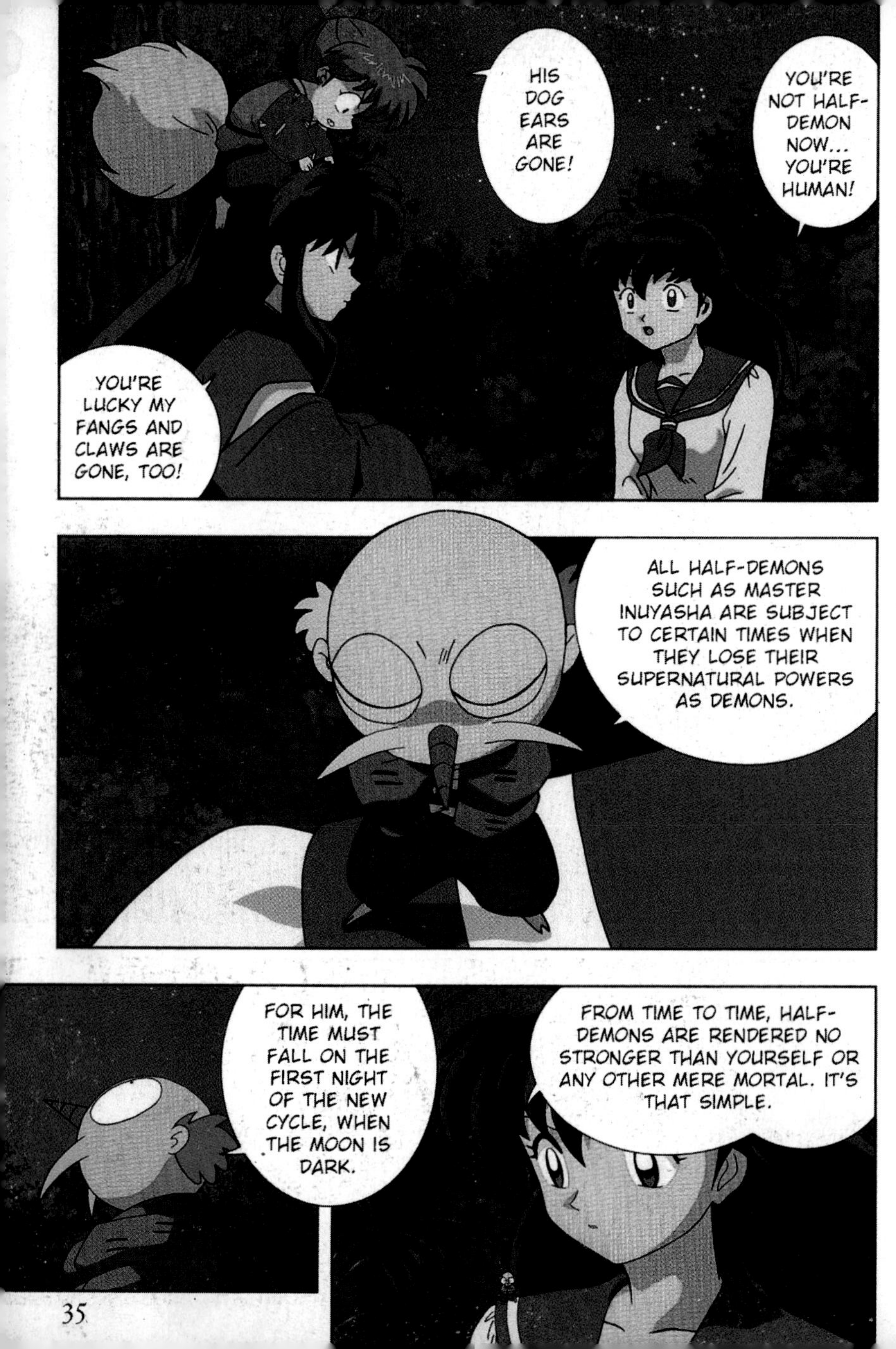
YOU'RE NOT HALF-DEMON NOW... YOU'RE HUMAN!
HIS DOG EARS ARE GONE!
YOU'RE LUCKY MY FANGS AND CLAWS ARE GONE, TOO!
ALL HALF-DEMONS SUCH AS MASTER INUYASHA ARE SUBJECT TO CERTAIN TIMES WHEN THEY LOSE THEIR SUPERNATURAL POWERS AS DEMONS.
FROM TIME TO TIME, HALF-DEMONS ARE RENDERED NO STRONGER THAN YOURSELF OR ANY OTHER MERE MORTAL. IT'S THAT SIMPLE.
FOR HIM, THE TIME MUST FALL ON THE FIRST NIGHT OF THE NEW CYCLE, WHEN THE MOON IS DARK.

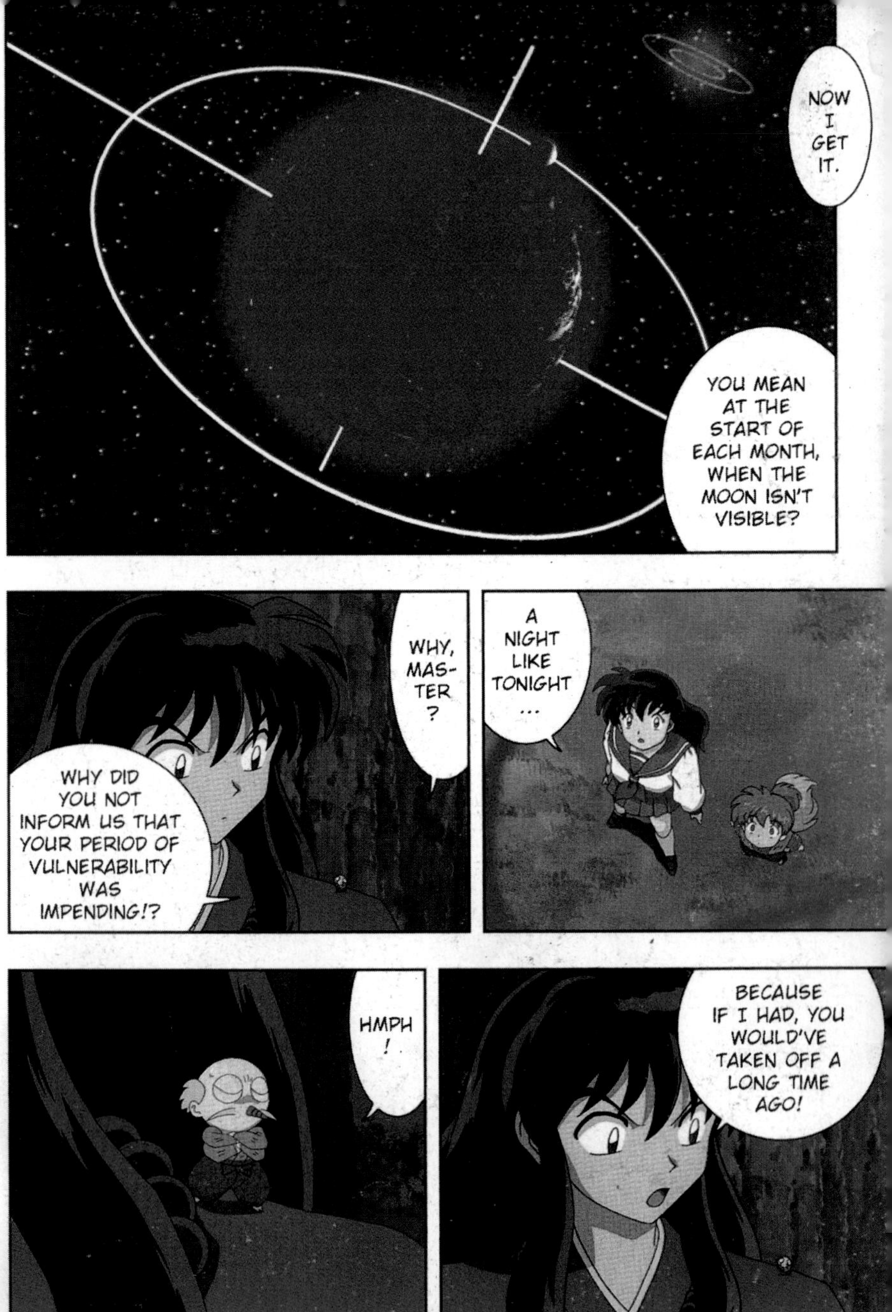
NOW I GET IT.
YOU MEAN AT THE START OF EACH MONTH, WHEN THE MOON ISN'T VISIBLE?
A NIGHT LIKE TONIGHT...
WHY, MASTER?
WHY DID YOU NOT INFORM US THAT YOUR PERIOD OF VULNERABILITY WAS IMPENDING!?
BECAUSE IF I HAD, YOU WOULD'VE TAKEN OFF A LONG TIME AGO!
HMPH!

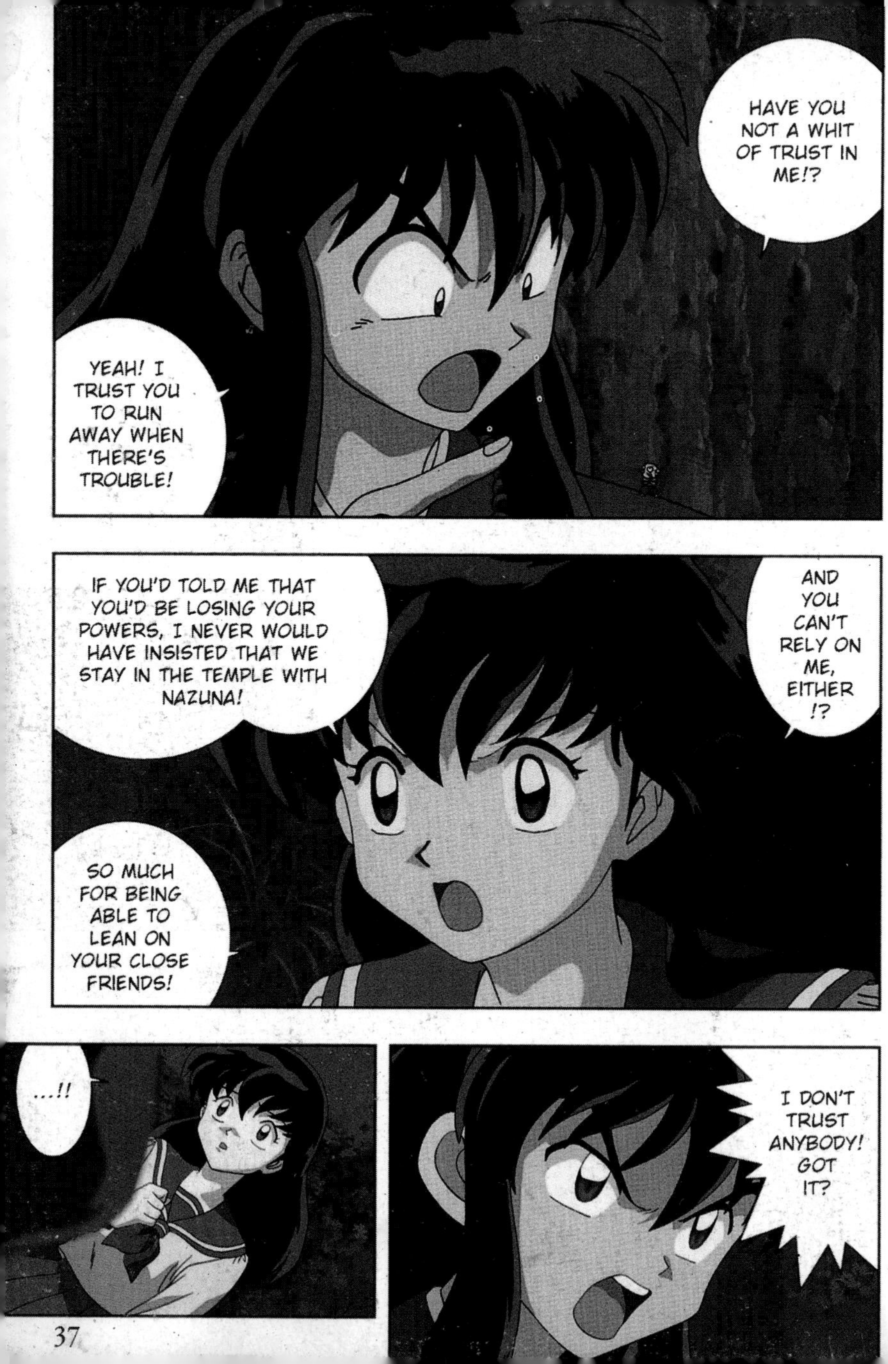
HAVE YOU NOT A WHIT OF TRUST IN ME!?
YEAH! I TRUST YOU TO RUN AWAY WHEN THERE'S TROUBLE!
AND YOU CAN'T RELY ON ME, EITHER!?
IF YOU'D TOLD ME THAT YOU'D BE LOSING YOUR POWERS, I NEVER WOULD HAVE INSISTED THAT WE STAY IN THE TEMPLE WITH NAZUNA!
SO MUCH FOR BEING ABLE TO LEAN ON YOUR CLOSE FRIENDS!
I DON'T TRUST ANYBODY! GOT IT?
...!!

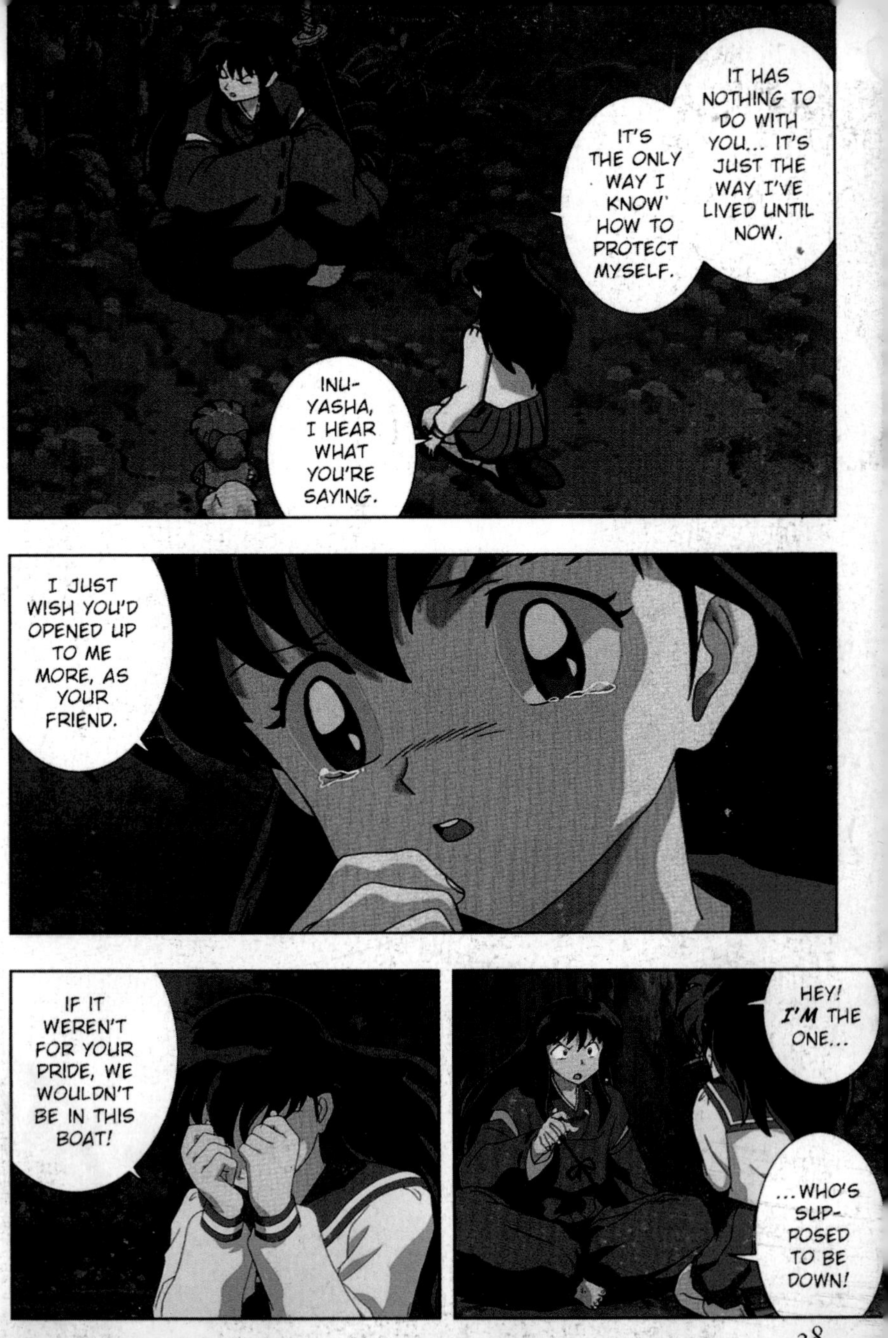
IT HAS NOTHING TO DO WITH YOU... IT'S JUST THE WAY I'VE LIVED UNTIL NOW.
IT'S THE ONLY WAY I KNOW HOW TO PROTECT MYSELF.
INU-YASHA, I HEAR WHAT YOU'RE SAYING.
I JUST WISH YOU'D OPENED UP TO ME MORE, AS YOUR FRIEND.
HEY! *I'M* THE ONE...
...WHO'S SUP-POSED TO BE DOWN!
IF IT WEREN'T FOR YOUR PRIDE, WE WOULDN'T BE IN THIS BOAT!

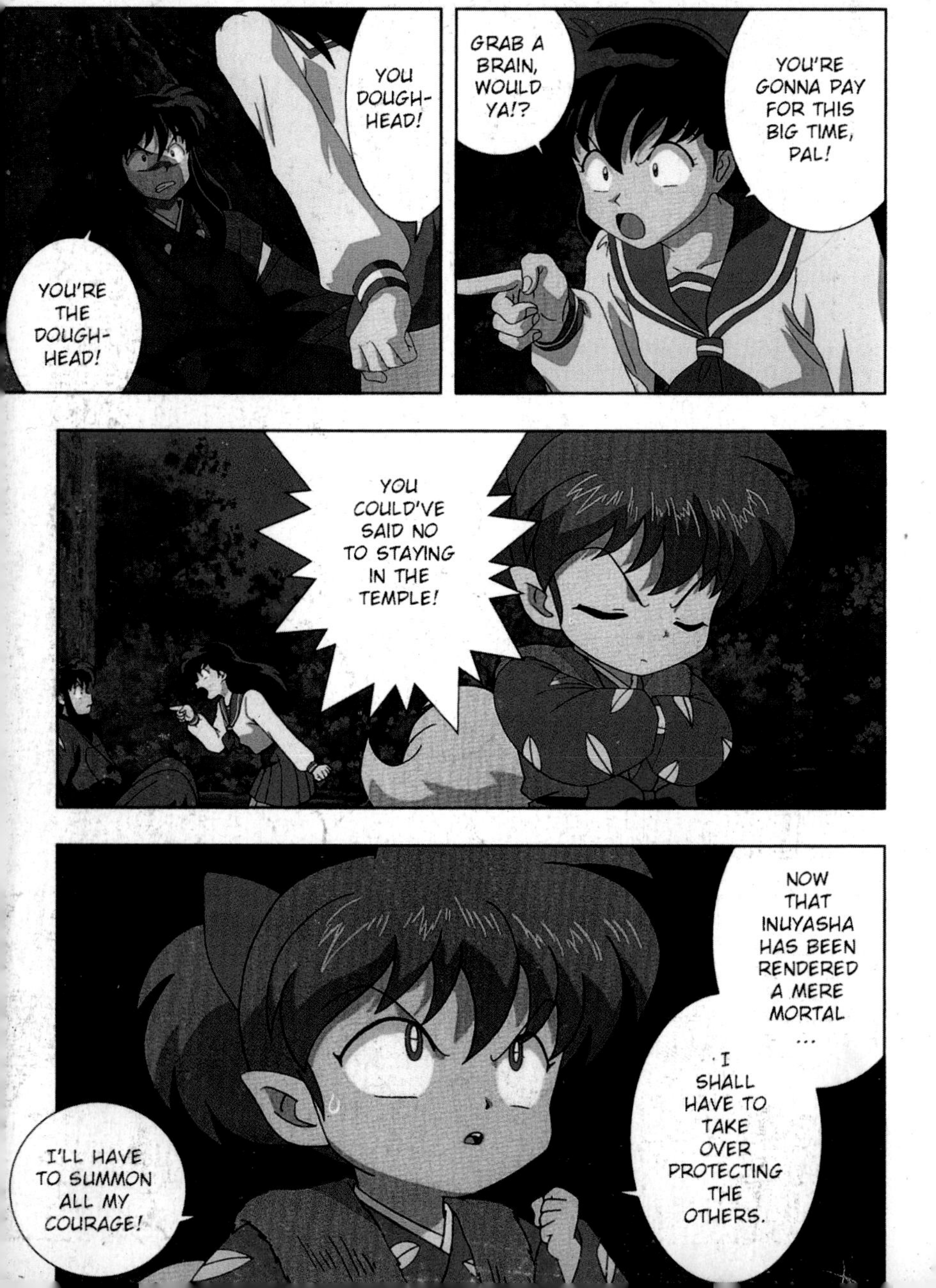
YOU'RE GONNA PAY FOR THIS BIG TIME, PAL!
GRAB A BRAIN, WOULD YA!?
YOU DOUGH-HEAD!
YOU'RE THE DOUGH-HEAD!
YOU COULD'VE SAID NO TO STAYING IN THE TEMPLE!
NOW THAT INUYASHA HAS BEEN RENDERED A MERE MORTAL ...
I SHALL HAVE TO TAKE OVER PROTECTING THE OTHERS.
I'LL HAVE TO SUMMON ALL MY COURAGE!

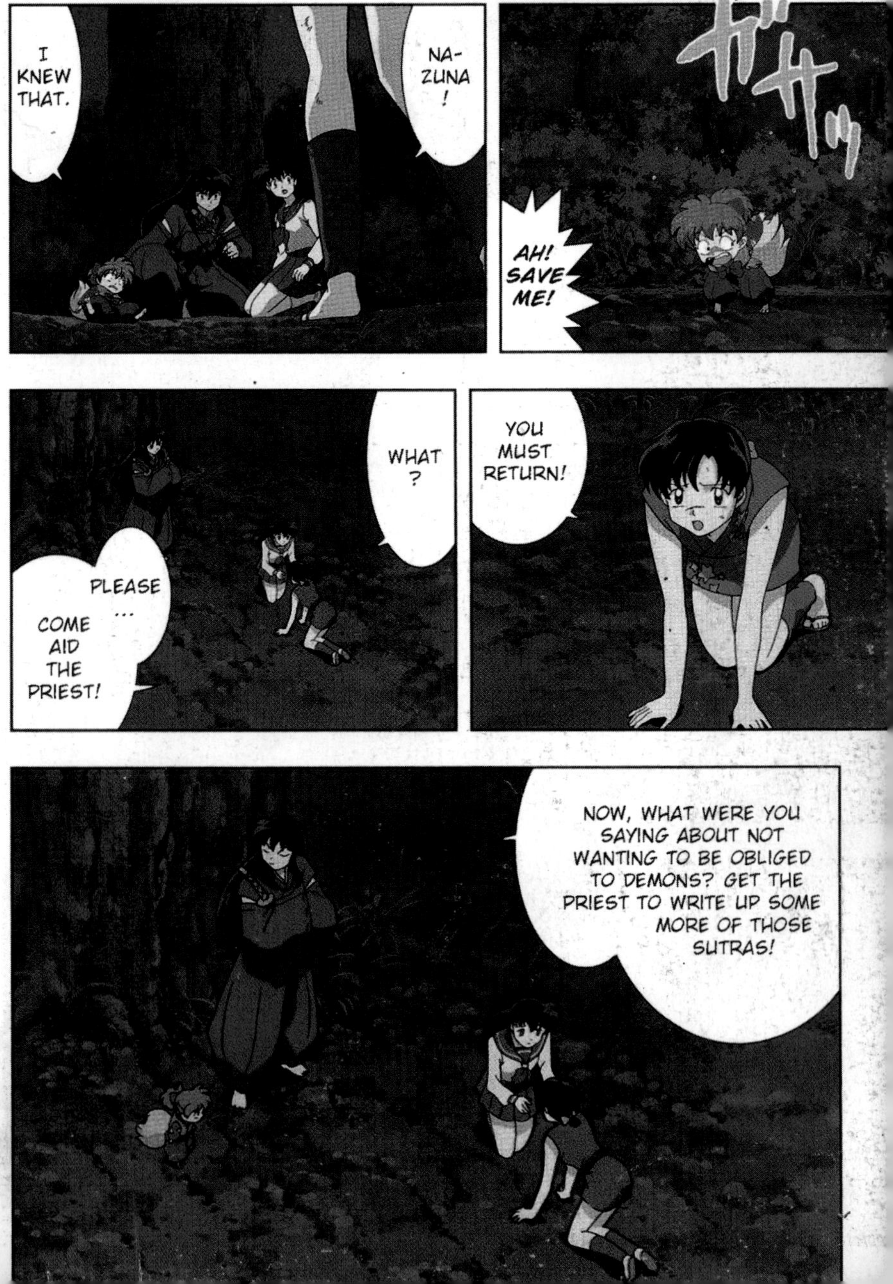
ガサッ
AH! SAVE ME!
NA-ZUNA!
I KNEW THAT.
YOU MUST RETURN!
WHAT?
PLEASE... COME AID THE PRIEST!
NOW, WHAT WERE YOU SAYING ABOUT NOT WANTING TO BE OBLIGED TO DEMONS? GET THE PRIEST TO WRITE UP SOME MORE OF THOSE SUTRAS!

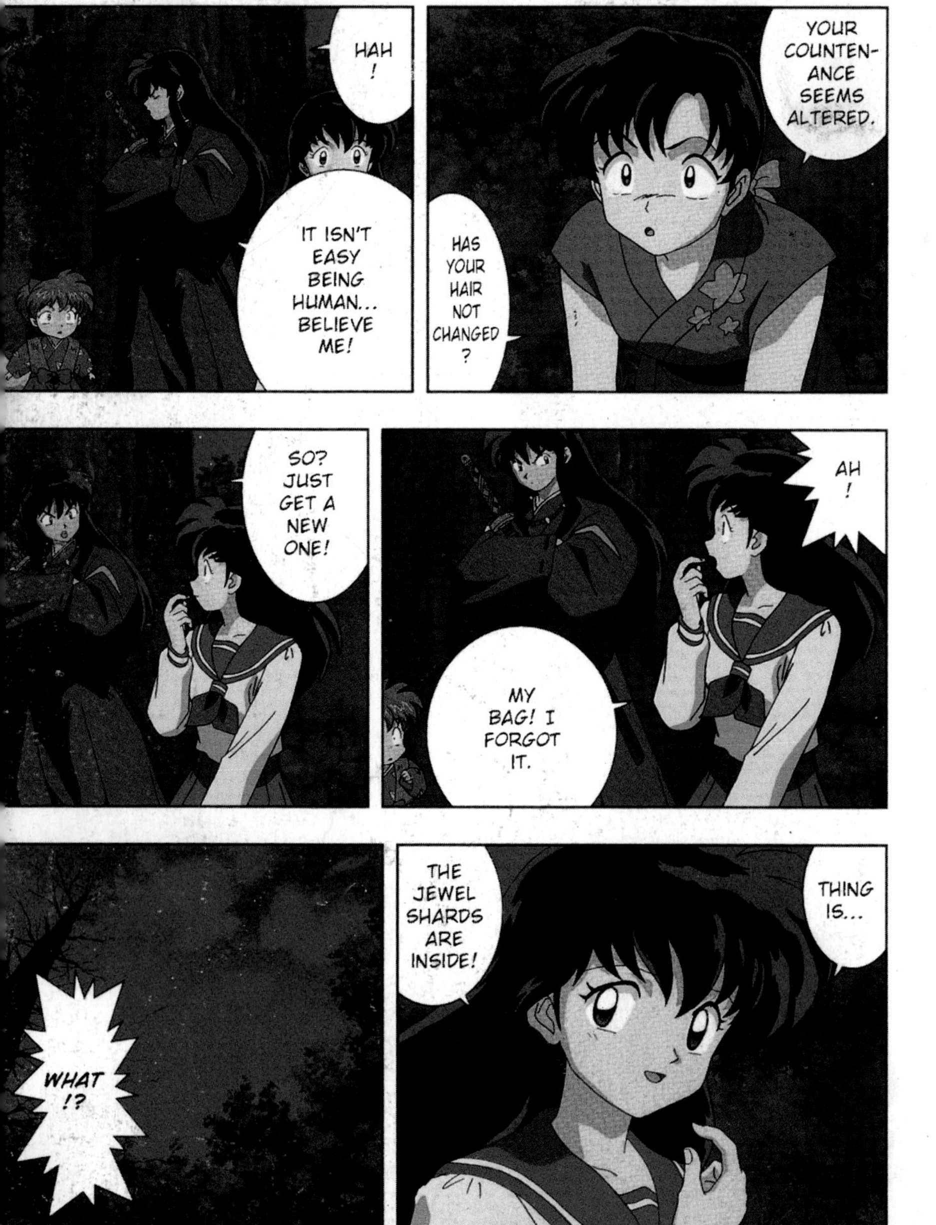
YOUR COUNTENANCE SEEMS ALTERED.
HAS YOUR HAIR NOT CHANGED?
HAH!
IT ISN'T EASY BEING HUMAN... BELIEVE ME!
AH!
MY BAG! I FORGOT IT.
SO? JUST GET A NEW ONE!
THING IS...
THE JEWEL SHARDS ARE INSIDE!
WHAT!?

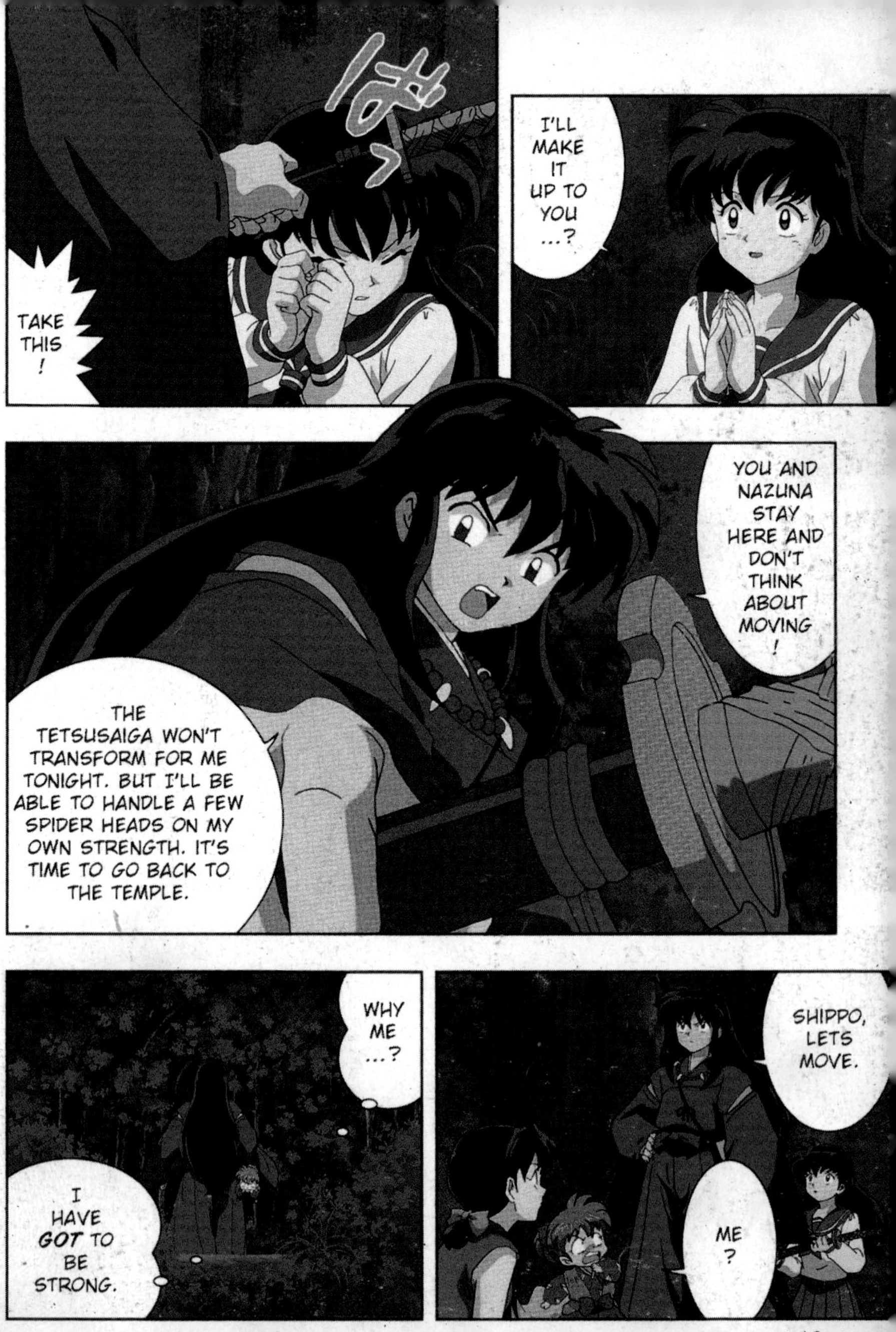
I'LL MAKE IT UP TO YOU ...?
はっ
TAKE THIS!
YOU AND NAZUNA STAY HERE AND DON'T THINK ABOUT MOVING!
THE TETSUSAIGA WON'T TRANSFORM FOR ME TONIGHT. BUT I'LL BE ABLE TO HANDLE A FEW SPIDER HEADS ON MY OWN STRENGTH. IT'S TIME TO GO BACK TO THE TEMPLE.
SHIPPO, LETS MOVE.
ME?
WHY ME ...?
I HAVE **GOT** TO BE STRONG.

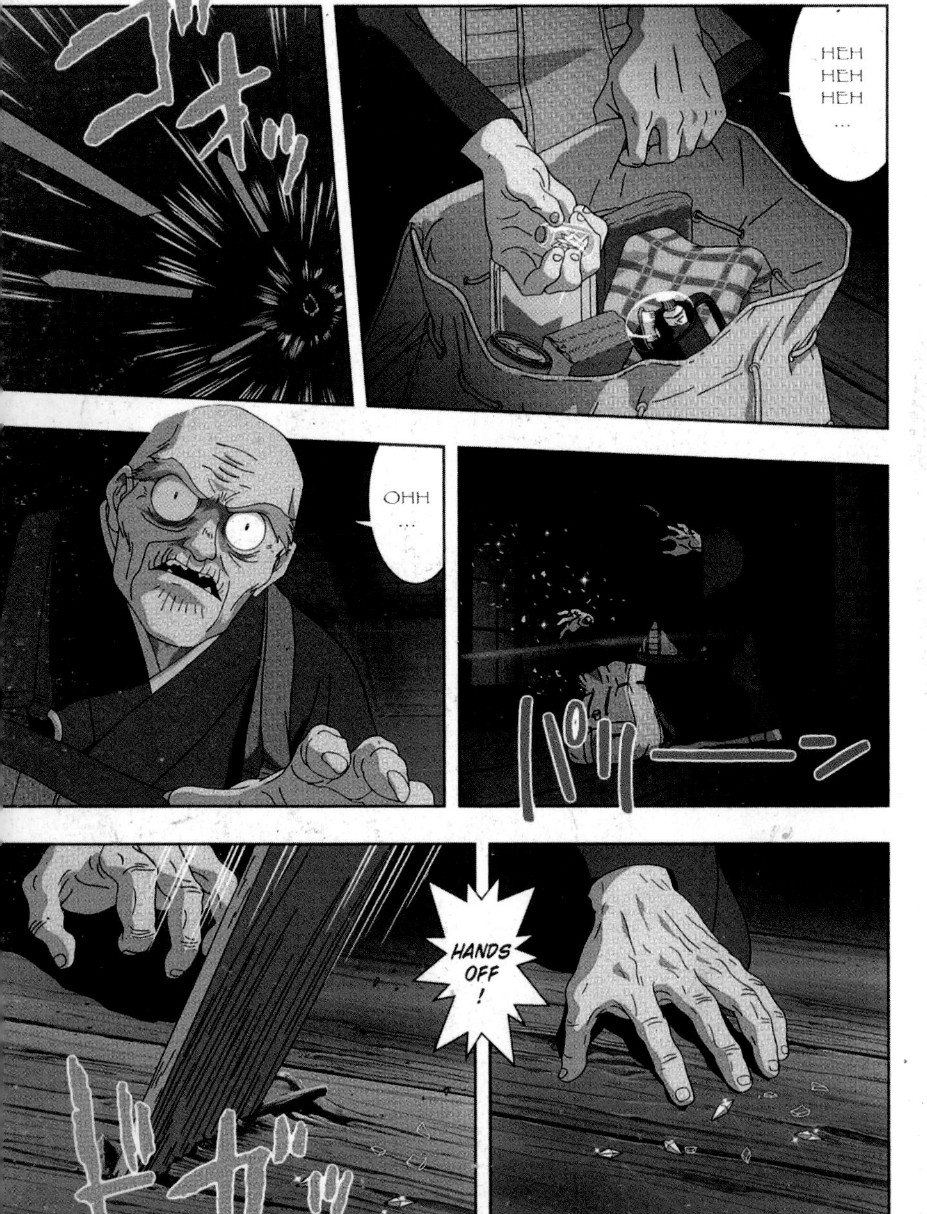
HEH HEH HEH ...
ゴォッ
パリーン
OHH ...
HANDS OFF !
ドガッ

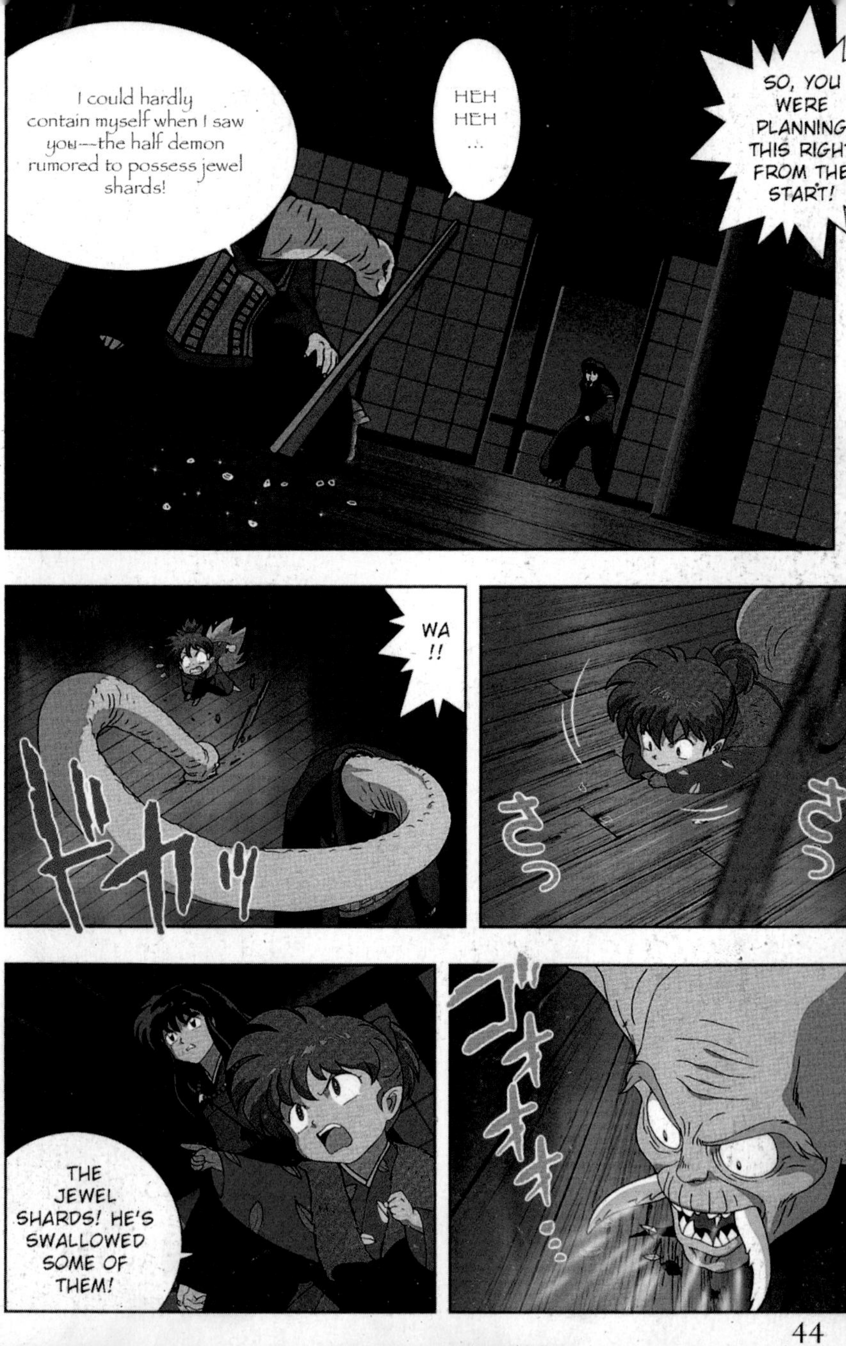
SO, YOU WERE PLANNING THIS RIGHT FROM THE START!
HEH HEH ...
I could hardly contain myself when I saw you---the half demon rumored to possess jewel shards!
さっ
さっ
WA !!
ドカッ
ゴォォォ...
THE JEWEL SHARDS! HE'S SWALLOWED SOME OF THEM!

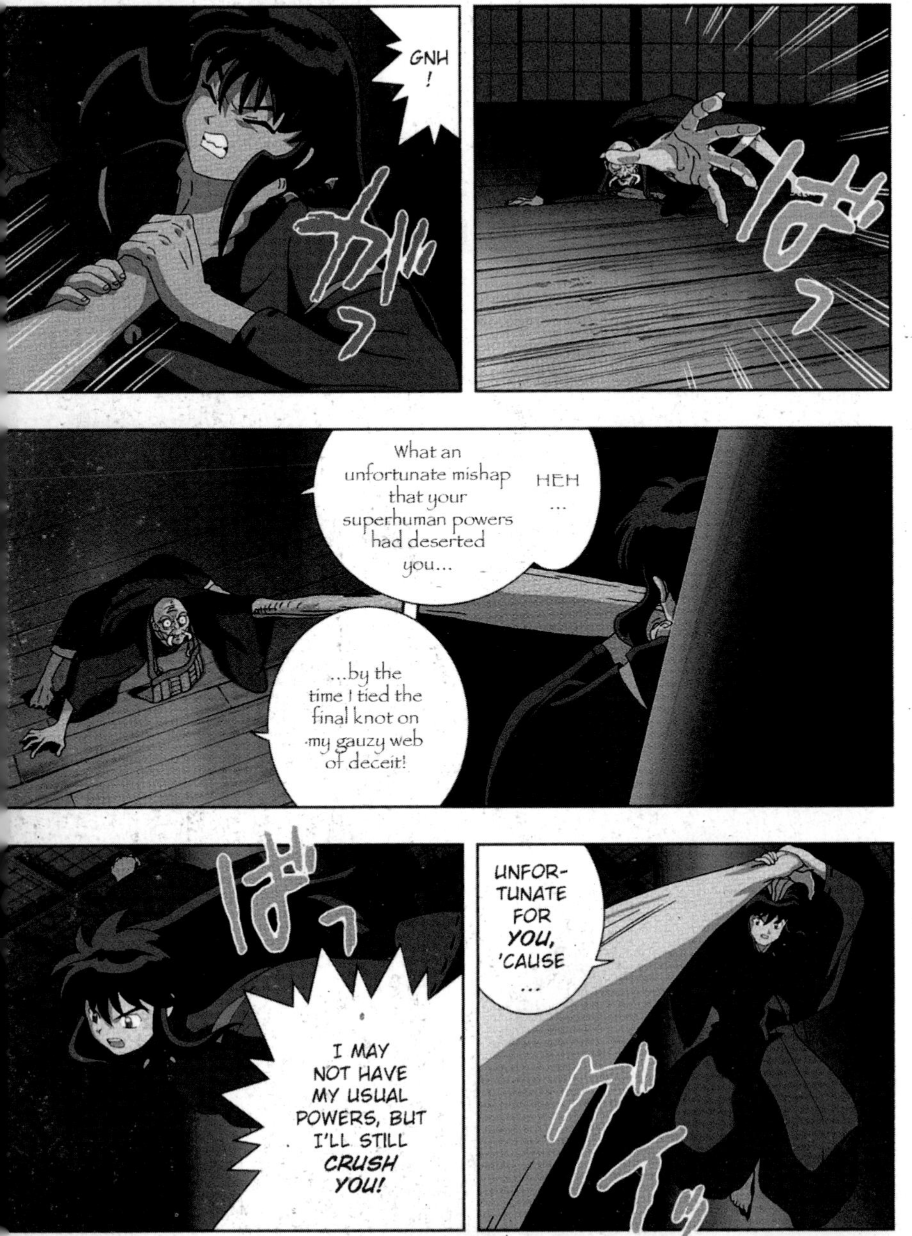

GNH!
HEH ...
What an unfortunate mishap that your superhuman powers had deserted you...
...by the time I tied the final knot on my gauzy web of deceit!
UNFORTUNATE FOR YOU, 'CAUSE ...
I MAY NOT HAVE MY USUAL POWERS, BUT I'LL STILL CRUSH YOU!

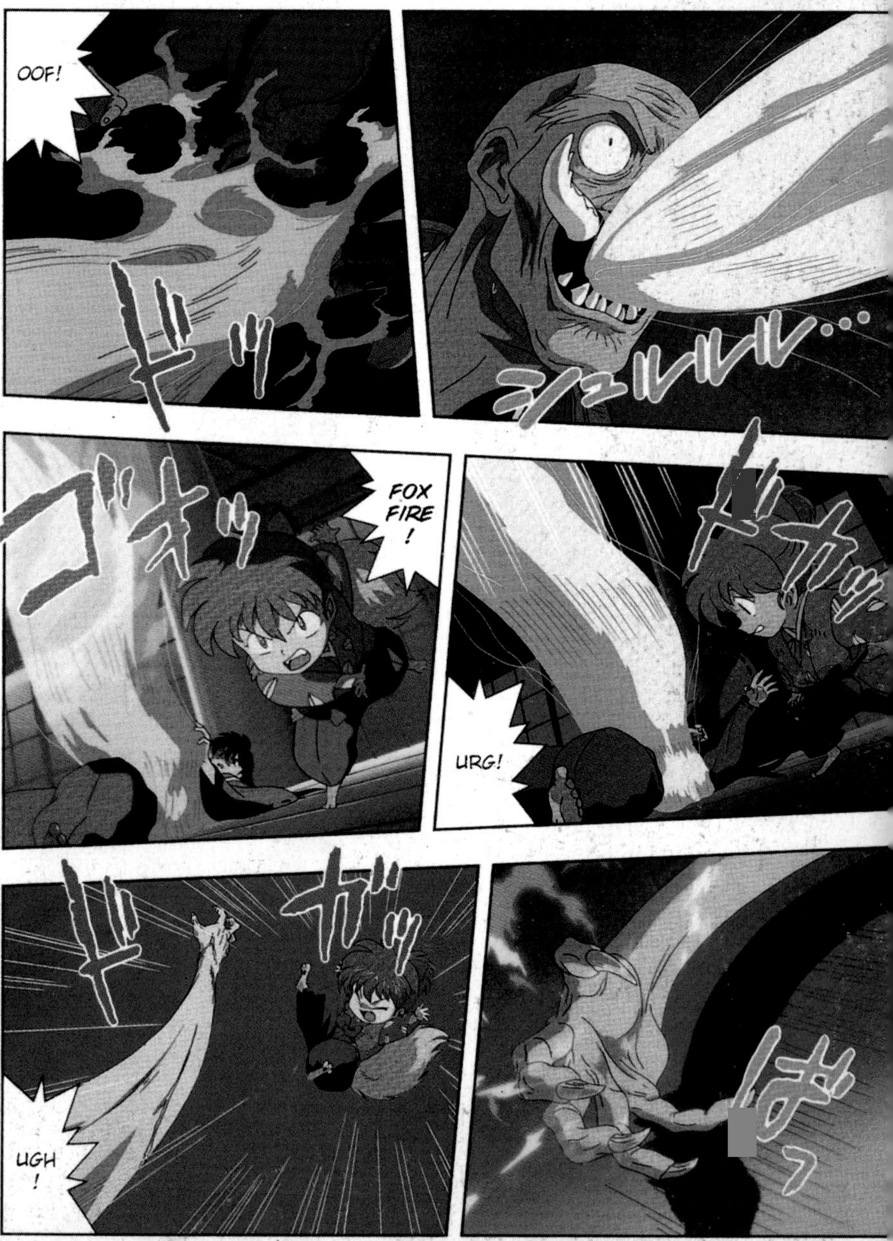
OOF!
URG!
FOX FIRE !
UGH !

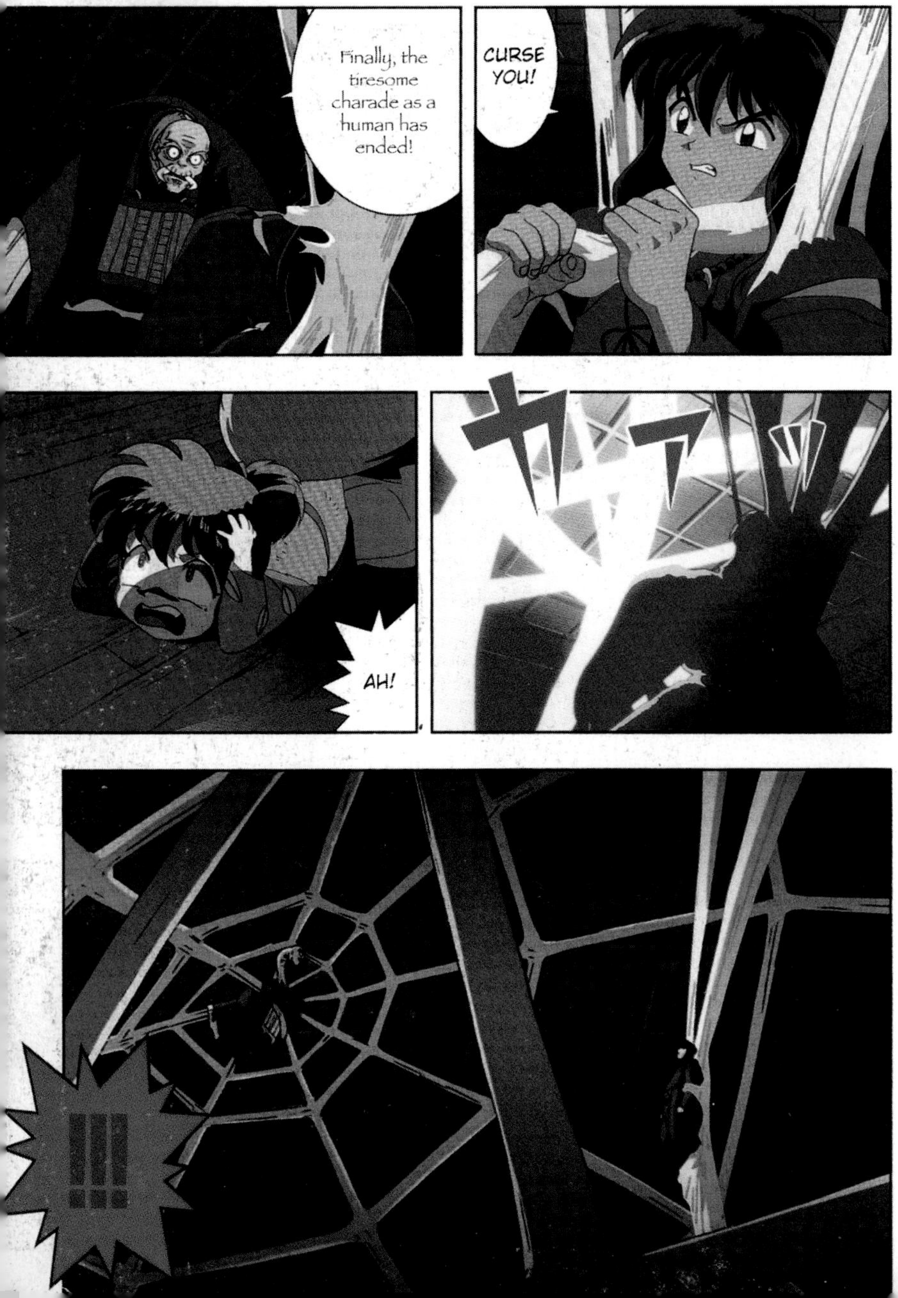

CURSE YOU!
Finally, the tiresome charade as a human has ended!
AH!
!!

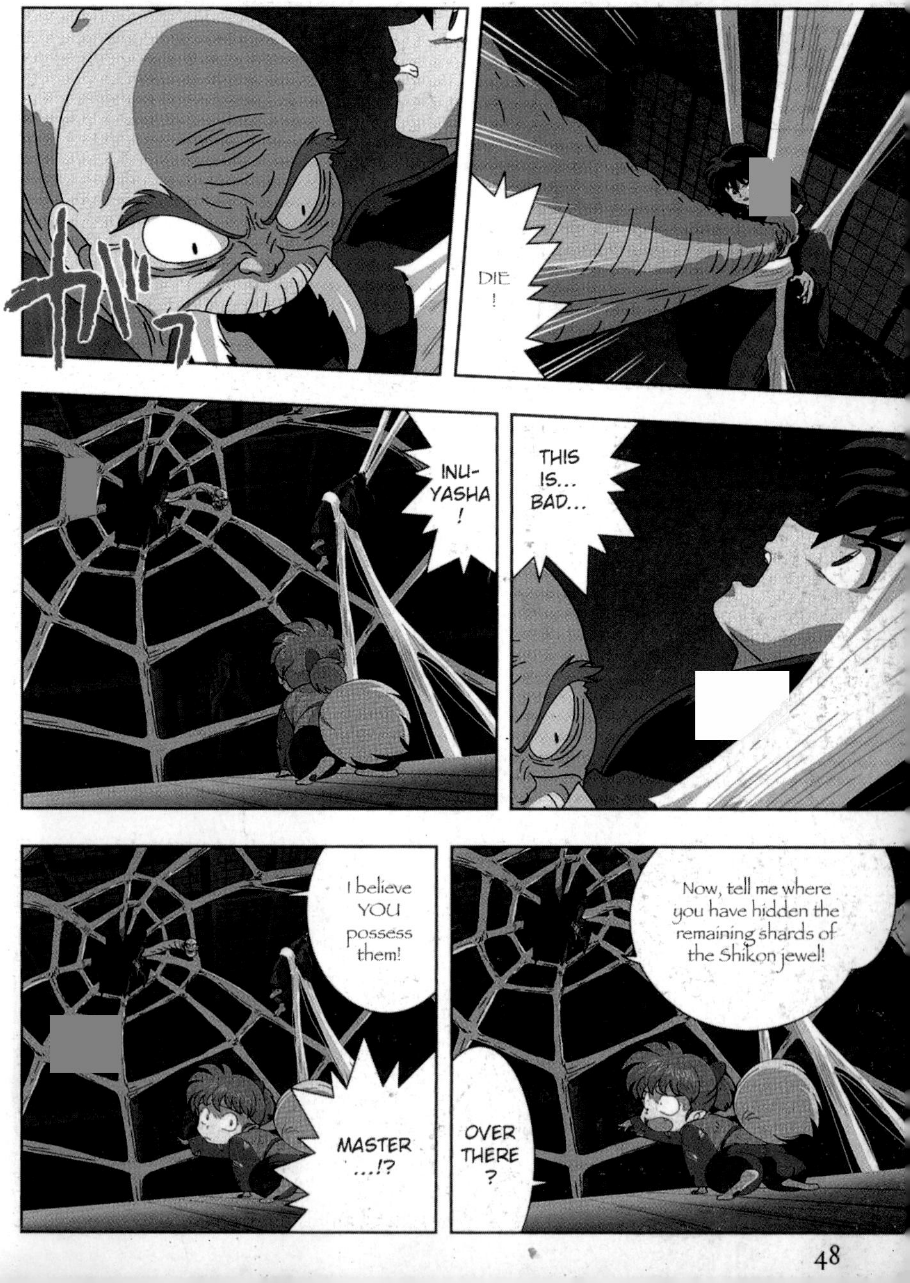
DIE !
THIS IS... BAD...
INU-YASHA !
Now, tell me where you have hidden the remaining shards of the Shikon jewel!
OVER THERE ?
I believe YOU possess them!
MASTER ...!?

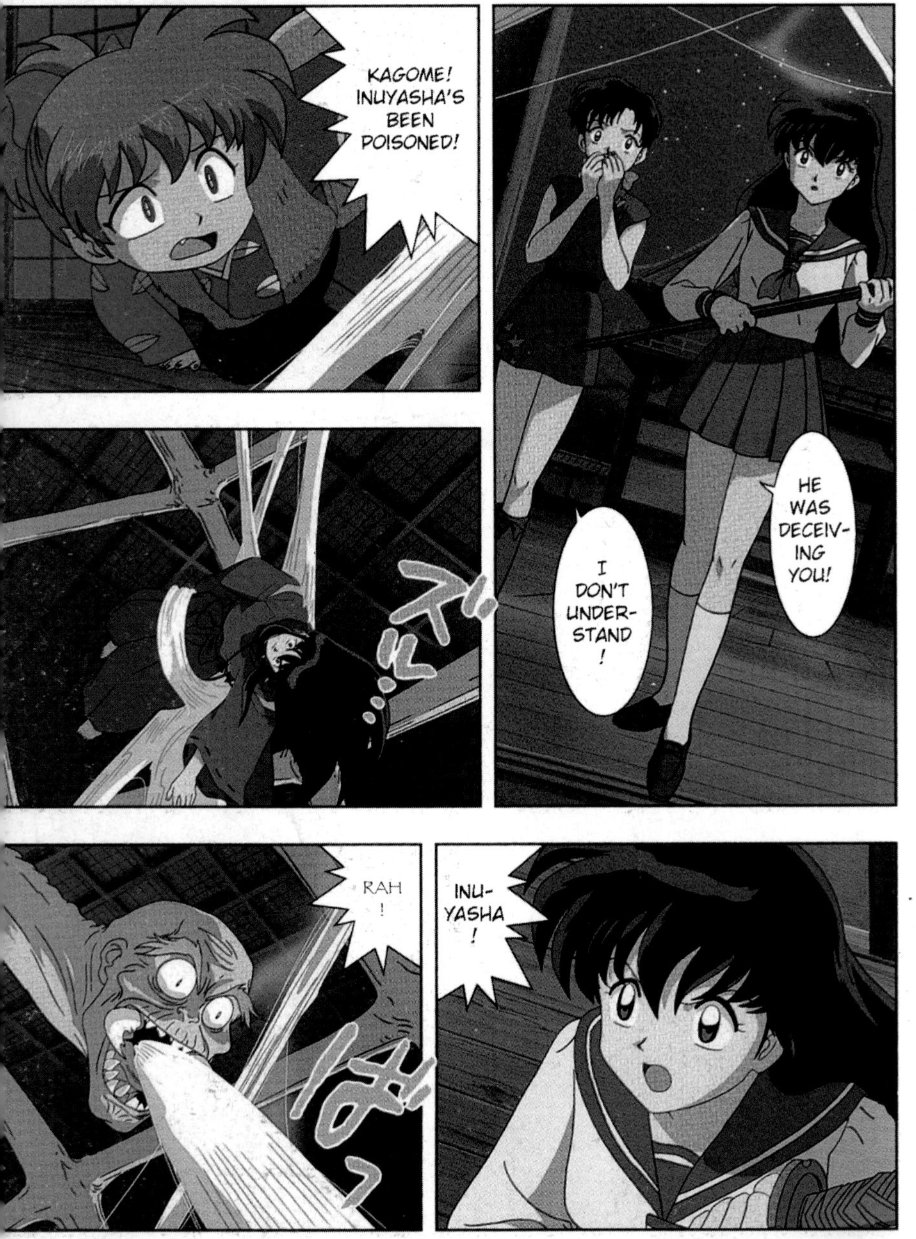
HE WAS DECEIV-ING YOU!
I DON'T UNDER-STAND!
KAGOME! INUYASHA'S BEEN POISONED!
INU-YASHA!
RAH!

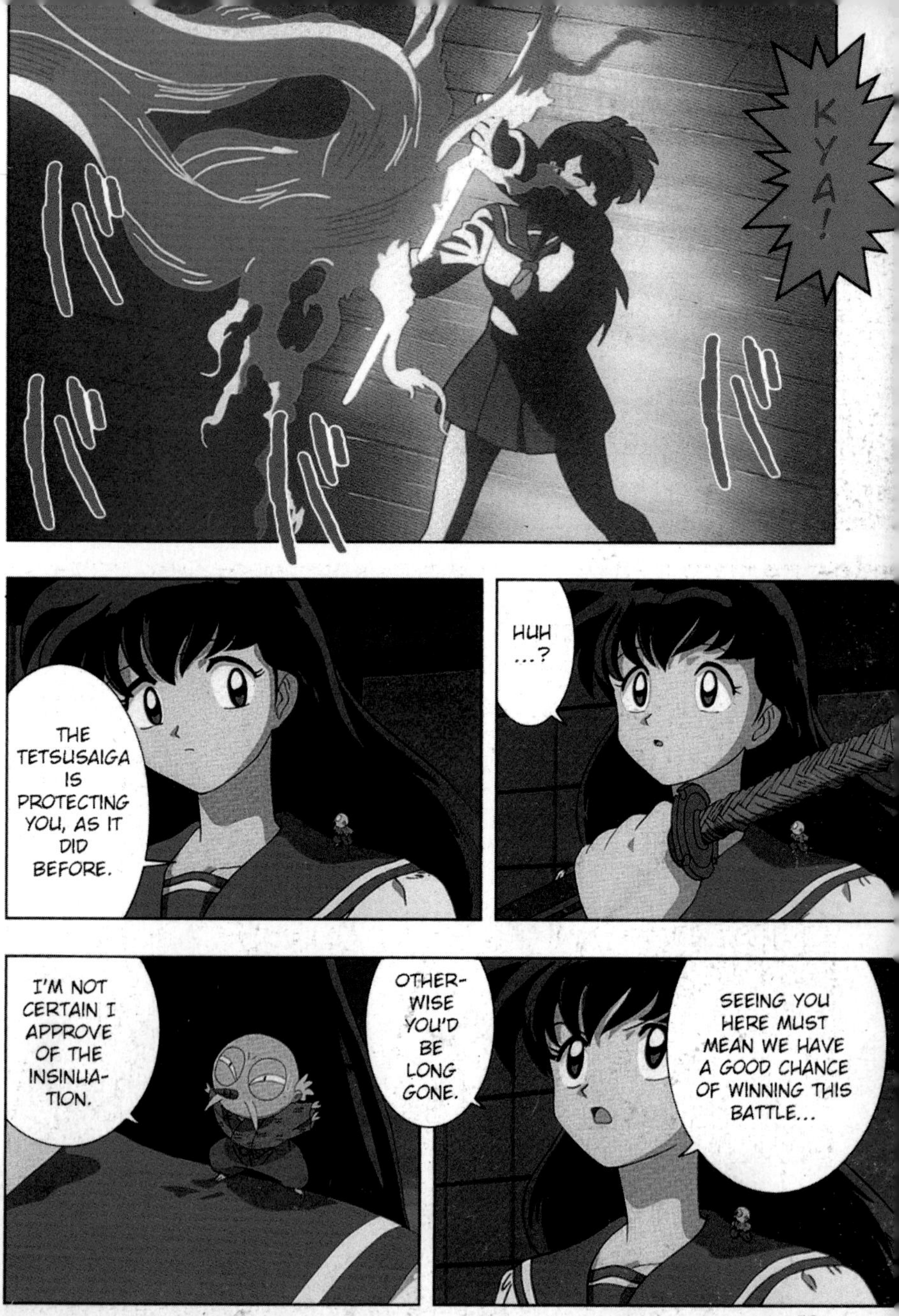
KYA!
HUH ...?
THE TETSUSAIGA IS PROTECTING YOU, AS IT DID BEFORE.
SEEING YOU HERE MUST MEAN WE HAVE A GOOD CHANCE OF WINNING THIS BATTLE...
OTHER-WISE YOU'D BE LONG GONE.
I'M NOT CERTAIN I APPROVE OF THE INSINUA-TION.

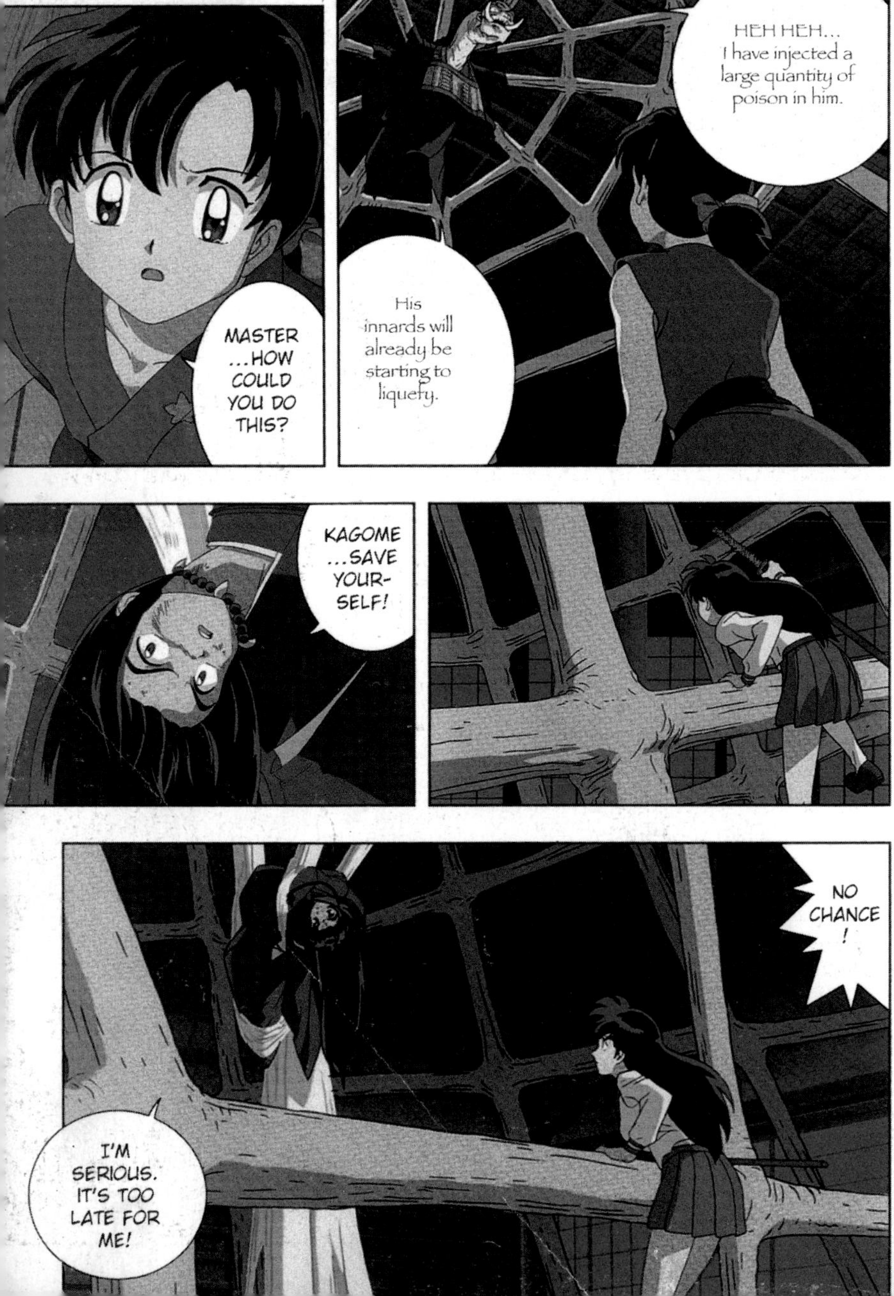
HEH HEH... I have injected a large quantity of poison in him.
His innards will already be starting to liquefy.
MASTER ...HOW COULD YOU DO THIS?
KAGOME ...SAVE YOUR-SELF!
NO CHANCE!
I'M SERIOUS. IT'S TOO LATE FOR ME!

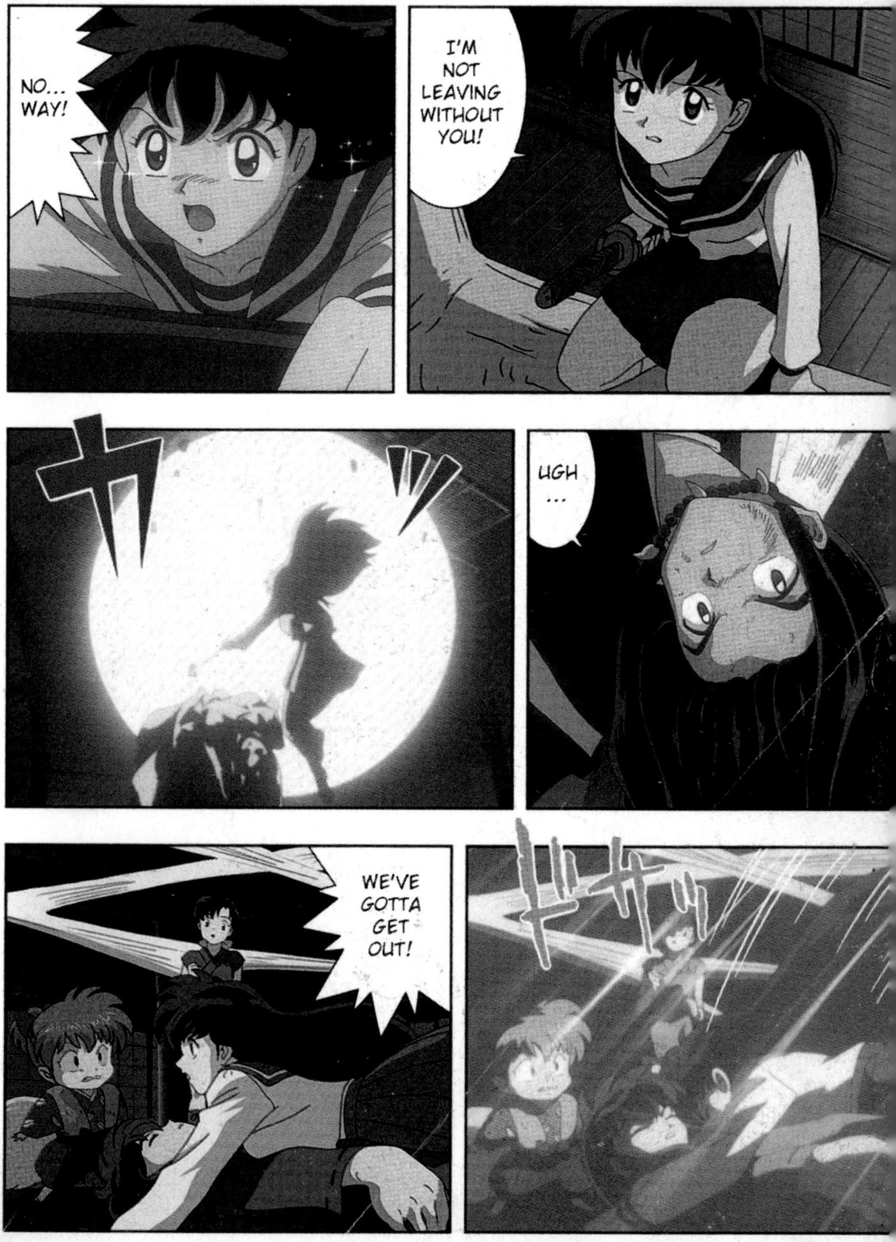
I'M NOT LEAVING WITHOUT YOU!
NO... WAY!
UGH ...
WE'VE GOTTA GET OUT!

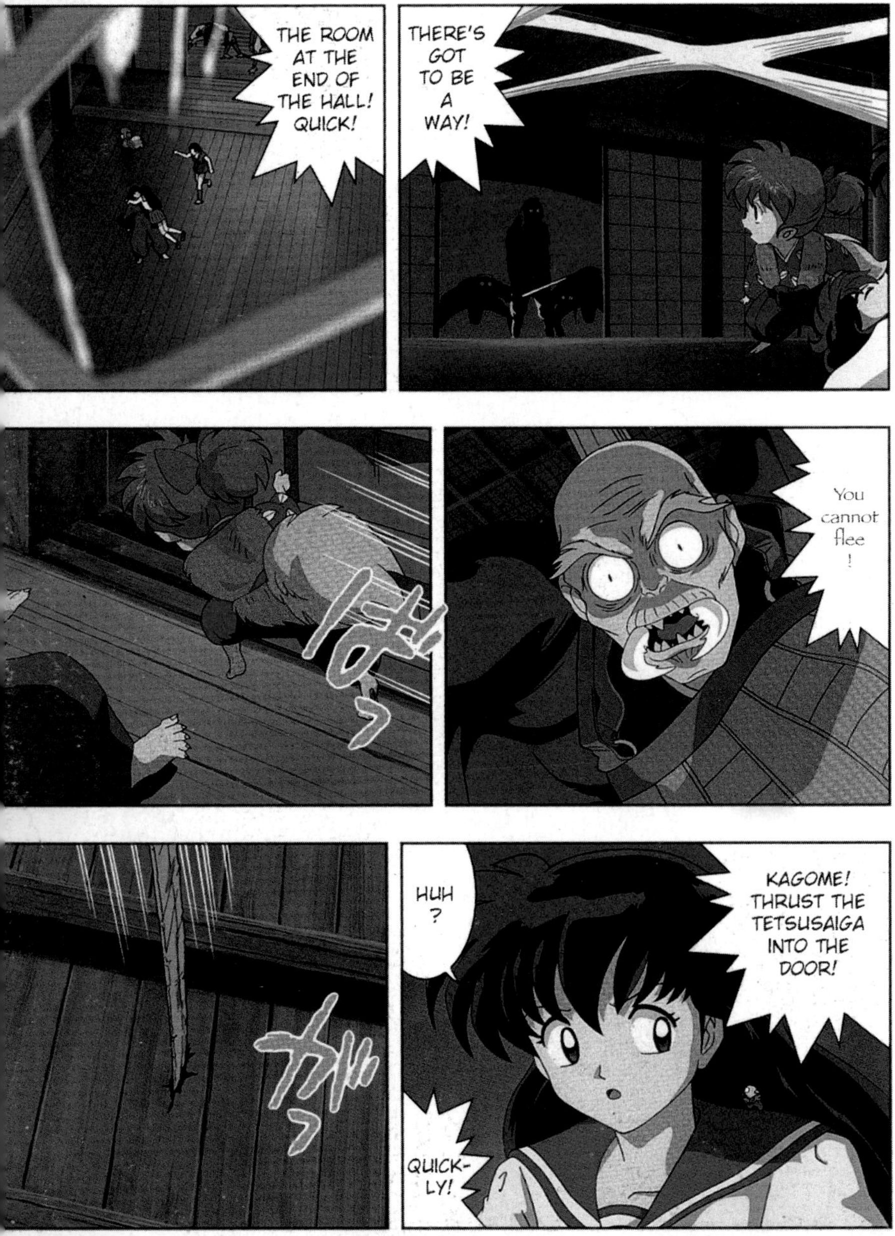

THERE'S GOT TO BE A WAY!
THE ROOM AT THE END OF THE HALL! QUICK!
You cannot flee!
ぱっ
KAGOME! THRUST THE TETSUSAIGA INTO THE DOOR!
HUH?
QUICK-LY!
ガッ

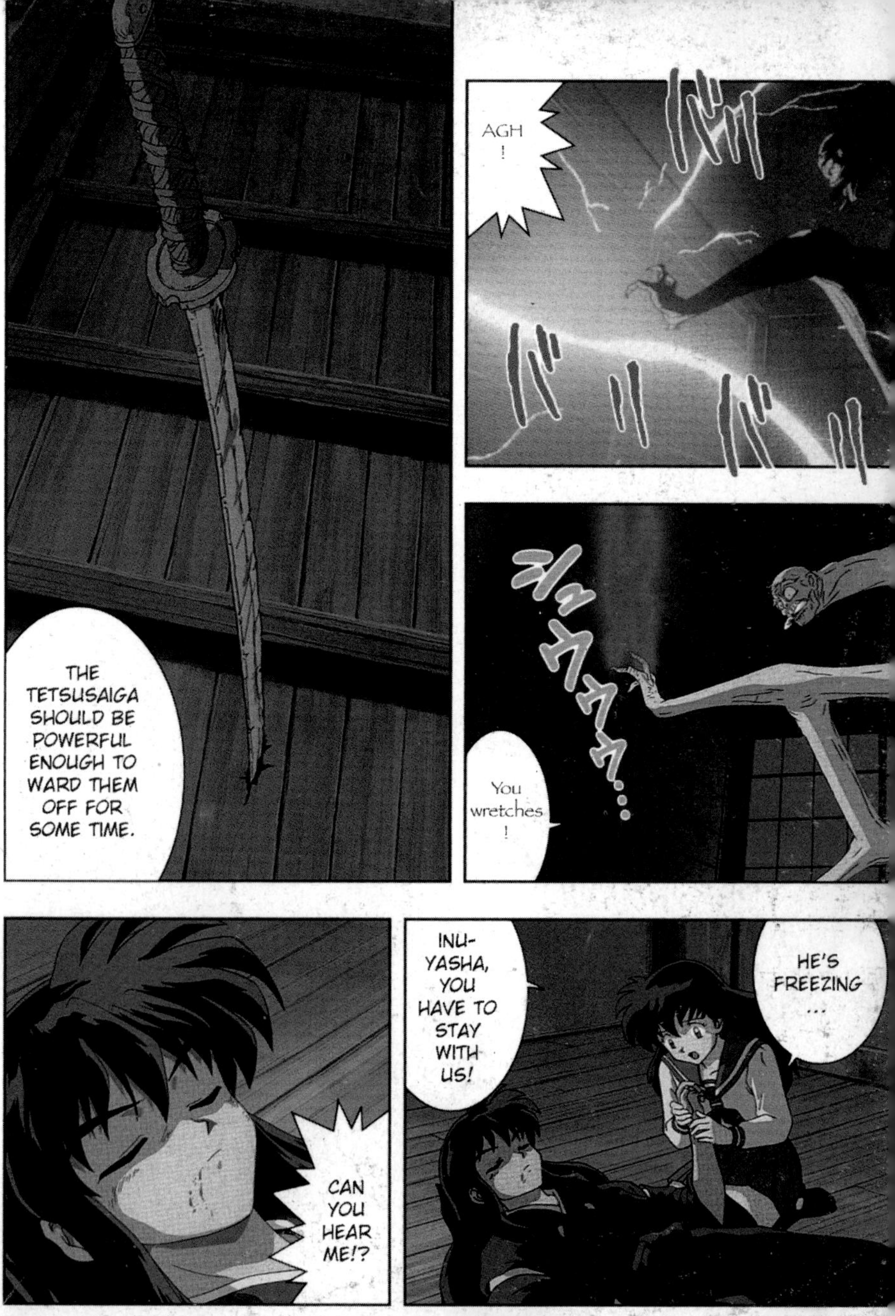
AGH!
You wretches!
THE TETSUSAIGA SHOULD BE POWERFUL ENOUGH TO WARD THEM OFF FOR SOME TIME.
HE'S FREEZING...
INU-YASHA, YOU HAVE TO STAY WITH US!
CAN YOU HEAR ME!?

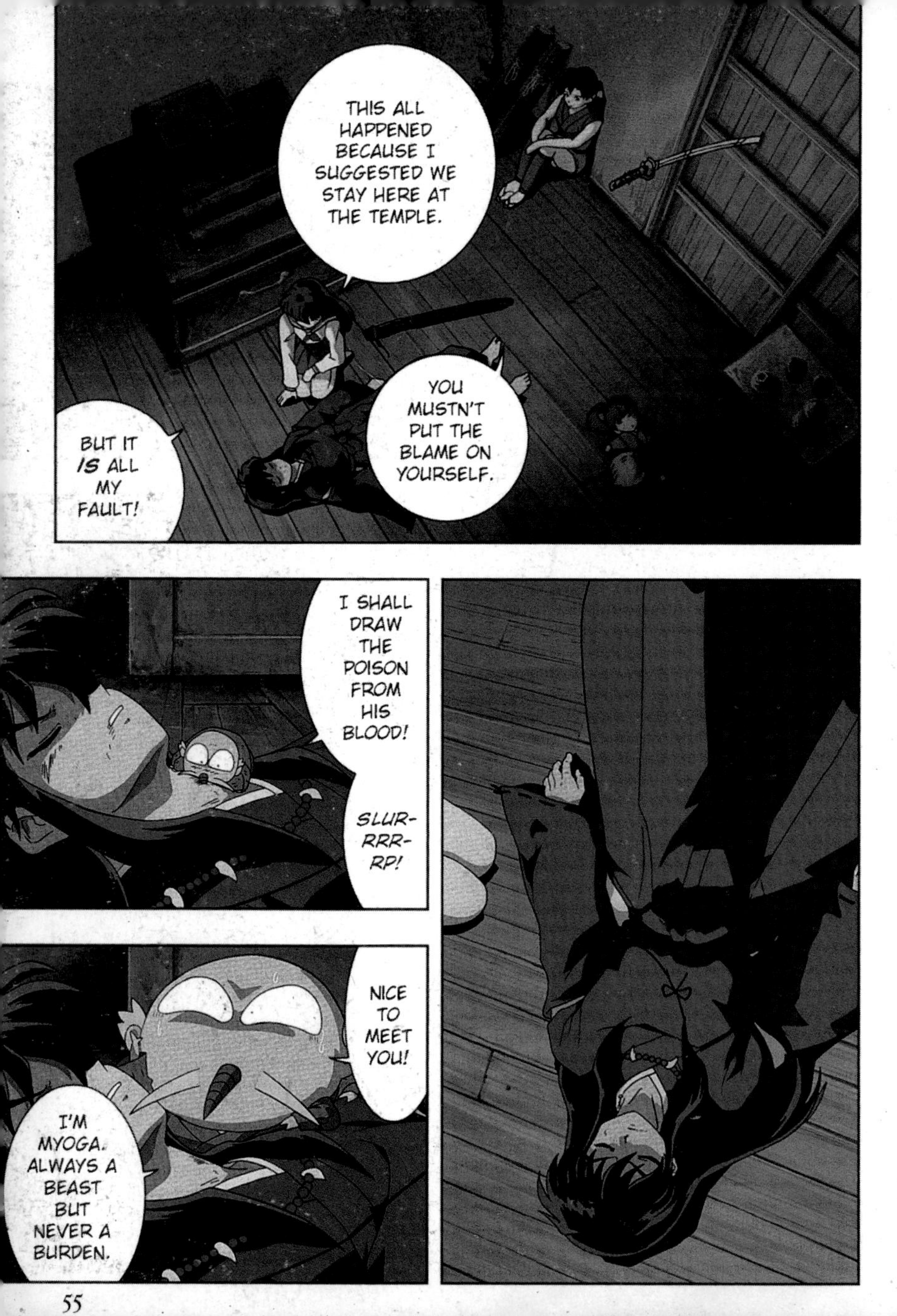
THIS ALL HAPPENED BECAUSE I SUGGESTED WE STAY HERE AT THE TEMPLE.
YOU MUSTN'T PUT THE BLAME ON YOURSELF.
BUT IT *IS* ALL MY FAULT!
I SHALL DRAW THE POISON FROM HIS BLOOD!
*SLURRRRP!*
NICE TO MEET YOU!
I'M MYOGA. ALWAYS A BEAST BUT NEVER A BURDEN.

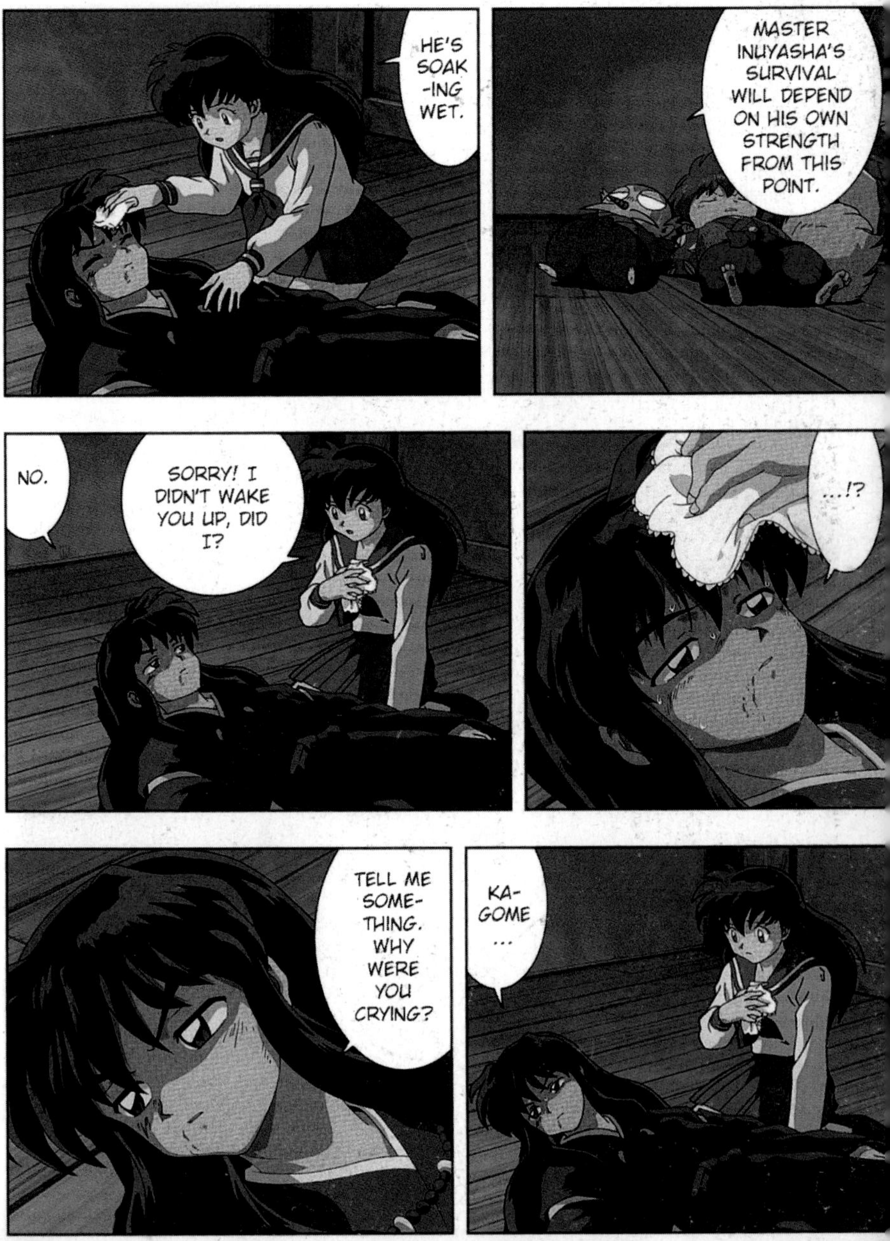
MASTER INUYASHA'S SURVIVAL WILL DEPEND ON HIS OWN STRENGTH FROM THIS POINT.
HE'S SOAK-ING WET.
...!?
SORRY! I DIDN'T WAKE YOU UP, DID I?
NO.
KA-GOME ...
TELL ME SOME-THING. WHY WERE YOU CRYING?

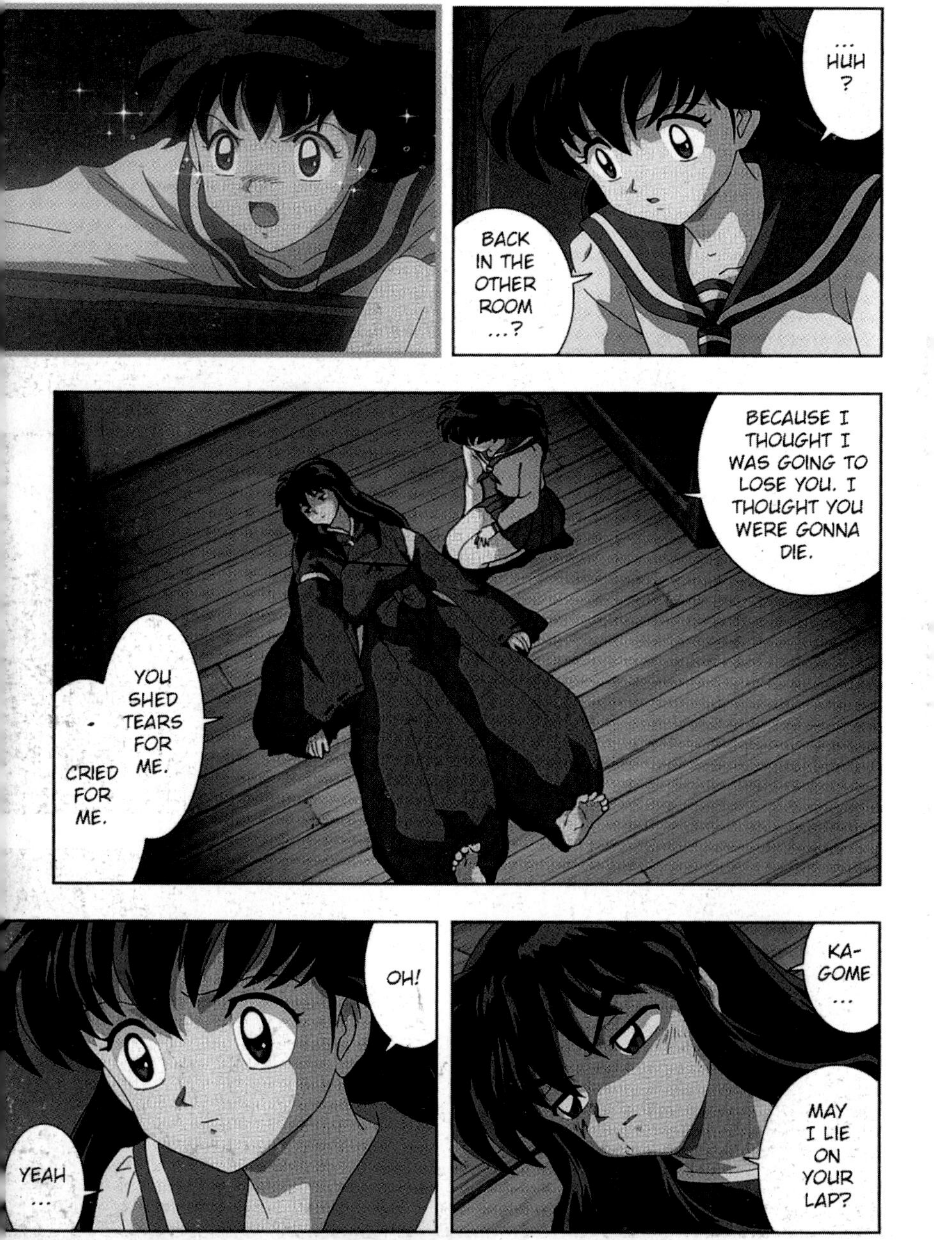
...HUH?
BACK IN THE OTHER ROOM...?
BECAUSE I THOUGHT I WAS GOING TO LOSE YOU. I THOUGHT YOU WERE GONNA DIE.
YOU SHED TEARS FOR ME.
CRIED FOR ME.
KA-GOME...
MAY I LIE ON YOUR LAP?
OH!
YEAH...

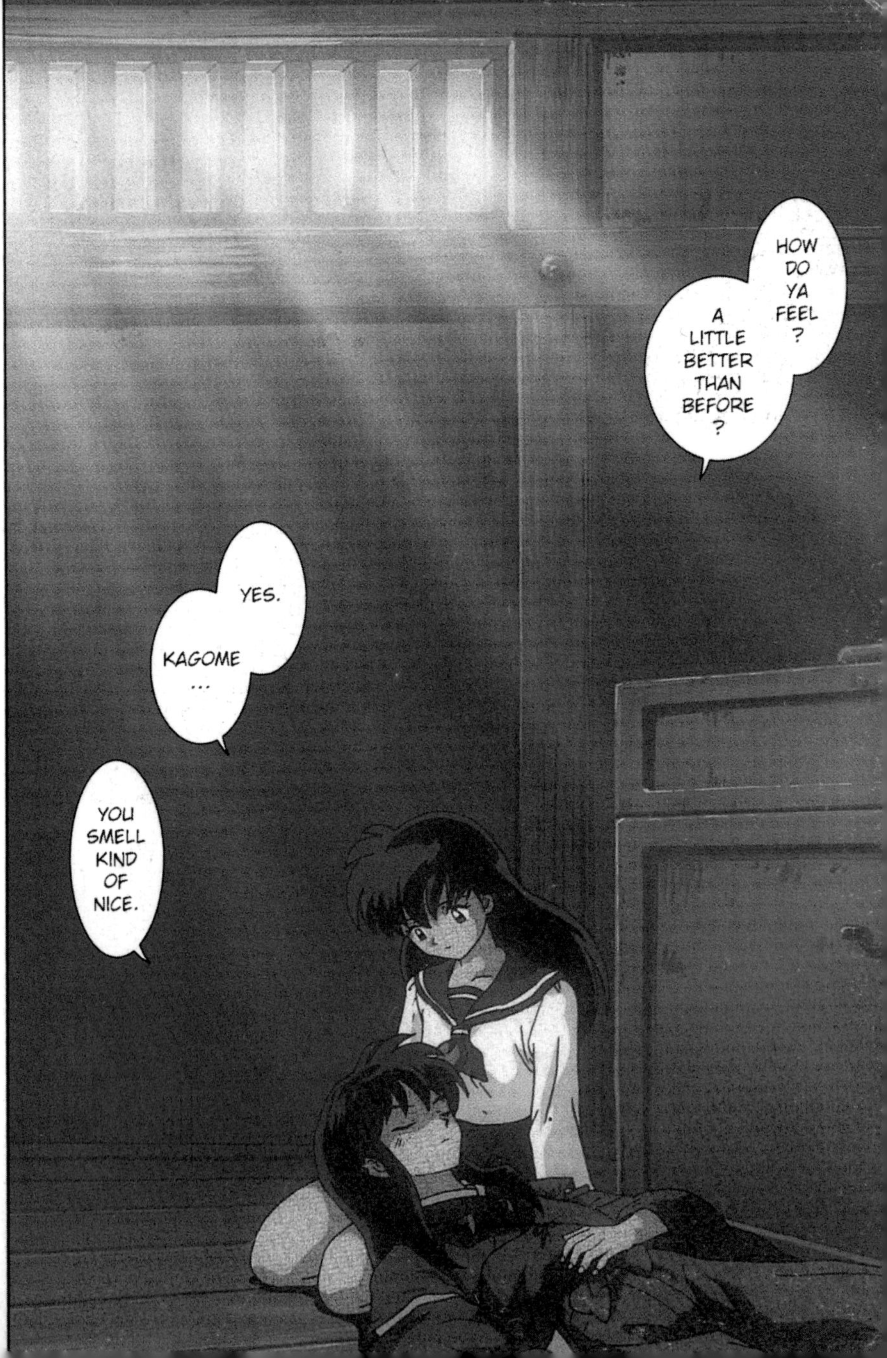
HOW DO YA FEEL?
A LITTLE BETTER THAN BEFORE?
YES.
KAGOME...
YOU SMELL KIND OF NICE.

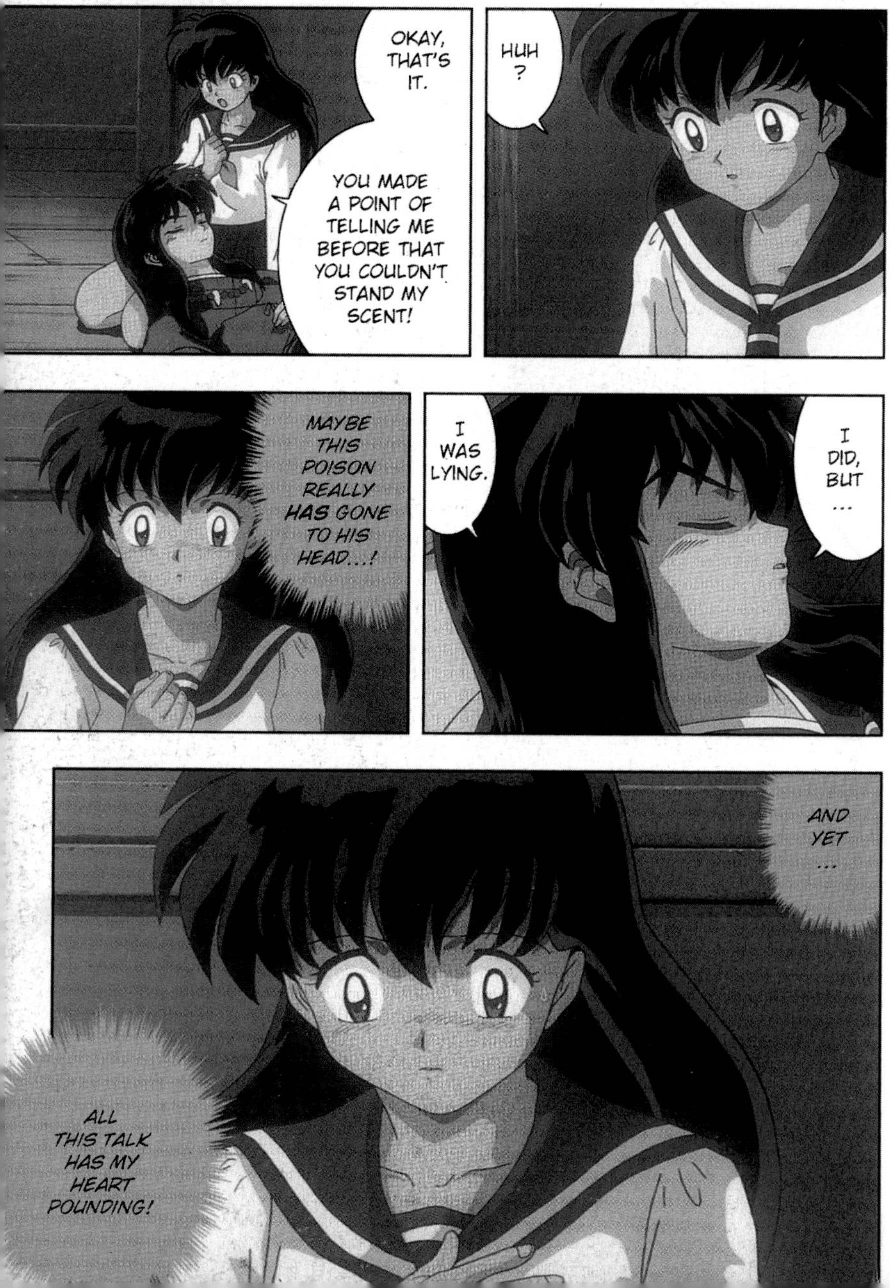
HUH?
OKAY, THAT'S IT.
YOU MADE A POINT OF TELLING ME BEFORE THAT YOU COULDN'T STAND MY SCENT!
I DID, BUT ...
I WAS LYING.
MAYBE THIS POISON REALLY **HAS** GONE TO HIS HEAD...!
AND YET ...
ALL THIS TALK HAS MY HEART POUNDING!

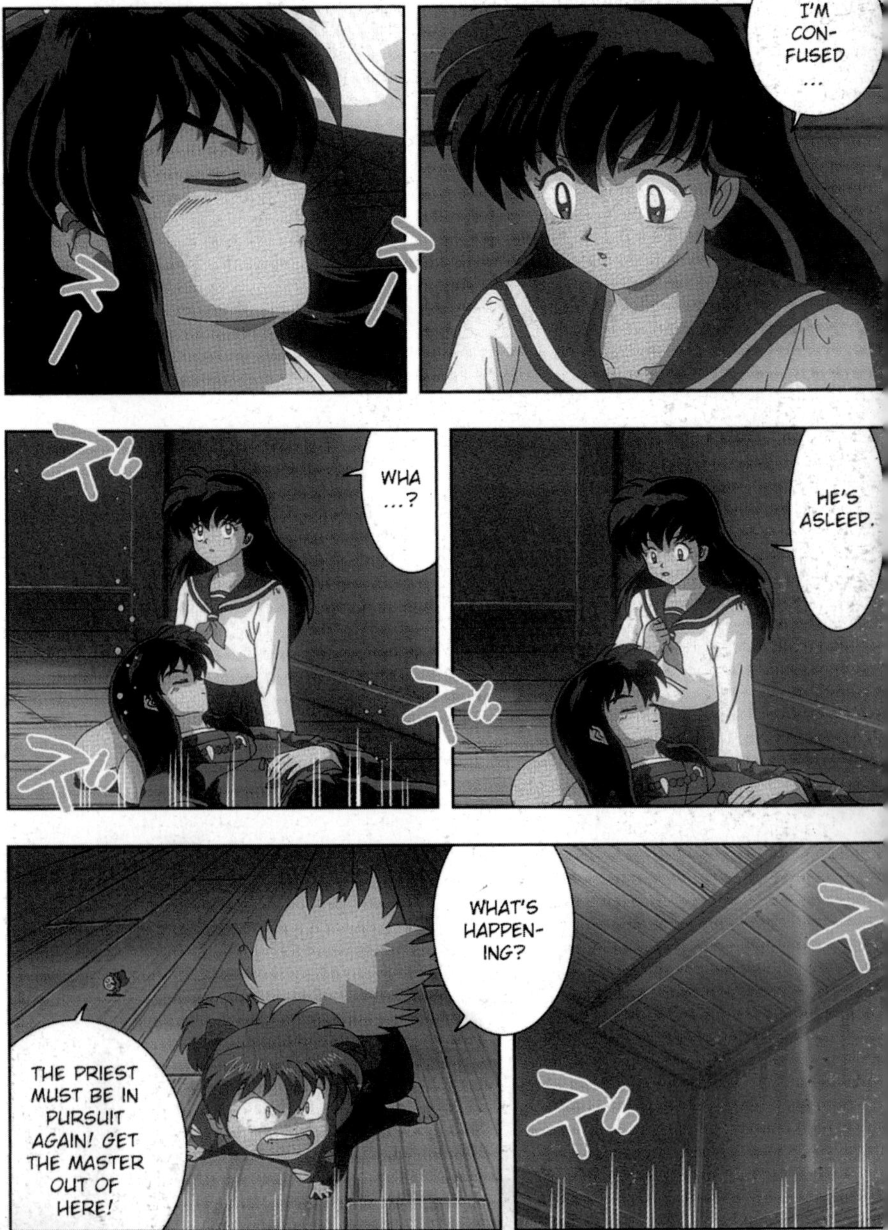
NOW I'M CON-FUSED ...
HE'S ASLEEP.
WHA ...?
WHAT'S HAPPEN-ING?
THE PRIEST MUST BE IN PURSUIT AGAIN! GET THE MASTER OUT OF HERE!

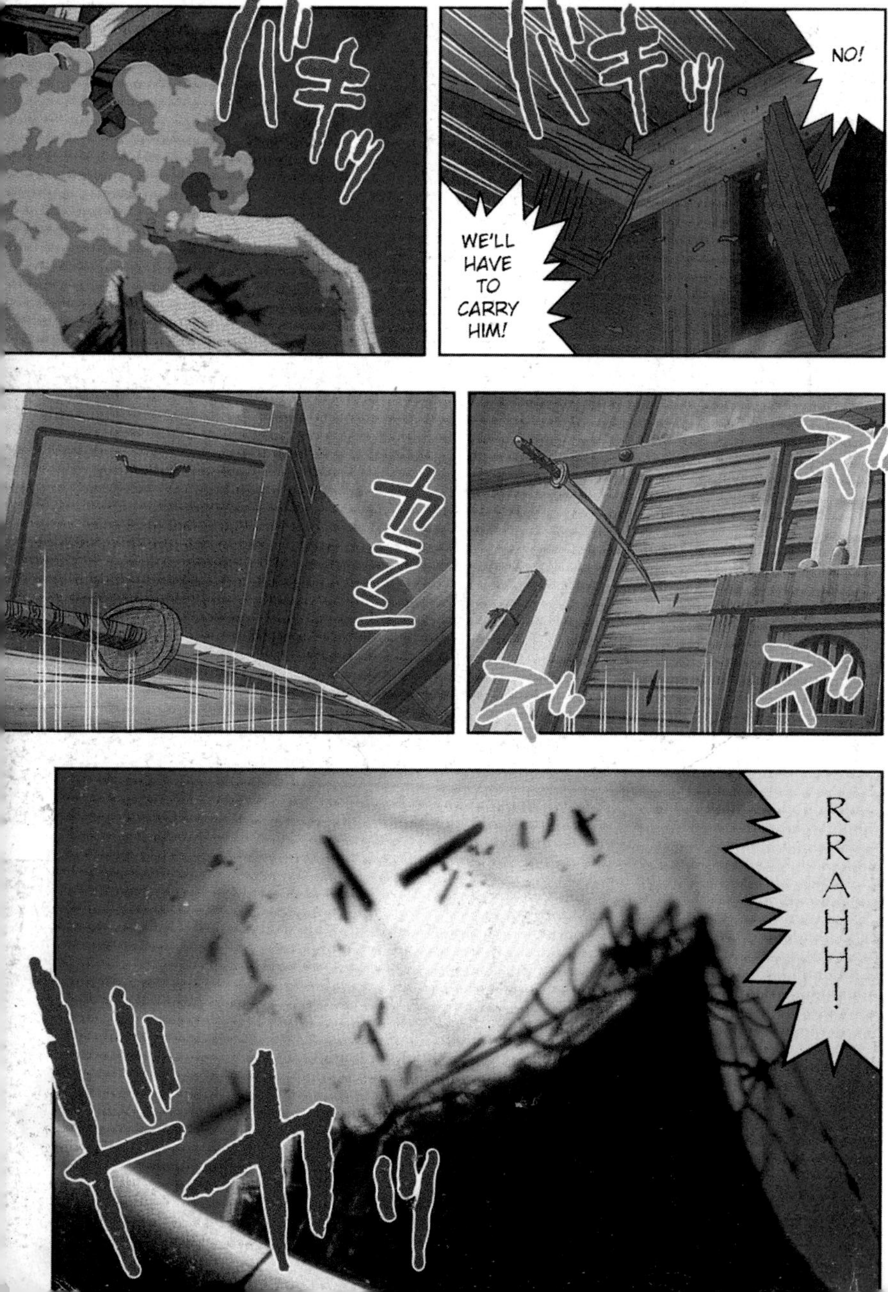
バキッ
NO!
WE'LL HAVE TO CARRY HIM!
バキッ
ズッ
ズッ
ズッ
カラン
RRAHH!
ドカッ

WATCH OUT!

グギッ

ガラ

ガラ

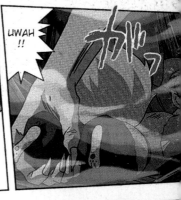

UWAH !!

WHOA!

カバッ

I must possess the remaining jewel fragments!

SHIPPO!

ブンッ

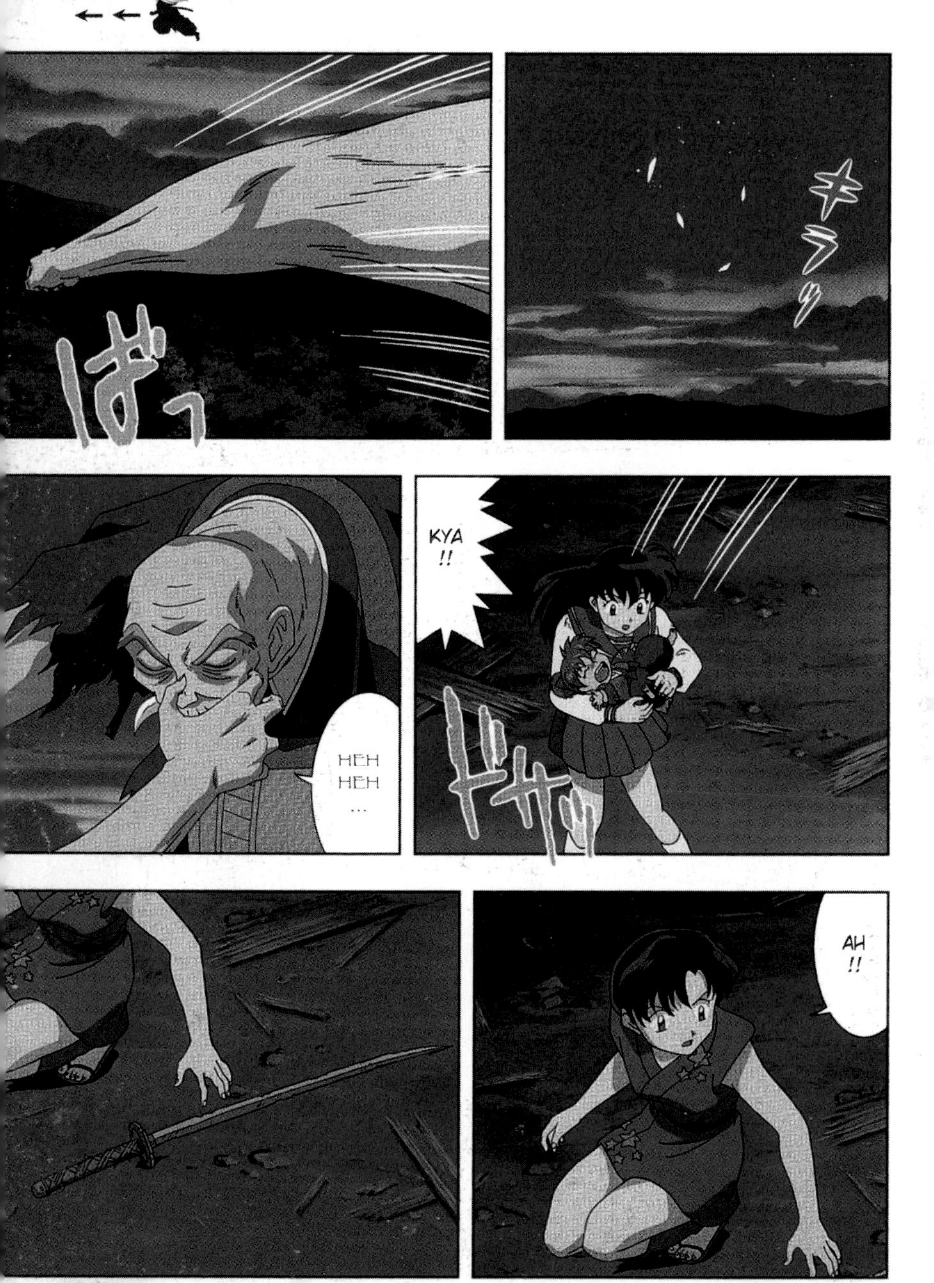
キラッ
ぱっ
KYA !!
ドサッ
HEH HEH ...
AH !!

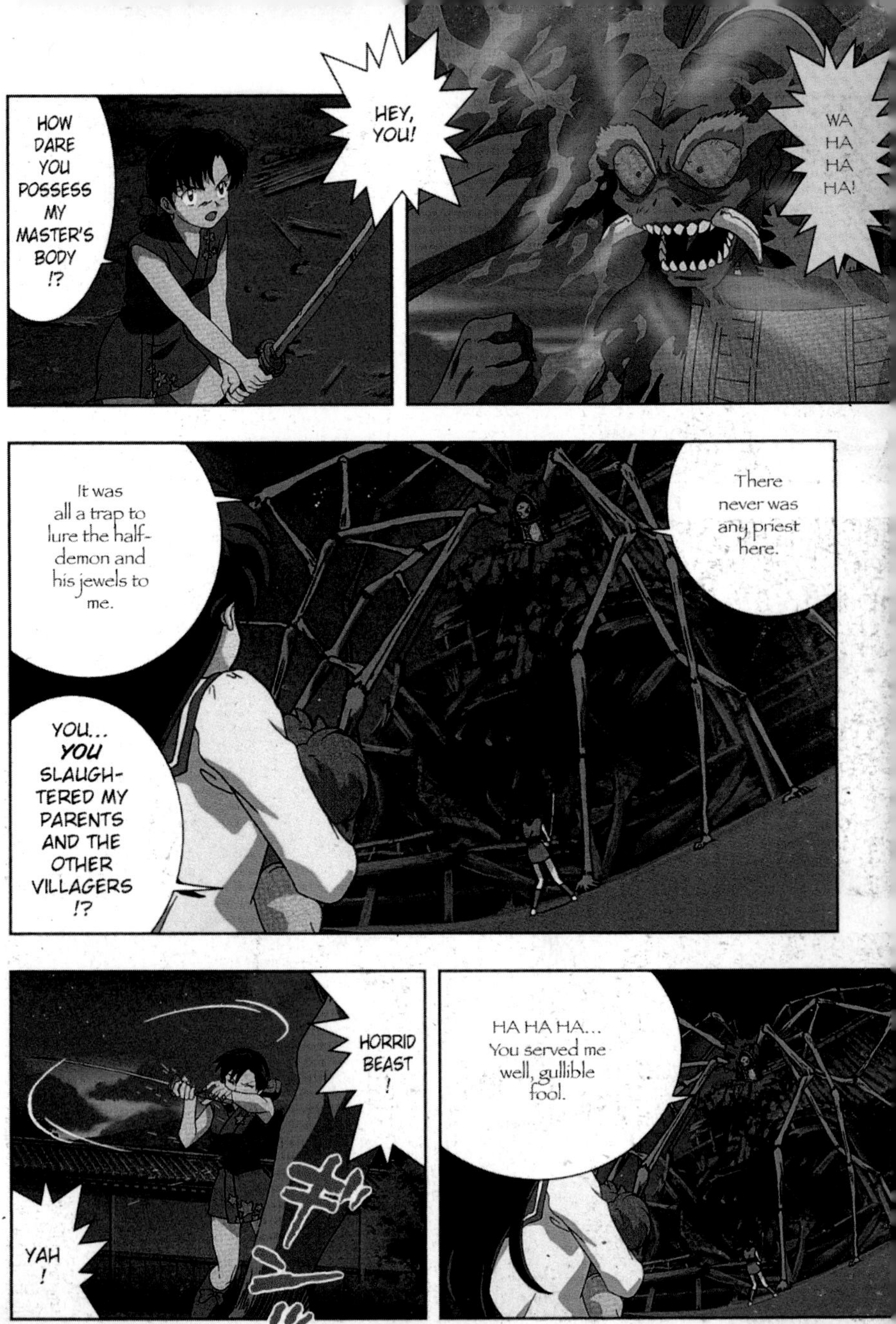
WA HA HA HA!
HEY, YOU!
HOW DARE YOU POSSESS MY MASTER'S BODY !?
There never was any priest here.
It was all a trap to lure the half-demon and his jewels to me.
YOU... *YOU* SLAUGHTERED MY PARENTS AND THE OTHER VILLAGERS !?
HA HA HA... You served me well, gullible fool.
HORRID BEAST !
YAH !

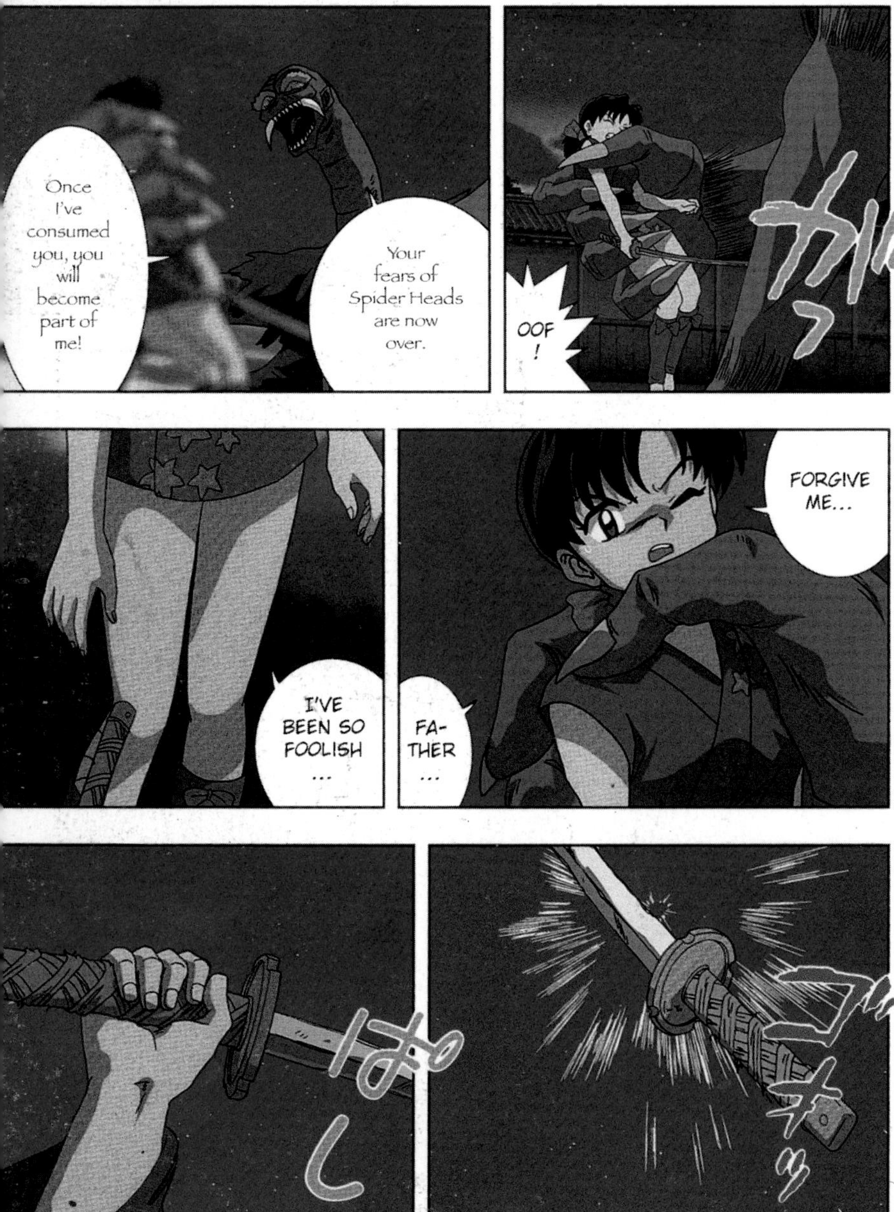
OOF!
Your fears of Spider Heads are now over.
Once I've consumed you, you will become part of me!
FORGIVE ME...
FA-THER...
I'VE BEEN SO FOOLISH...

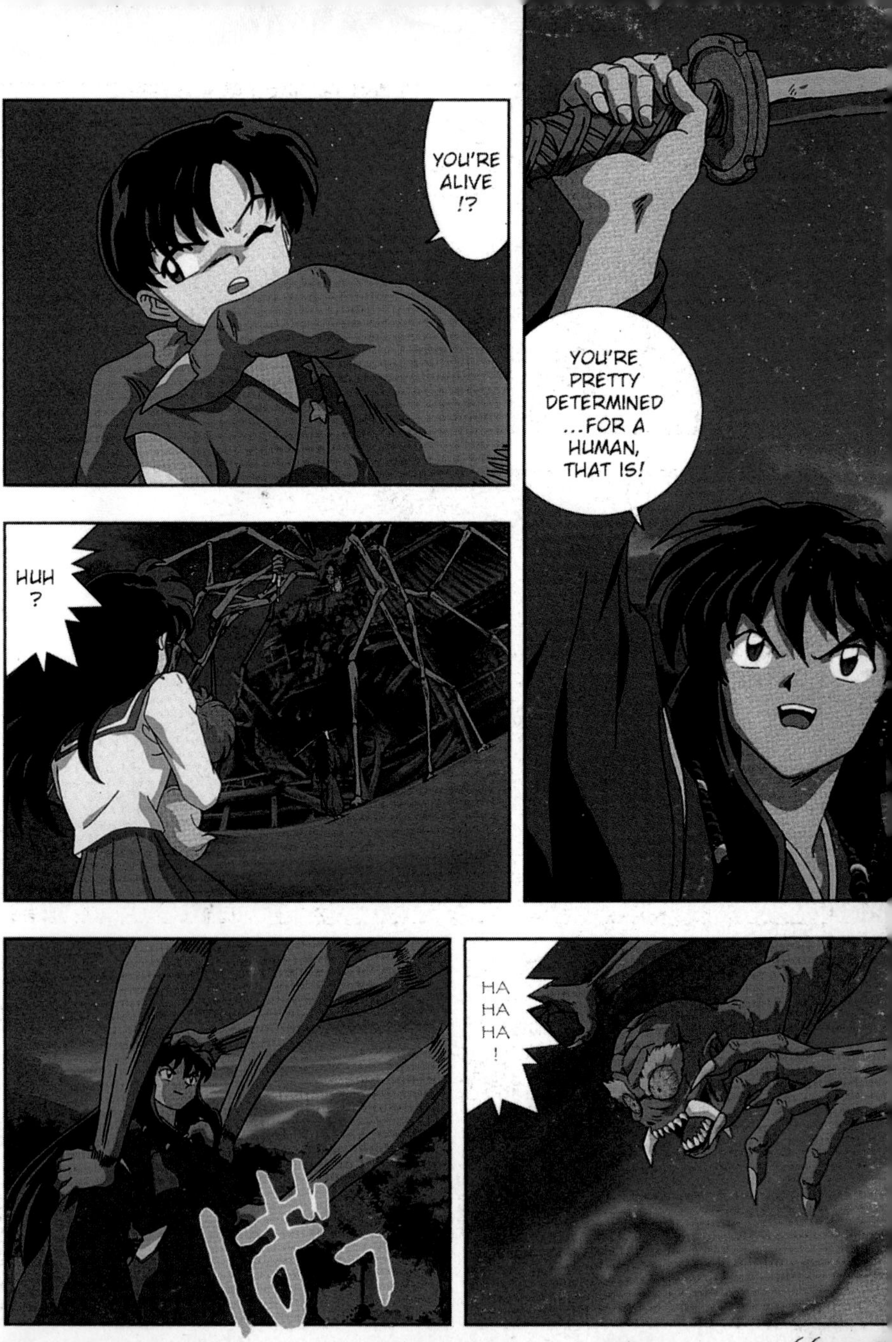
YOU'RE PRETTY DETERMINED ...FOR A HUMAN, THAT IS!
YOU'RE ALIVE !?
HUH ?
HA HA HA !
ばっ

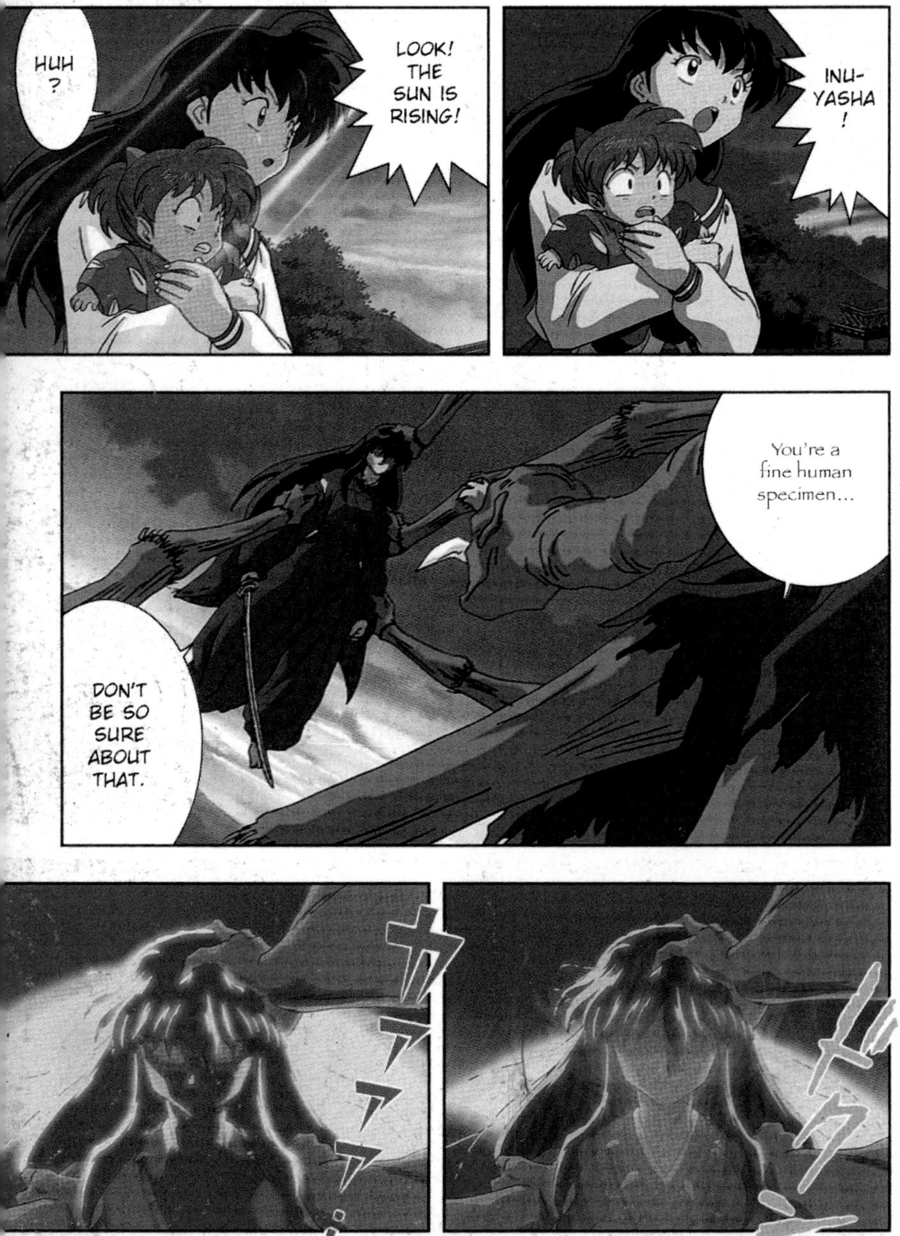
INU-YASHA!
LOOK! THE SUN IS RISING!
HUH?
You're a fine human specimen...
DON'T BE SO SURE ABOUT THAT.

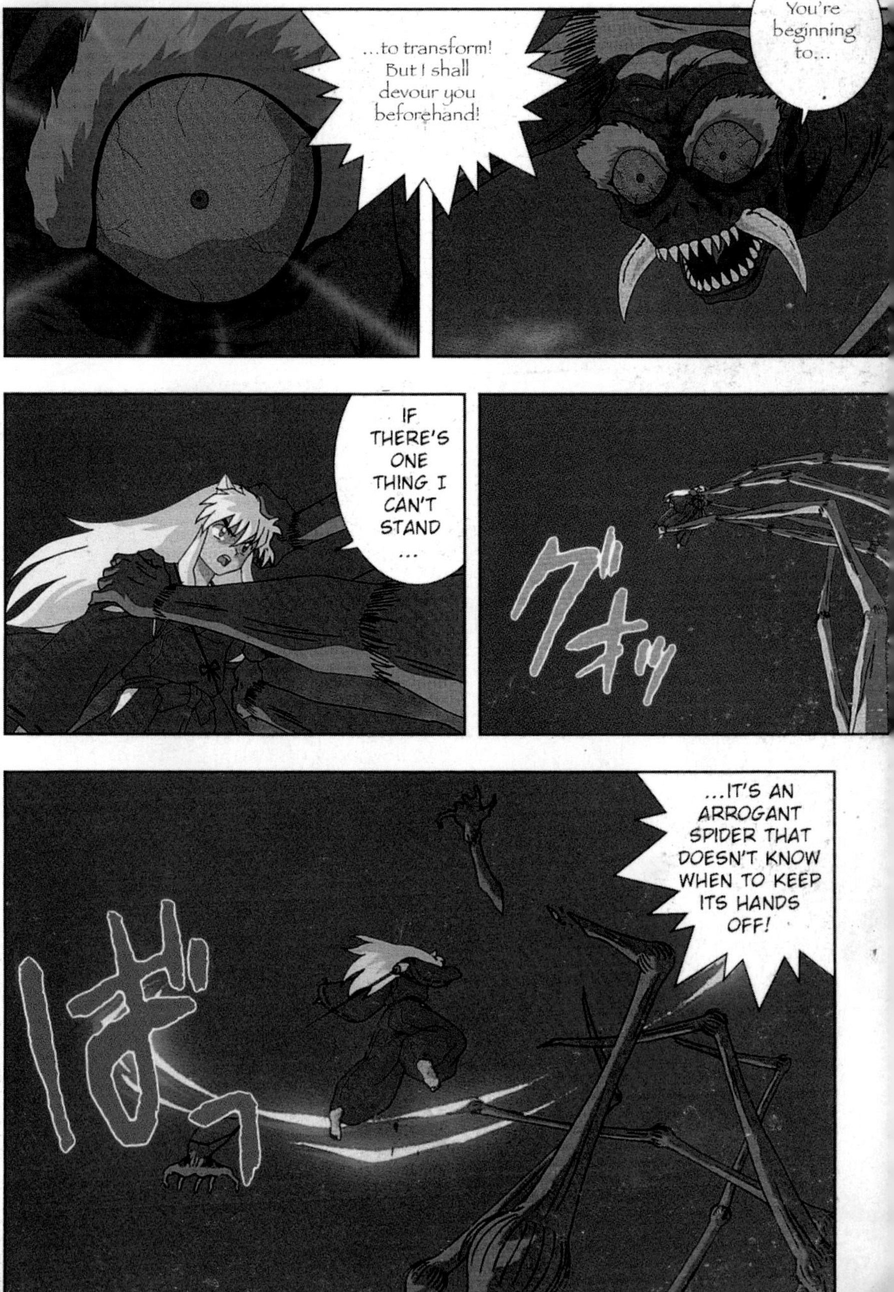
You're beginning to...
...to transform! But I shall devour you beforehand!
グオッ
IF THERE'S ONE THING I CAN'T STAND ...
...IT'S AN ARROGANT SPIDER THAT DOESN'T KNOW WHEN TO KEEP ITS HANDS OFF!
ばっ

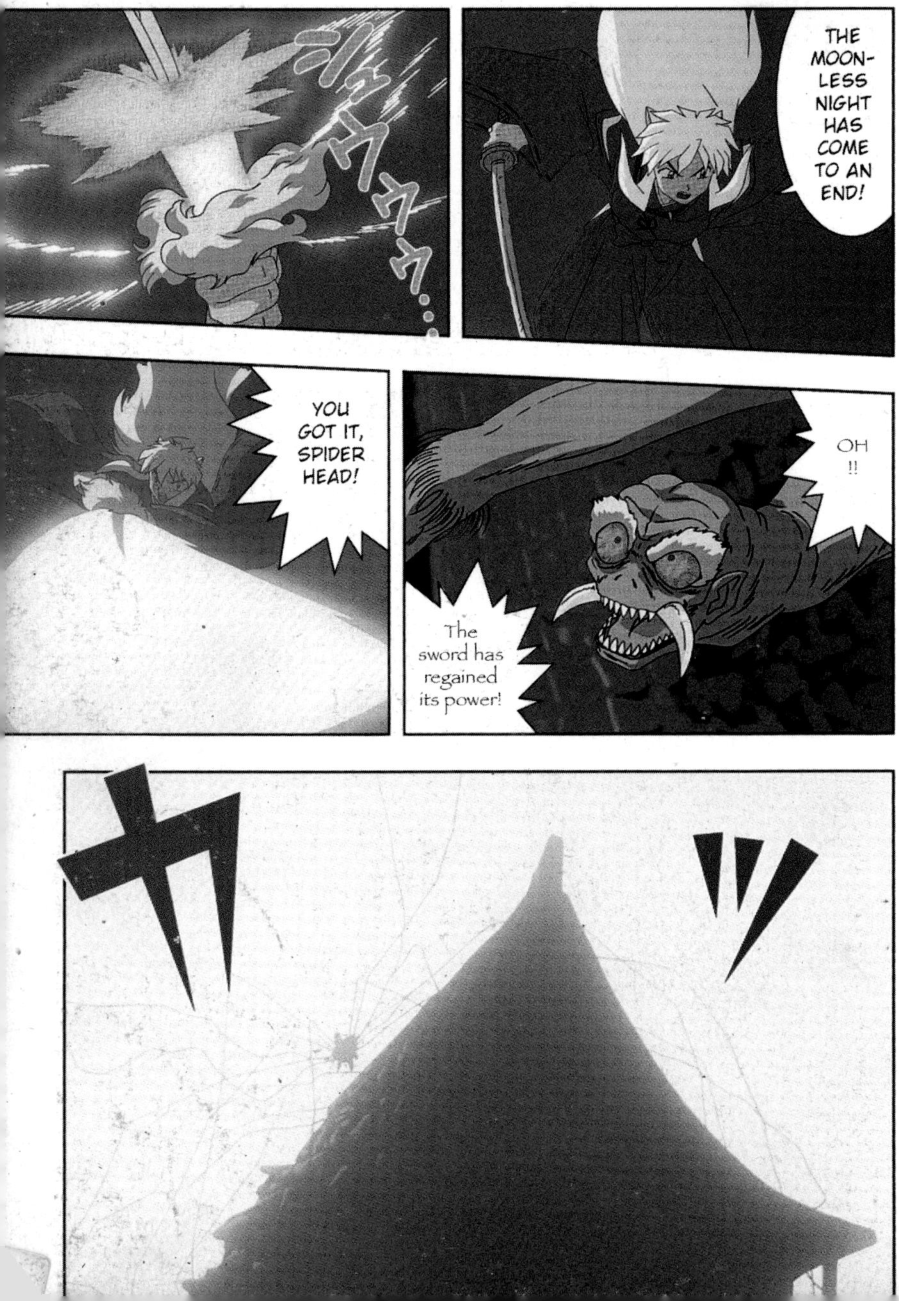
THE MOON-LESS NIGHT HAS COME TO AN END!
OH !!
The sword has regained its power!
YOU GOT IT, SPIDER HEAD!

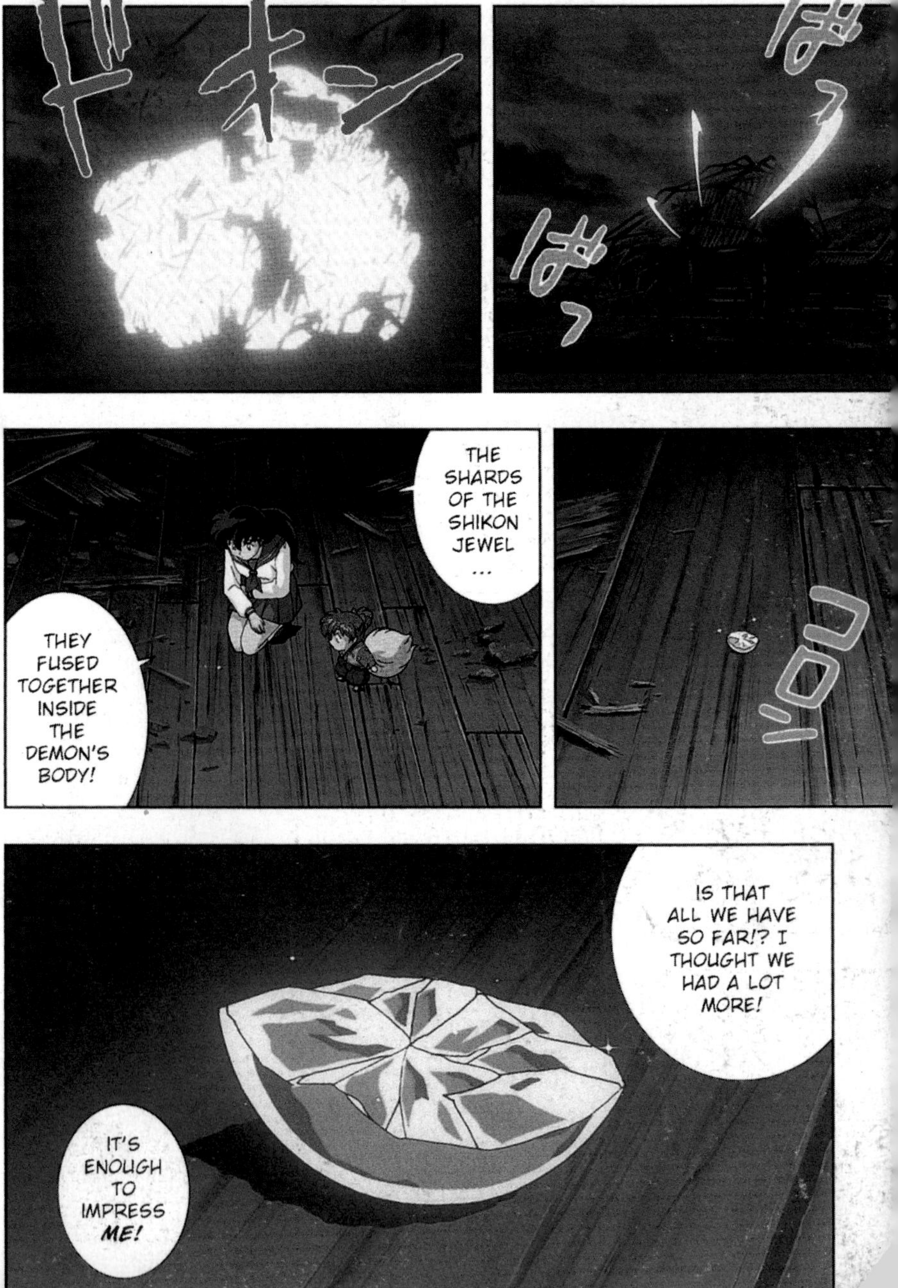
ぼっ
ぼっ
ドオーン
コロン
THE SHARDS OF THE SHIKON JEWEL ...
THEY FUSED TOGETHER INSIDE THE DEMON'S BODY!
IS THAT ALL WE HAVE SO FAR!? I THOUGHT WE HAD A LOT MORE!
IT'S ENOUGH TO IMPRESS *ME!*

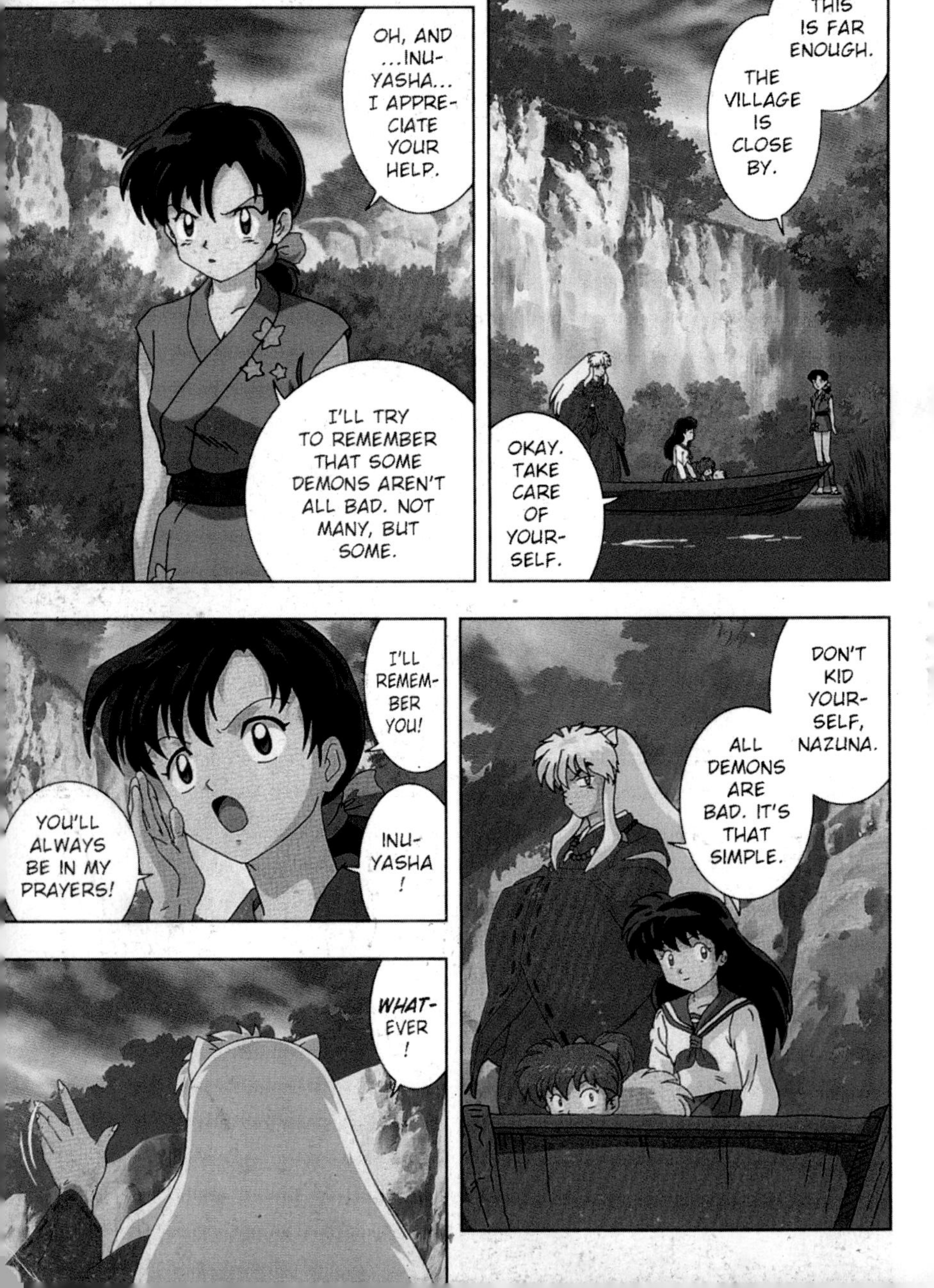
THIS IS FAR ENOUGH.
THE VILLAGE IS CLOSE BY.
OKAY. TAKE CARE OF YOUR-SELF.
OH, AND ...INU-YASHA... I APPRE-CIATE YOUR HELP.
I'LL TRY TO REMEMBER THAT SOME DEMONS AREN'T ALL BAD. NOT MANY, BUT SOME.
DON'T KID YOUR-SELF, NAZUNA.
ALL DEMONS ARE BAD. IT'S THAT SIMPLE.
I'LL REMEM-BER YOU!
INU-YASHA!
YOU'LL ALWAYS BE IN MY PRAYERS!
WHAT-EVER!

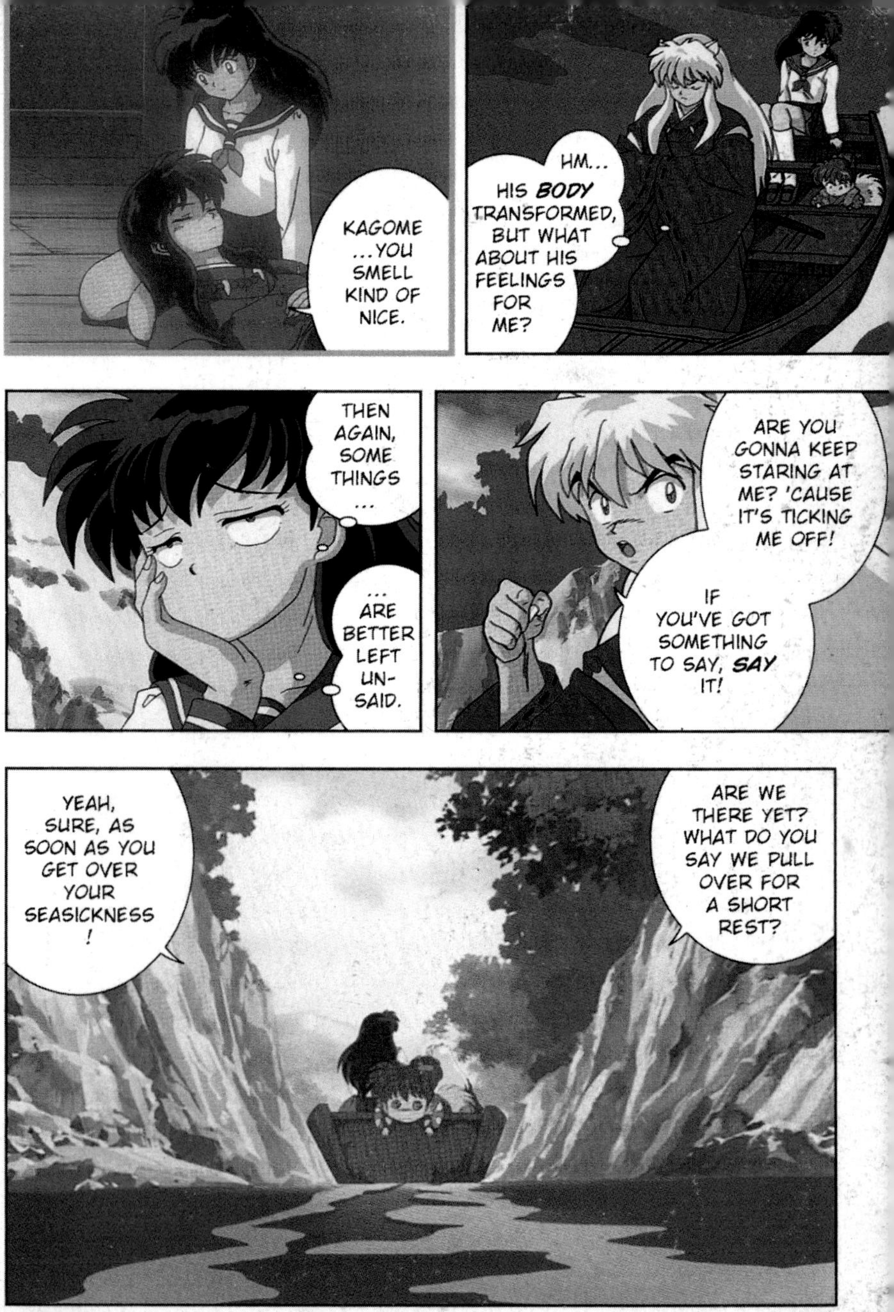
HM... HIS BODY TRANSFORMED, BUT WHAT ABOUT HIS FEELINGS FOR ME?
KAGOME ...YOU SMELL KIND OF NICE.
ARE YOU GONNA KEEP STARING AT ME? 'CAUSE IT'S TICKING ME OFF!
IF YOU'VE GOT SOMETHING TO SAY, SAY IT!
THEN AGAIN, SOME THINGS ...
... ARE BETTER LEFT UN-SAID.
ARE WE THERE YET? WHAT DO YOU SAY WE PULL OVER FOR A SHORT REST?
YEAH, SURE, AS SOON AS YOU GET OVER YOUR SEASICKNESS!

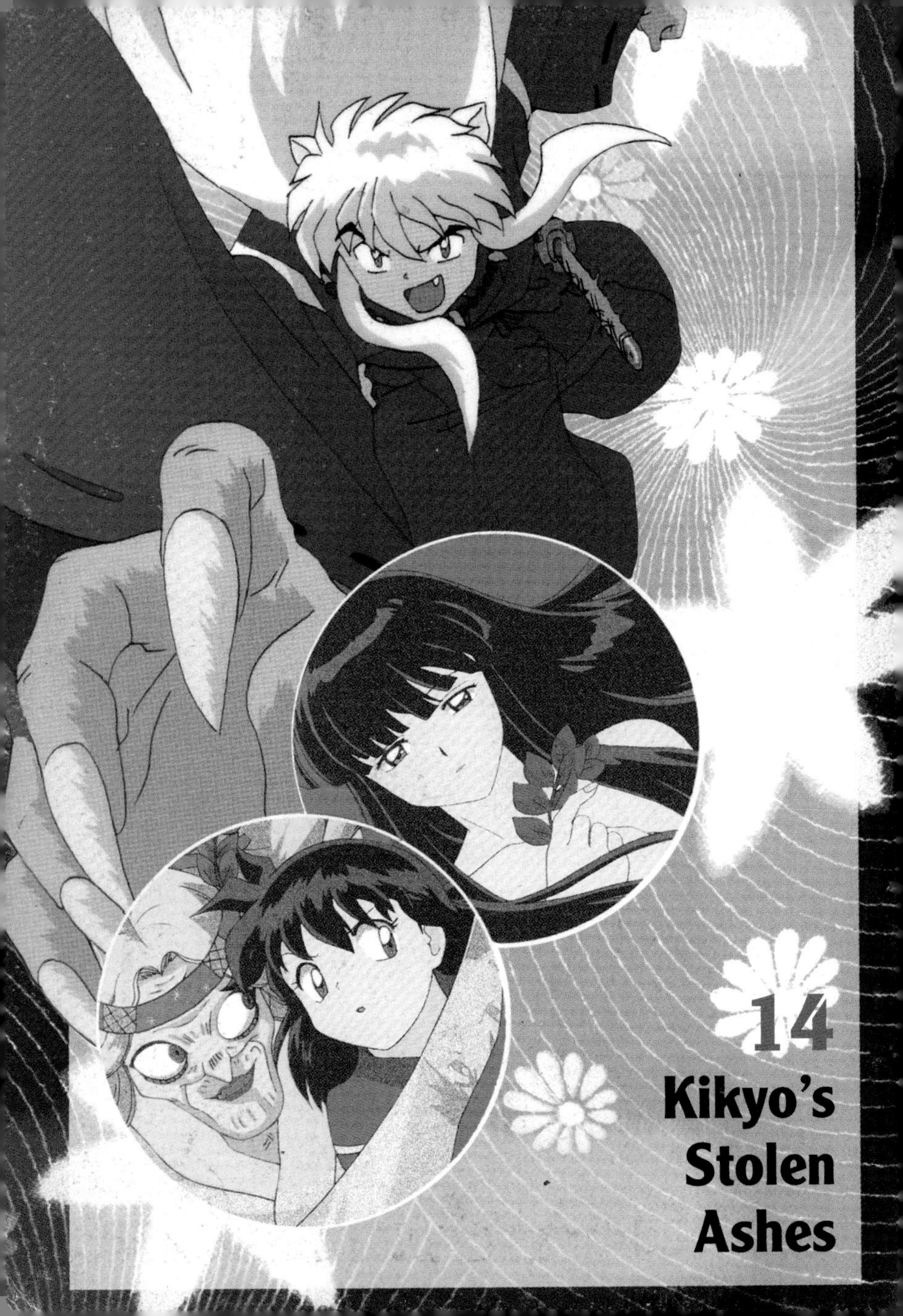

# 14 Kikyo's Stolen Ashes

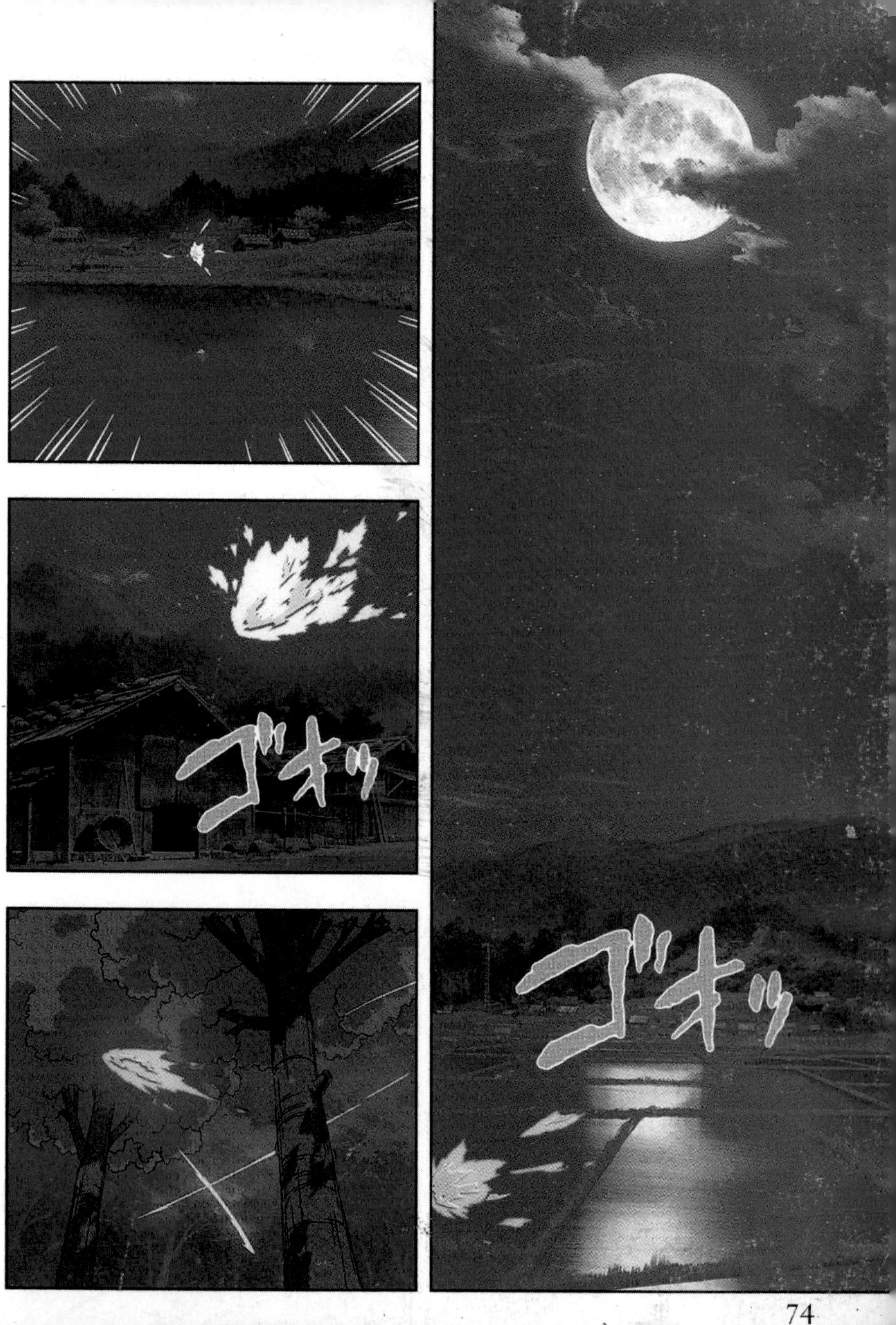
ゴオッ
ゴオッ

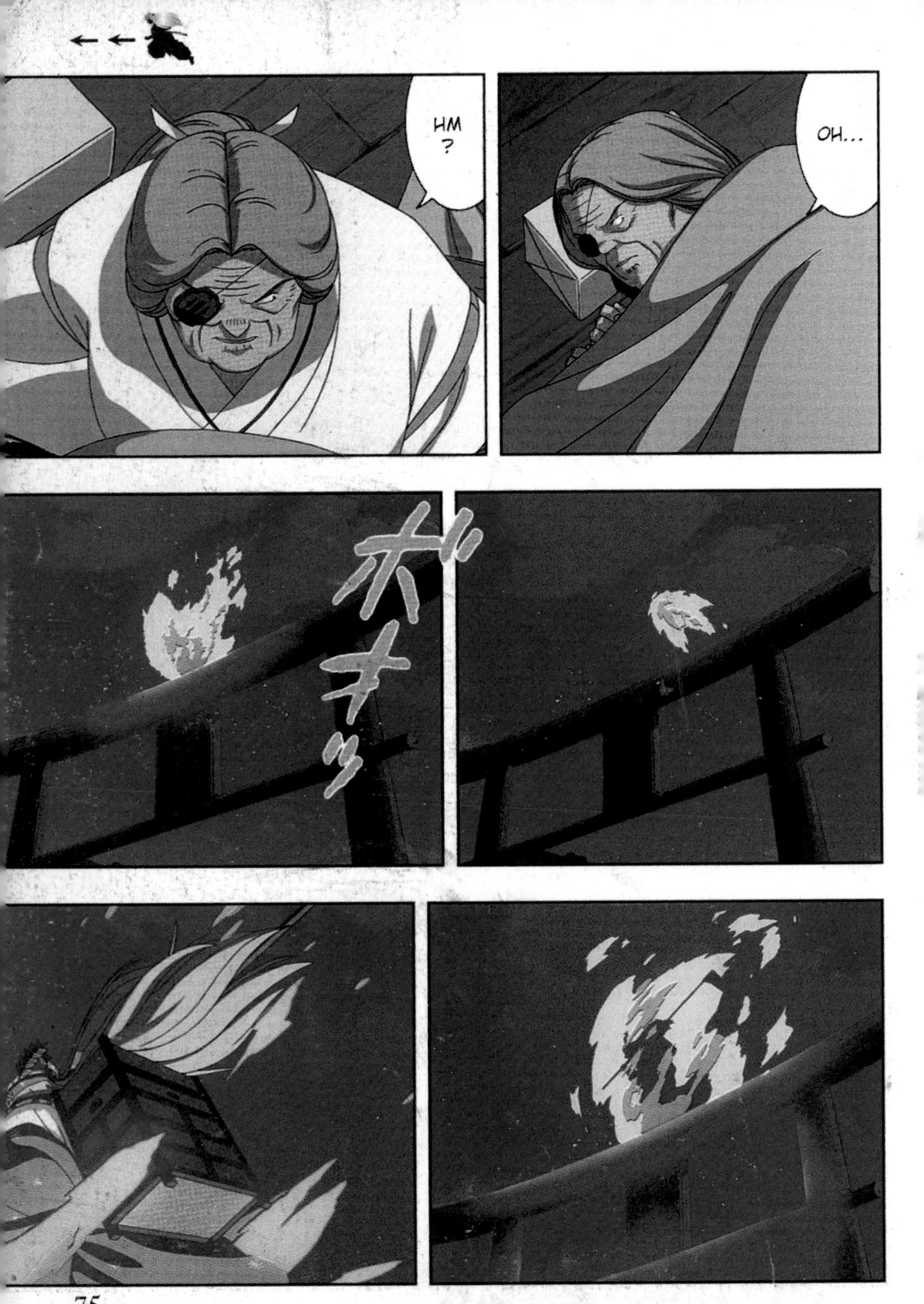
OH...
HM ?
ボキッ

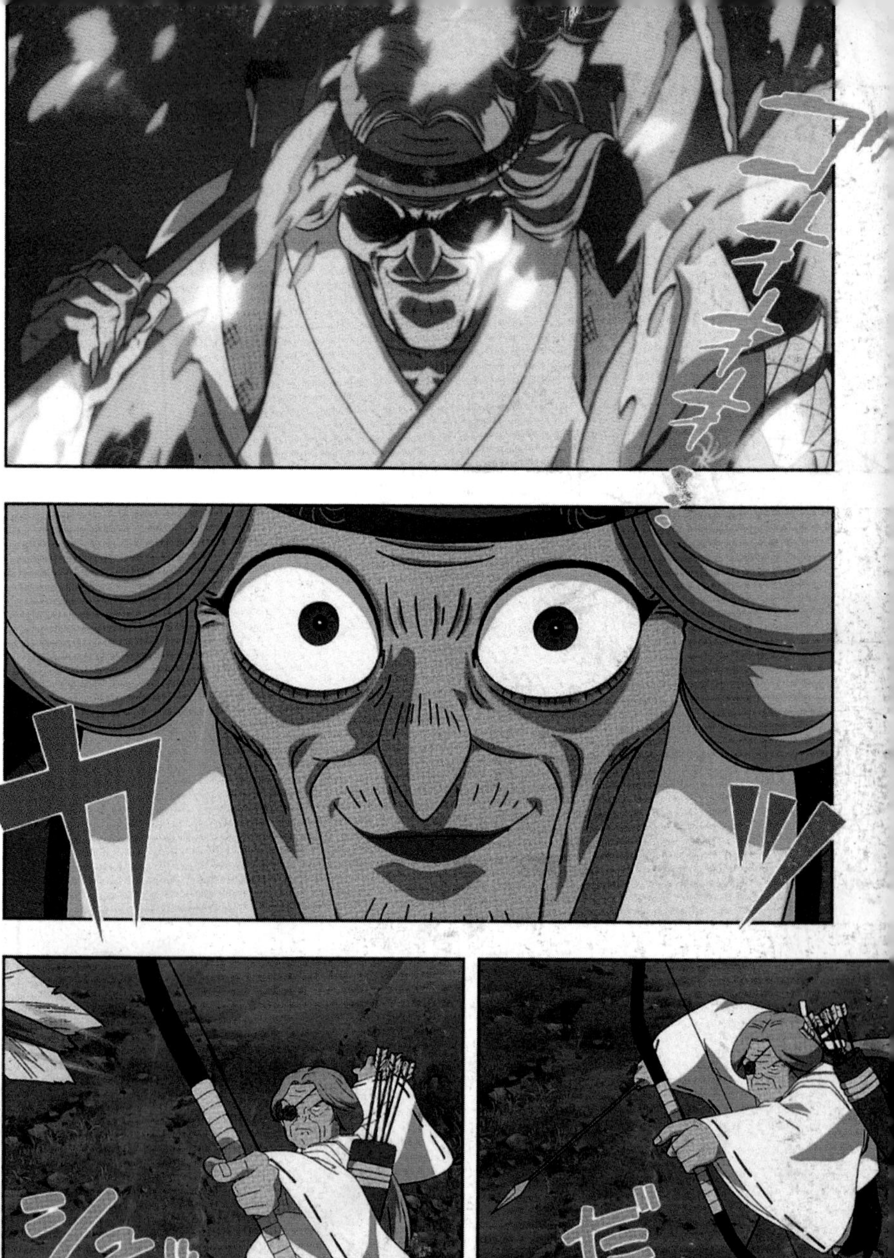
ゴキキキキ
カッ
だッ
シュッ

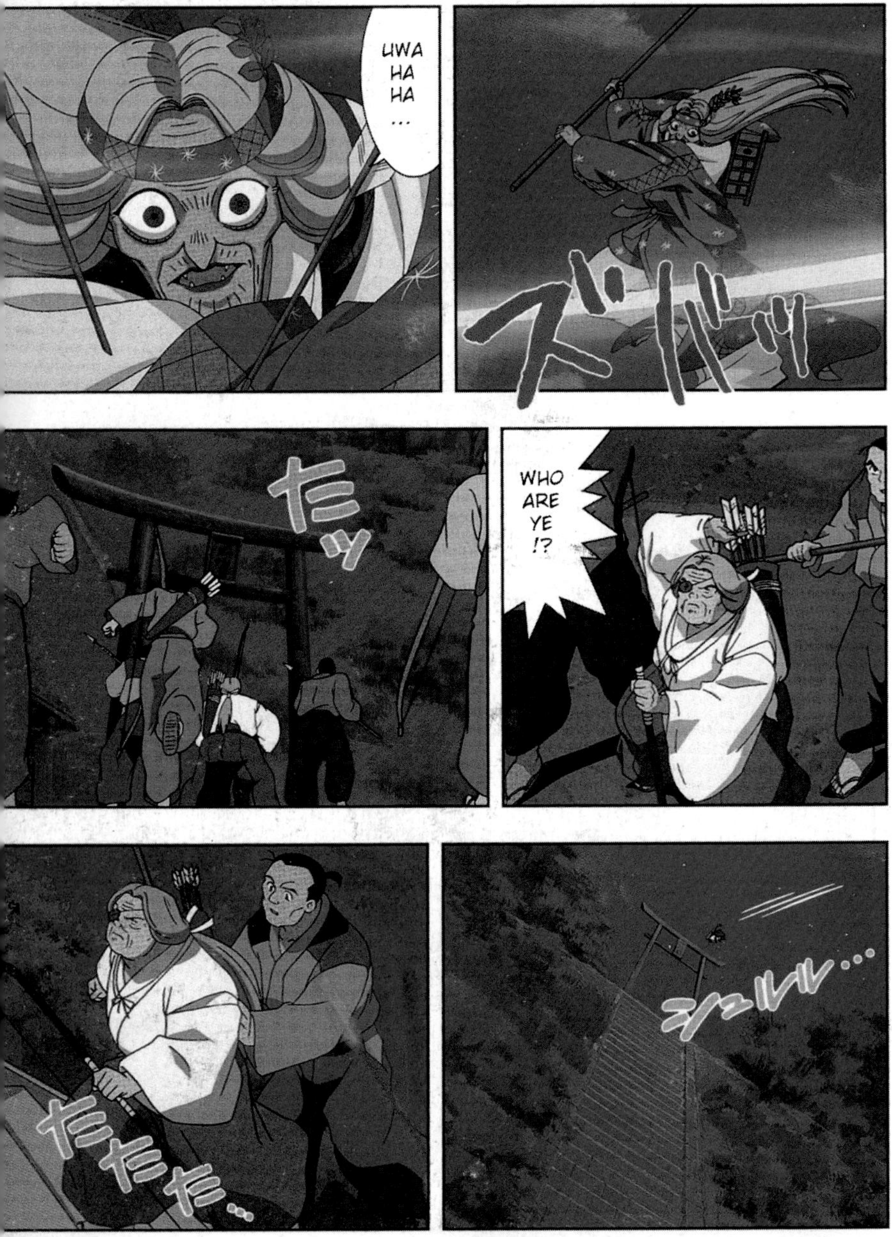
ズバッ
UWA HA HA ...
WHO ARE YE !?
たッ
シュルル...
たたた...

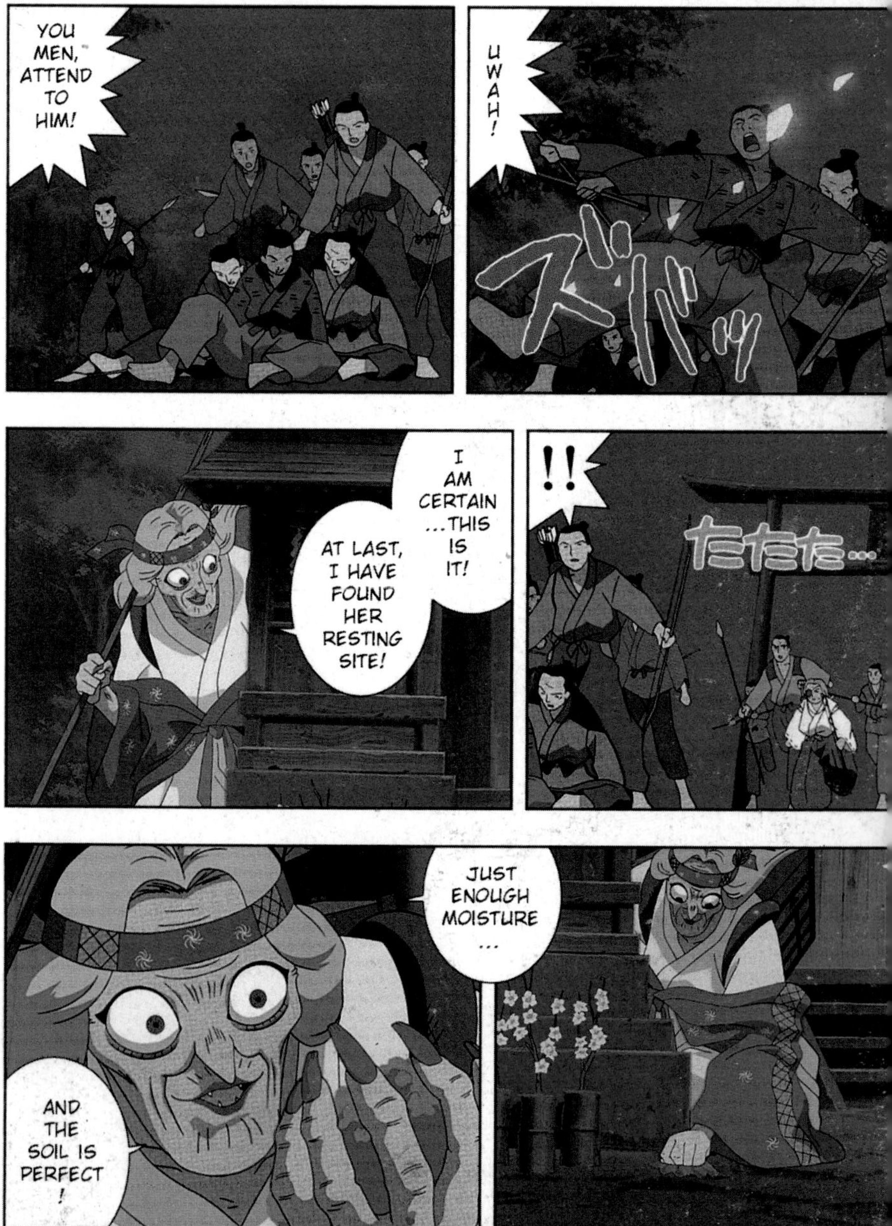
UWAH!
ズバッ
YOU MEN, ATTEND TO HIM!
!!
たたた…
I AM CERTAIN ...THIS IS IT!
AT LAST, I HAVE FOUND HER RESTING SITE!
JUST ENOUGH MOISTURE ...
AND THE SOIL IS PERFECT!

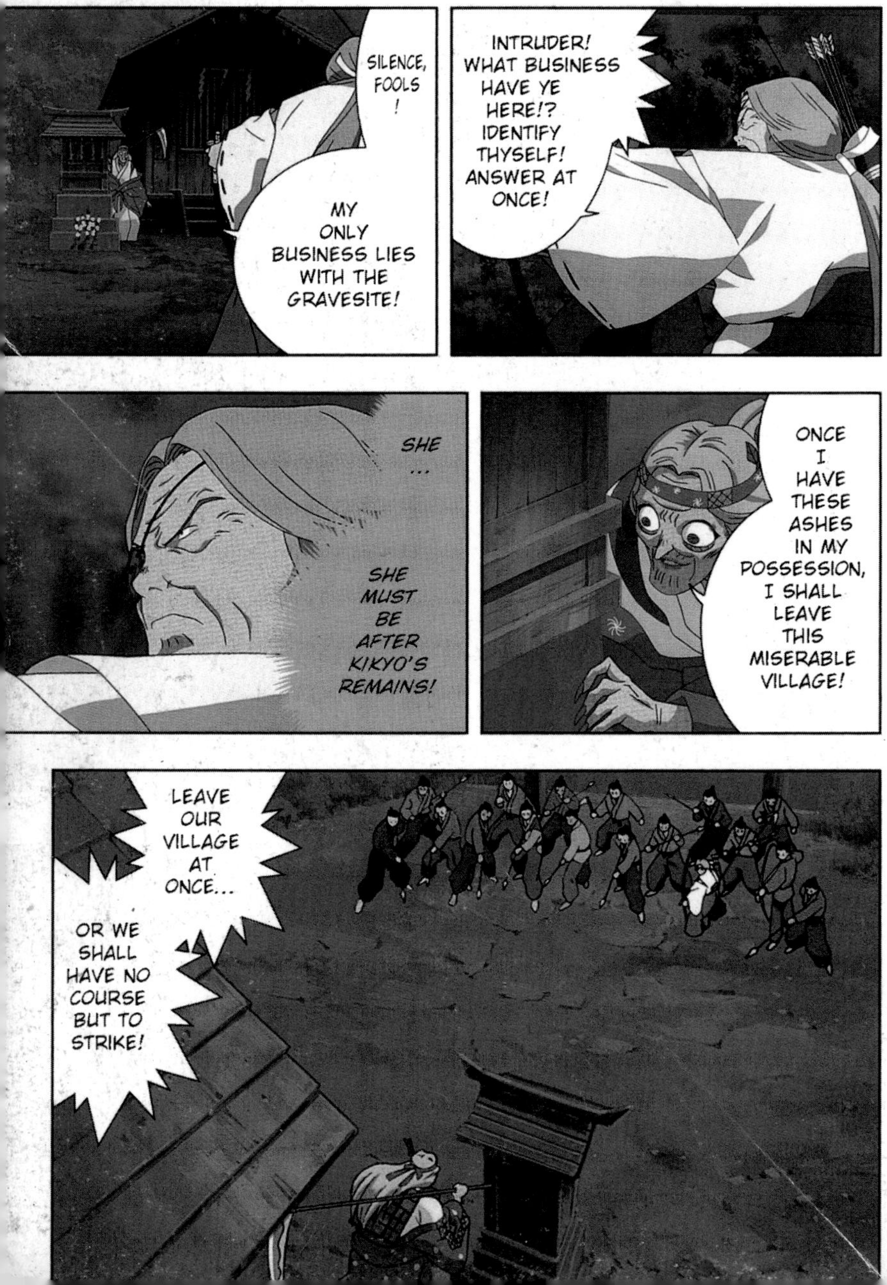
INTRUDER! WHAT BUSINESS HAVE YE HERE!? IDENTIFY THYSELF! ANSWER AT ONCE!
SILENCE, FOOLS!
MY ONLY BUSINESS LIES WITH THE GRAVESITE!
ONCE I HAVE THESE ASHES IN MY POSSESSION, I SHALL LEAVE THIS MISERABLE VILLAGE!
SHE...
SHE MUST BE AFTER KIKYO'S REMAINS!
LEAVE OUR VILLAGE AT ONCE...
OR WE SHALL HAVE NO COURSE BUT TO STRIKE!

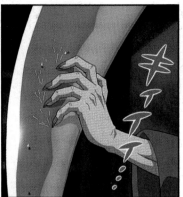

PER-
SISTENT
WRETCH
!

YOU
WOULD
HAVE DONE
WELL NOT
TO CROSS
MY PATH!

A
G
H
H
H
!

HYAH
!

NOW,
YOU SHALL
PAY FOR YOUR
MEDDLING!

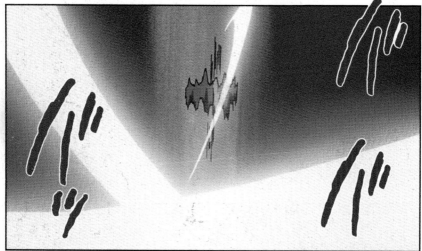

WAHHH!

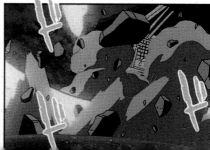

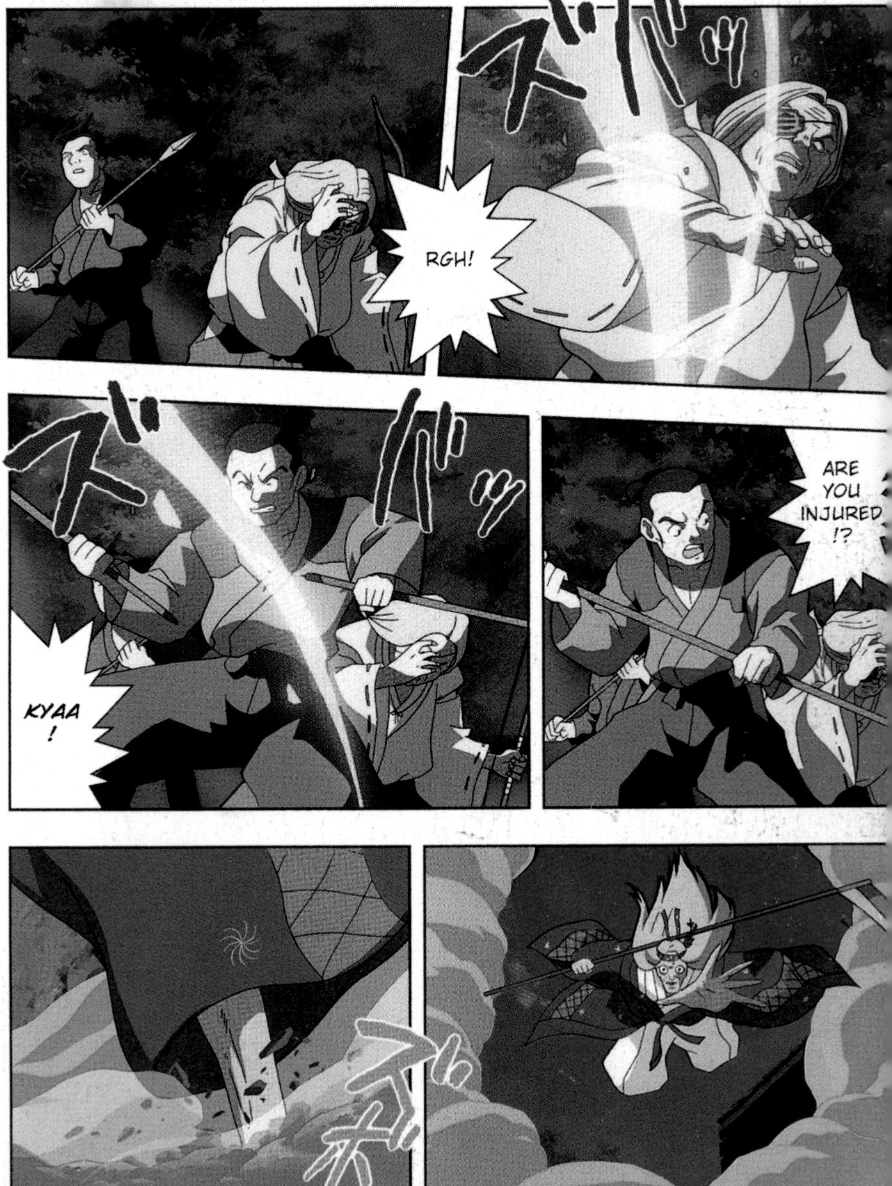

ズバッ
RGH!
ARE YOU INJURED !?
ズバッ
KYAA !

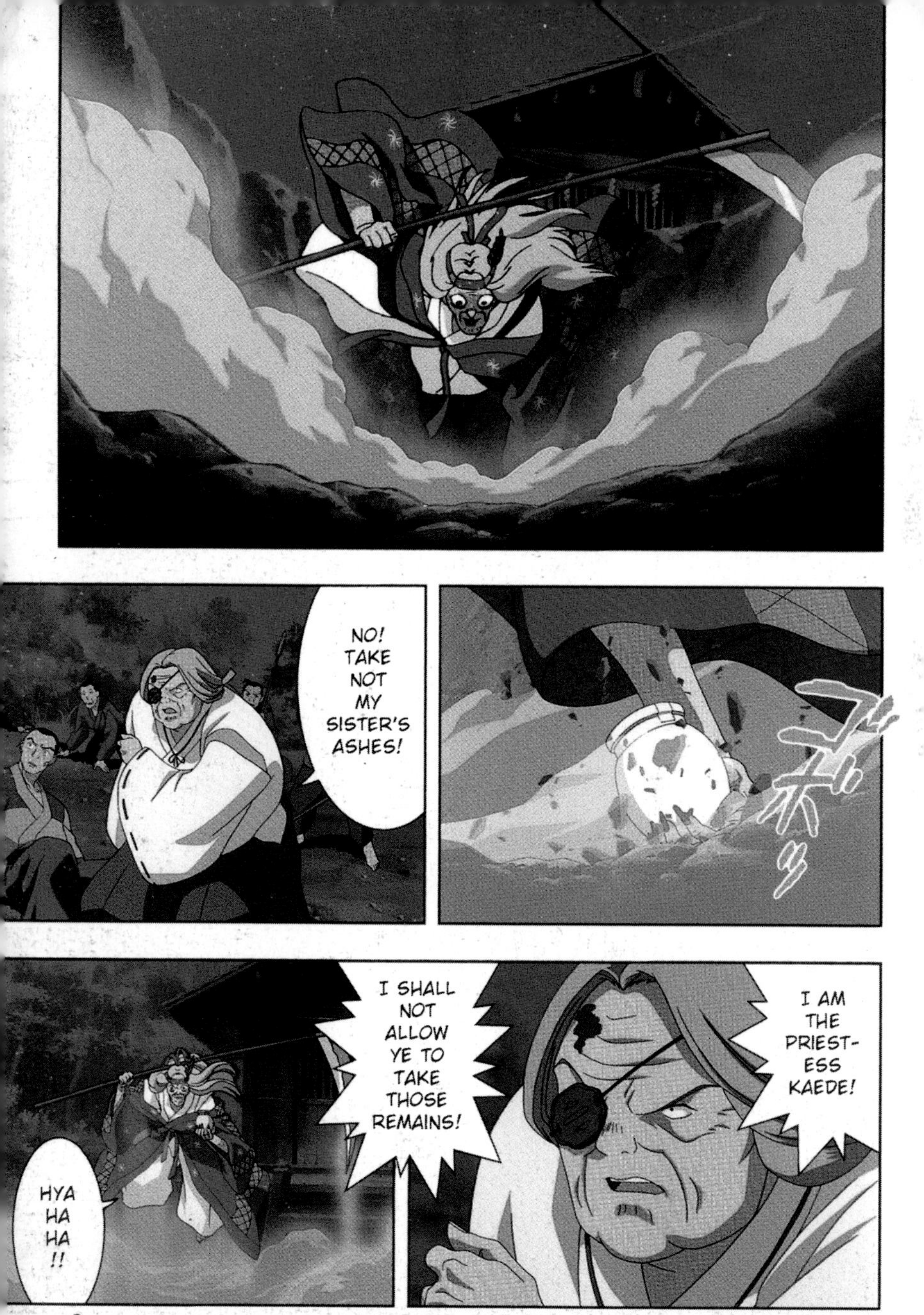
NO! TAKE NOT MY SISTER'S ASHES!
I AM THE PRIEST-ESS KAEDE!
I SHALL NOT ALLOW YE TO TAKE THOSE REMAINS!
HYA HA HA!!

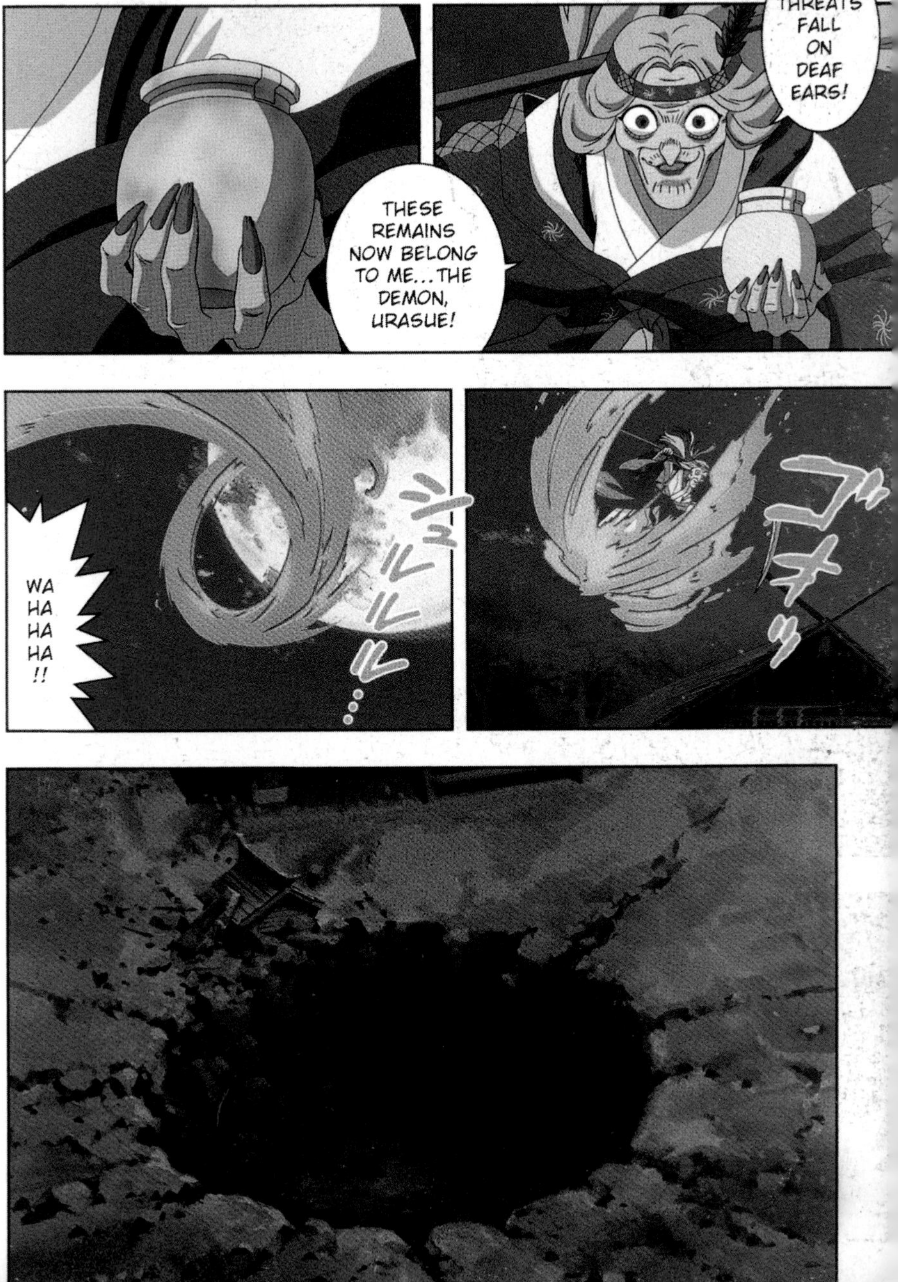
YOUR THREATS FALL ON DEAF EARS!
THESE REMAINS NOW BELONG TO ME...THE DEMON, URASUE!
ゴオッ
WA HA HA HA!!
シュルルル…

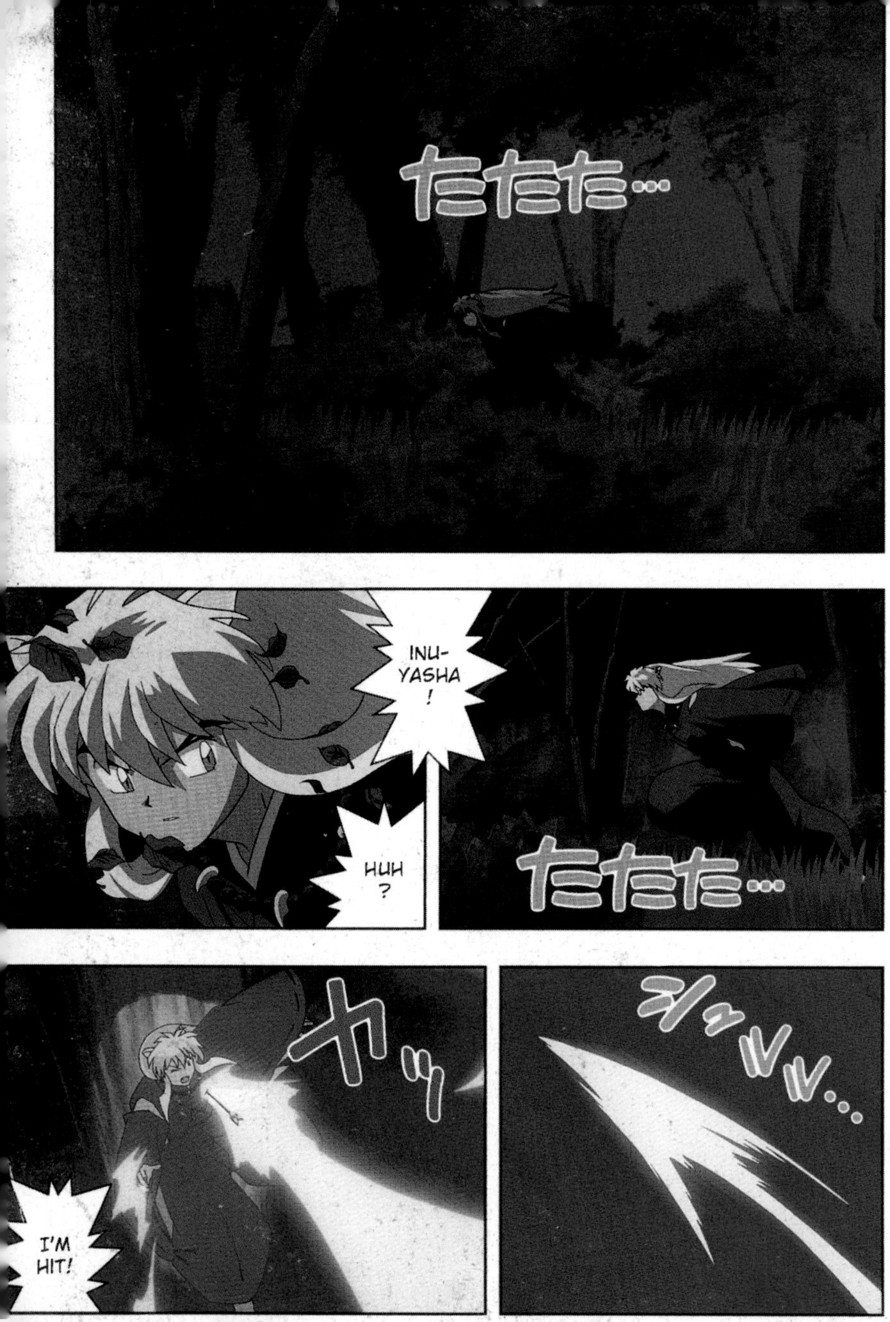
たたた…
たたた…
INU-YASHA!
HUH?
シュゥゥ...
ヤッ
I'M HIT!

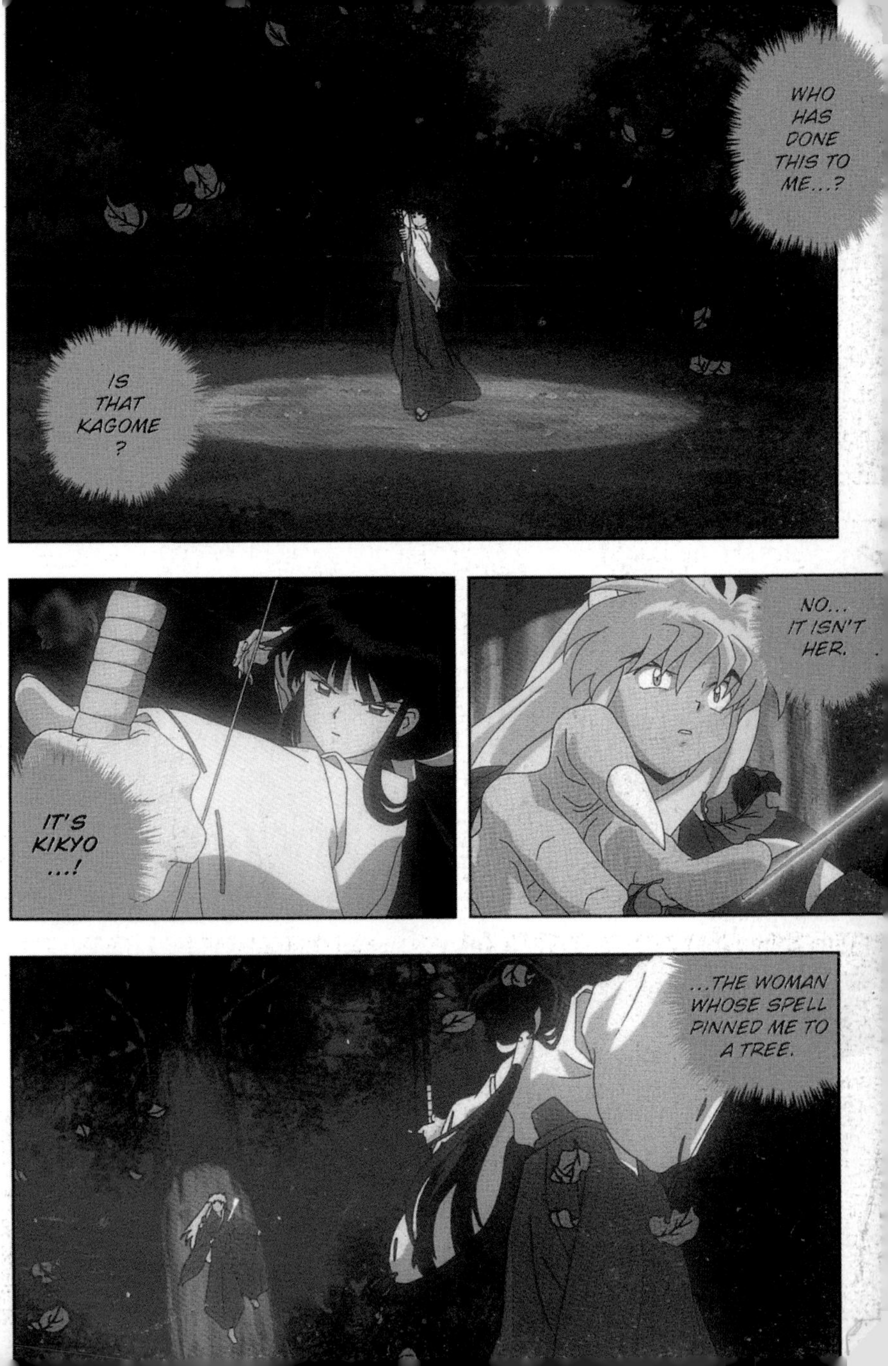
WHO HAS DONE THIS TO ME...?
IS THAT KAGOME?
NO... IT ISN'T HER.
IT'S KIKYO...!
...THE WOMAN WHOSE SPELL PINNED ME TO A TREE.

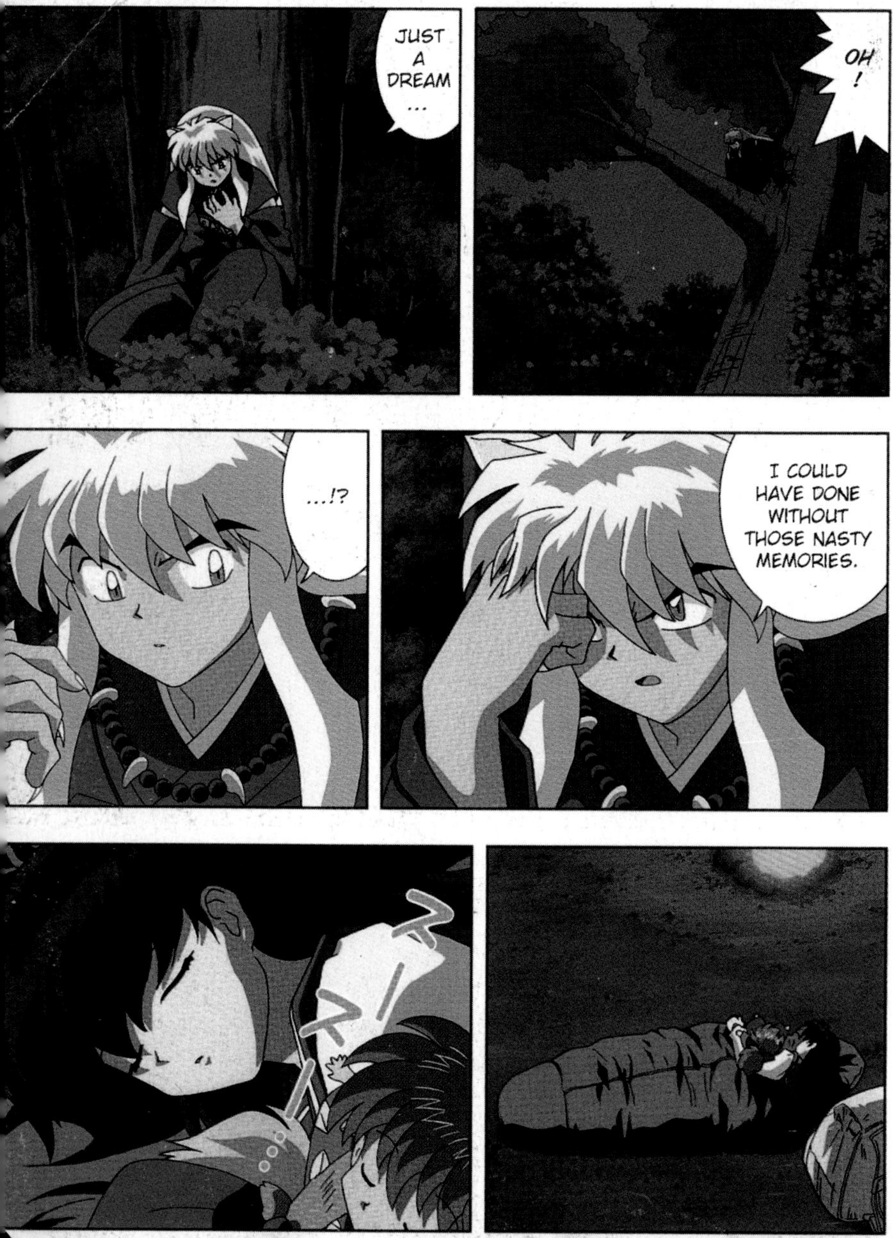
OH!
JUST A DREAM...
I COULD HAVE DONE WITHOUT THOSE NASTY MEMORIES.
...!?

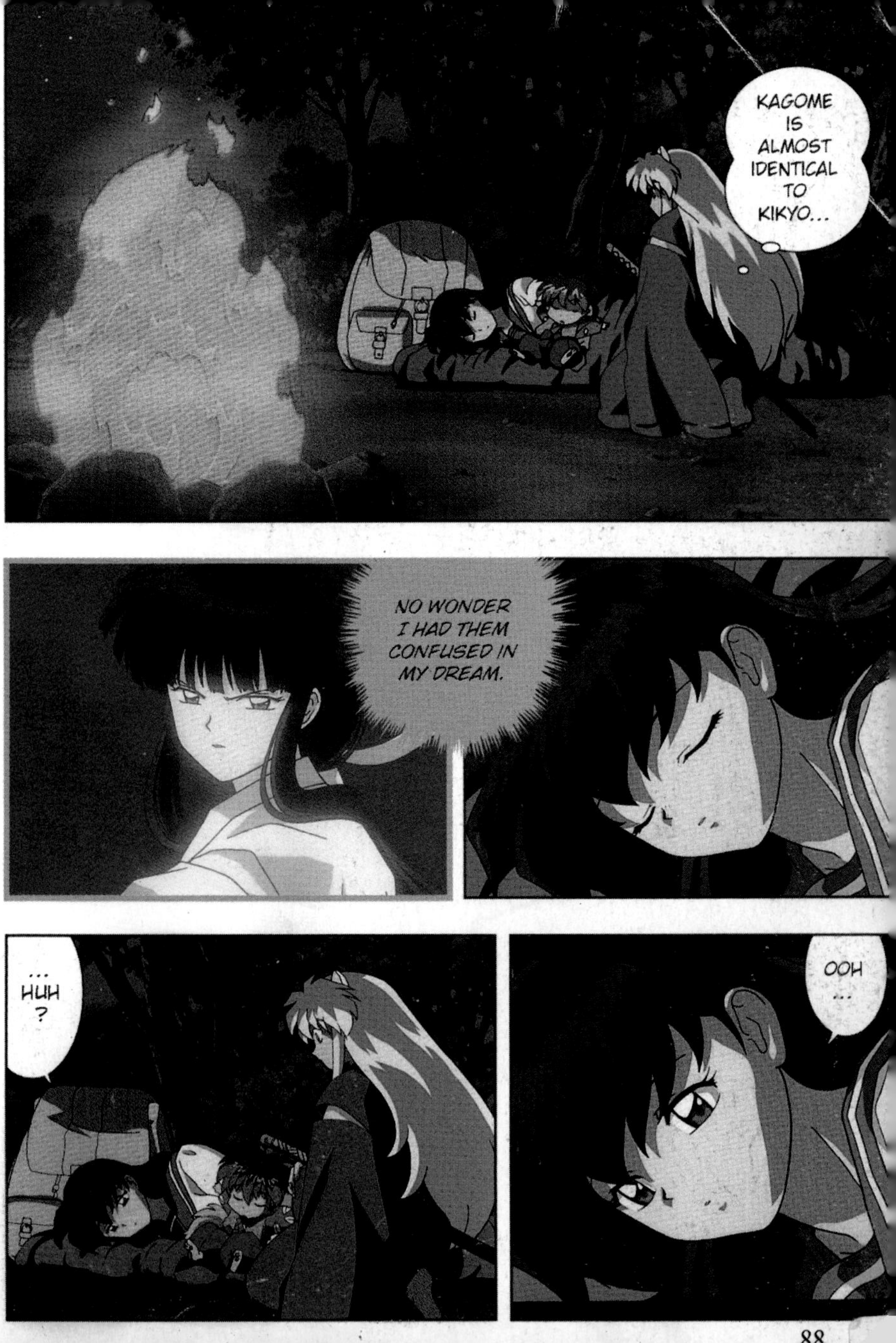
KAGOME IS ALMOST IDENTICAL TO KIKYO...
NO WONDER I HAD THEM CONFUSED IN MY DREAM.
OOH ...
... HUH ?

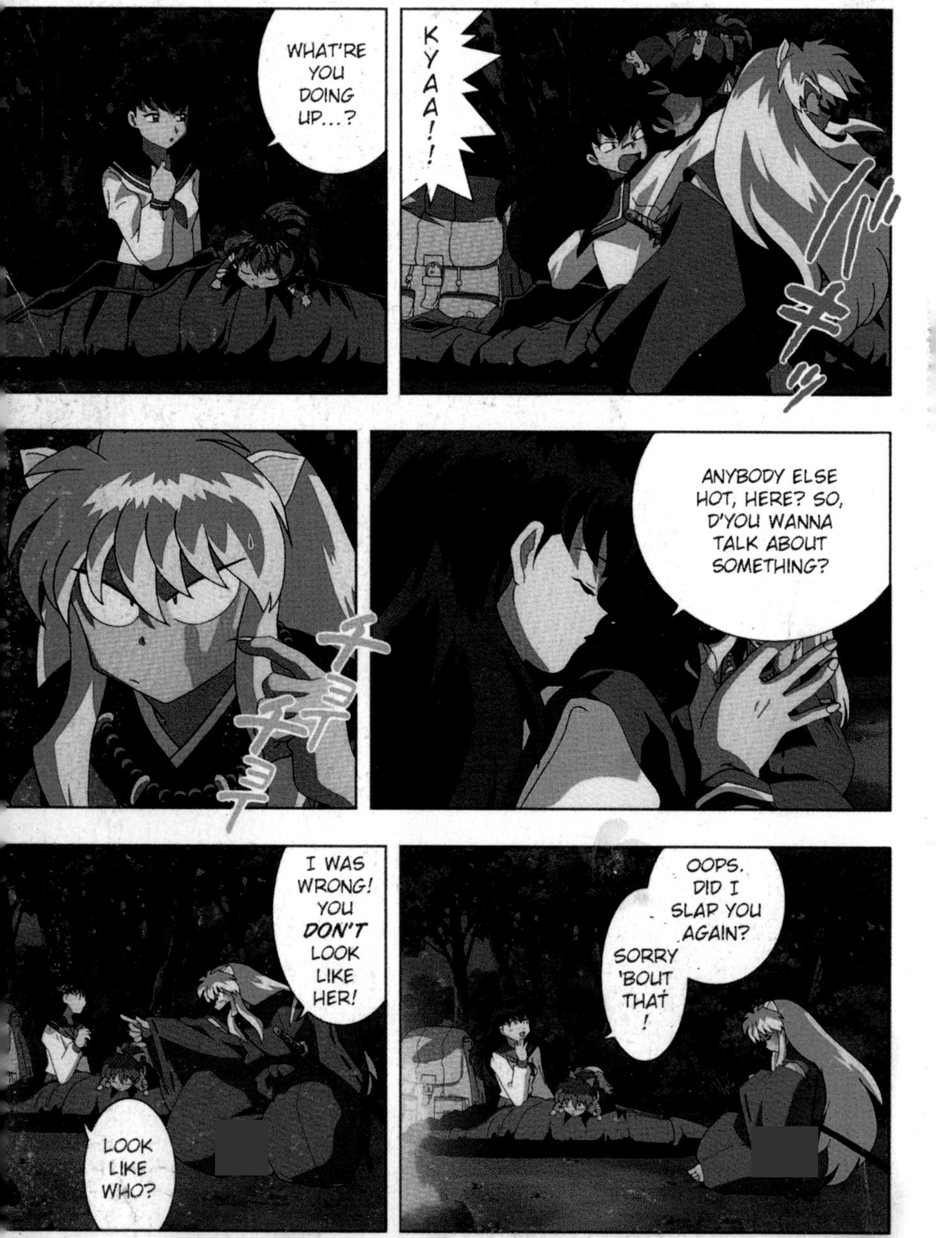
KYAA!!
WHAT'RE YOU DOING UP...?
ANYBODY ELSE HOT, HERE? SO, D'YOU WANNA TALK ABOUT SOMETHING?
OOPS. DID I SLAP YOU AGAIN?
SORRY 'BOUT THAT!
I WAS WRONG! YOU **DON'T** LOOK LIKE HER!
LOOK LIKE WHO?

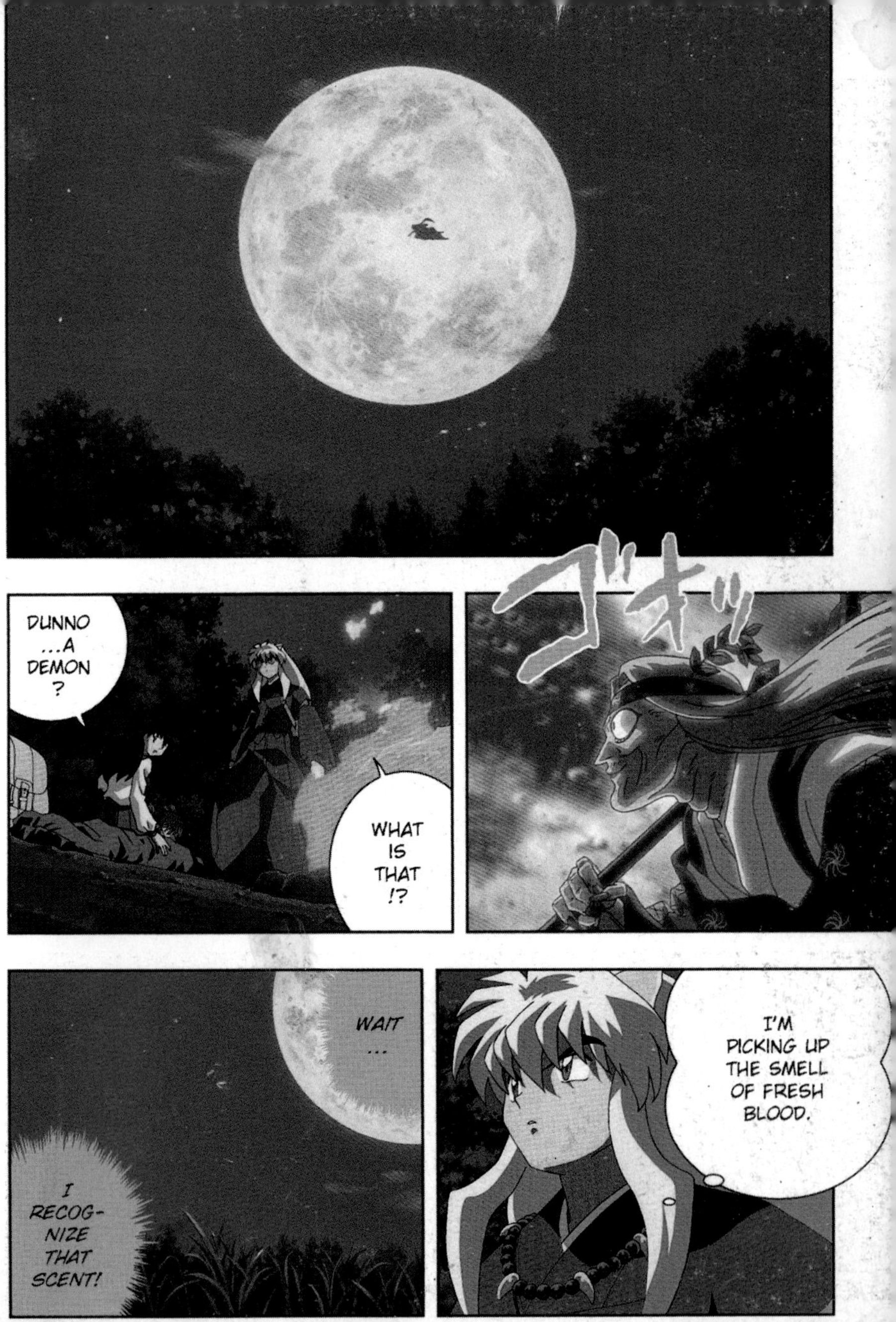
ゴオッ
WHAT IS THAT !?
DUNNO ...A DEMON ?
I'M PICKING UP THE SMELL OF FRESH BLOOD.
WAIT ...
I RECOG- NIZE THAT SCENT!

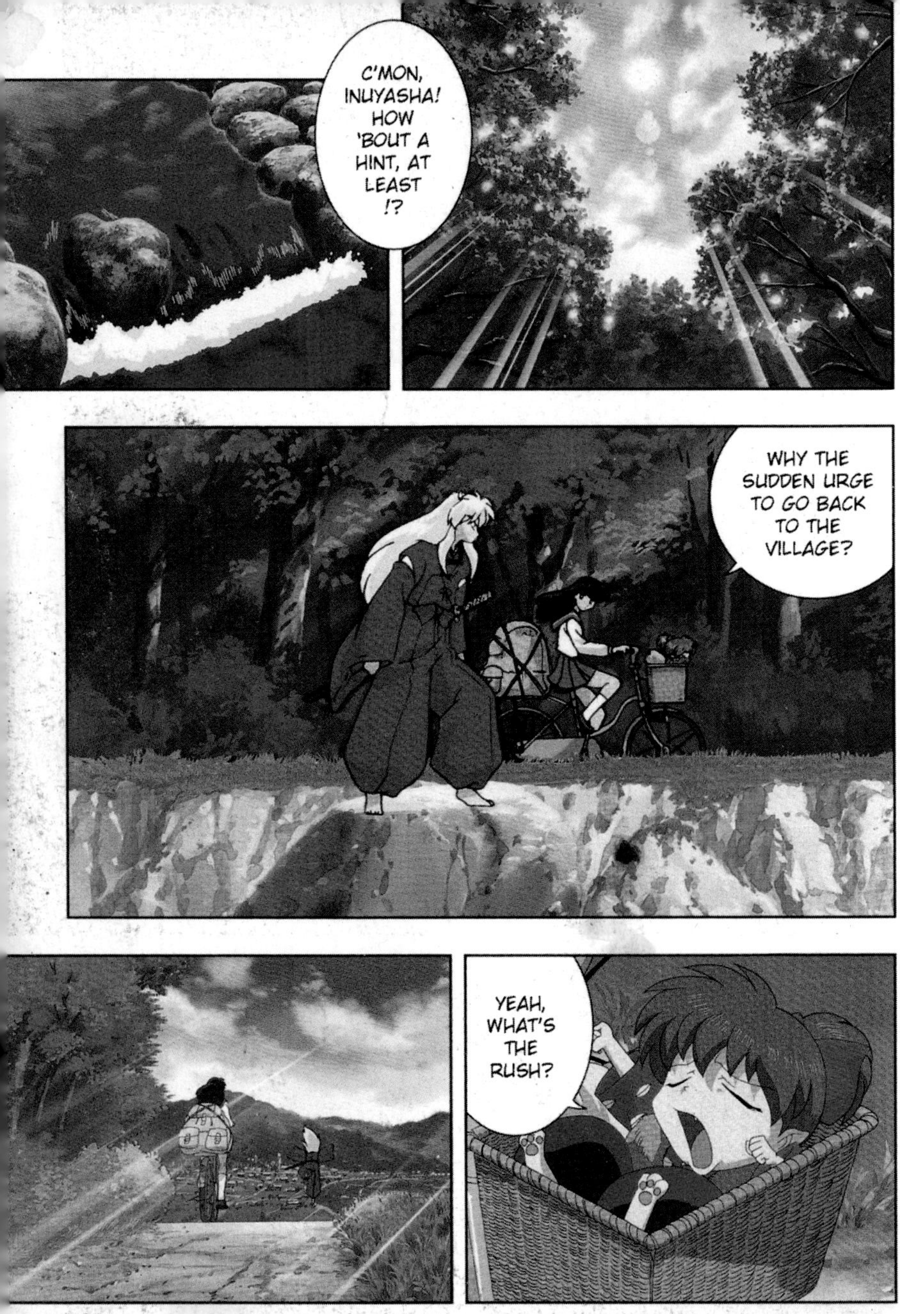
C'MON, INUYASHA! HOW 'BOUT A HINT, AT LEAST !?
WHY THE SUDDEN URGE TO GO BACK TO THE VILLAGE?
YEAH, WHAT'S THE RUSH?

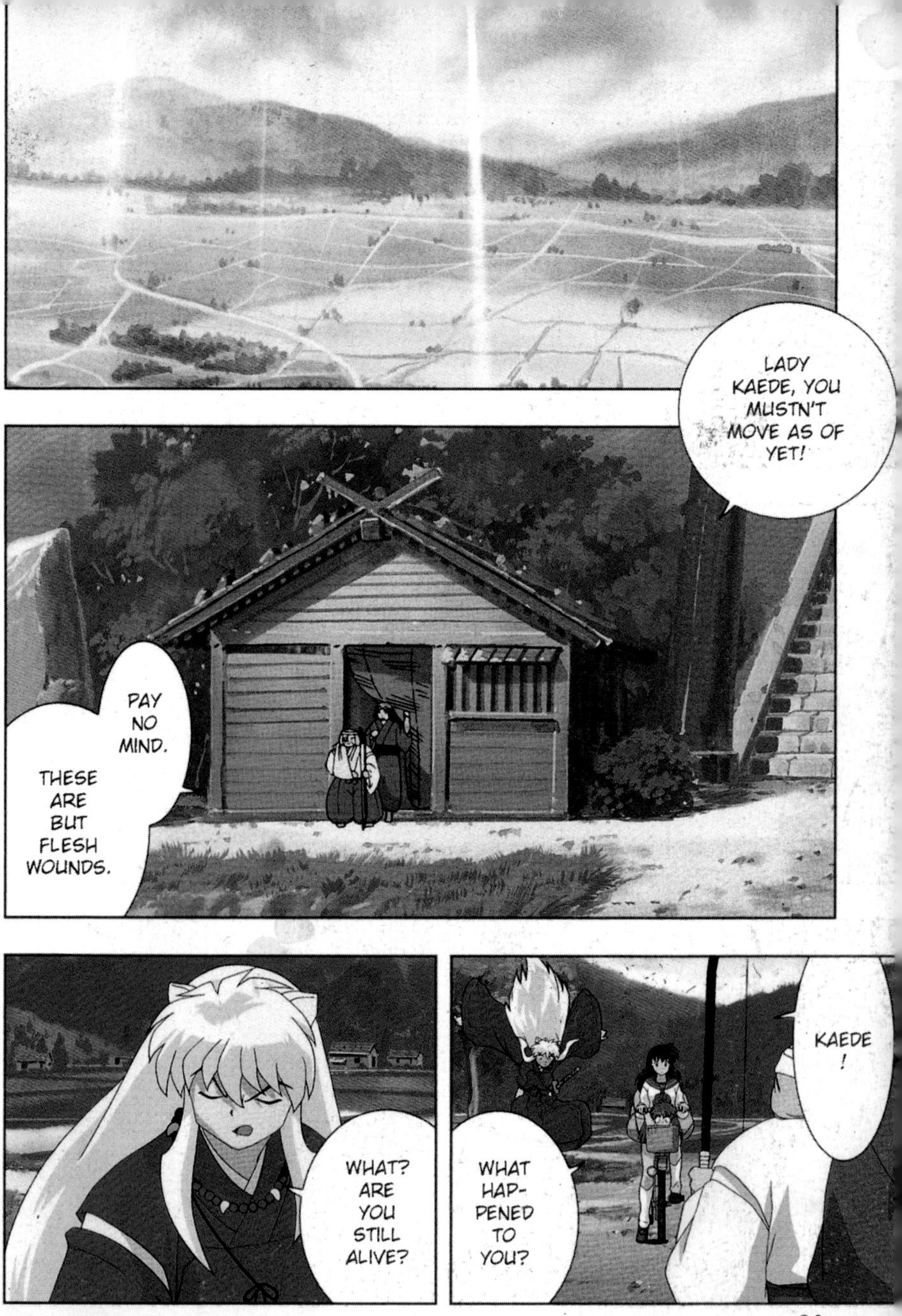
LADY KAEDE, YOU MUSTN'T MOVE AS OF YET!
PAY NO MIND.
THESE ARE BUT FLESH WOUNDS.
KAEDE!
WHAT HAPPENED TO YOU?
WHAT? ARE YOU STILL ALIVE?

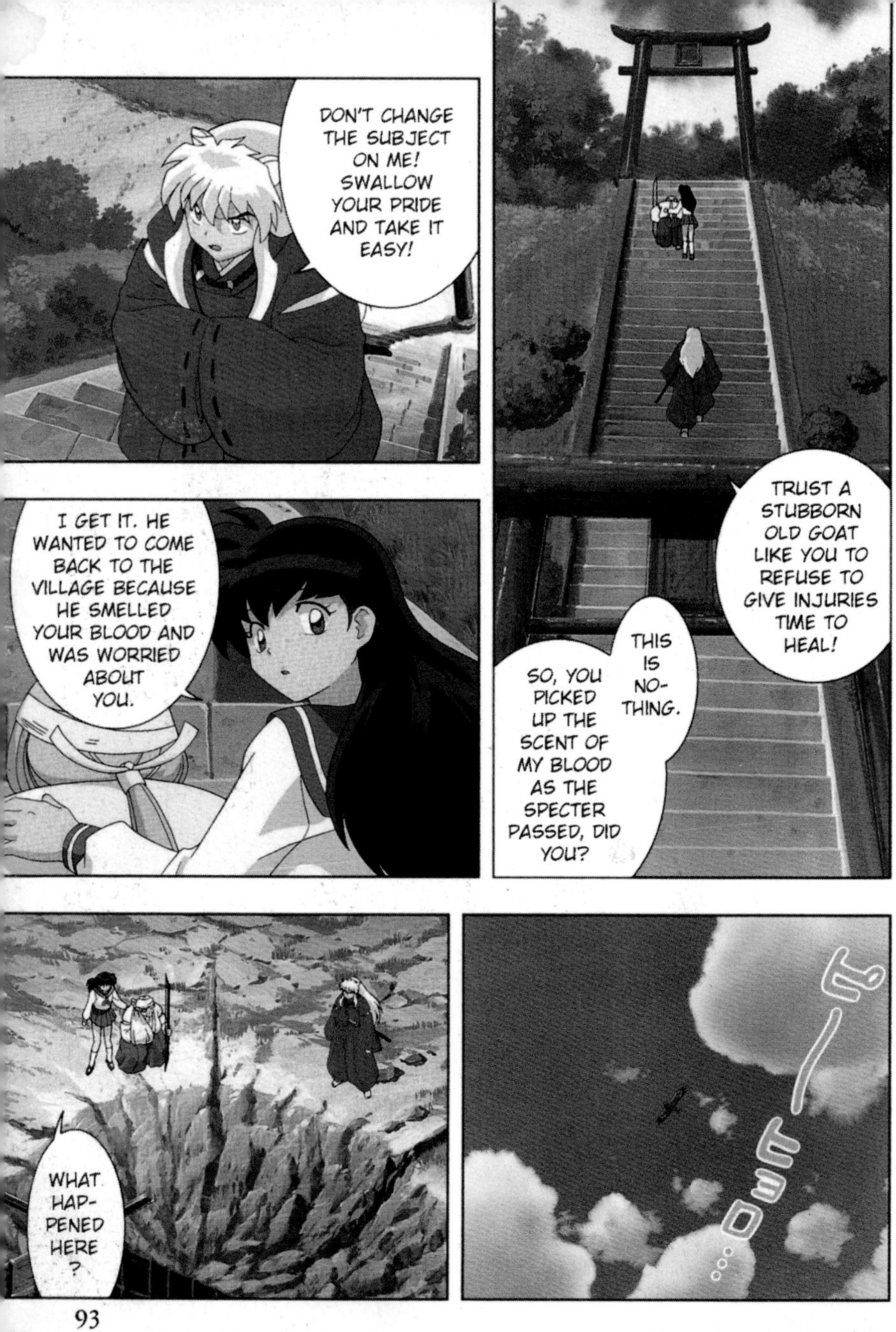
TRUST A STUBBORN OLD GOAT LIKE YOU TO REFUSE TO GIVE INJURIES TIME TO HEAL!
THIS IS NO-THING.
SO, YOU PICKED UP THE SCENT OF MY BLOOD AS THE SPECTER PASSED, DID YOU?
DON'T CHANGE THE SUBJECT ON ME! SWALLOW YOUR PRIDE AND TAKE IT EASY!
I GET IT. HE WANTED TO COME BACK TO THE VILLAGE BECAUSE HE SMELLED YOUR BLOOD AND WAS WORRIED ABOUT YOU.
ピーヒョロ…
WHAT HAP-PENED HERE ?

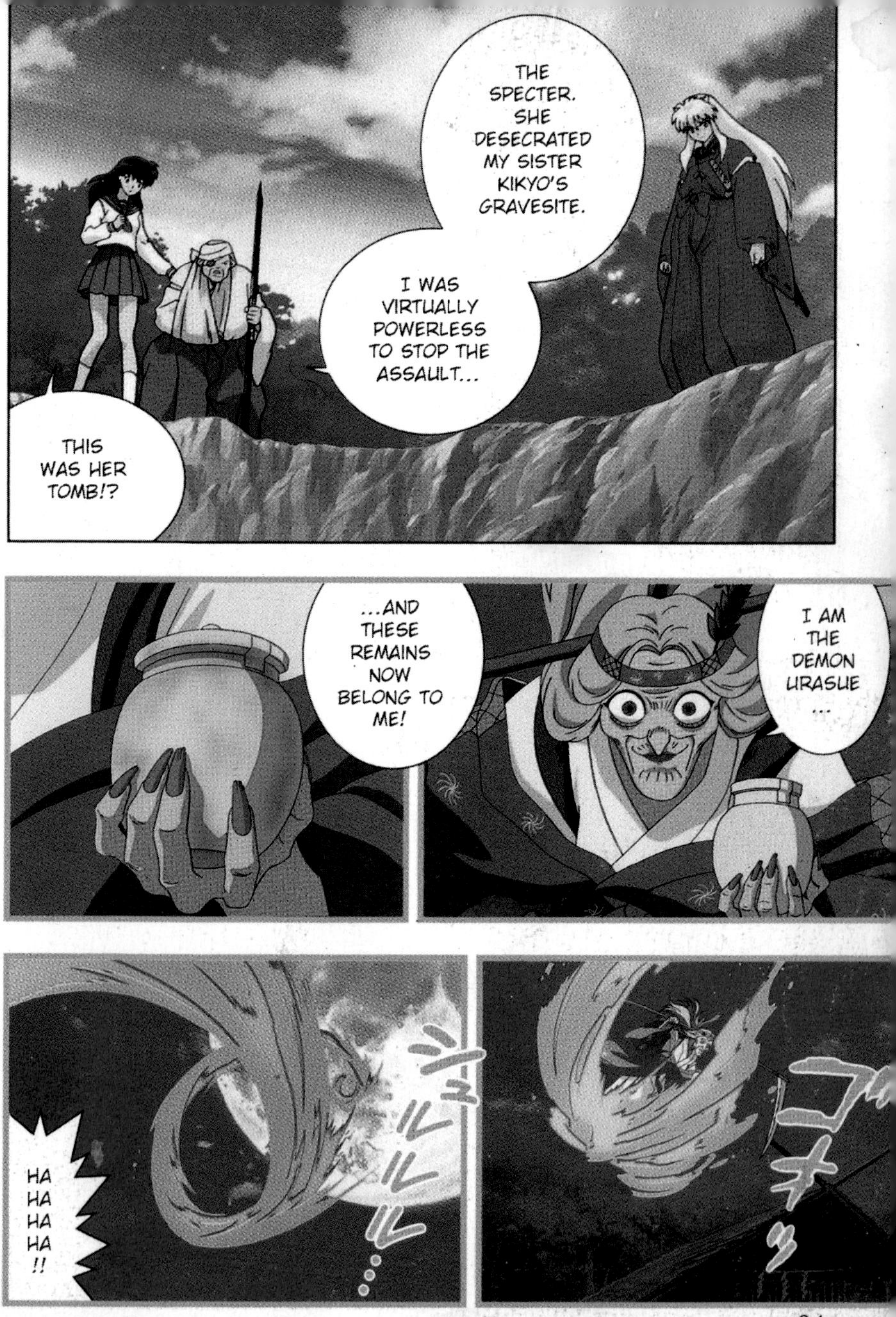
THE SPECTER. SHE DESECRATED MY SISTER KIKYO'S GRAVESITE.
I WAS VIRTUALLY POWERLESS TO STOP THE ASSAULT...
THIS WAS HER TOMB!?
I AM THE DEMON URASUE ...
...AND THESE REMAINS NOW BELONG TO ME!
シュルルル…
HA HA HA HA !!

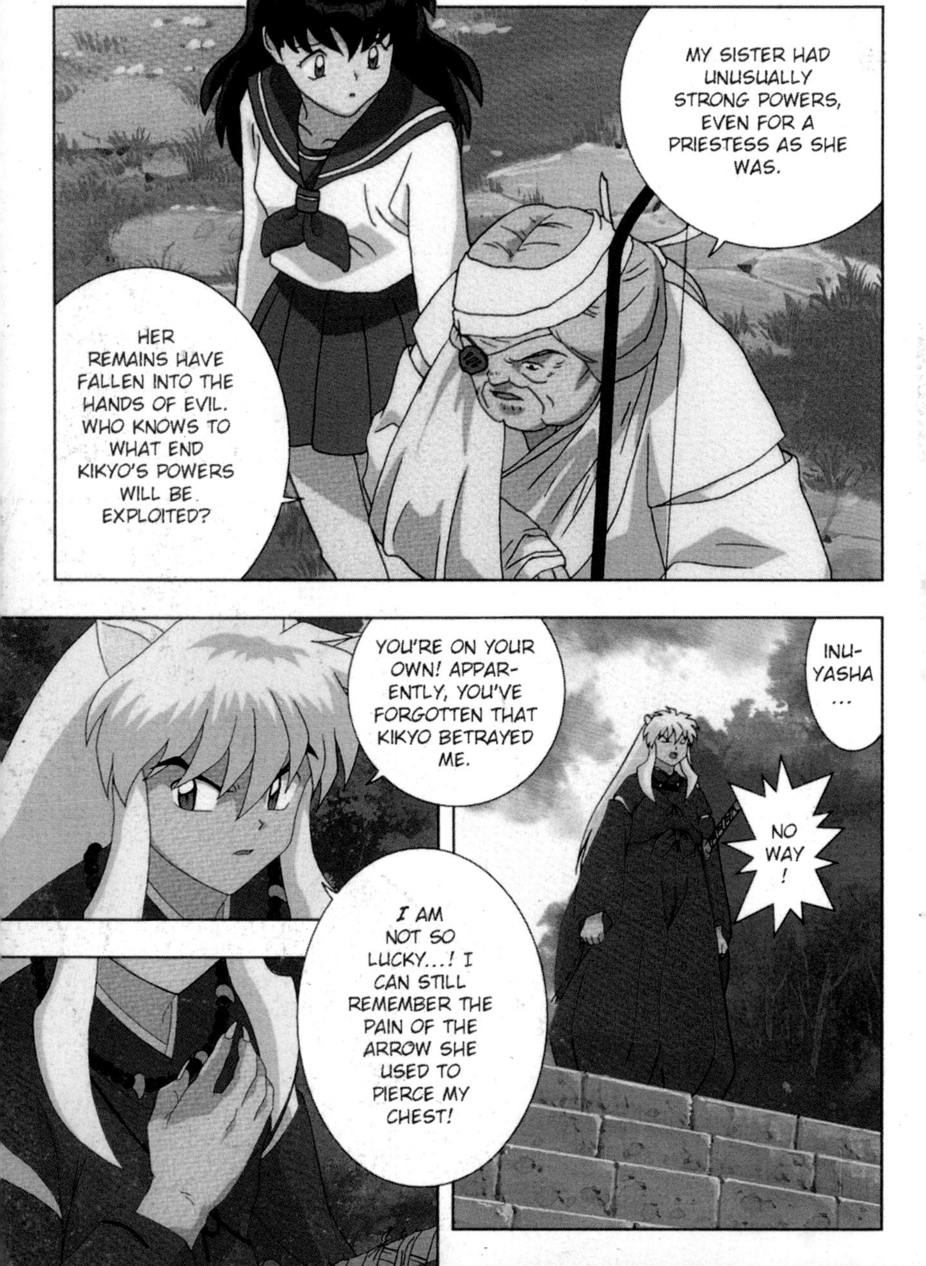
MY SISTER HAD UNUSUALLY STRONG POWERS, EVEN FOR A PRIESTESS AS SHE WAS.
HER REMAINS HAVE FALLEN INTO THE HANDS OF EVIL. WHO KNOWS TO WHAT END KIKYO'S POWERS WILL BE EXPLOITED?
INU-YASHA ...
NO WAY!
YOU'RE ON YOUR OWN! APPAR-ENTLY, YOU'VE FORGOTTEN THAT KIKYO BETRAYED ME.
I AM NOT SO LUCKY...! I CAN STILL REMEMBER THE PAIN OF THE ARROW SHE USED TO PIERCE MY CHEST!

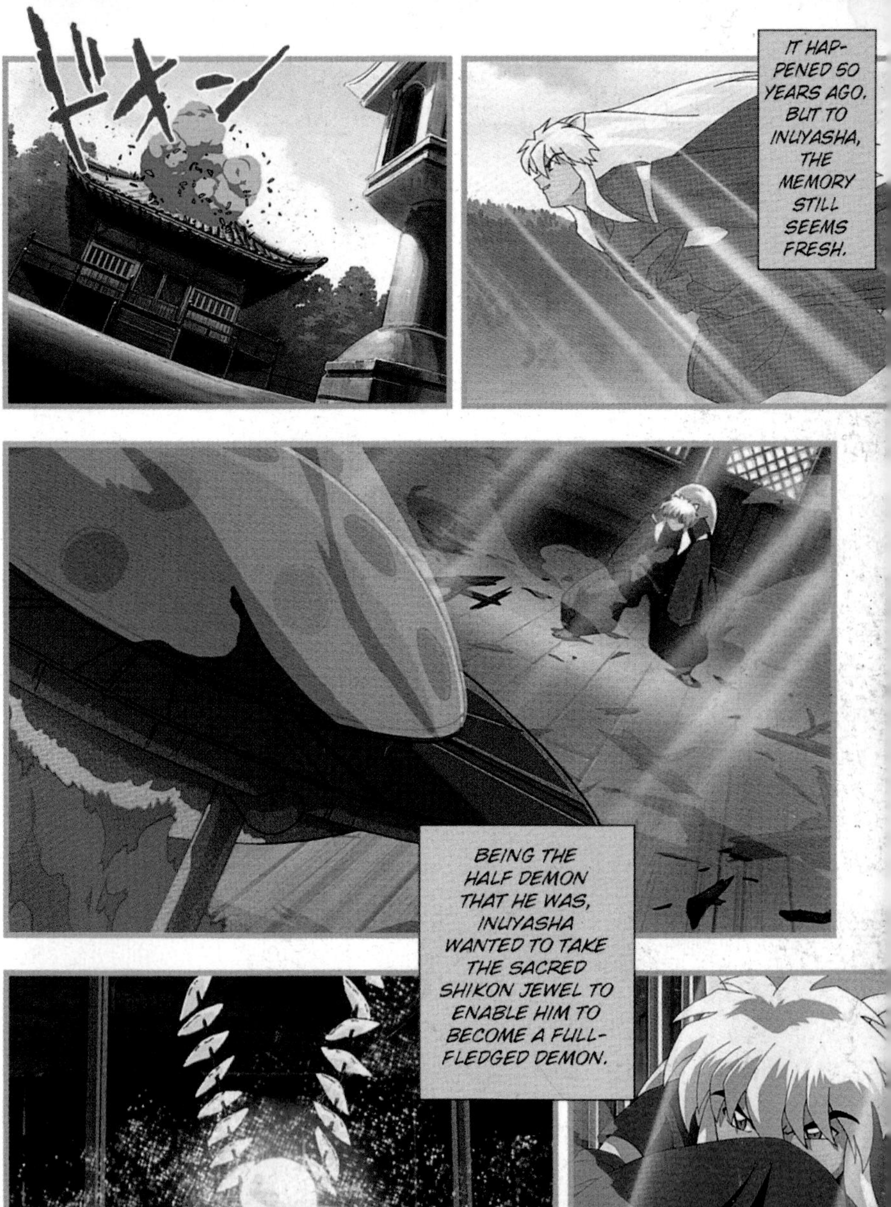
IT HAPPENED 50 YEARS AGO. BUT TO INUYASHA, THE MEMORY STILL SEEMS FRESH.
BEING THE HALF DEMON THAT HE WAS, INUYASHA WANTED TO TAKE THE SACRED SHIKON JEWEL TO ENABLE HIM TO BECOME A FULL-FLEDGED DEMON.

SO THERE!

FINALLY, A WAY FOR ME TO BECOME ALL DEMON AT LAST! HAH!

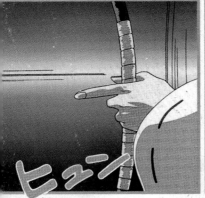

INU-YASHA!

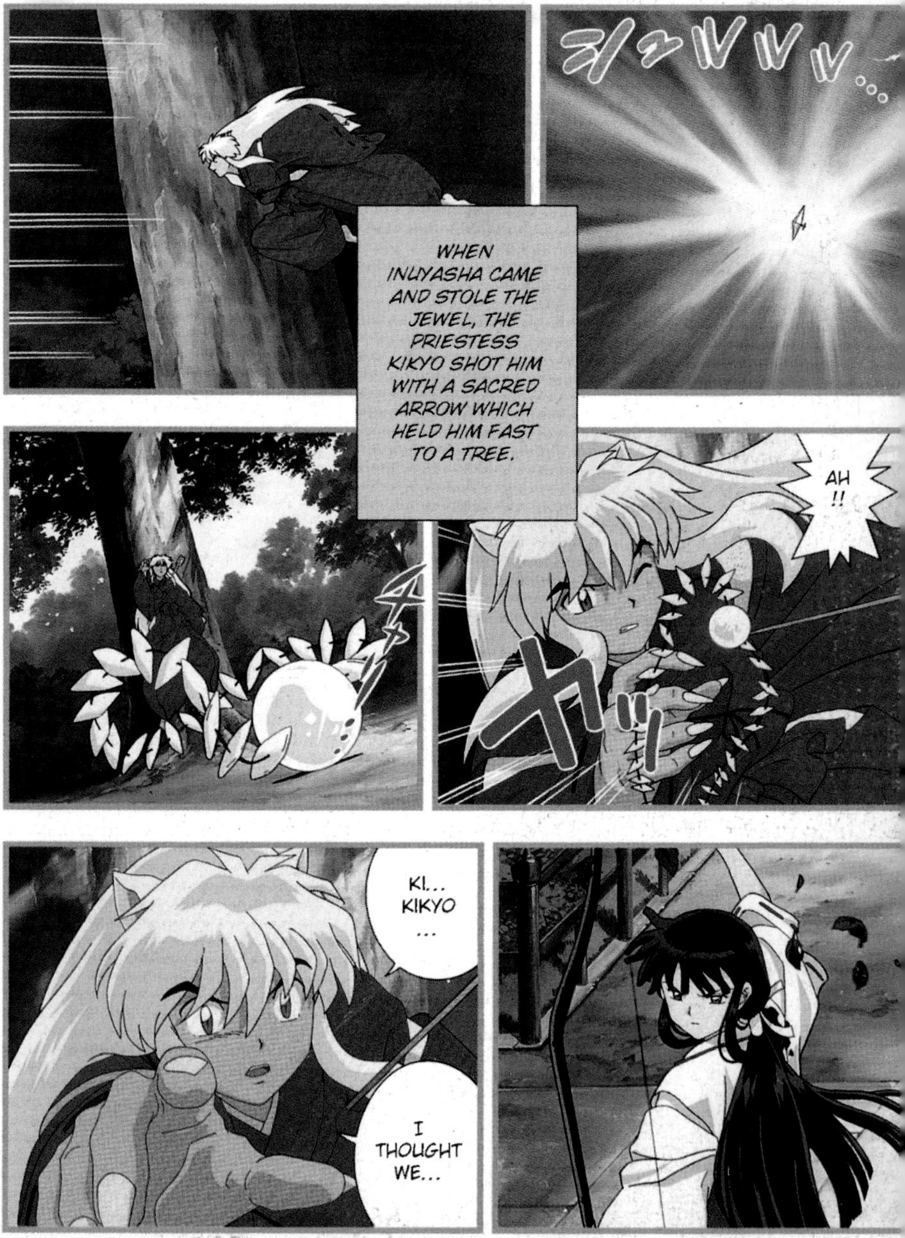
シュルルル…
WHEN INUYASHA CAME AND STOLE THE JEWEL, THE PRIESTESS KIKYO SHOT HIM WITH A SACRED ARROW WHICH HELD HIM FAST TO A TREE.
AH !!
ヤッ
KI... KIKYO ...
I THOUGHT WE...

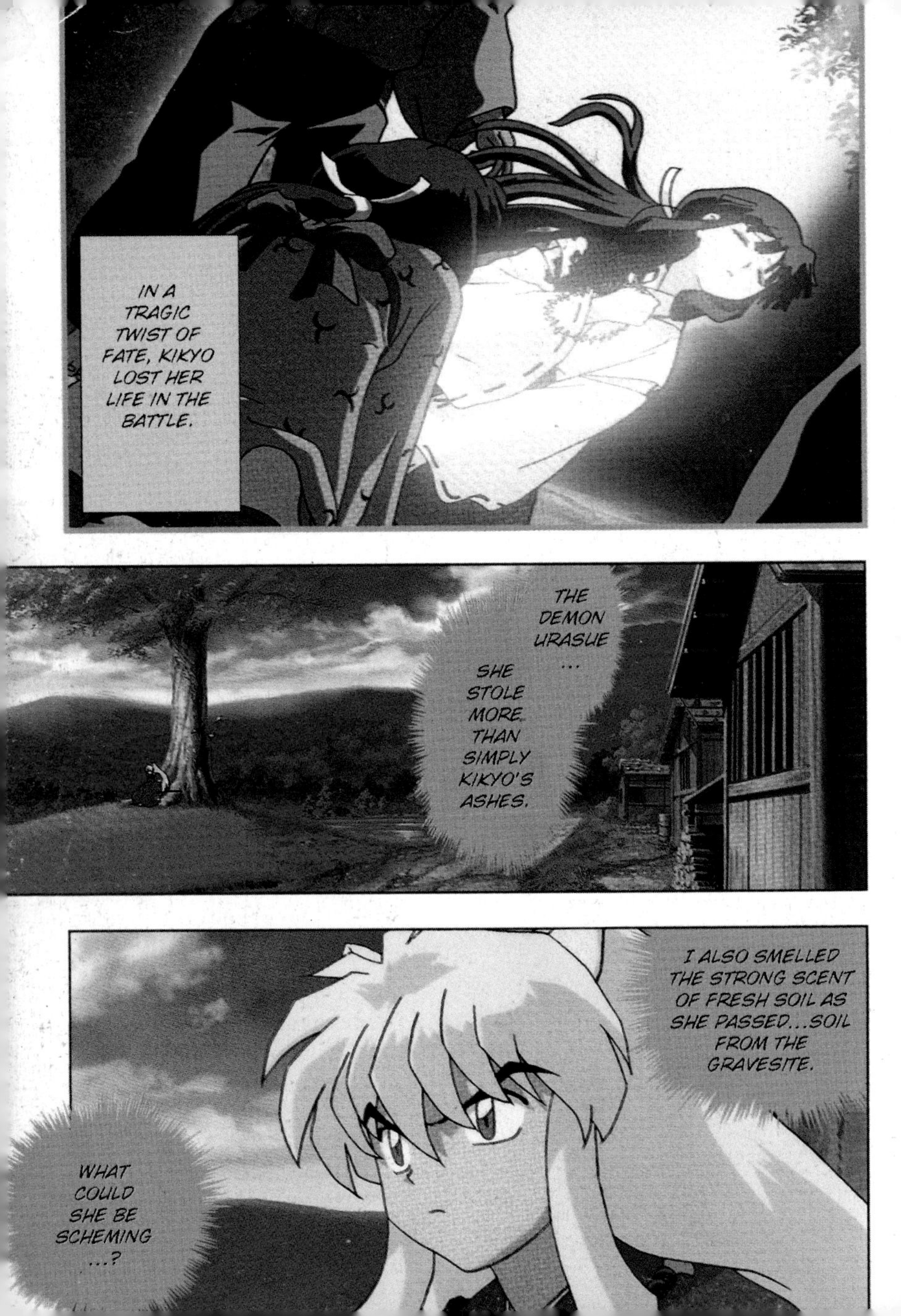
IN A TRAGIC TWIST OF FATE, KIKYO LOST HER LIFE IN THE BATTLE.
THE DEMON URASUE...
SHE STOLE MORE THAN SIMPLY KIKYO'S ASHES.
I ALSO SMELLED THE STRONG SCENT OF FRESH SOIL AS SHE PASSED...SOIL FROM THE GRAVESITE.
WHAT COULD SHE BE SCHEMING...?

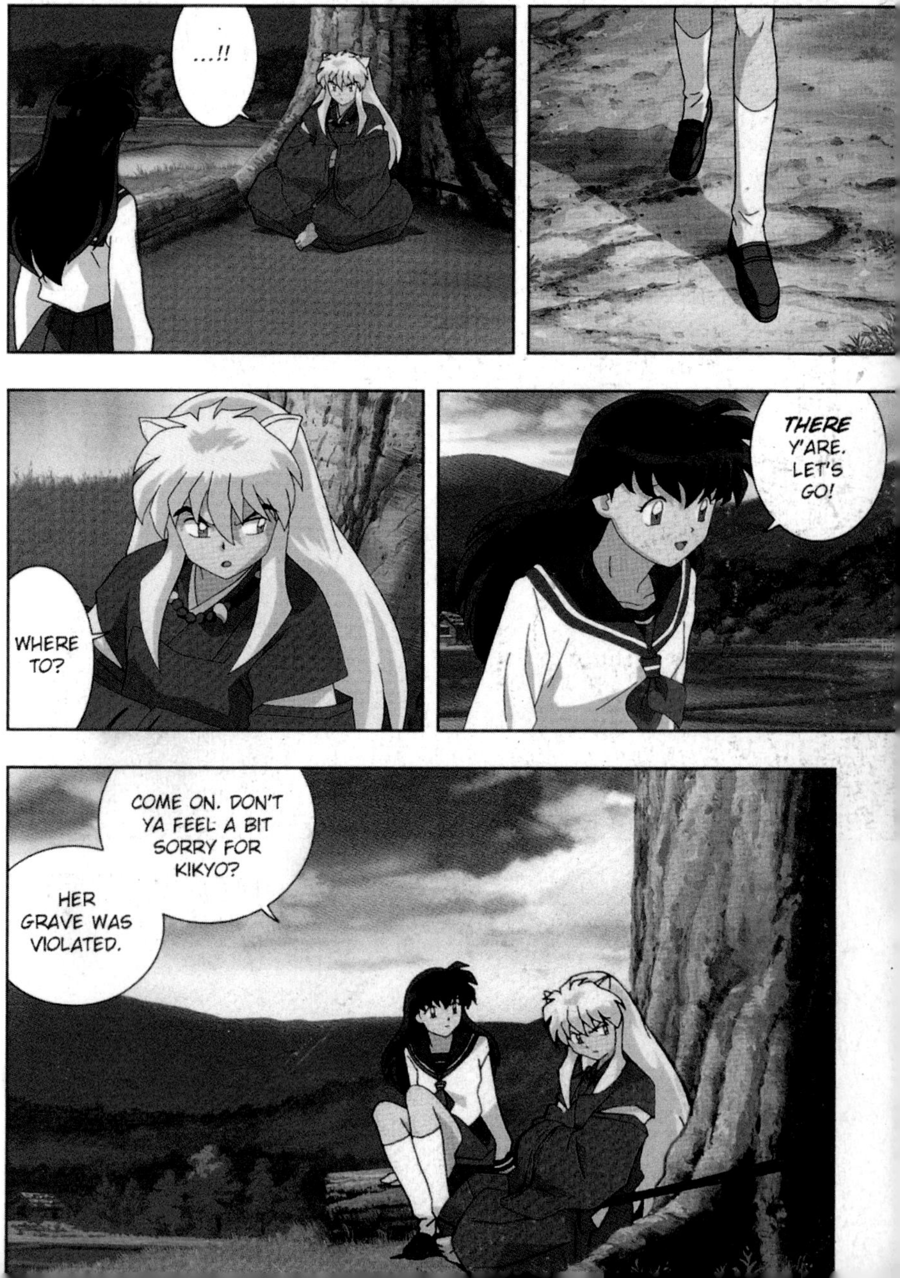
...!!
THERE Y'ARE. LET'S GO!
WHERE TO?
COME ON. DON'T YA FEEL A BIT SORRY FOR KIKYO?
HER GRAVE WAS VIOLATED.

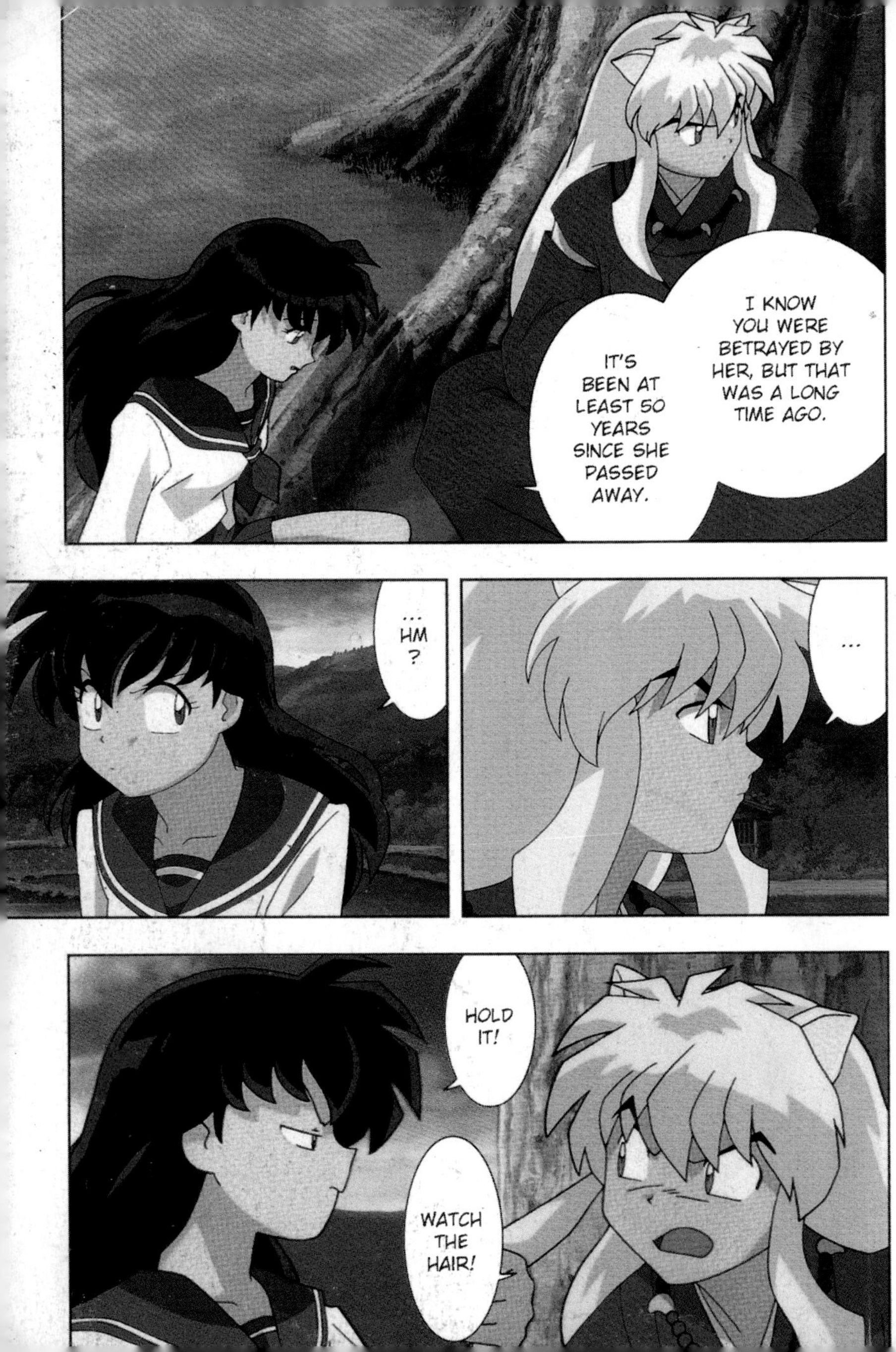

I KNOW YOU WERE BETRAYED BY HER, BUT THAT WAS A LONG TIME AGO.
IT'S BEEN AT LEAST 50 YEARS SINCE SHE PASSED AWAY.
...
...HM?
HOLD IT!
WATCH THE HAIR!

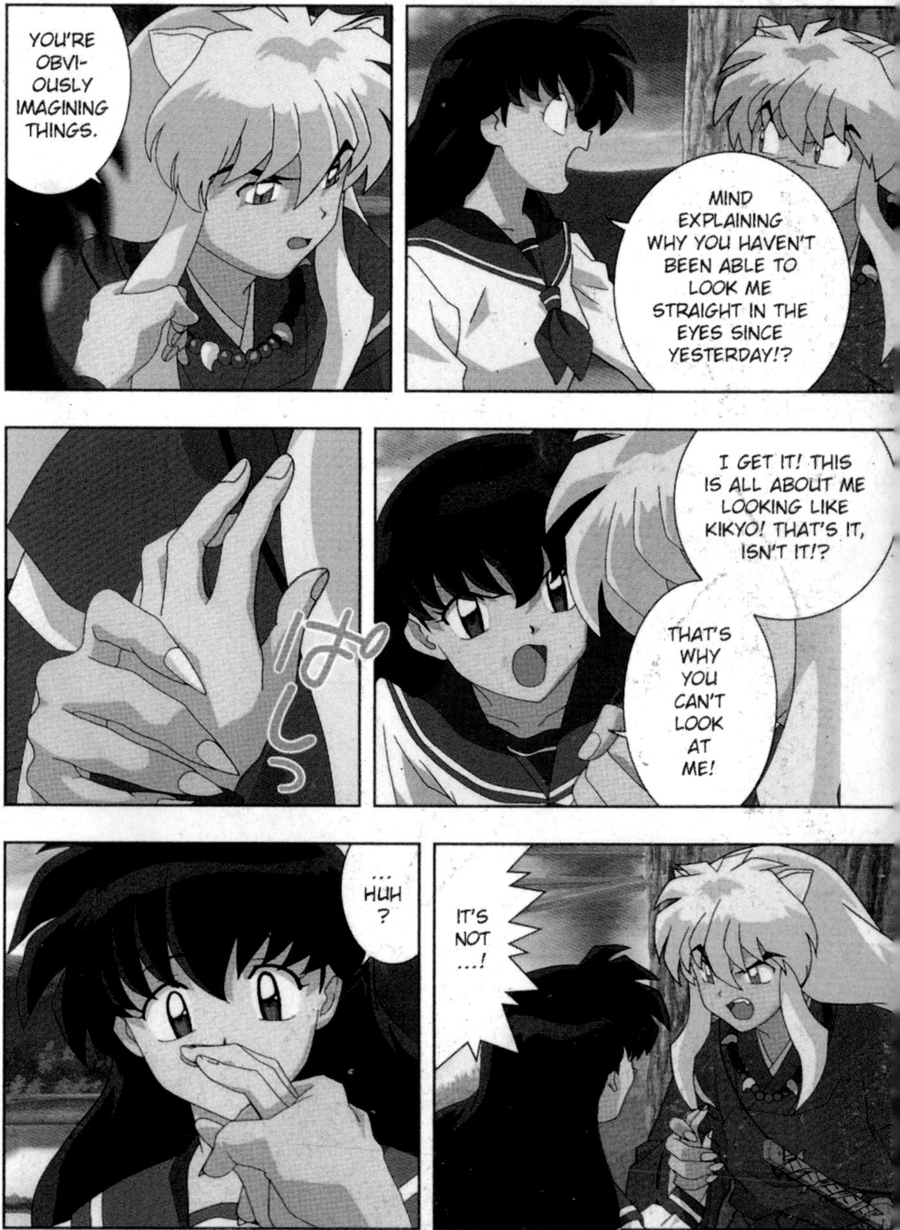
MIND EXPLAINING WHY YOU HAVEN'T BEEN ABLE TO LOOK ME STRAIGHT IN THE EYES SINCE YESTERDAY!?
YOU'RE OBVI-OUSLY IMAGINING THINGS.
I GET IT! THIS IS ALL ABOUT ME LOOKING LIKE KIKYO! THAT'S IT, ISN'T IT!?
THAT'S WHY YOU CAN'T LOOK AT ME!
ぱしっ
IT'S NOT ...!
... HUH ?

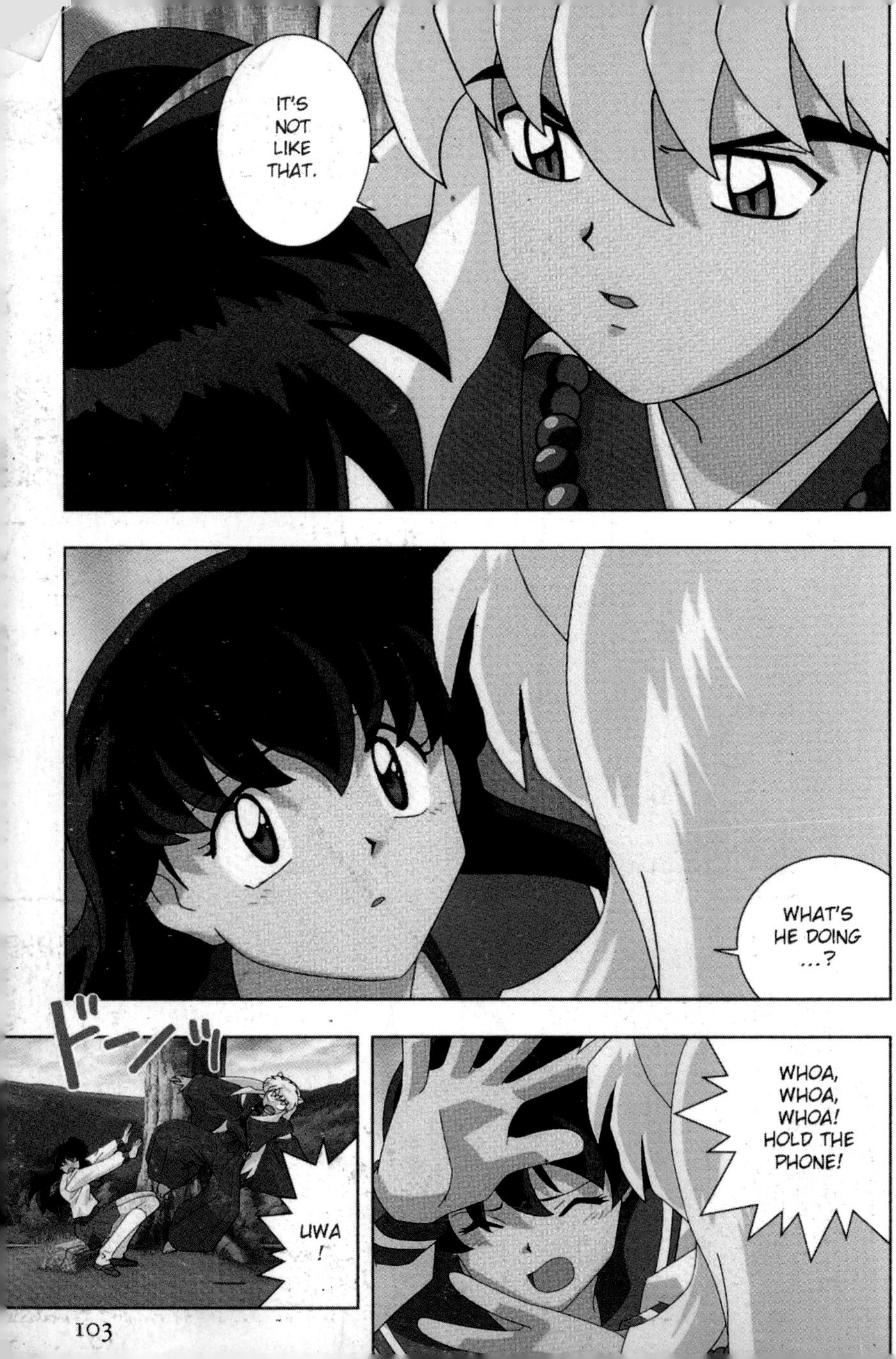
IT'S NOT LIKE THAT.
WHAT'S HE DOING ...?
WHOA, WHOA, WHOA! HOLD THE PHONE!
ドーンッ
UWA!

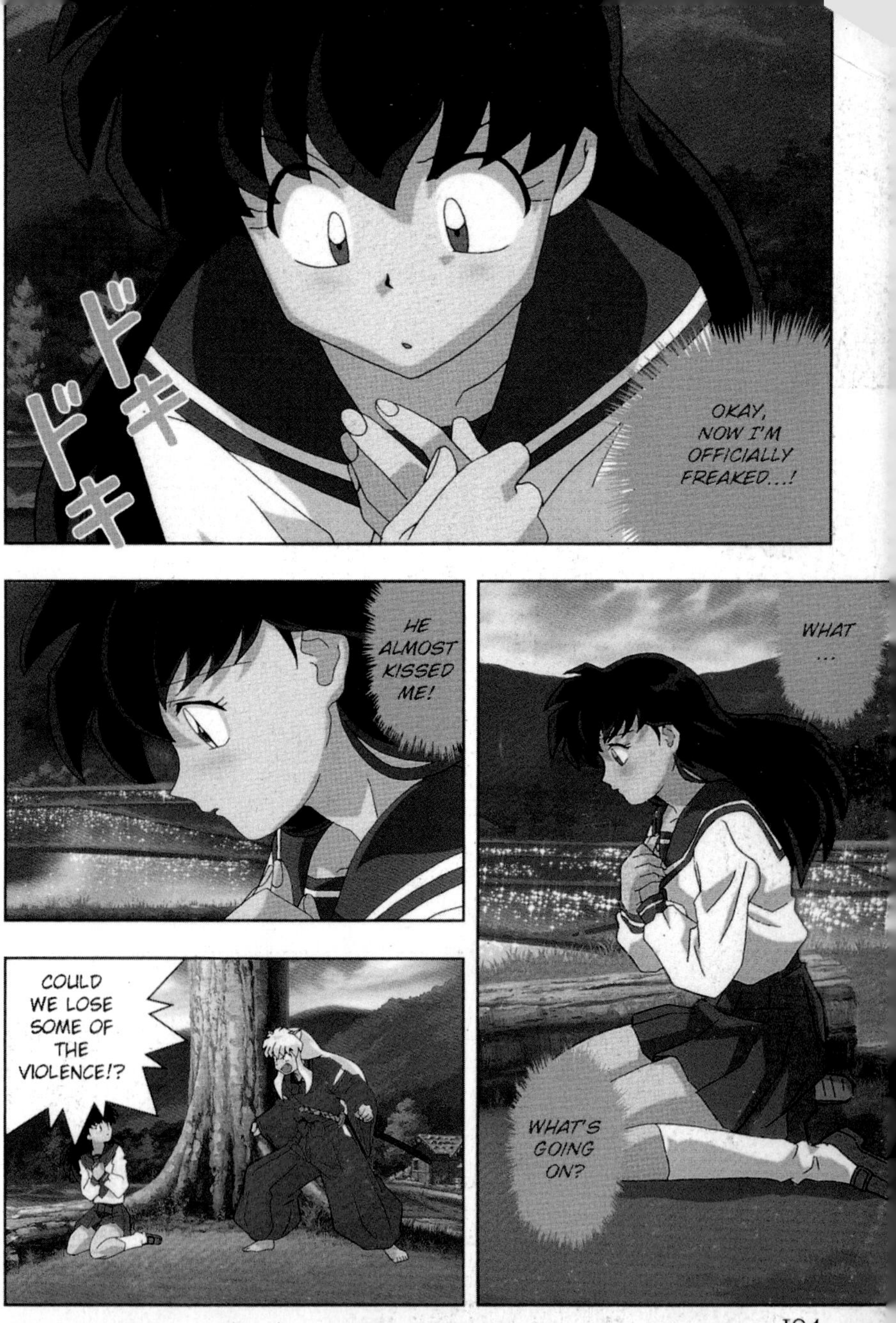
ドキ
ドキ
OKAY, NOW I'M OFFICIALLY FREAKED...!
WHAT ...
WHAT'S GOING ON?
HE ALMOST KISSED ME!
COULD WE LOSE SOME OF THE VIOLENCE!?

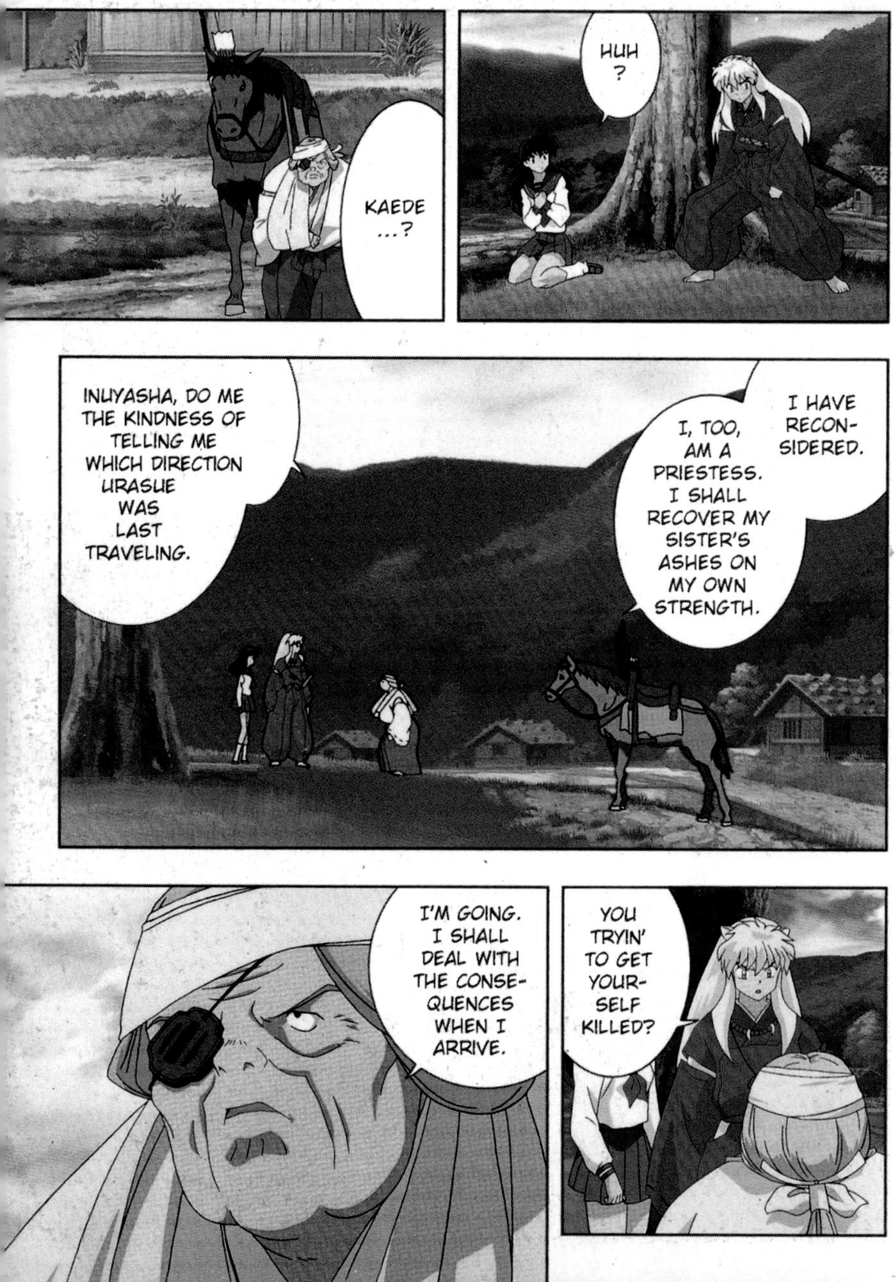
HUH ?
KAEDE ...?
I HAVE RECON-SIDERED.
I, TOO, AM A PRIESTESS. I SHALL RECOVER MY SISTER'S ASHES ON MY OWN STRENGTH.
INUYASHA, DO ME THE KINDNESS OF TELLING ME WHICH DIRECTION URASUE WAS LAST TRAVELING.
YOU TRYIN' TO GET YOUR-SELF KILLED?
I'M GOING. I SHALL DEAL WITH THE CONSE-QUENCES WHEN I ARRIVE.

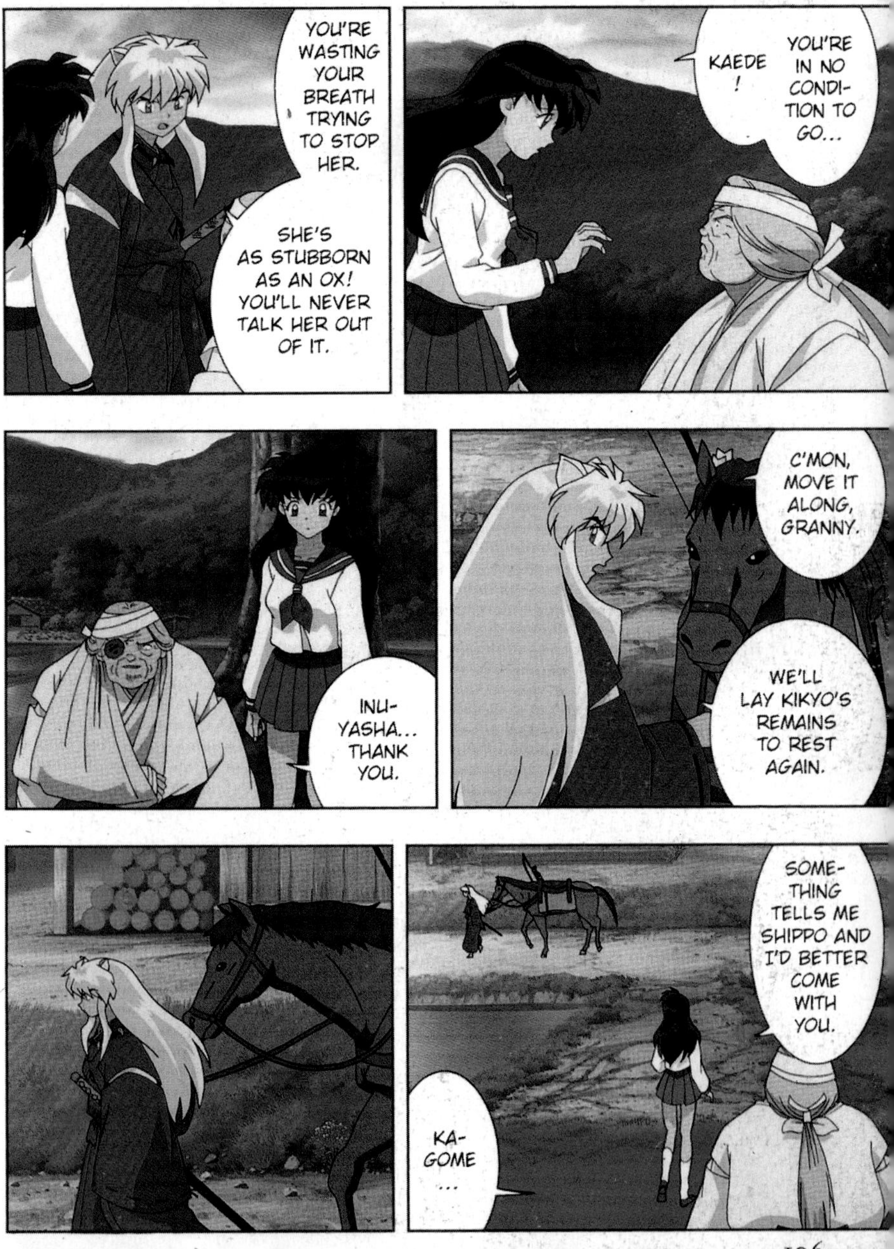
KAEDE!
YOU'RE IN NO CONDITION TO GO...
YOU'RE WASTING YOUR BREATH TRYING TO STOP HER.
SHE'S AS STUBBORN AS AN OX! YOU'LL NEVER TALK HER OUT OF IT.
C'MON, MOVE IT ALONG, GRANNY.
WE'LL LAY KIKYO'S REMAINS TO REST AGAIN.
INU-YASHA... THANK YOU.
SOME-THING TELLS ME SHIPPO AND I'D BETTER COME WITH YOU.
KA-GOME...

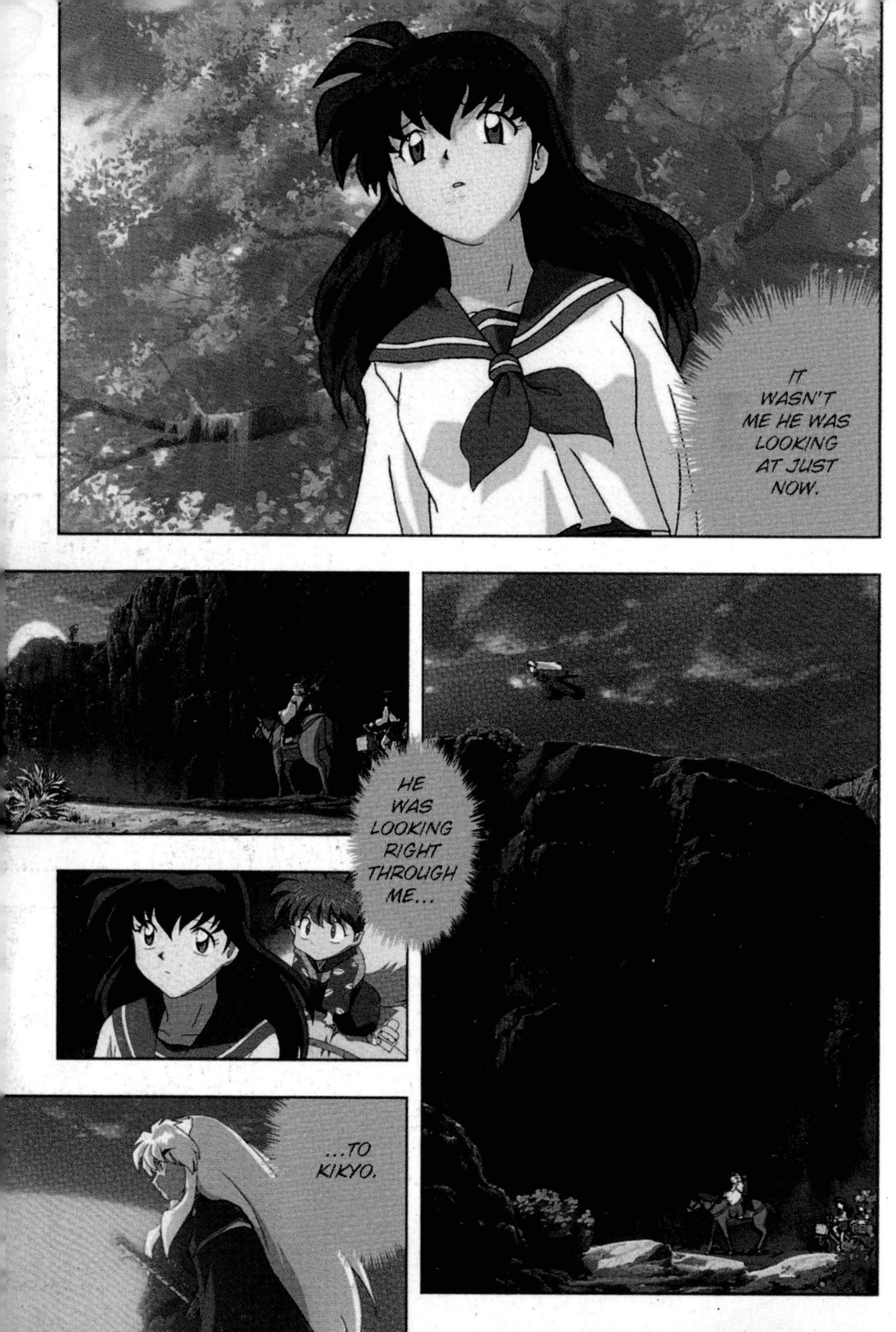
IT WASN'T ME HE WAS LOOKING AT JUST NOW.
HE WAS LOOKING RIGHT THROUGH ME...
...TO KIKYO.

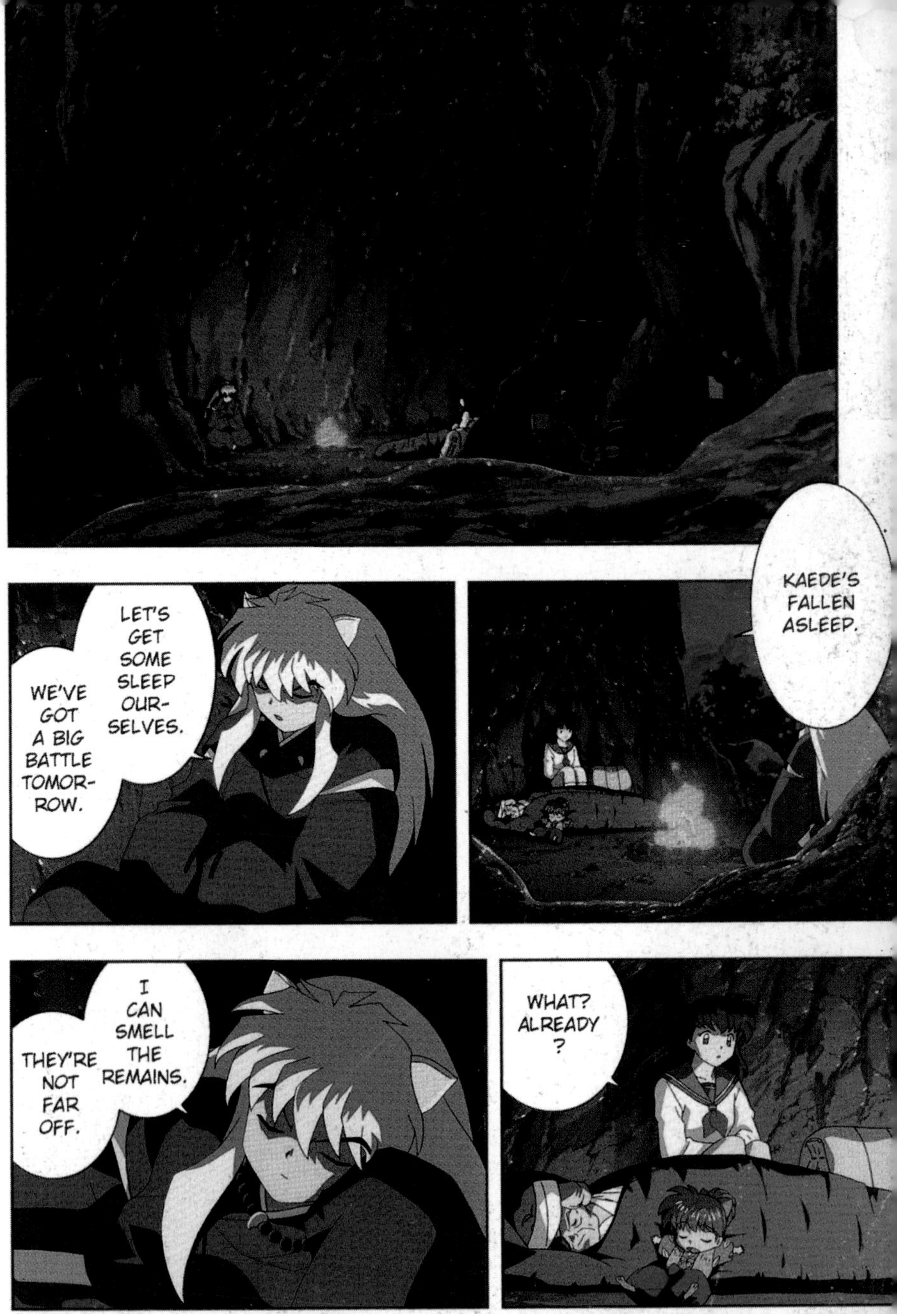
KAEDE'S FALLEN ASLEEP.
LET'S GET SOME SLEEP OUR-SELVES.
WE'VE GOT A BIG BATTLE TOMOR-ROW.
WHAT? ALREADY?
I CAN SMELL THE REMAINS.
THEY'RE NOT FAR OFF.

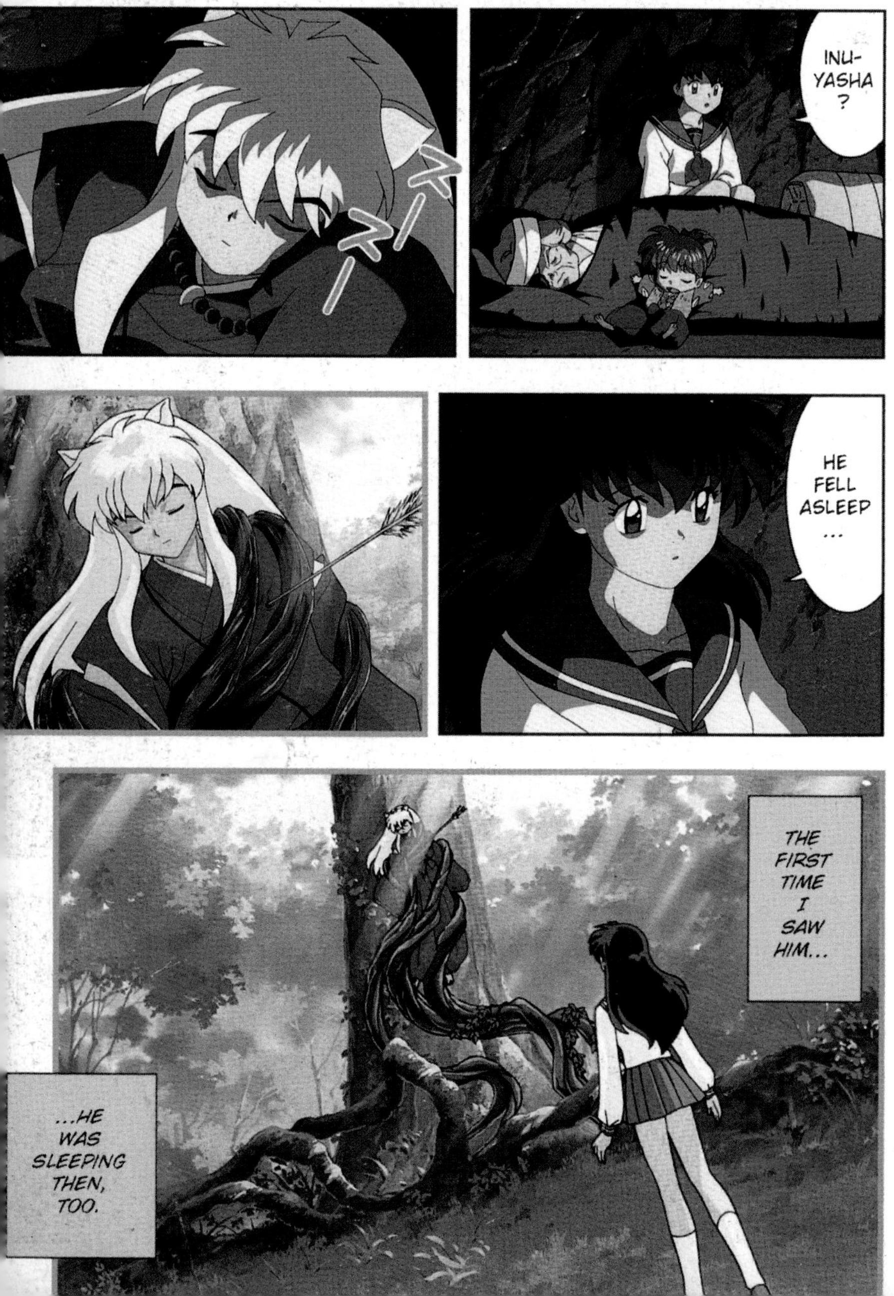
INU-YASHA ?
スースー
HE FELL ASLEEP ...
THE FIRST TIME I SAW HIM...
...HE WAS SLEEPING THEN, TOO.

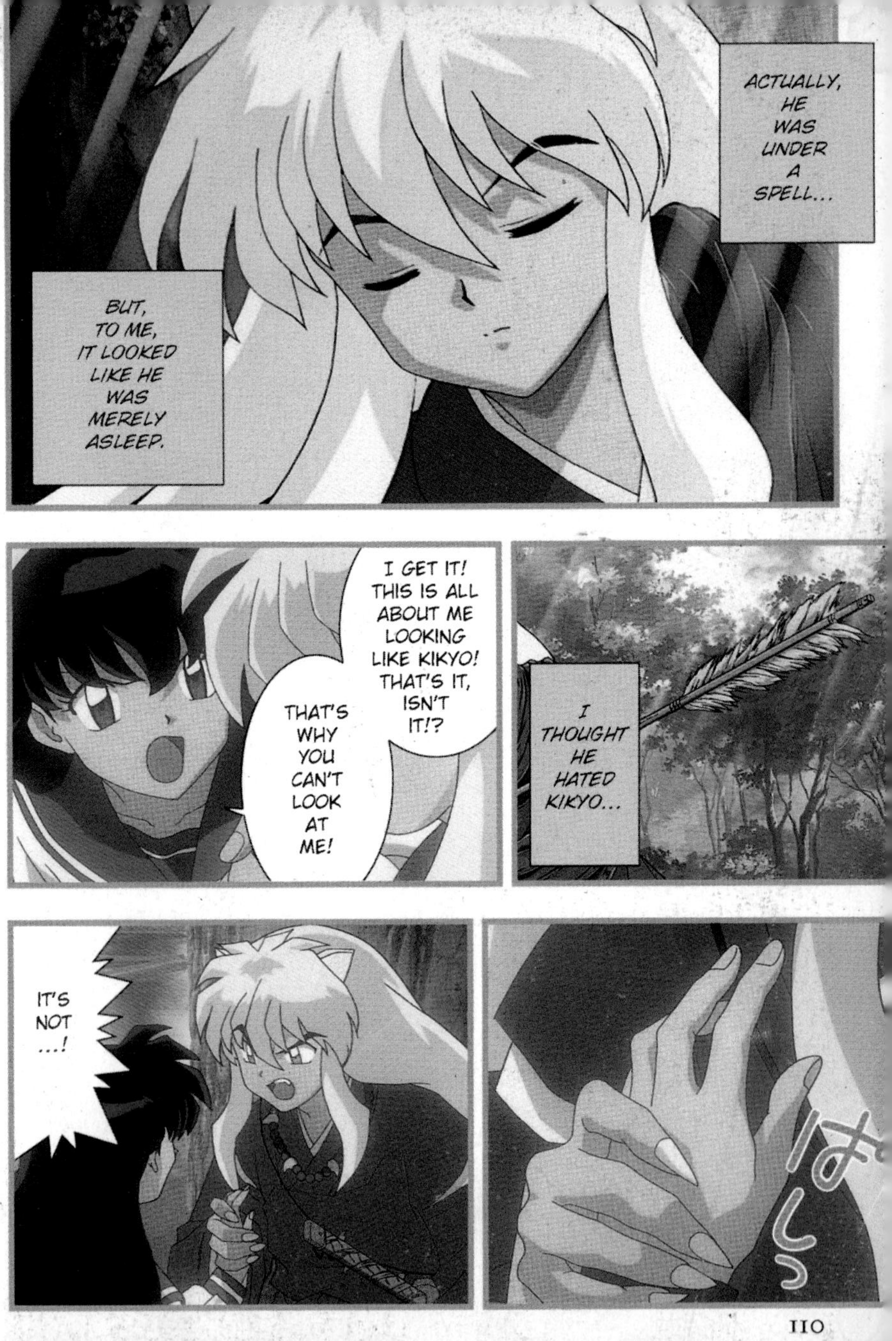
ACTUALLY, HE WAS UNDER A SPELL...
BUT, TO ME, IT LOOKED LIKE HE WAS MERELY ASLEEP.
I GET IT! THIS IS ALL ABOUT ME LOOKING LIKE KIKYO! THAT'S IT, ISN'T IT!?
THAT'S WHY YOU CAN'T LOOK AT ME!
I THOUGHT HE HATED KIKYO...
IT'S NOT ...!
はしっ

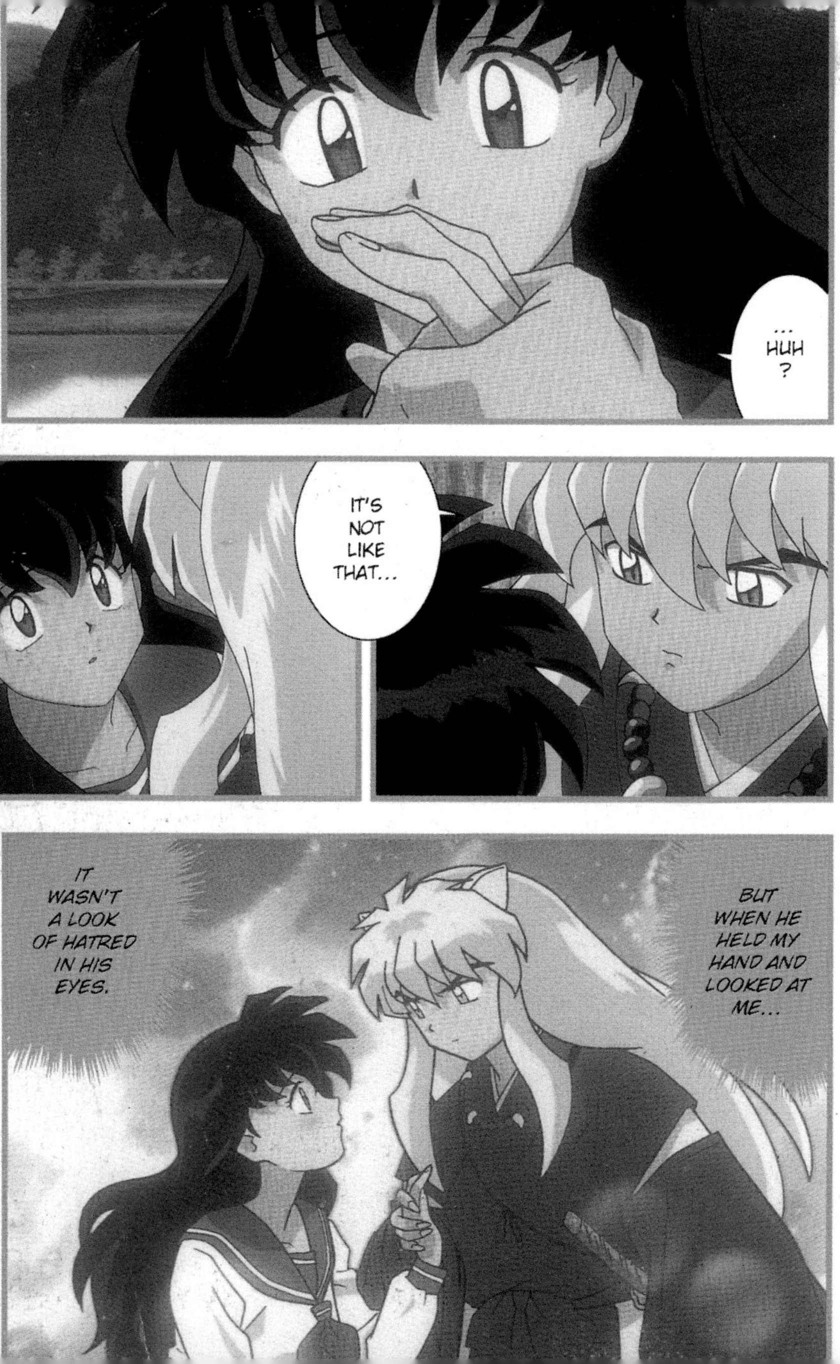
...HUH?
IT'S NOT LIKE THAT...
BUT WHEN HE HELD MY HAND AND LOOKED AT ME...
IT WASN'T A LOOK OF HATRED IN HIS EYES.

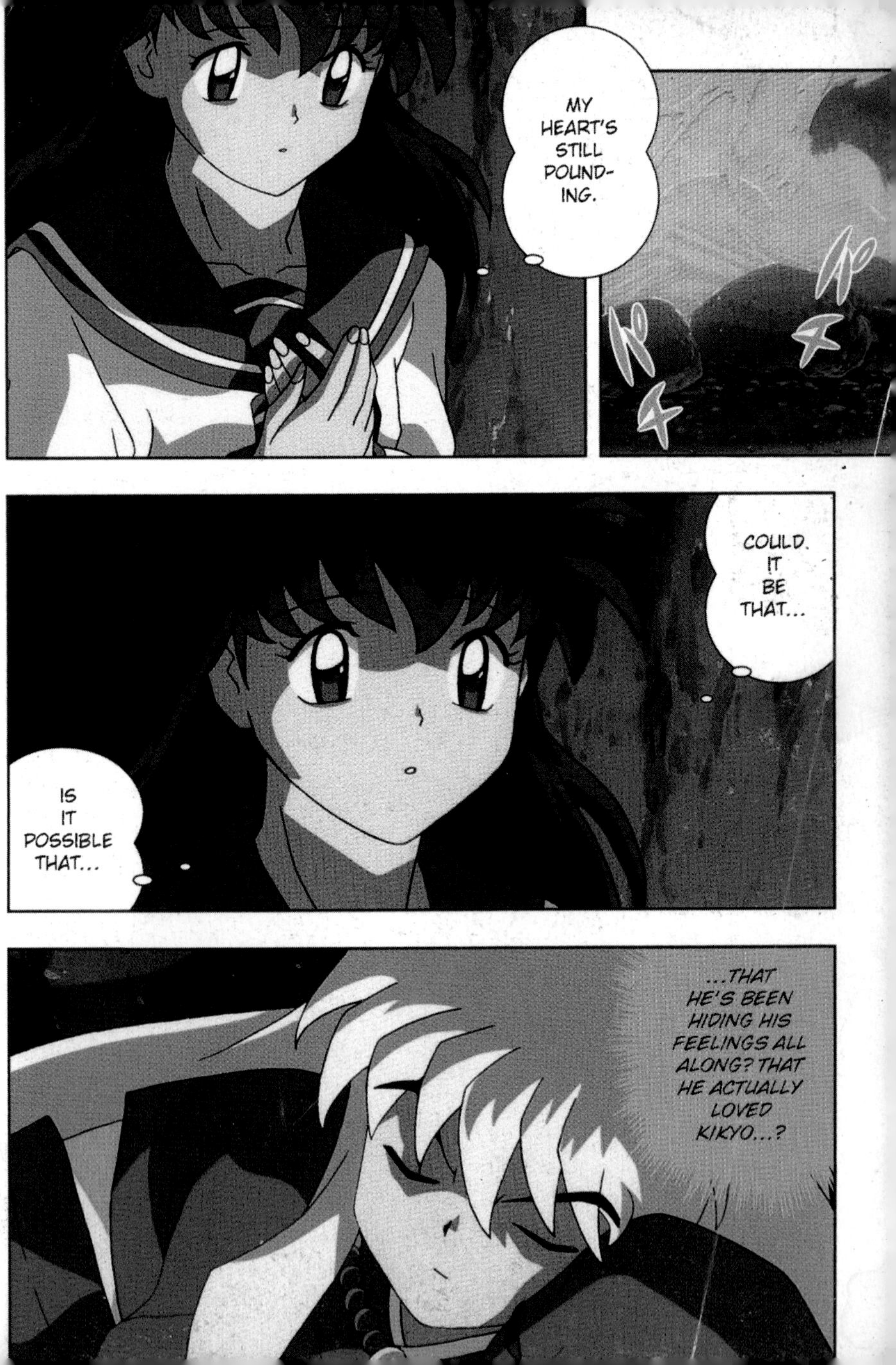
MY HEART'S STILL POUNDING.
COULD IT BE THAT...
IS IT POSSIBLE THAT...
...THAT HE'S BEEN HIDING HIS FEELINGS ALL ALONG? THAT HE ACTUALLY LOVED KIKYO...?

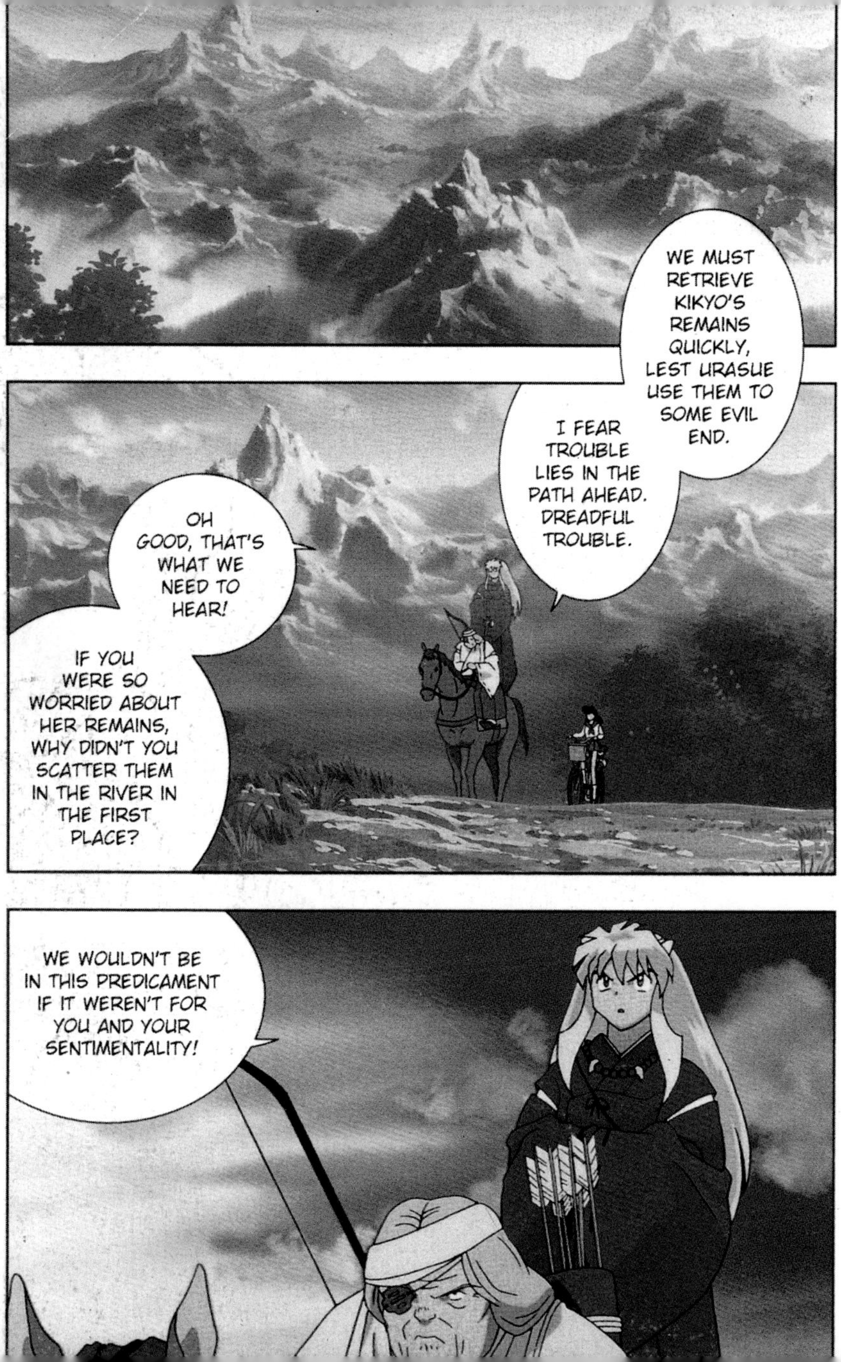
WE MUST RETRIEVE KIKYO'S REMAINS QUICKLY, LEST URASUE USE THEM TO SOME EVIL END.
I FEAR TROUBLE LIES IN THE PATH AHEAD. DREADFUL TROUBLE.
OH GOOD, THAT'S WHAT WE NEED TO HEAR!
IF YOU WERE SO WORRIED ABOUT HER REMAINS, WHY DIDN'T YOU SCATTER THEM IN THE RIVER IN THE FIRST PLACE?
WE WOULDN'T BE IN THIS PREDICAMENT IF IT WEREN'T FOR YOU AND YOUR SENTIMENTALITY!

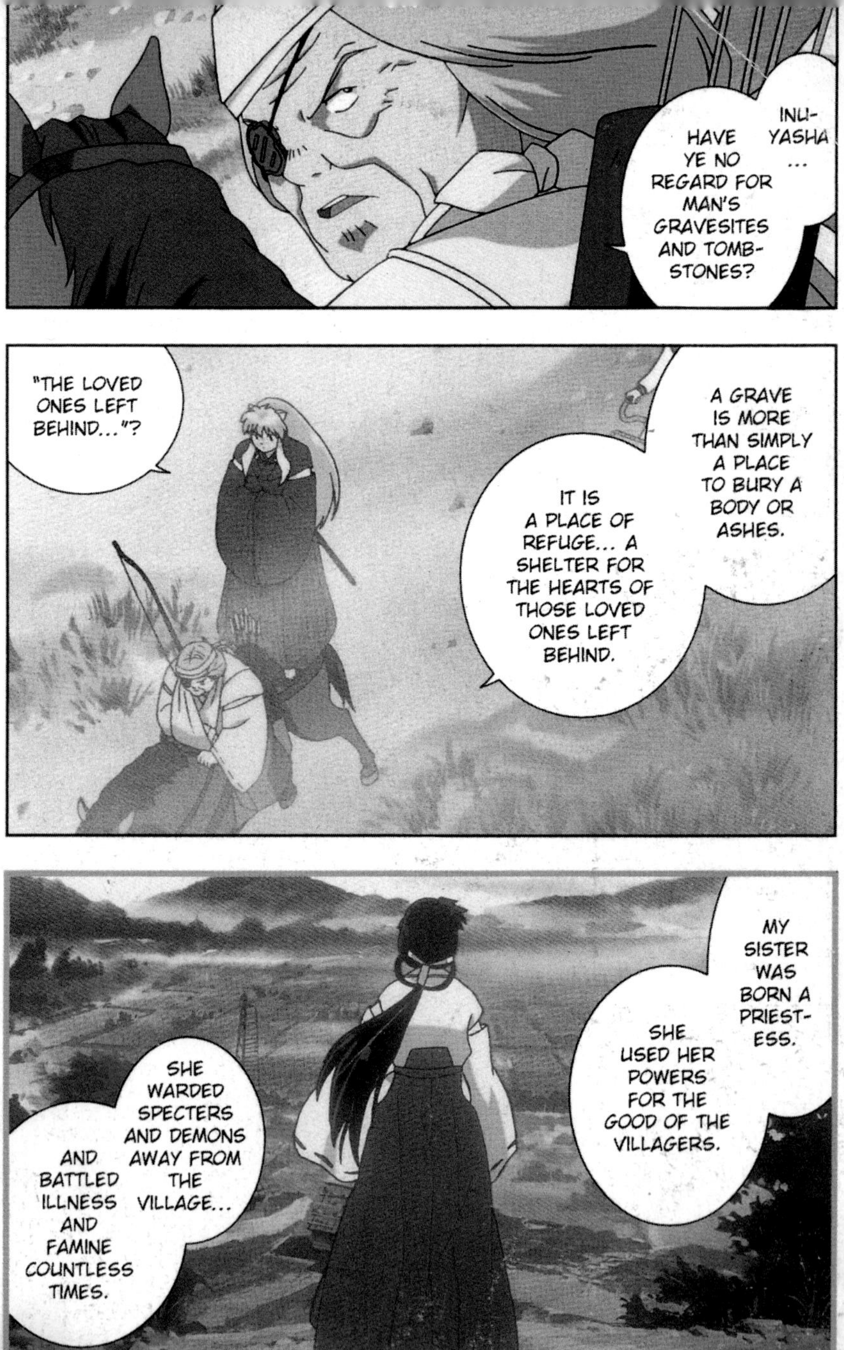
INU-YASHA...
HAVE YE NO REGARD FOR MAN'S GRAVESITES AND TOMB-STONES?
A GRAVE IS MORE THAN SIMPLY A PLACE TO BURY A BODY OR ASHES.
IT IS A PLACE OF REFUGE... A SHELTER FOR THE HEARTS OF THOSE LOVED ONES LEFT BEHIND.
"THE LOVED ONES LEFT BEHIND..."?
MY SISTER WAS BORN A PRIEST-ESS.
SHE USED HER POWERS FOR THE GOOD OF THE VILLAGERS.
SHE WARDED SPECTERS AND DEMONS AWAY FROM THE VILLAGE...
AND BATTLED ILLNESS AND FAMINE COUNTLESS TIMES.

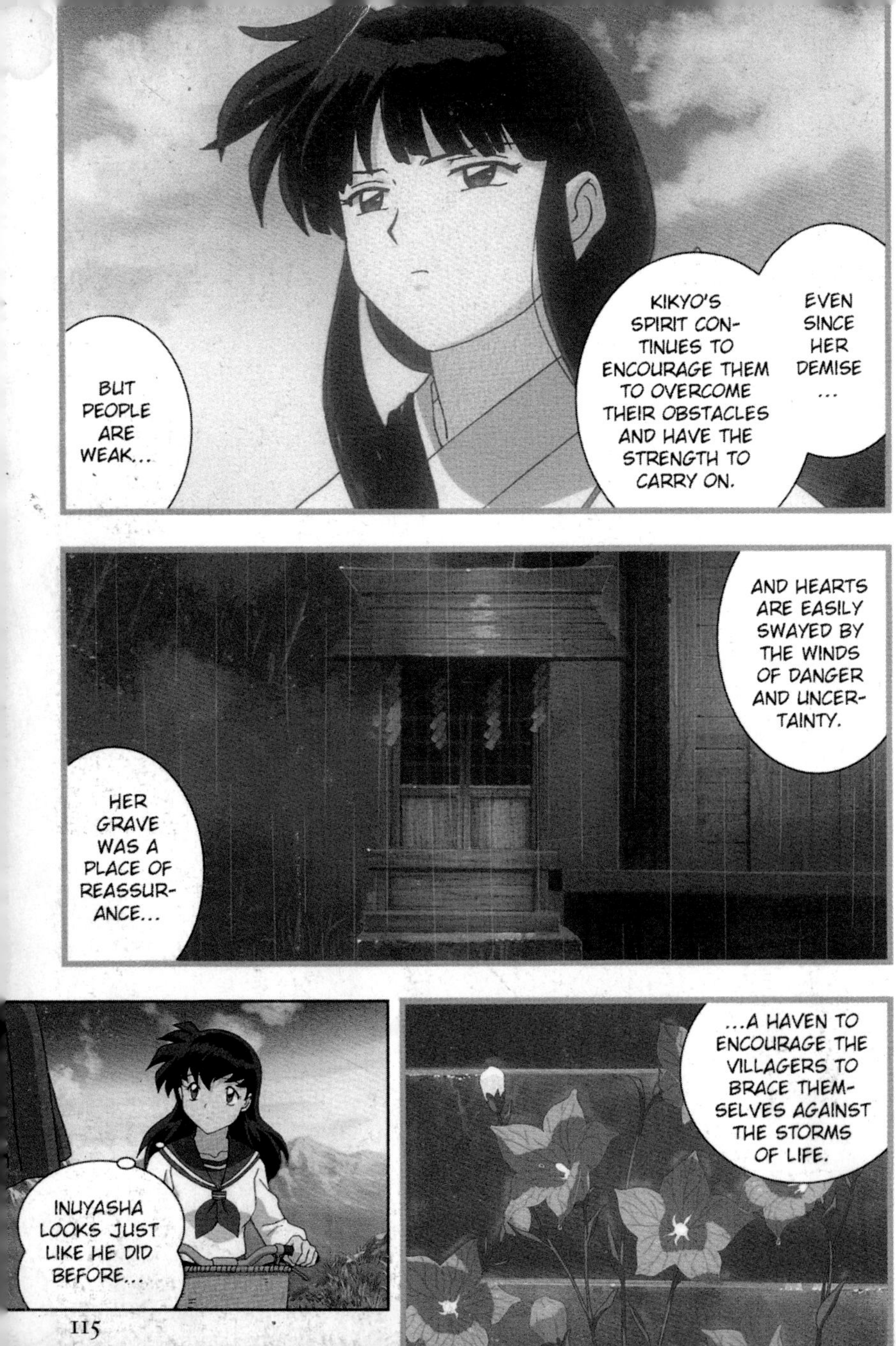
EVEN SINCE HER DEMISE...
KIKYO'S SPIRIT CONTINUES TO ENCOURAGE THEM TO OVERCOME THEIR OBSTACLES AND HAVE THE STRENGTH TO CARRY ON.
BUT PEOPLE ARE WEAK...
AND HEARTS ARE EASILY SWAYED BY THE WINDS OF DANGER AND UNCERTAINTY.
HER GRAVE WAS A PLACE OF REASSURANCE...
...A HAVEN TO ENCOURAGE THE VILLAGERS TO BRACE THEMSELVES AGAINST THE STORMS OF LIFE.
INUYASHA LOOKS JUST LIKE HE DID BEFORE...

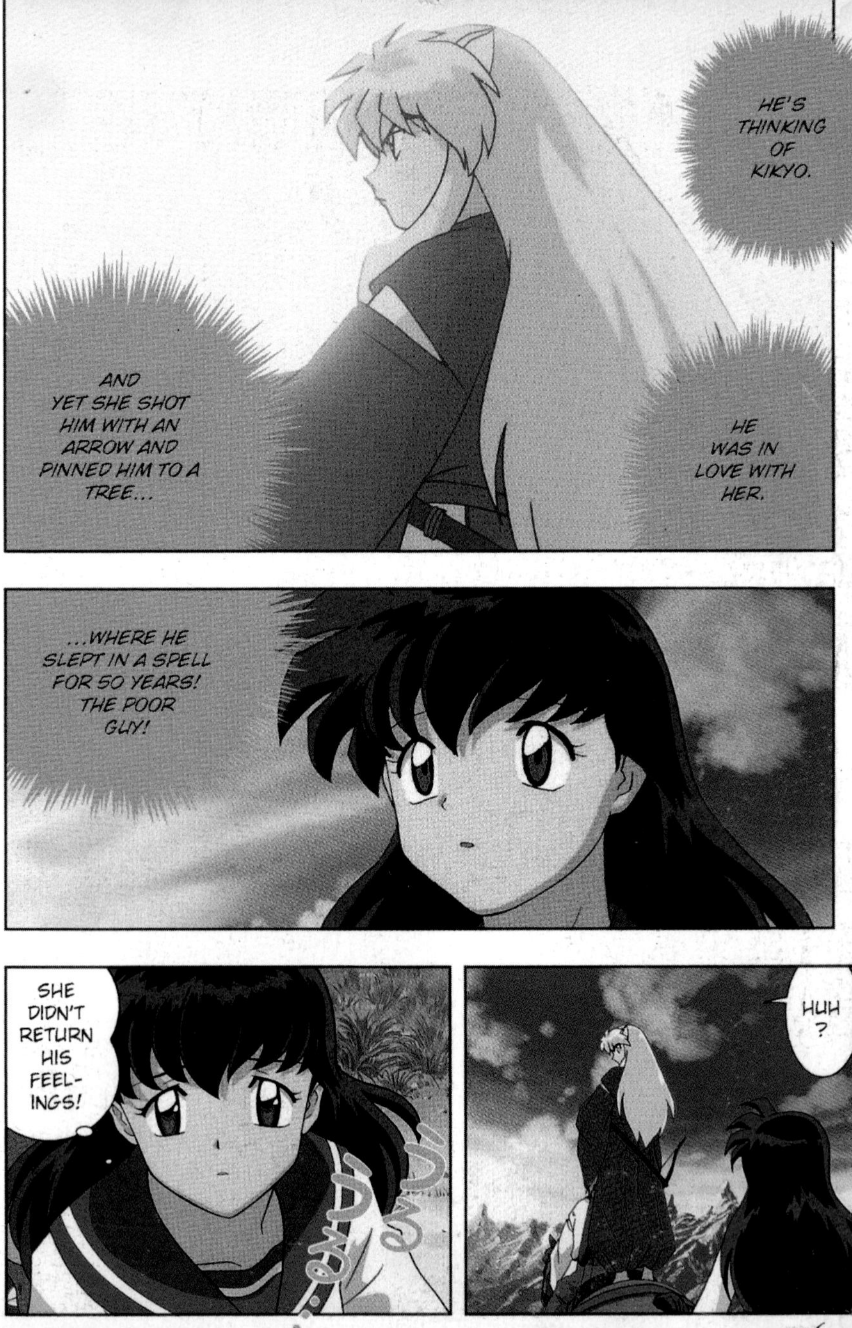
HE'S THINKING OF KIKYO.
HE WAS IN LOVE WITH HER.
AND YET SHE SHOT HIM WITH AN ARROW AND PINNED HIM TO A TREE...
...WHERE HE SLEPT IN A SPELL FOR 50 YEARS! THE POOR GUY!
HUH?
SHE DIDN'T RETURN HIS FEEL-INGS!

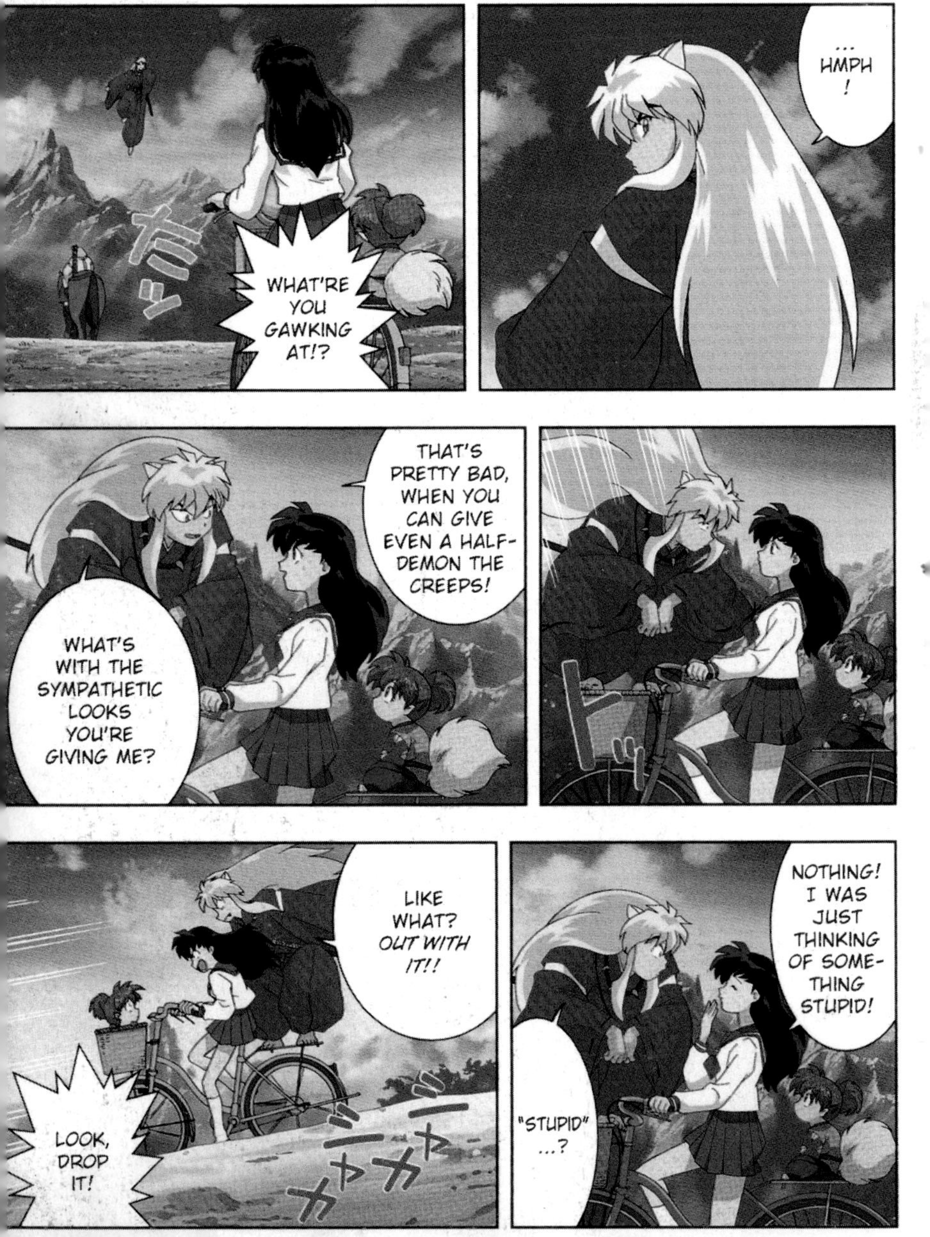
...HMPH!
WHAT'RE YOU GAWKING AT!?
THAT'S PRETTY BAD, WHEN YOU CAN GIVE EVEN A HALF-DEMON THE CREEPS!
WHAT'S WITH THE SYMPATHETIC LOOKS YOU'RE GIVING ME?
NOTHING! I WAS JUST THINKING OF SOME-THING STUPID!
"STUPID" ...?
LIKE WHAT? *OUT WITH IT!!*
LOOK, DROP IT!

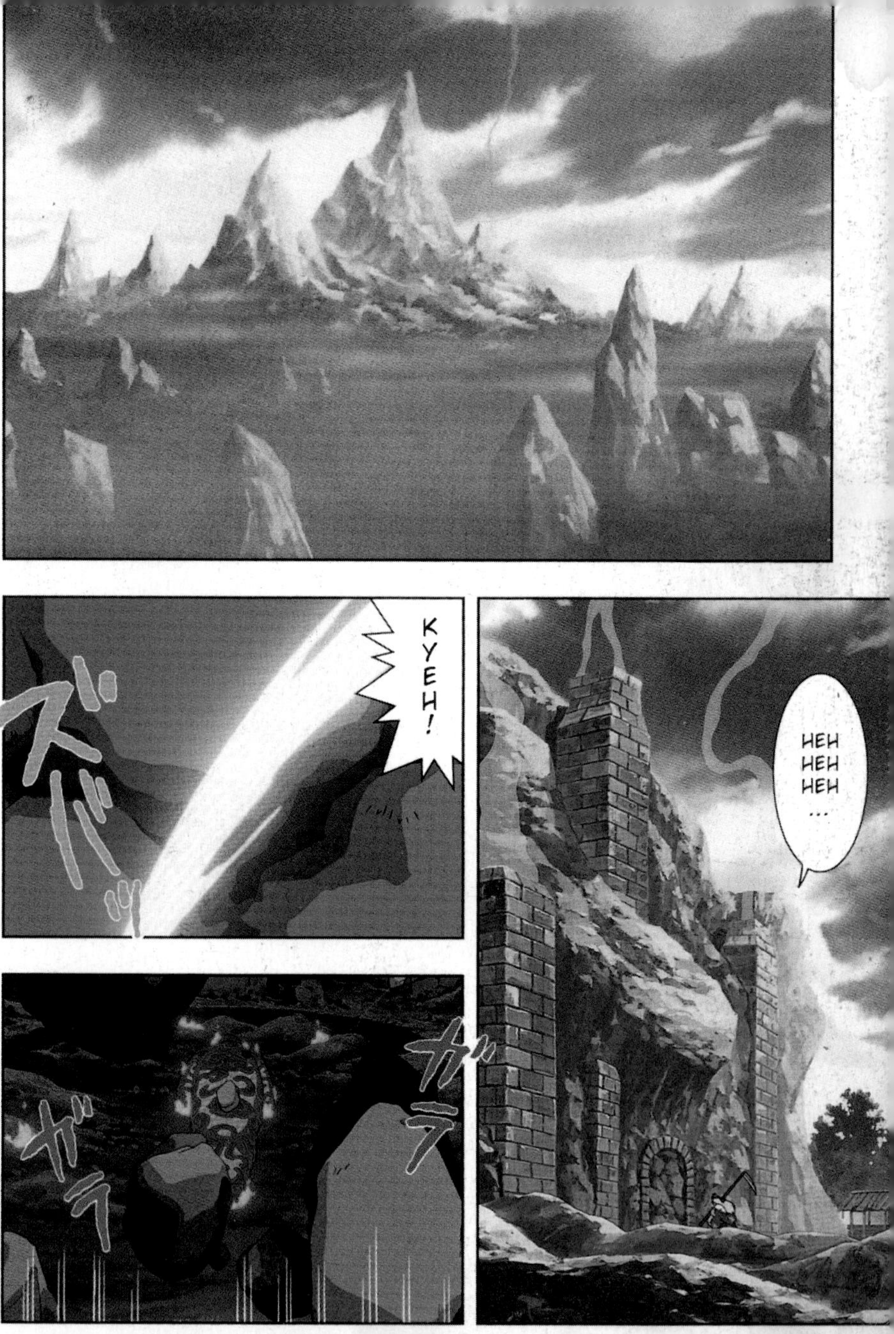
HEH HEH HEH ...
KYEH!
ズバッ
ガラ
ガラ

NOW THEN... LET'S SEE WHAT MAGIC MY DEMON KILN...
HAS BROUGHT TO THE MIXTURE OF ASHES AND GRAVESIDE SOIL.
AH, YES!
THIS COULD BE MY FINEST CREATION YET!
NOW ...

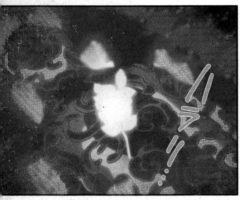

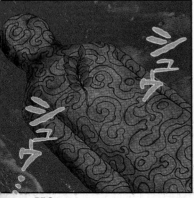

ARISE!
ARISE, KIKYO!
COME TO ME!

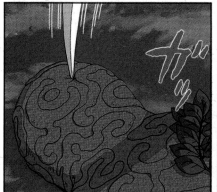

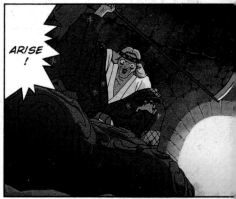

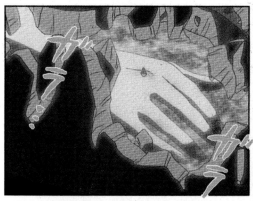

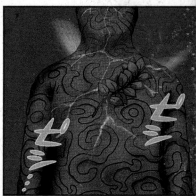

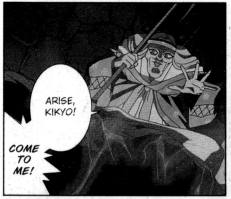

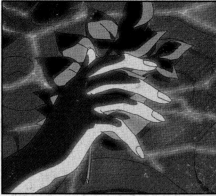

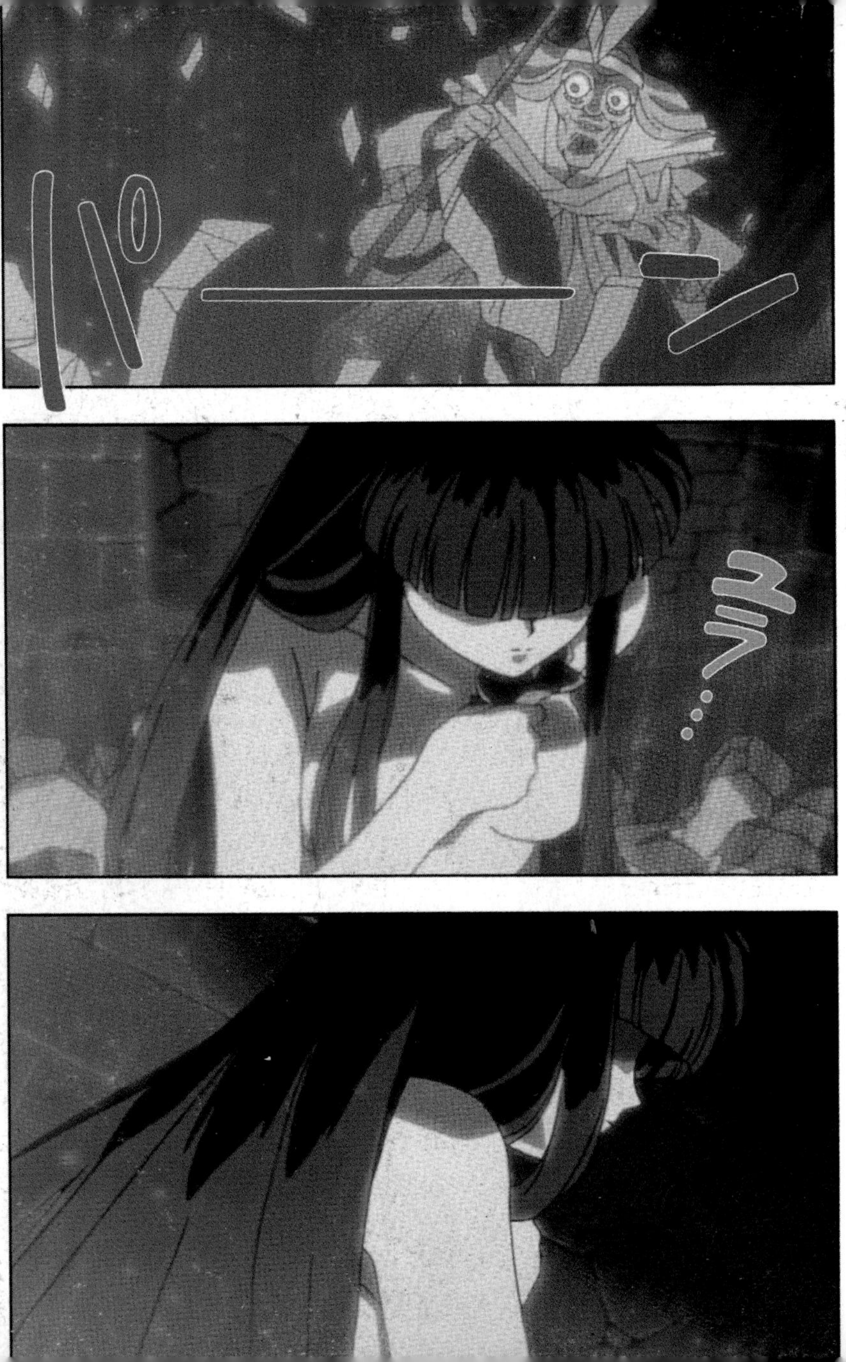
パーーン
ユラ…

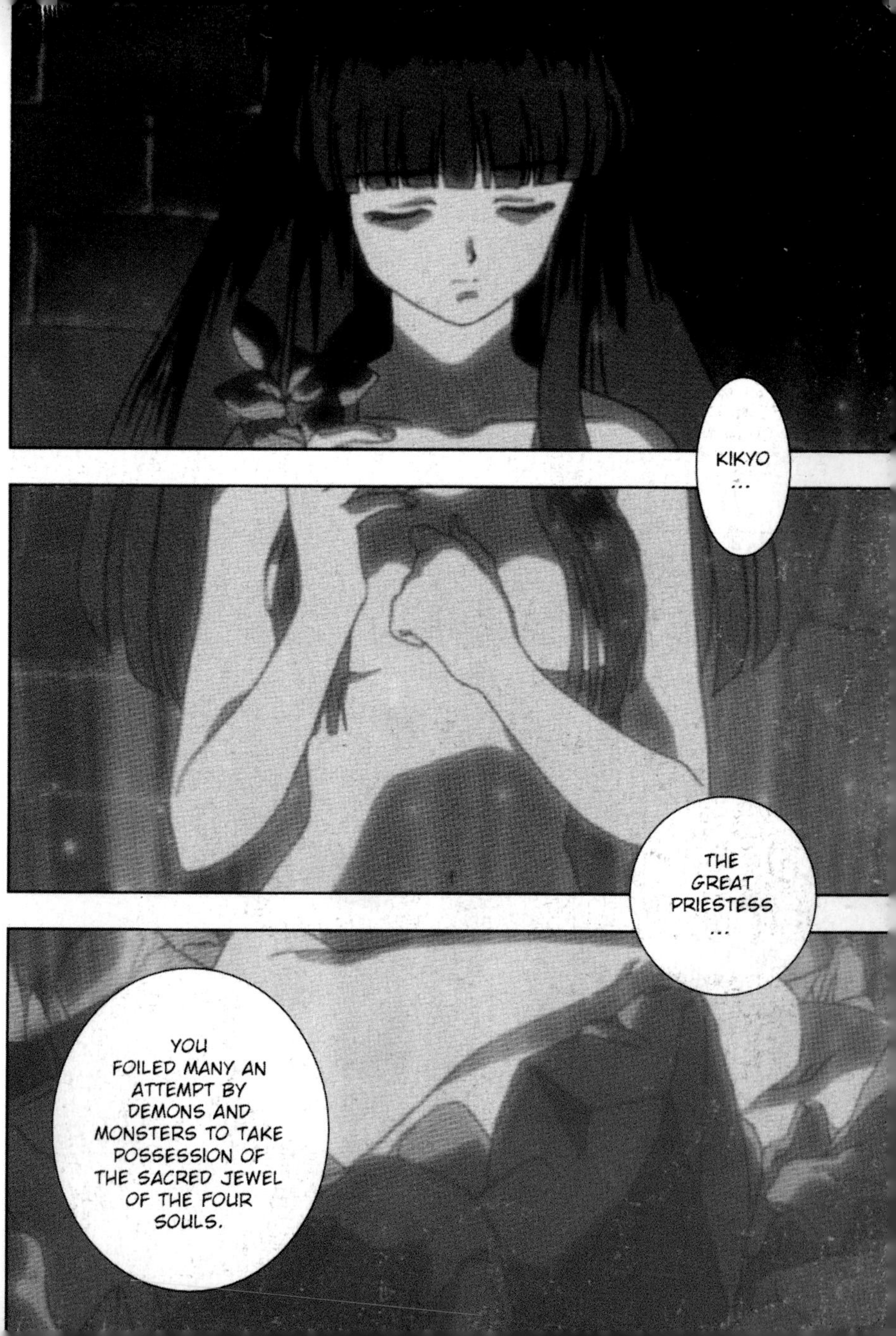
KIKYO ...
THE GREAT PRIESTESS ...
YOU FOILED MANY AN ATTEMPT BY DEMONS AND MONSTERS TO TAKE POSSESSION OF THE SACRED JEWEL OF THE FOUR SOULS.

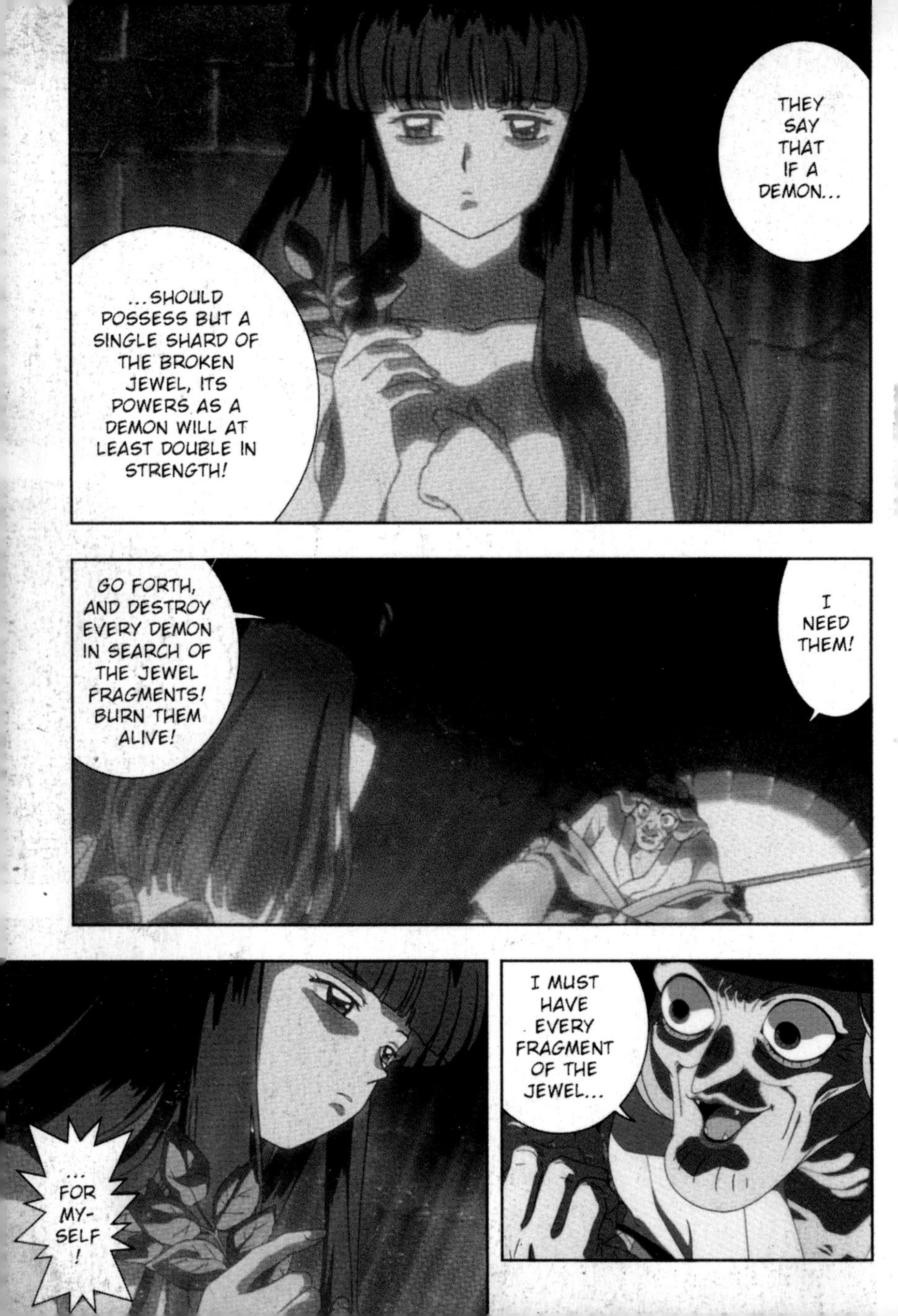
THEY SAY THAT IF A DEMON...
...SHOULD POSSESS BUT A SINGLE SHARD OF THE BROKEN JEWEL, ITS POWERS AS A DEMON WILL AT LEAST DOUBLE IN STRENGTH!
I NEED THEM!
GO FORTH, AND DESTROY EVERY DEMON IN SEARCH OF THE JEWEL FRAGMENTS! BURN THEM ALIVE!
I MUST HAVE EVERY FRAGMENT OF THE JEWEL...
...FOR MY-SELF!

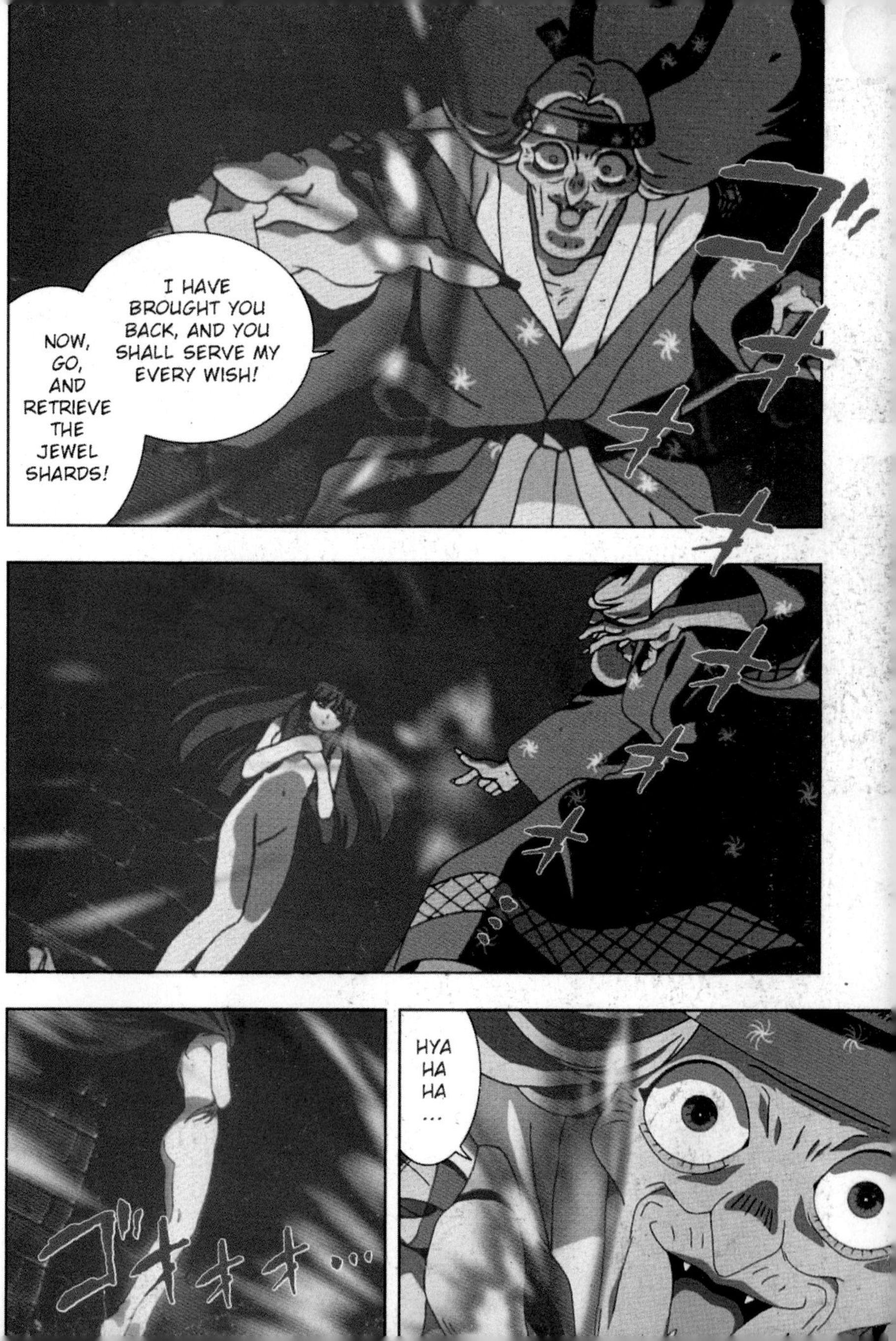
I HAVE BROUGHT YOU BACK, AND YOU SHALL SERVE MY EVERY WISH!
NOW, GO, AND RETRIEVE THE JEWEL SHARDS!
HYA HA HA ...
ゴオオオ…

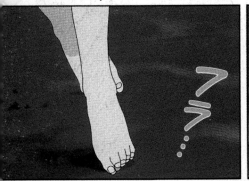

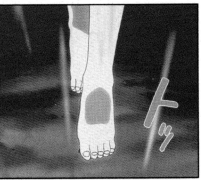

IMPOS-
SIBLE!
I DON'T
UNDER-
STAND...

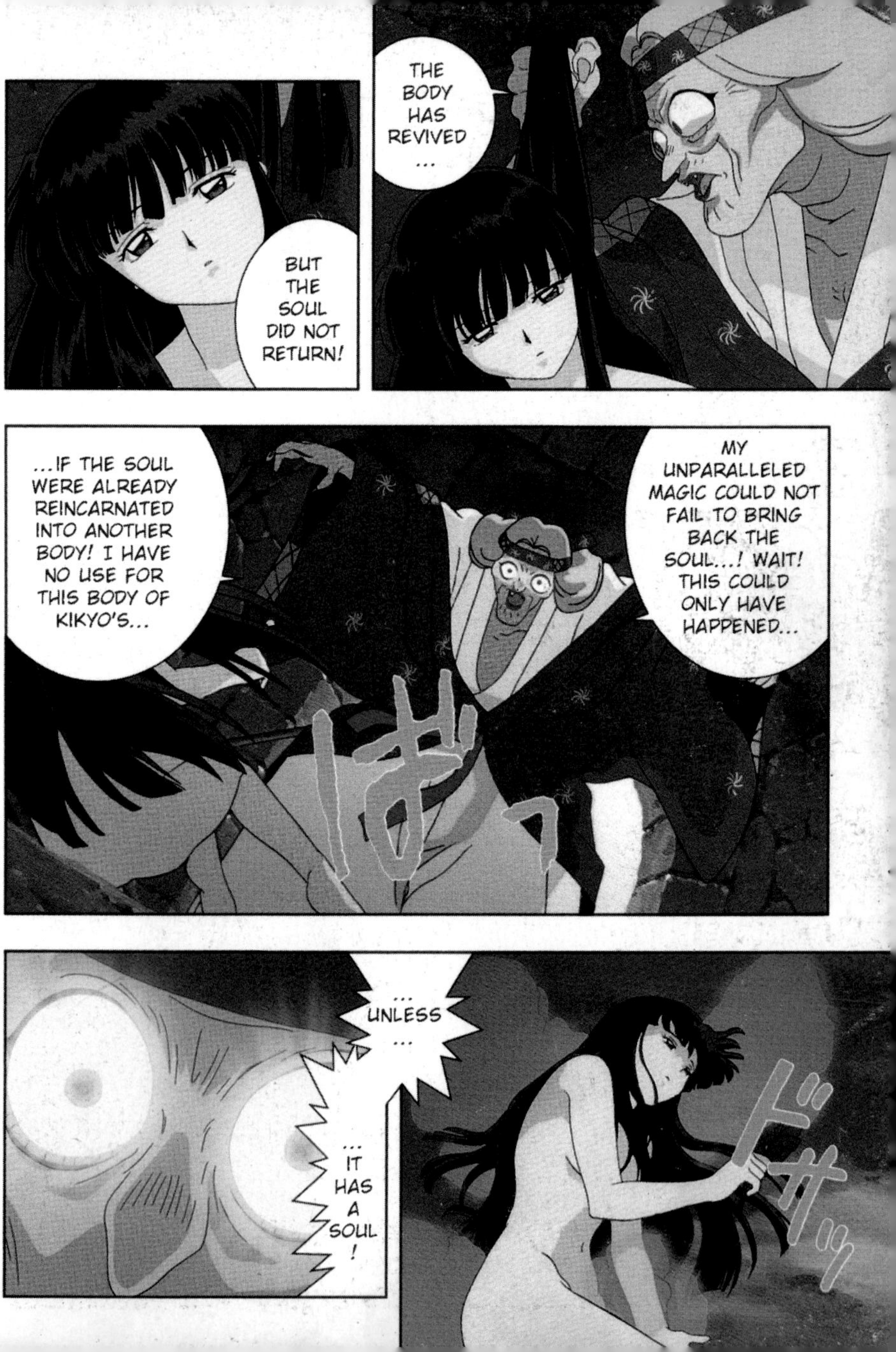
THE BODY HAS REVIVED ...
BUT THE SOUL DID NOT RETURN!
MY UNPARALLELED MAGIC COULD NOT FAIL TO BRING BACK THE SOUL...! WAIT! THIS COULD ONLY HAVE HAPPENED...
...IF THE SOUL WERE ALREADY REINCARNATED INTO ANOTHER BODY! I HAVE NO USE FOR THIS BODY OF KIKYO'S...
ぱっ
ドサッ
...UNLESS...
...IT HAS A SOUL!

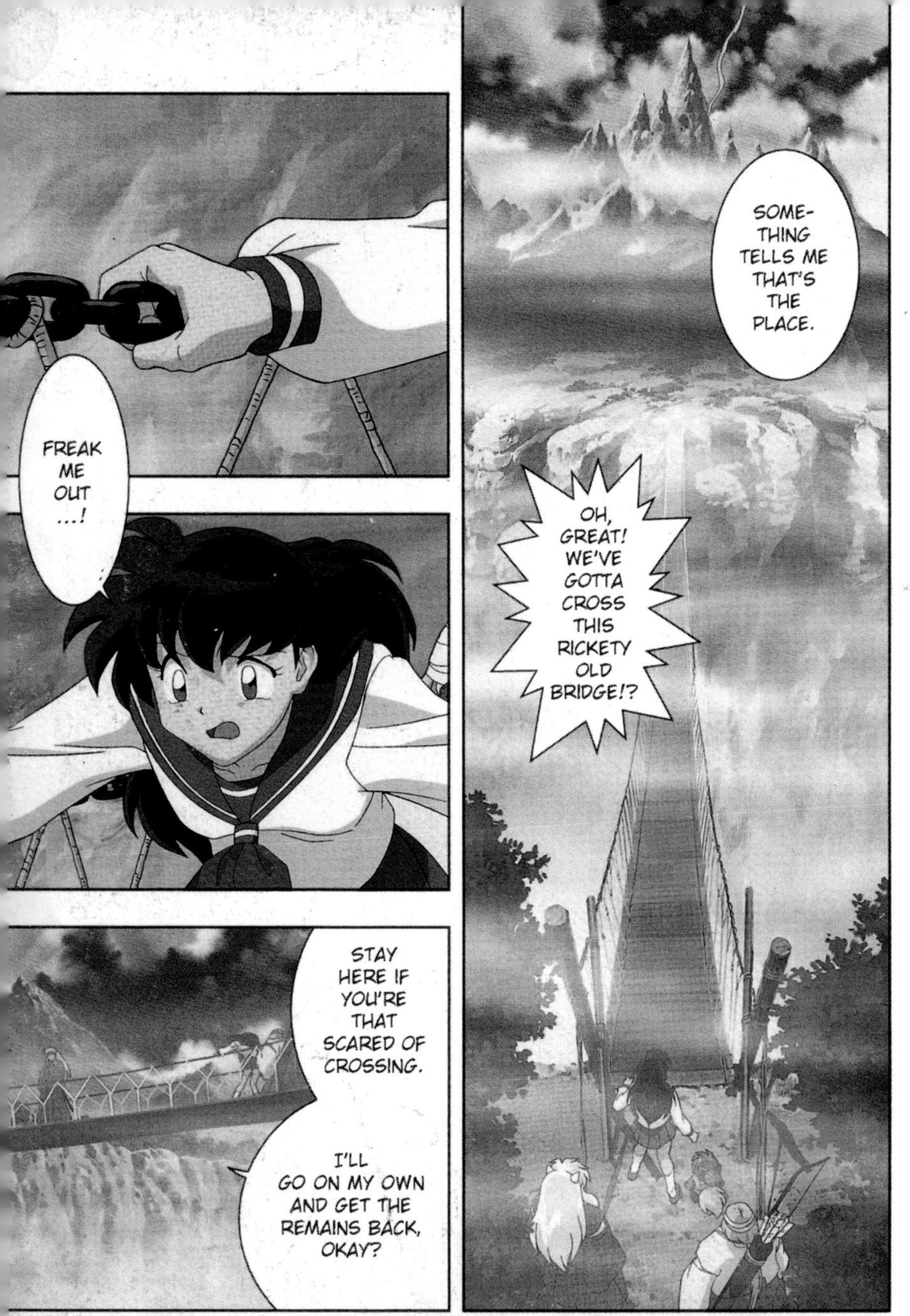
SOME-THING TELLS ME THAT'S THE PLACE.
OH, GREAT! WE'VE GOTTA CROSS THIS RICKETY OLD BRIDGE!?
FREAK ME OUT ...!
STAY HERE IF YOU'RE THAT SCARED OF CROSSING.
I'LL GO ON MY OWN AND GET THE REMAINS BACK, OKAY?

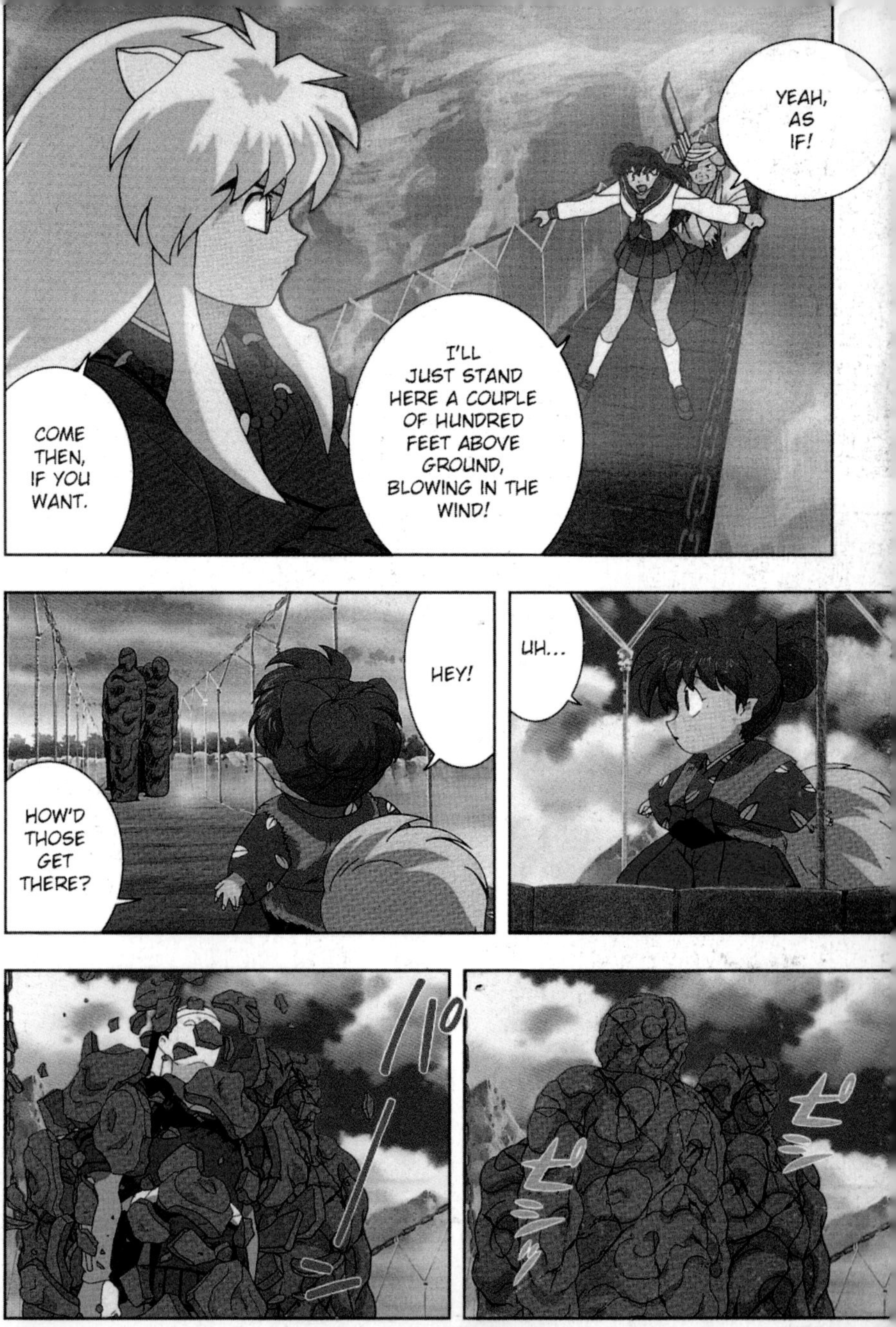
YEAH, AS IF!
I'LL JUST STAND HERE A COUPLE OF HUNDRED FEET ABOVE GROUND, BLOWING IN THE WIND!
COME THEN, IF YOU WANT.
UH...
HEY!
HOW'D THOSE GET THERE?

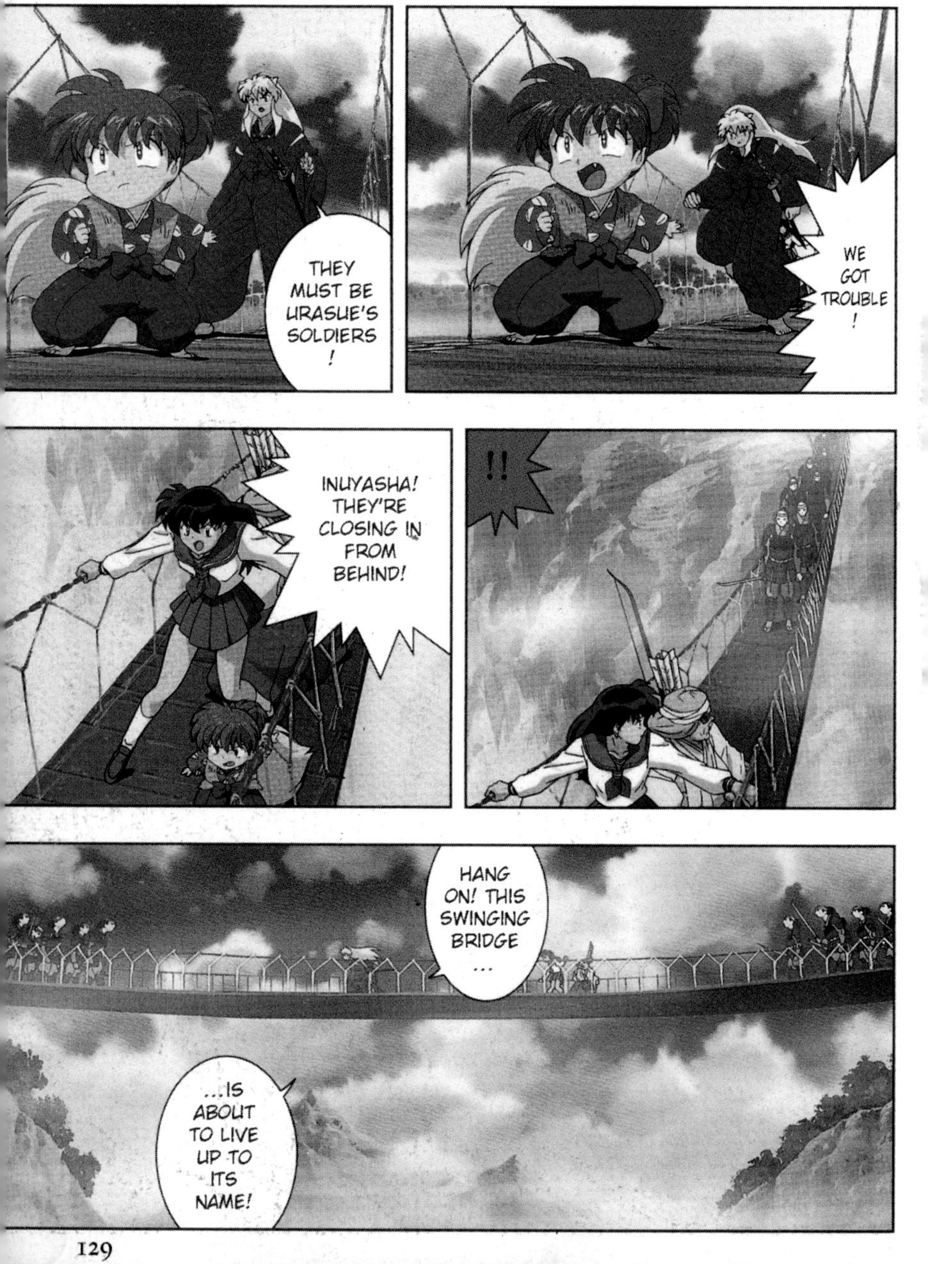
WE GOT TROUBLE!
THEY MUST BE URASUE'S SOLDIERS!
!!
INUYASHA! THEY'RE CLOSING IN FROM BEHIND!
HANG ON! THIS SWINGING BRIDGE ...
...IS ABOUT TO LIVE UP TO ITS NAME!

IRON REAVER, SOUL STEALER!

たたた…

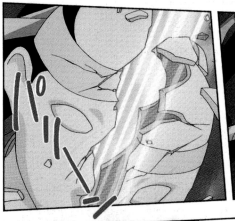

THESE THINGS REALLY *ARE* MADE OF MUD ...!

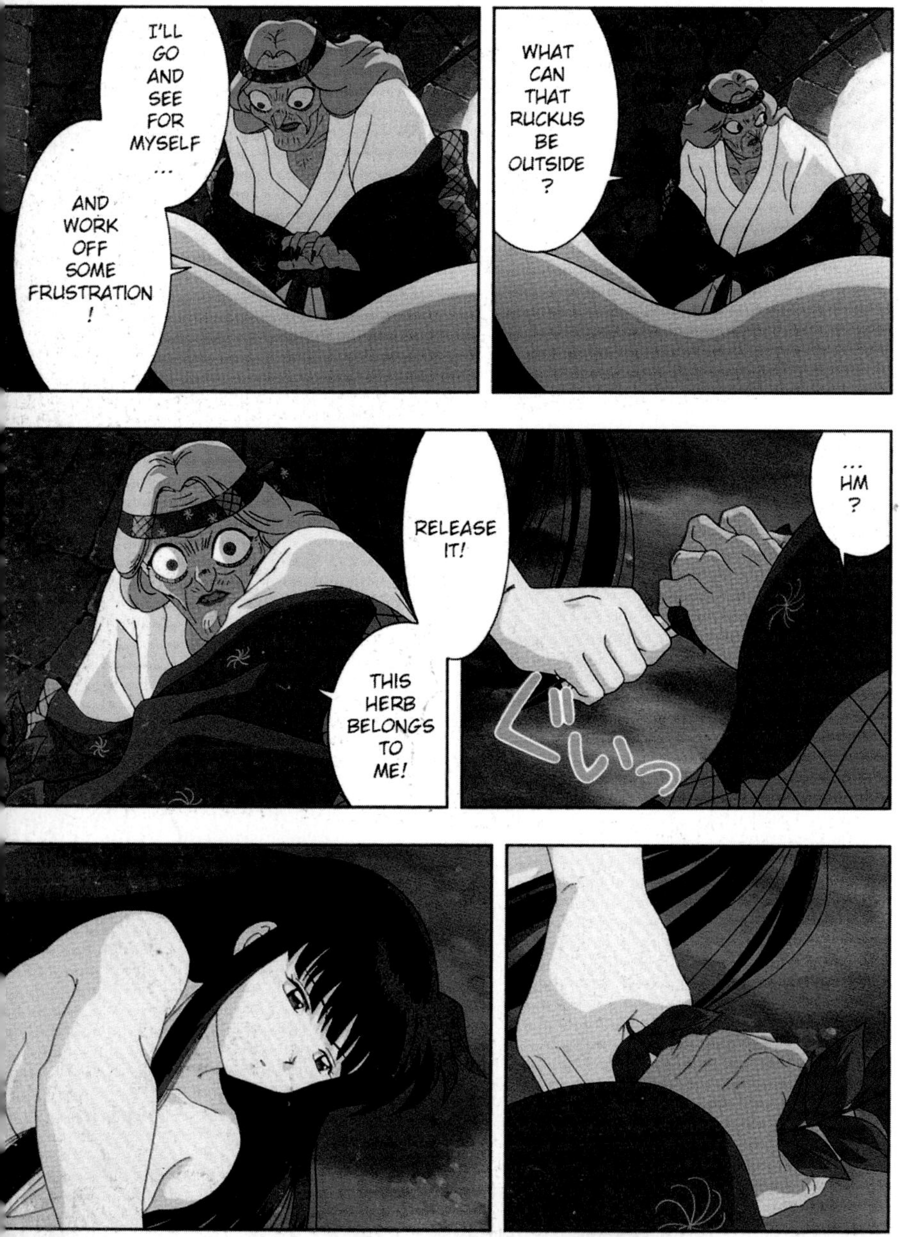
WHAT CAN THAT RUCKUS BE OUTSIDE?
I'LL GO AND SEE FOR MYSELF...
AND WORK OFF SOME FRUSTRATION!
...HM?
RELEASE IT!
THIS HERB BELONGS TO ME!
ぐいっ

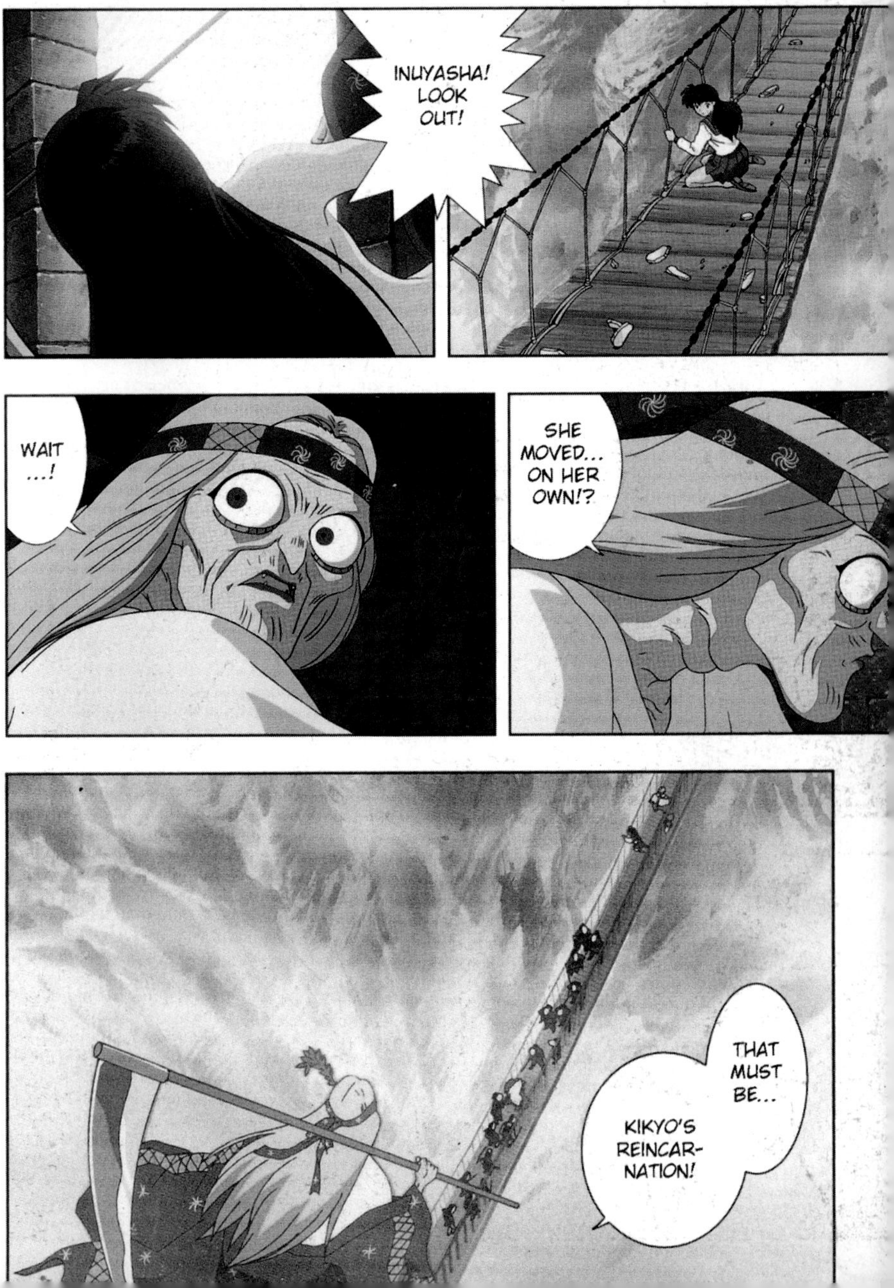
INUYASHA! LOOK OUT!
SHE MOVED... ON HER OWN!?
WAIT ...!
THAT MUST BE...
KIKYO'S REINCAR-NATION!

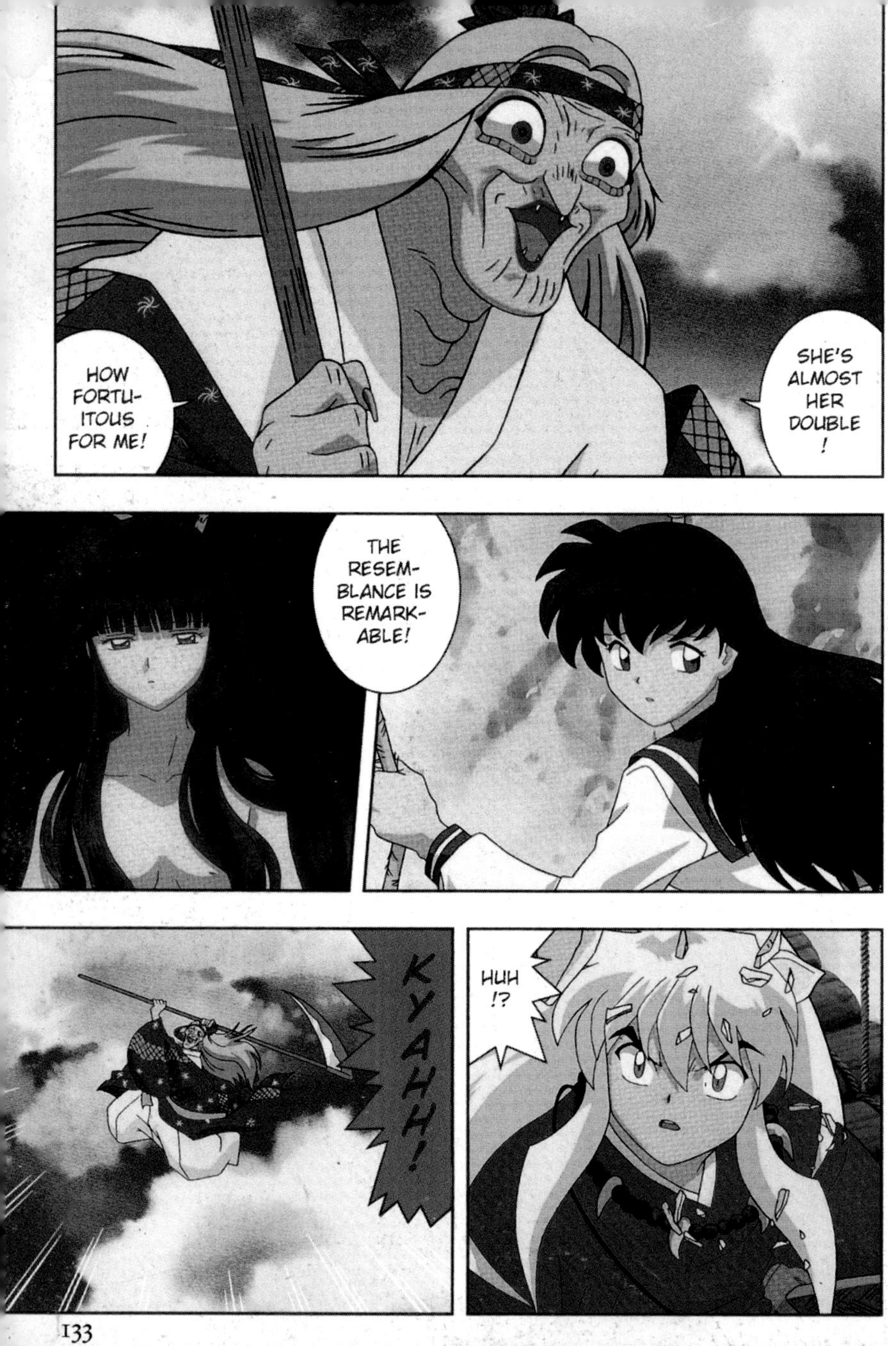
SHE'S ALMOST HER DOUBLE!
HOW FORTUITOUS FOR ME!
THE RESEMBLANCE IS REMARKABLE!
HUH!?
KYAHH!

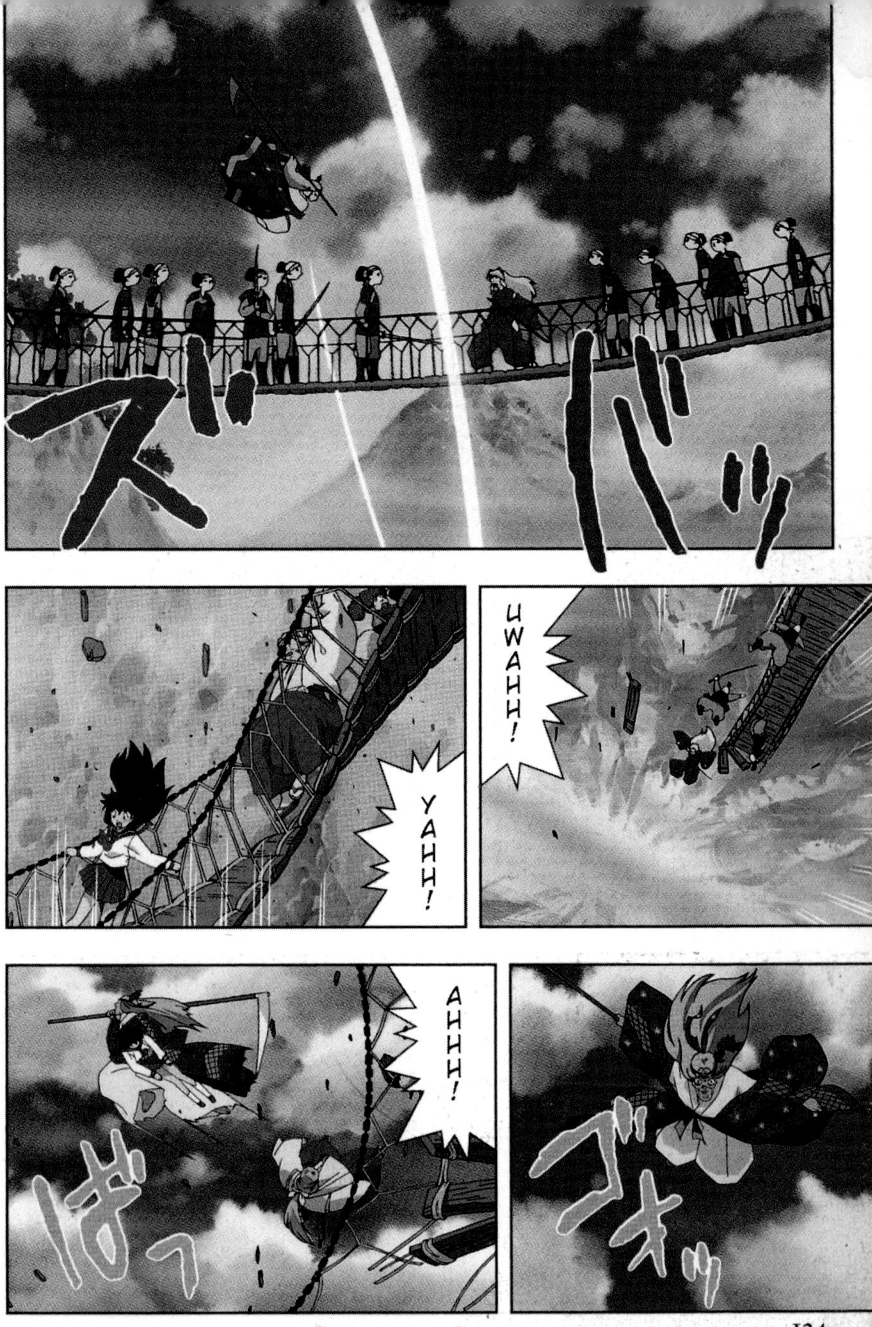
ズバッ
UWAHH!
YAHH!
ゴキッ
AHHH!
ぱっ

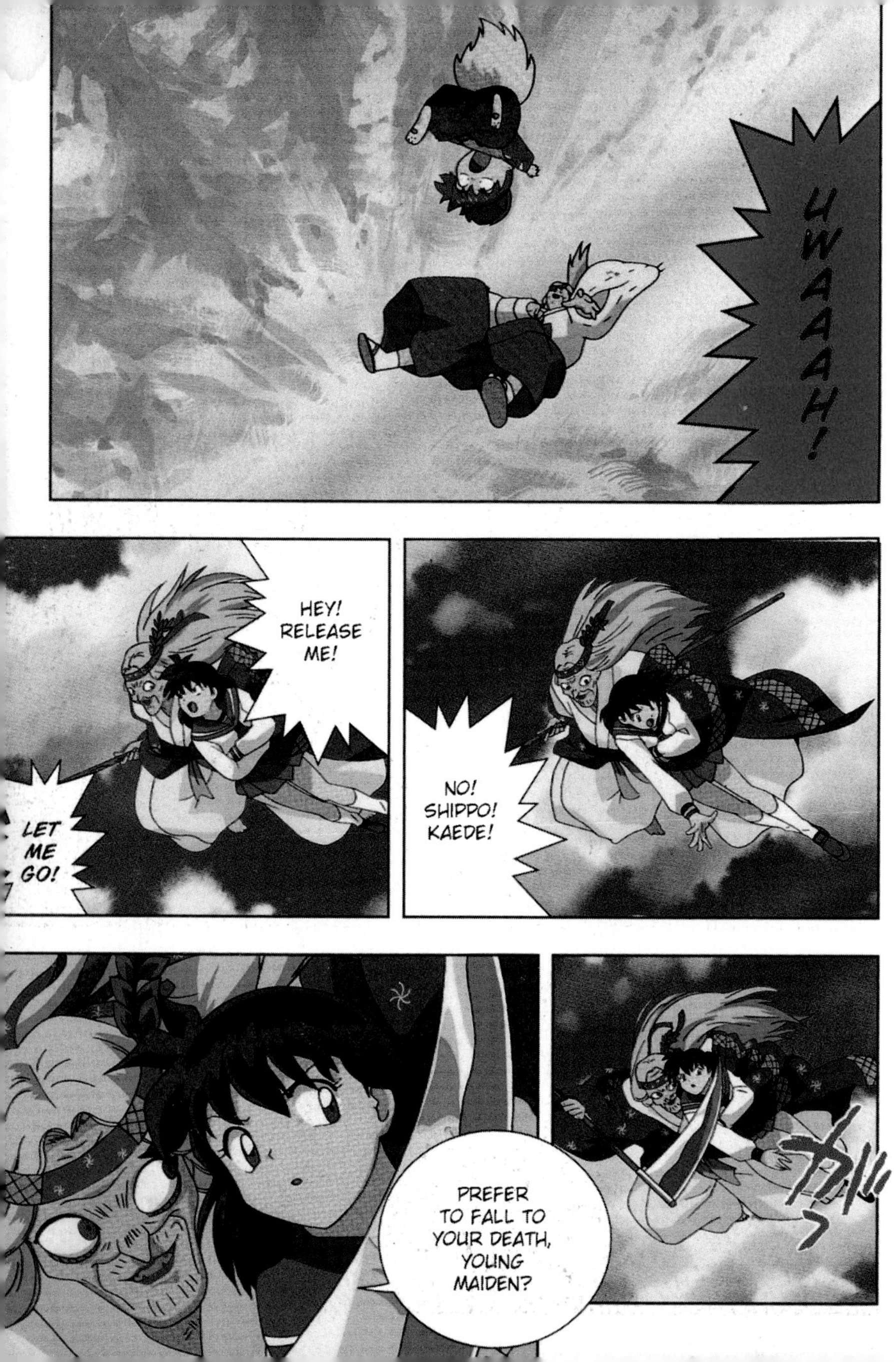
UWAAAAH!
NO! SHIPPO! KAEDE!
HEY! RELEASE ME!
LET ME GO!
PREFER TO FALL TO YOUR DEATH, YOUNG MAIDEN?

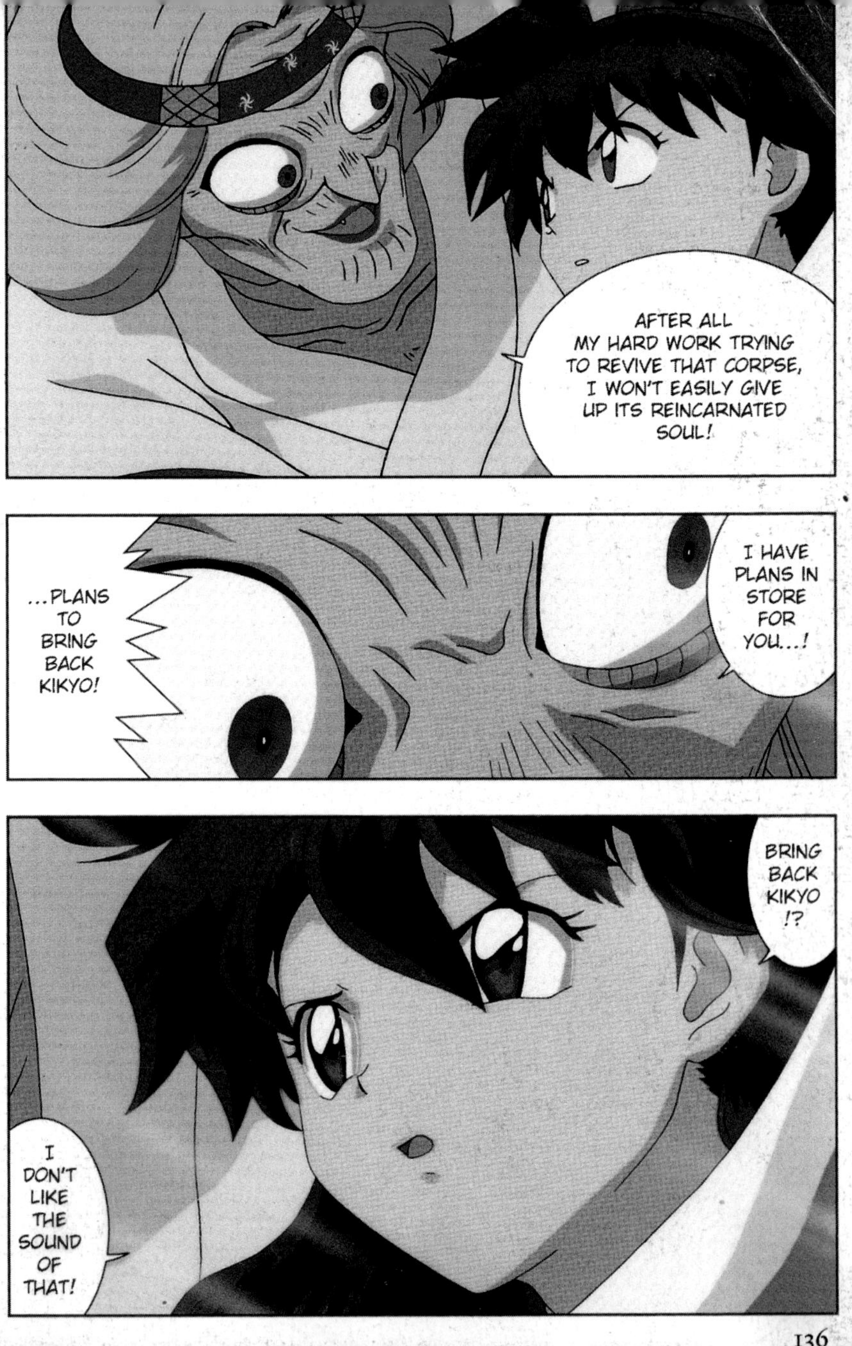
AFTER ALL MY HARD WORK TRYING TO REVIVE THAT CORPSE, I WON'T EASILY GIVE UP ITS REINCARNATED SOUL!
I HAVE PLANS IN STORE FOR YOU...!
...PLANS TO BRING BACK KIKYO!
BRING BACK KIKYO!?
I DON'T LIKE THE SOUND OF THAT!

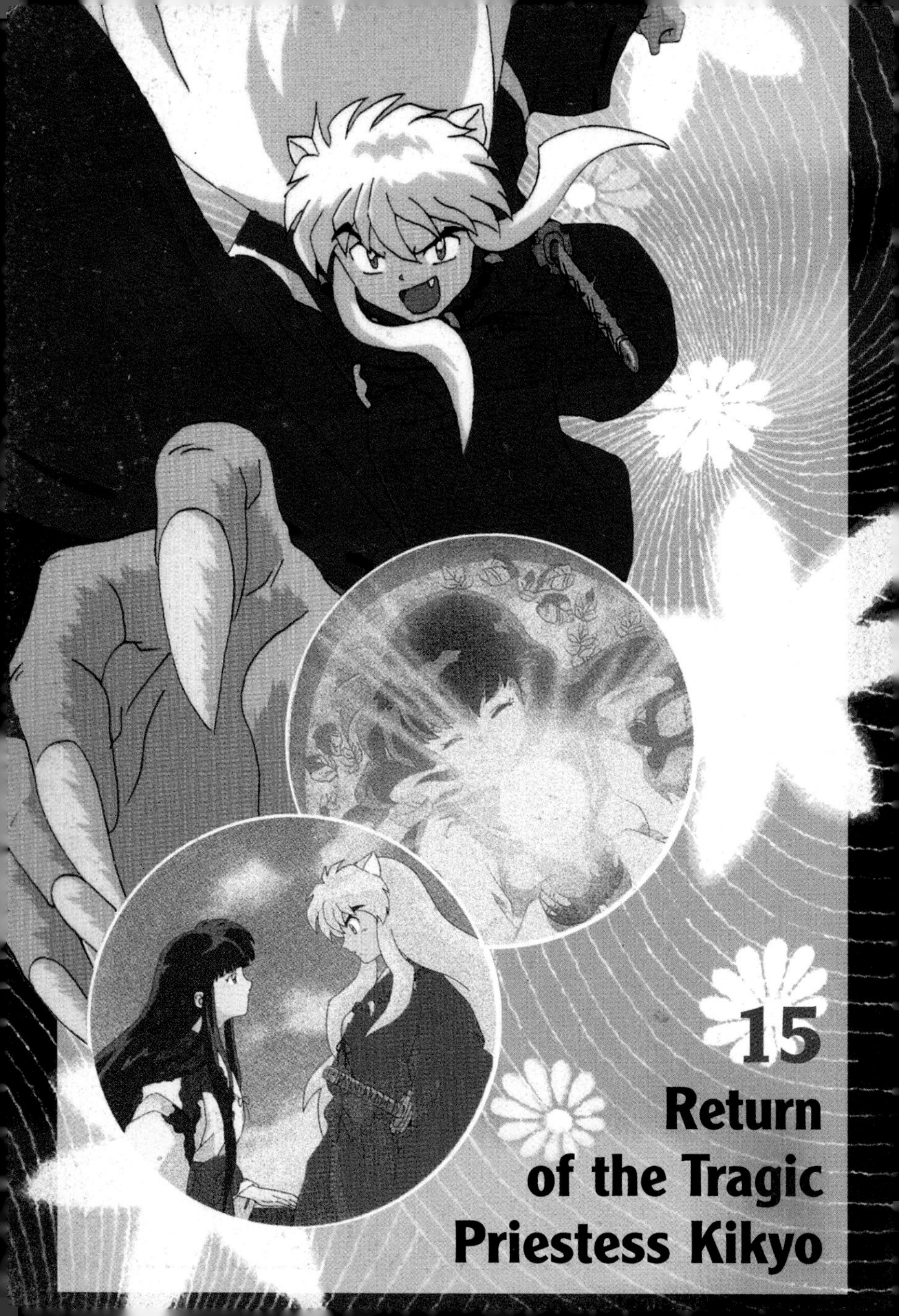

# 15
# Return of the Tragic Priestess Kikyo

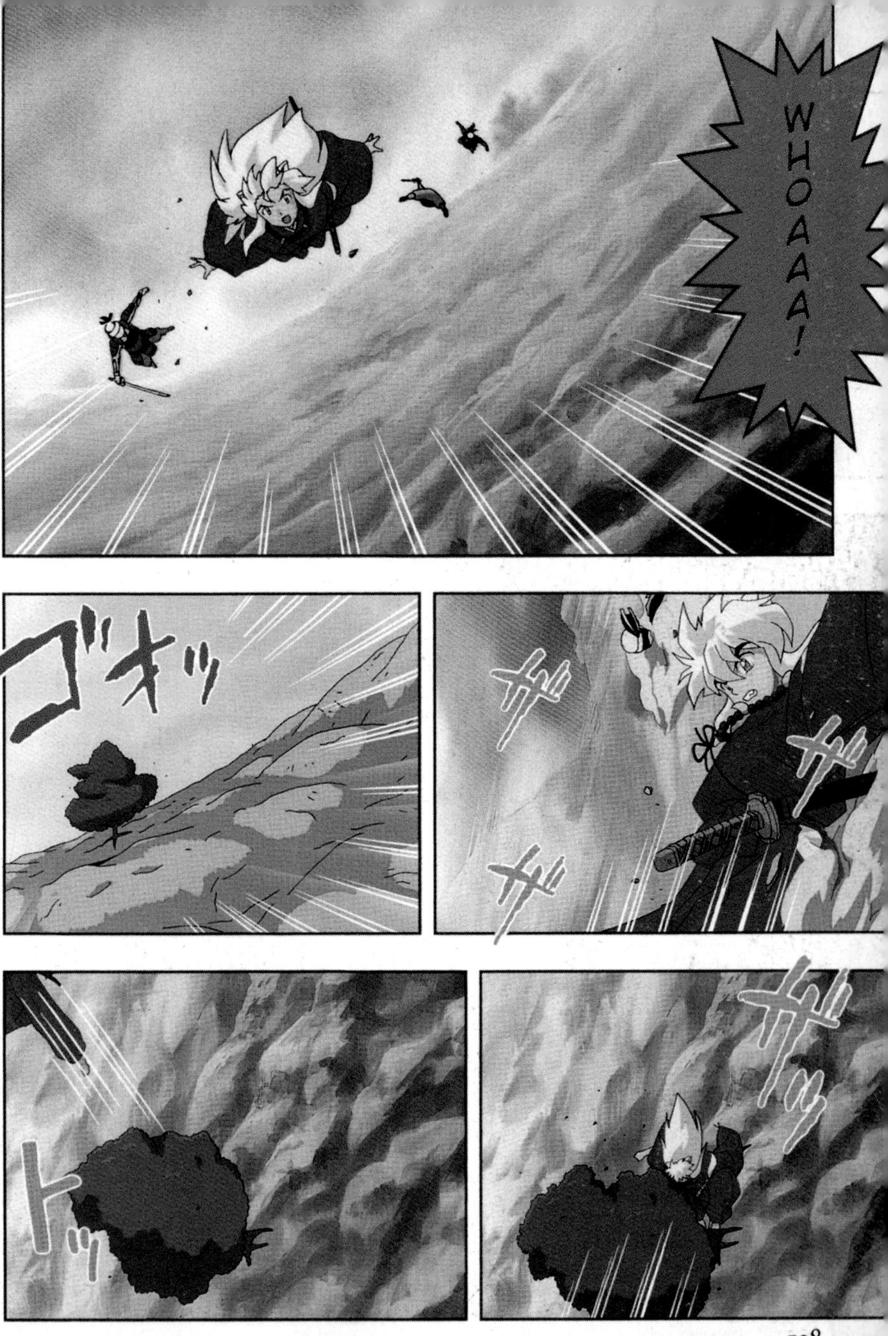
WHOAAAA!
ザ
ザ
ザ
ゴオッ
ザザッ
ドッ

AHH!

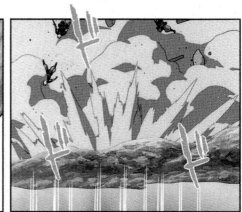

OOF!

HUH!?

WHERE ARE KAGOME AND THE OTHERS!?

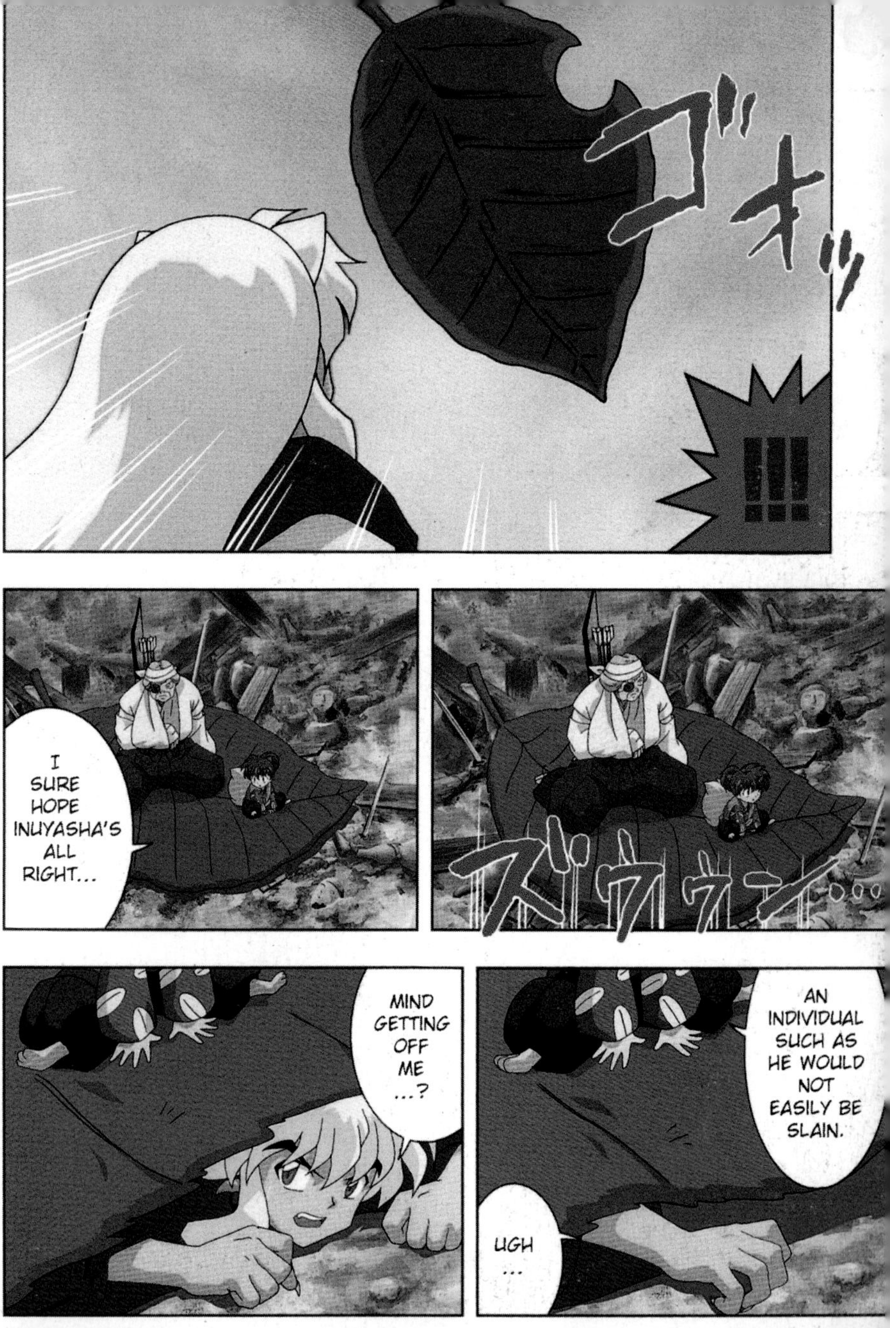
ゴオッ
!!!
ズウヴン…
I SURE HOPE INUYASHA'S ALL RIGHT...
AN INDIVIDUAL SUCH AS HE WOULD NOT EASILY BE SLAIN.
UGH ...
MIND GETTING OFF ME ...?

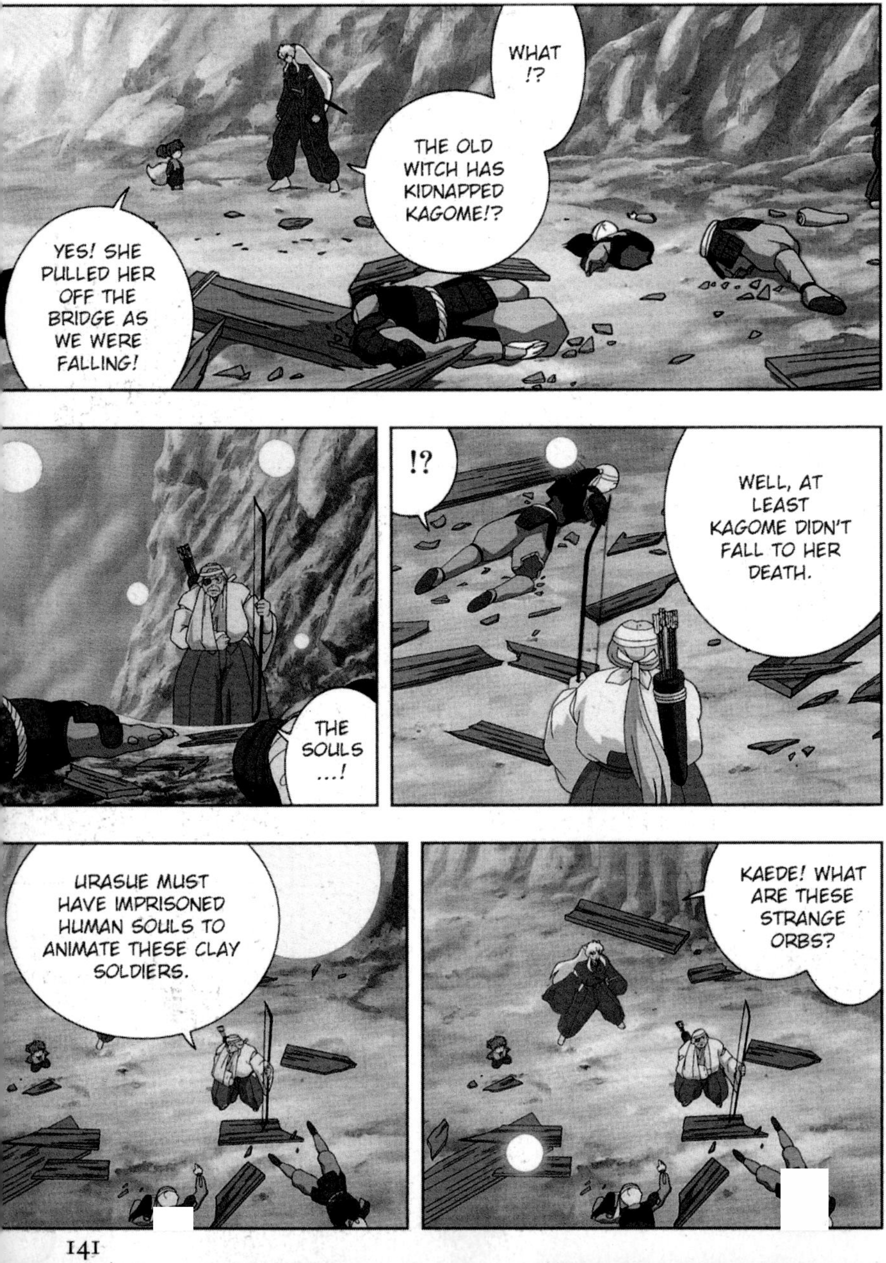
WHAT !?
THE OLD WITCH HAS KIDNAPPED KAGOME!?
YES! SHE PULLED HER OFF THE BRIDGE AS WE WERE FALLING!
WELL, AT LEAST KAGOME DIDN'T FALL TO HER DEATH.
!?
THE SOULS ...!
KAEDE! WHAT ARE THESE STRANGE ORBS?
URASUE MUST HAVE IMPRISONED HUMAN SOULS TO ANIMATE THESE CLAY SOLDIERS.

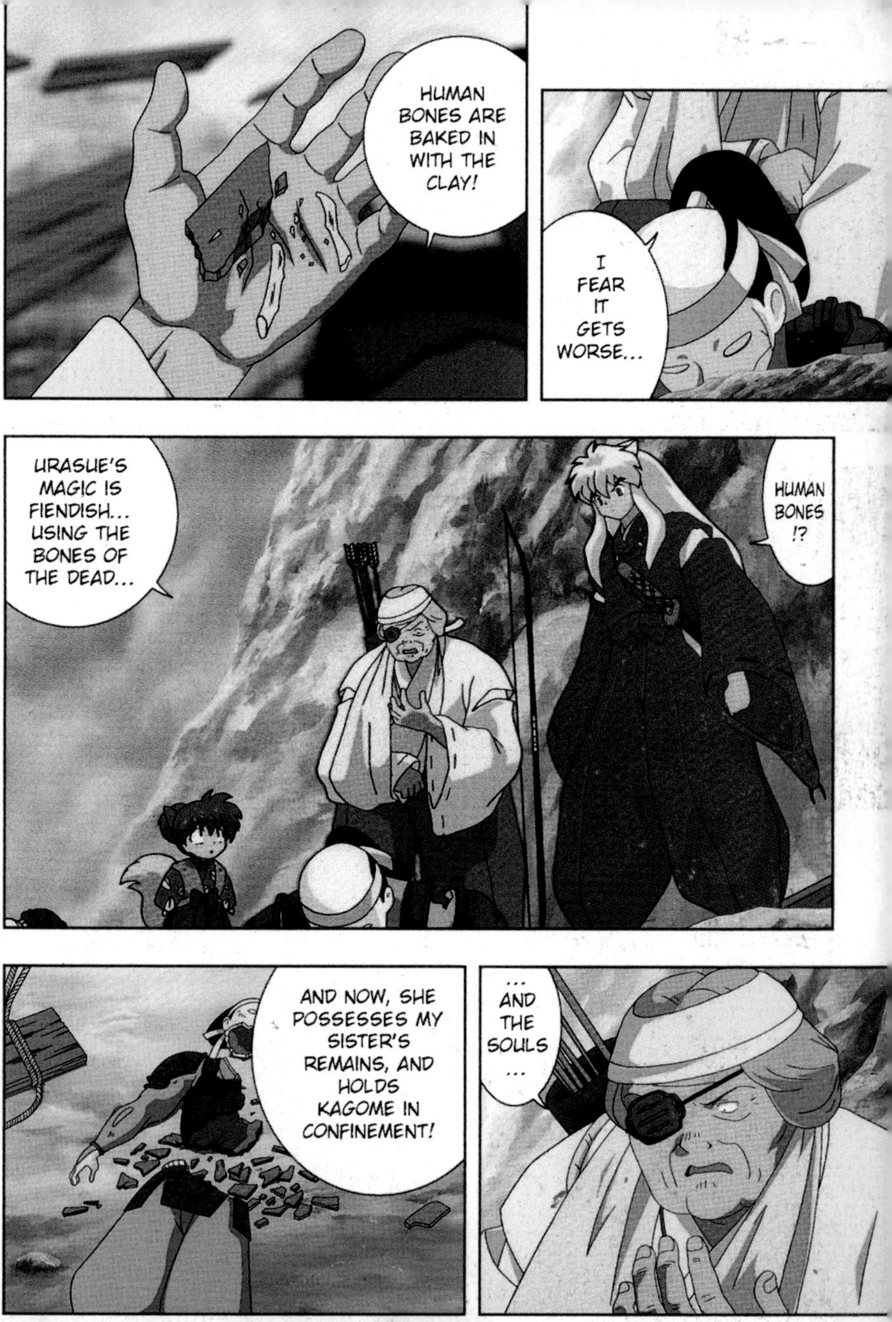

HUMAN BONES ARE BAKED IN WITH THE CLAY!
I FEAR IT GETS WORSE...
URASUE'S MAGIC IS FIENDISH... USING THE BONES OF THE DEAD...
HUMAN BONES !?
AND NOW, SHE POSSESSES MY SISTER'S REMAINS, AND HOLDS KAGOME IN CONFINEMENT!
... AND THE SOULS ...

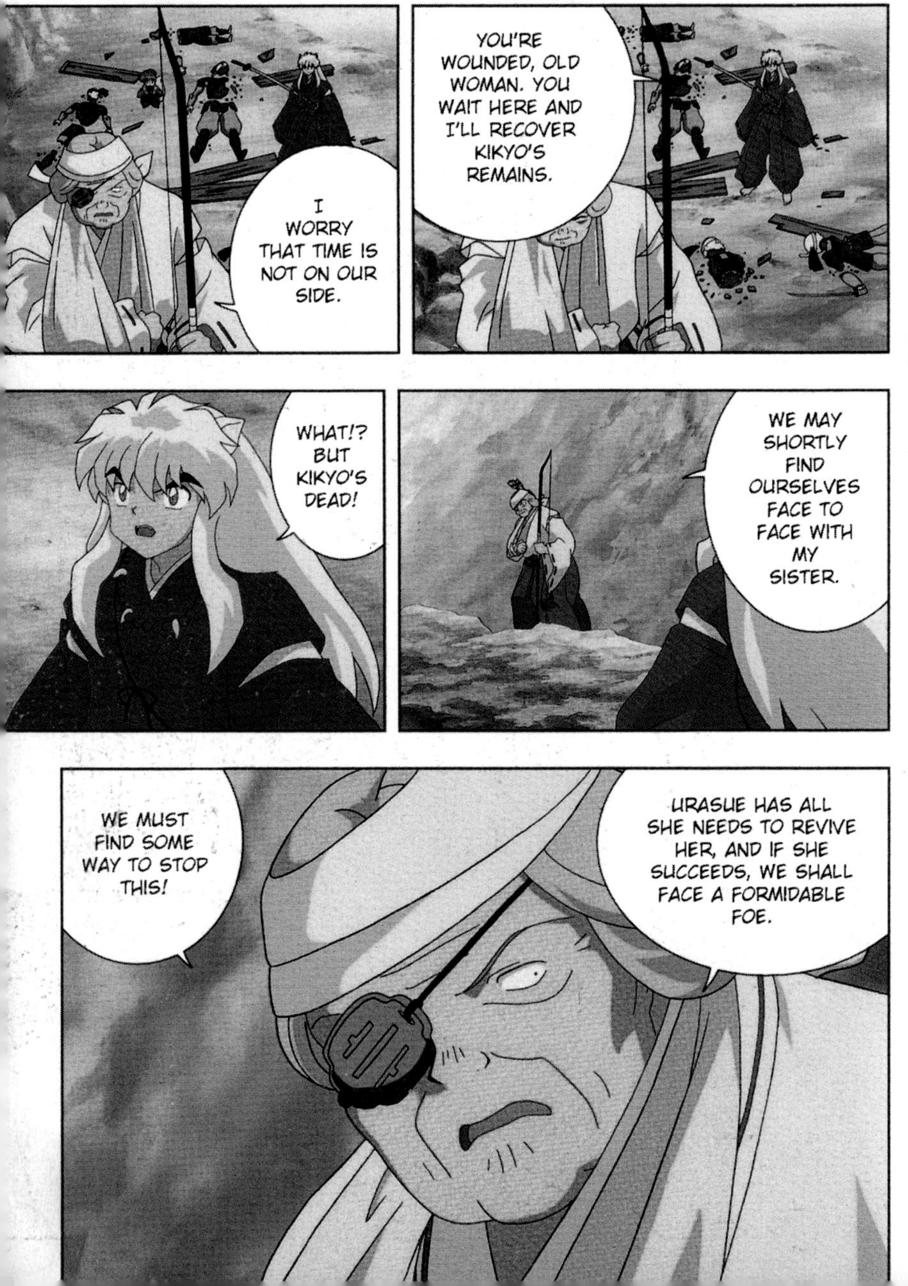
YOU'RE WOUNDED, OLD WOMAN. YOU WAIT HERE AND I'LL RECOVER KIKYO'S REMAINS.
I WORRY THAT TIME IS NOT ON OUR SIDE.
WE MAY SHORTLY FIND OURSELVES FACE TO FACE WITH MY SISTER.
WHAT!? BUT KIKYO'S DEAD!
URASUE HAS ALL SHE NEEDS TO REVIVE HER, AND IF SHE SUCCEEDS, WE SHALL FACE A FORMIDABLE FOE.
WE MUST FIND SOME WAY TO STOP THIS!

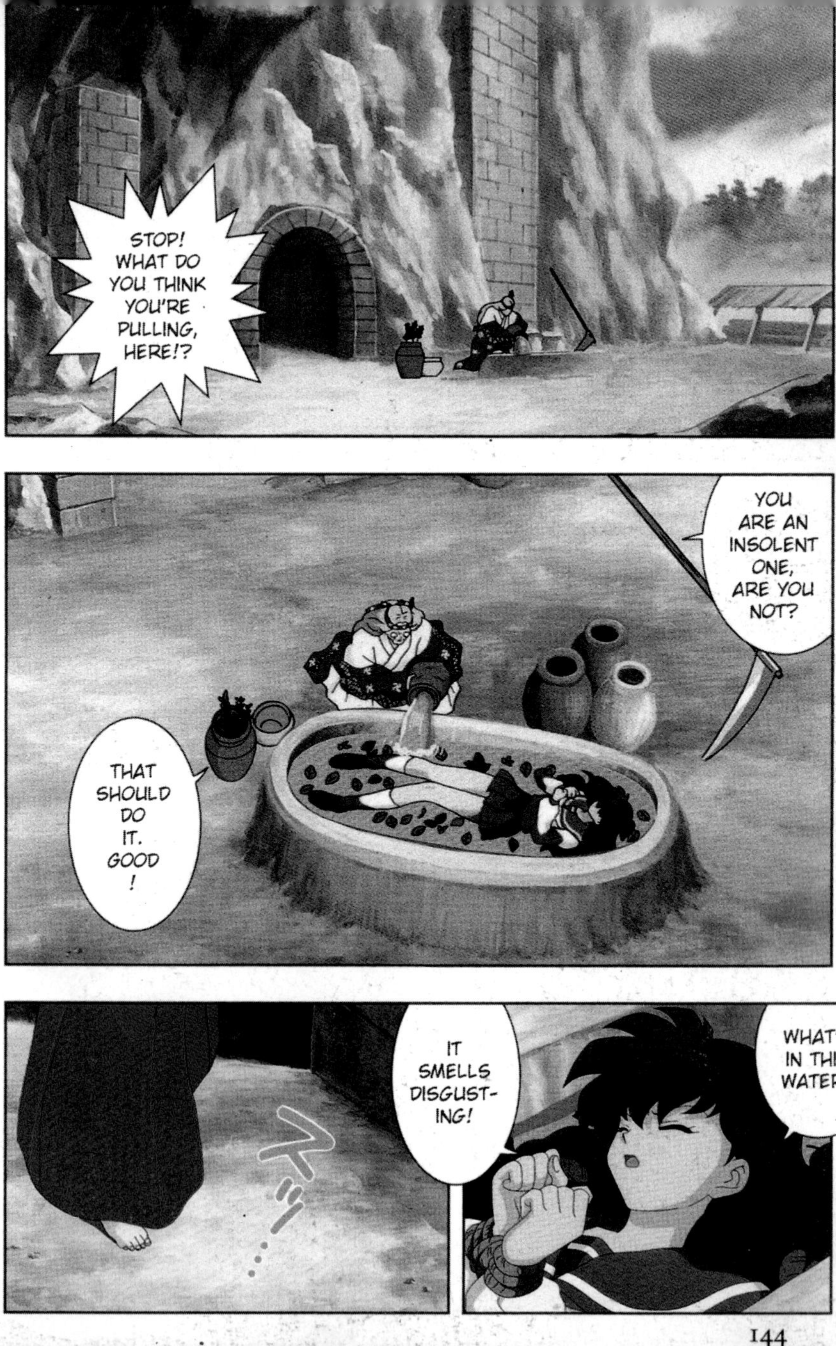
STOP! WHAT DO YOU THINK YOU'RE PULLING, HERE!?
YOU ARE AN INSOLENT ONE, ARE YOU NOT?
THAT SHOULD DO IT. GOOD!
WHAT'S IN THIS WATER?
IT SMELLS DISGUST-ING!
スッ…

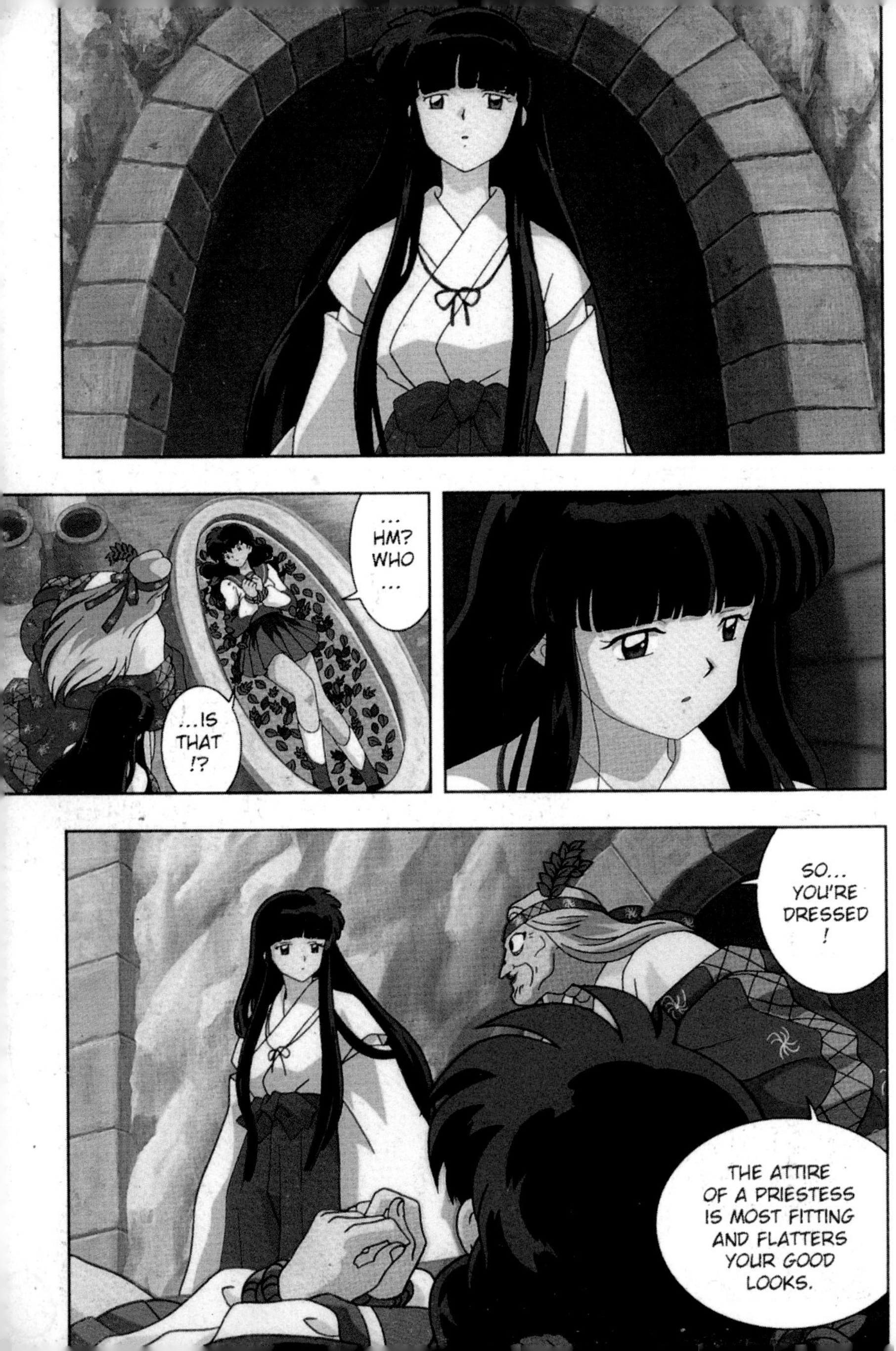
...HM? WHO ...
...IS THAT !?
SO... YOU'RE DRESSED !
THE ATTIRE OF A PRIESTESS IS MOST FITTING AND FLATTERS YOUR GOOD LOOKS.

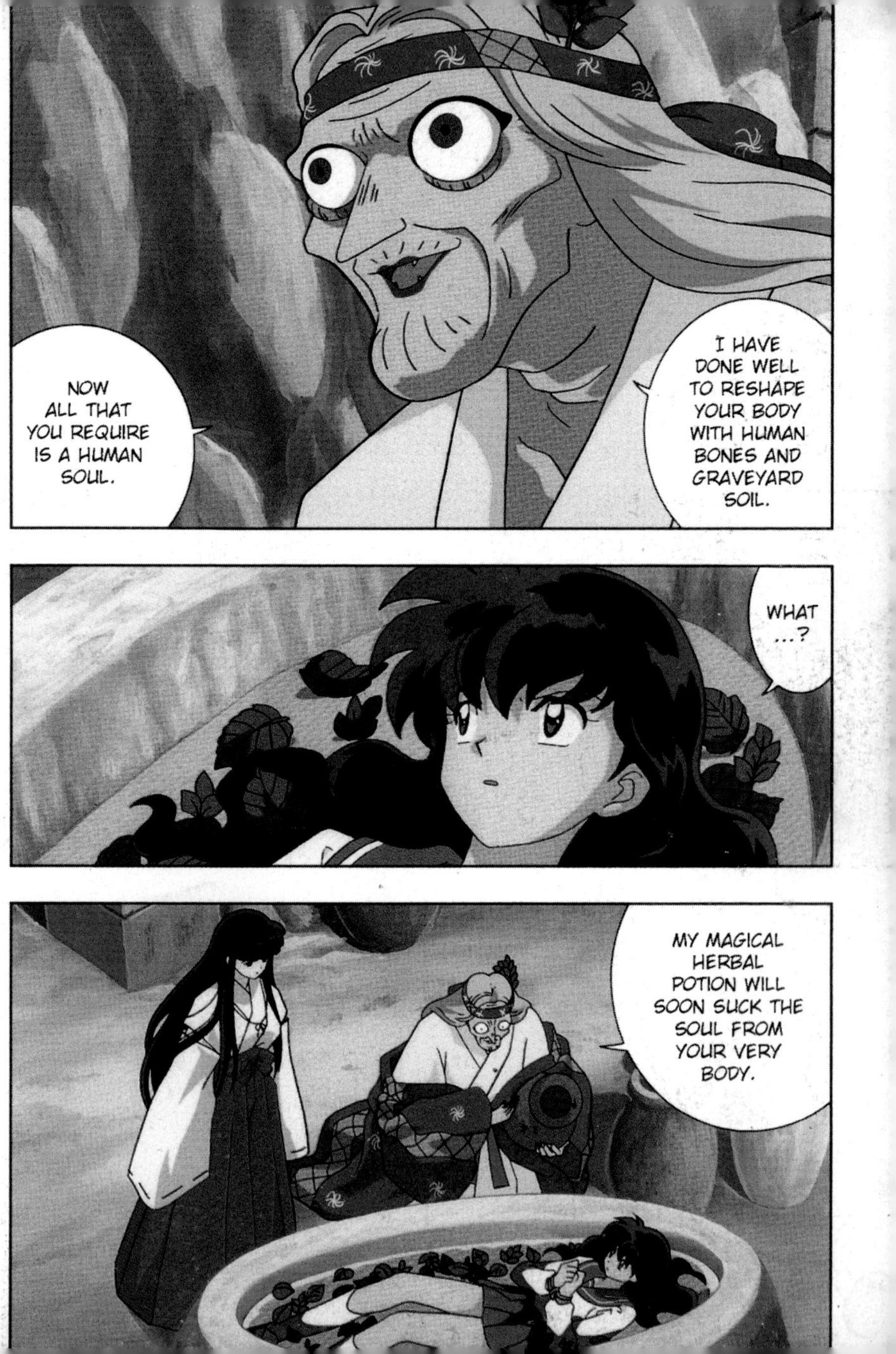
I HAVE DONE WELL TO RESHAPE YOUR BODY WITH HUMAN BONES AND GRAVEYARD SOIL.
NOW ALL THAT YOU REQUIRE IS A HUMAN SOUL.
WHAT ...?
MY MAGICAL HERBAL POTION WILL SOON SUCK THE SOUL FROM YOUR VERY BODY.

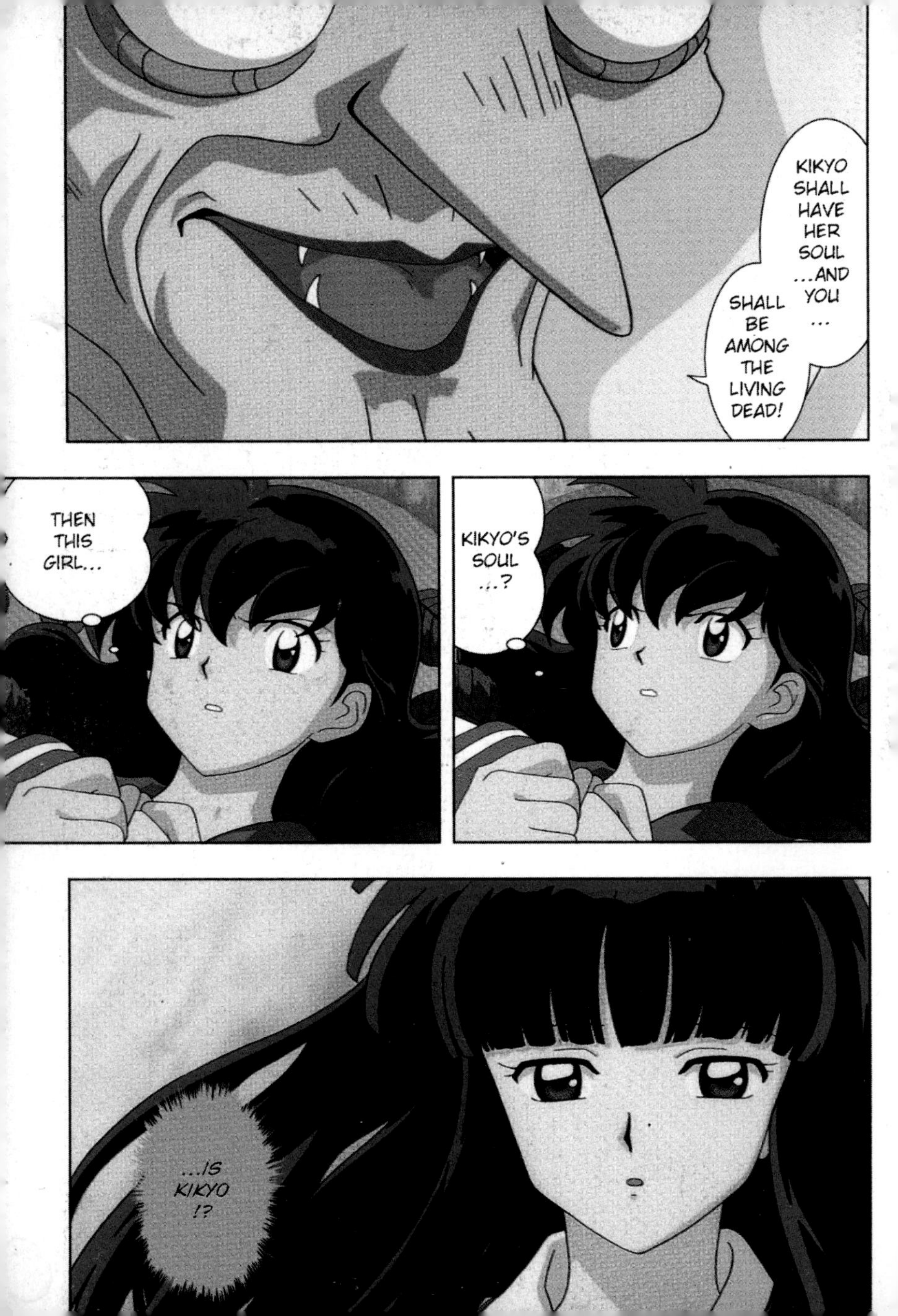
KIKYO SHALL HAVE HER SOUL ...AND YOU ...
SHALL BE AMONG THE LIVING DEAD!
KIKYO'S SOUL ...?
THEN THIS GIRL...
...IS KIKYO !?

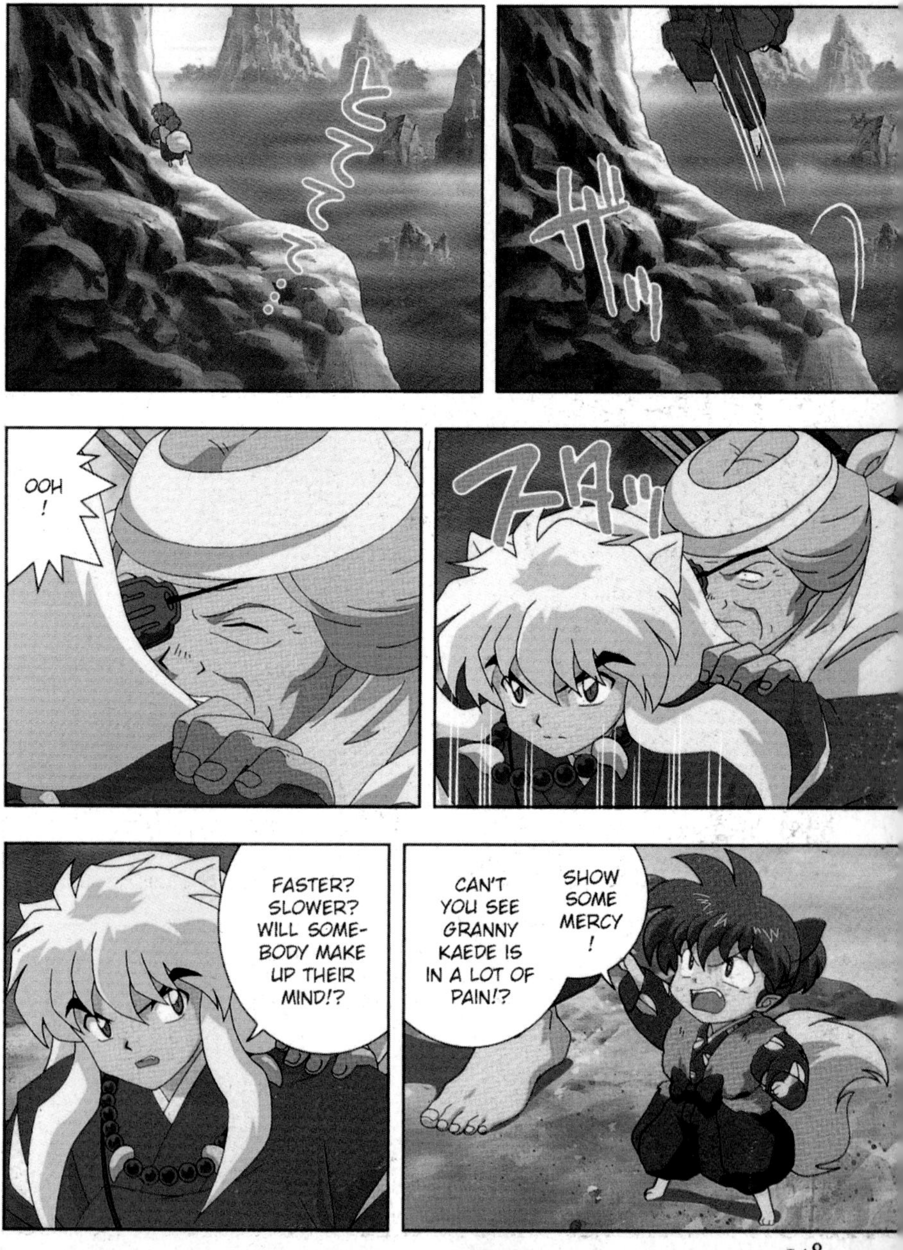
ザッ
スタッ
OOH!
SHOW SOME MERCY!
CAN'T YOU SEE GRANNY KAEDE IS IN A LOT OF PAIN!?
FASTER? SLOWER? WILL SOMEBODY MAKE UP THEIR MIND!?

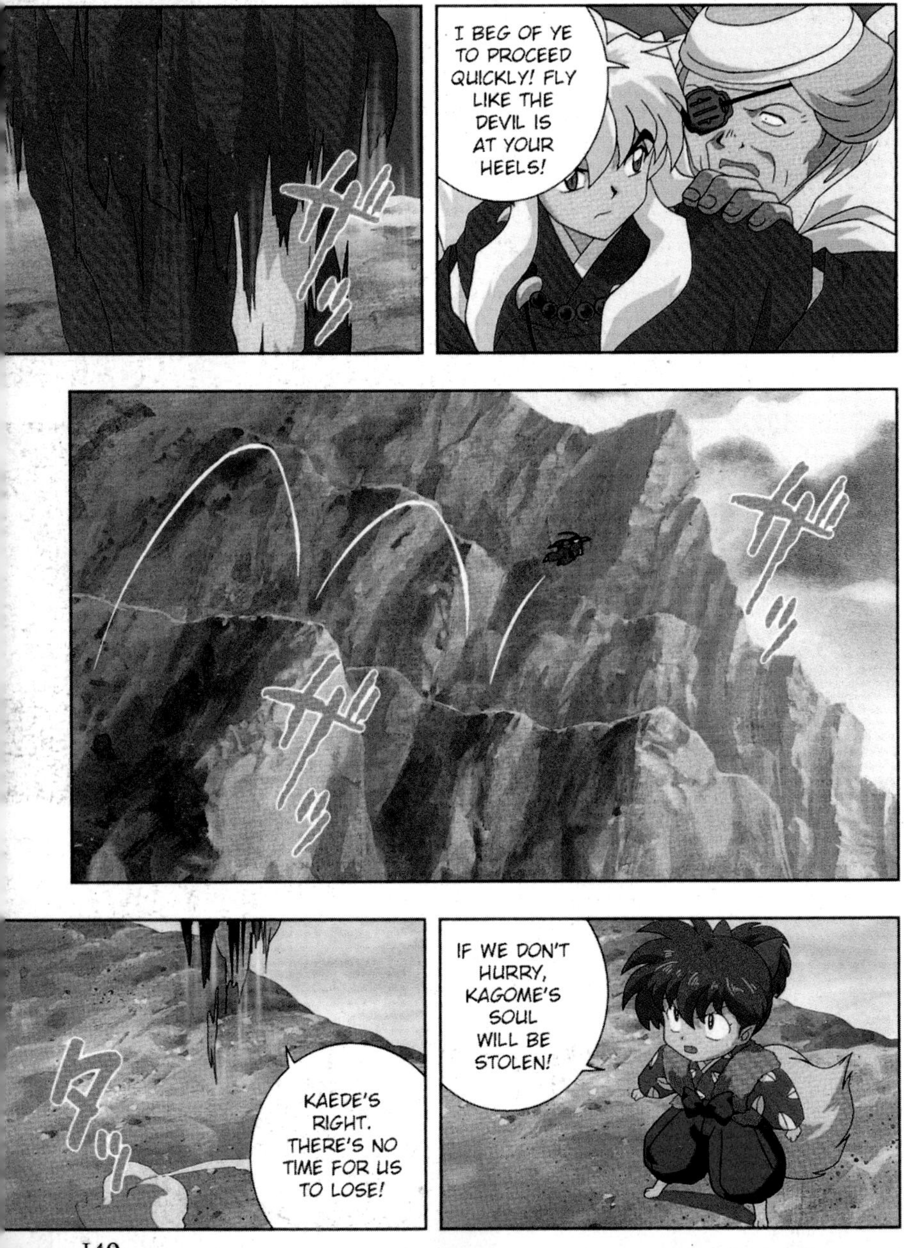
I BEG OF YE TO PROCEED QUICKLY! FLY LIKE THE DEVIL IS AT YOUR HEELS!
IF WE DON'T HURRY, KAGOME'S SOUL WILL BE STOLEN!
KAEDE'S RIGHT. THERE'S NO TIME FOR US TO LOSE!

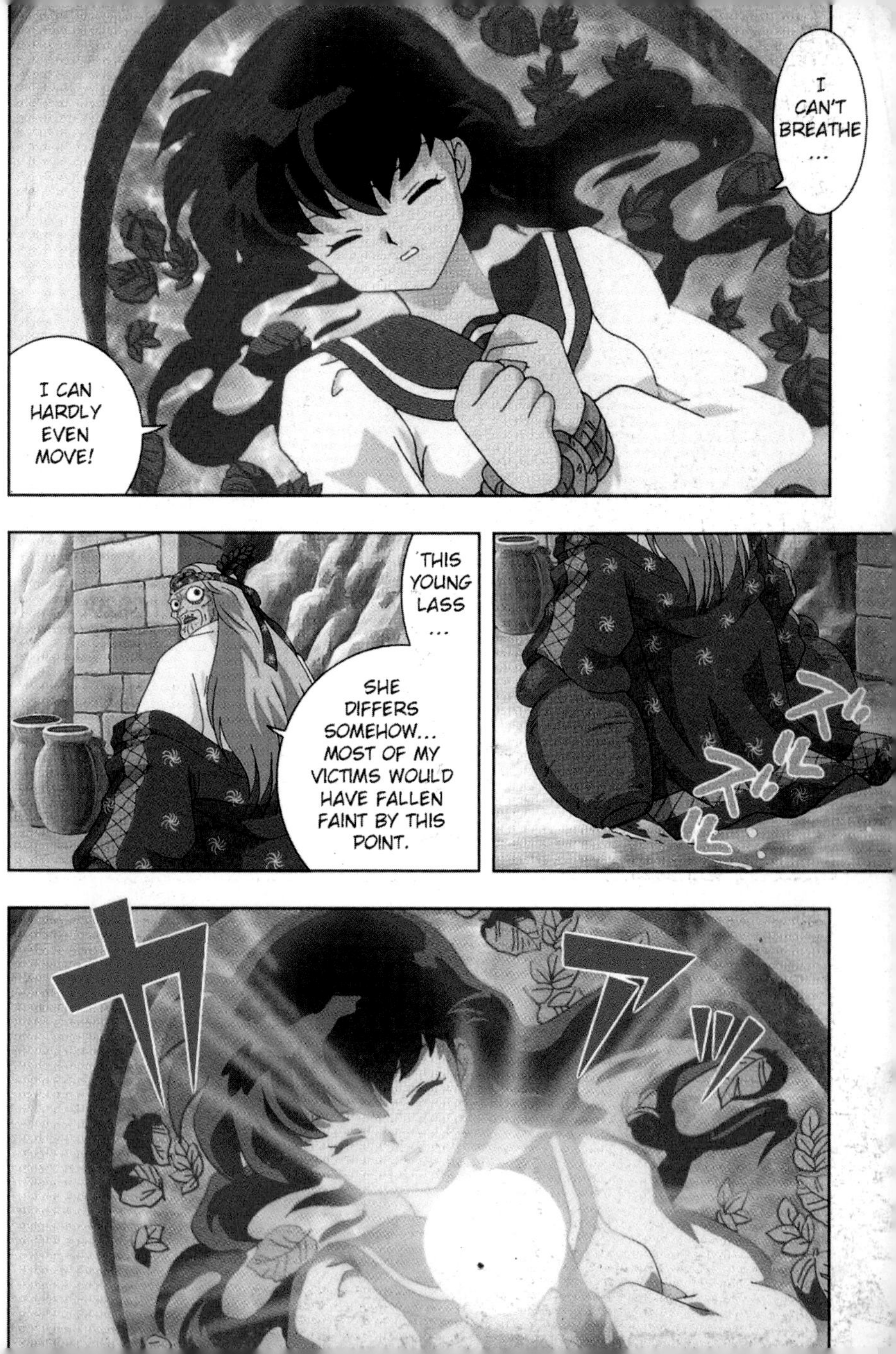
I CAN'T BREATHE ...
I CAN HARDLY EVEN MOVE!
THIS YOUNG LASS ...
SHE DIFFERS SOMEHOW... MOST OF MY VICTIMS WOULD HAVE FALLEN FAINT BY THIS POINT.

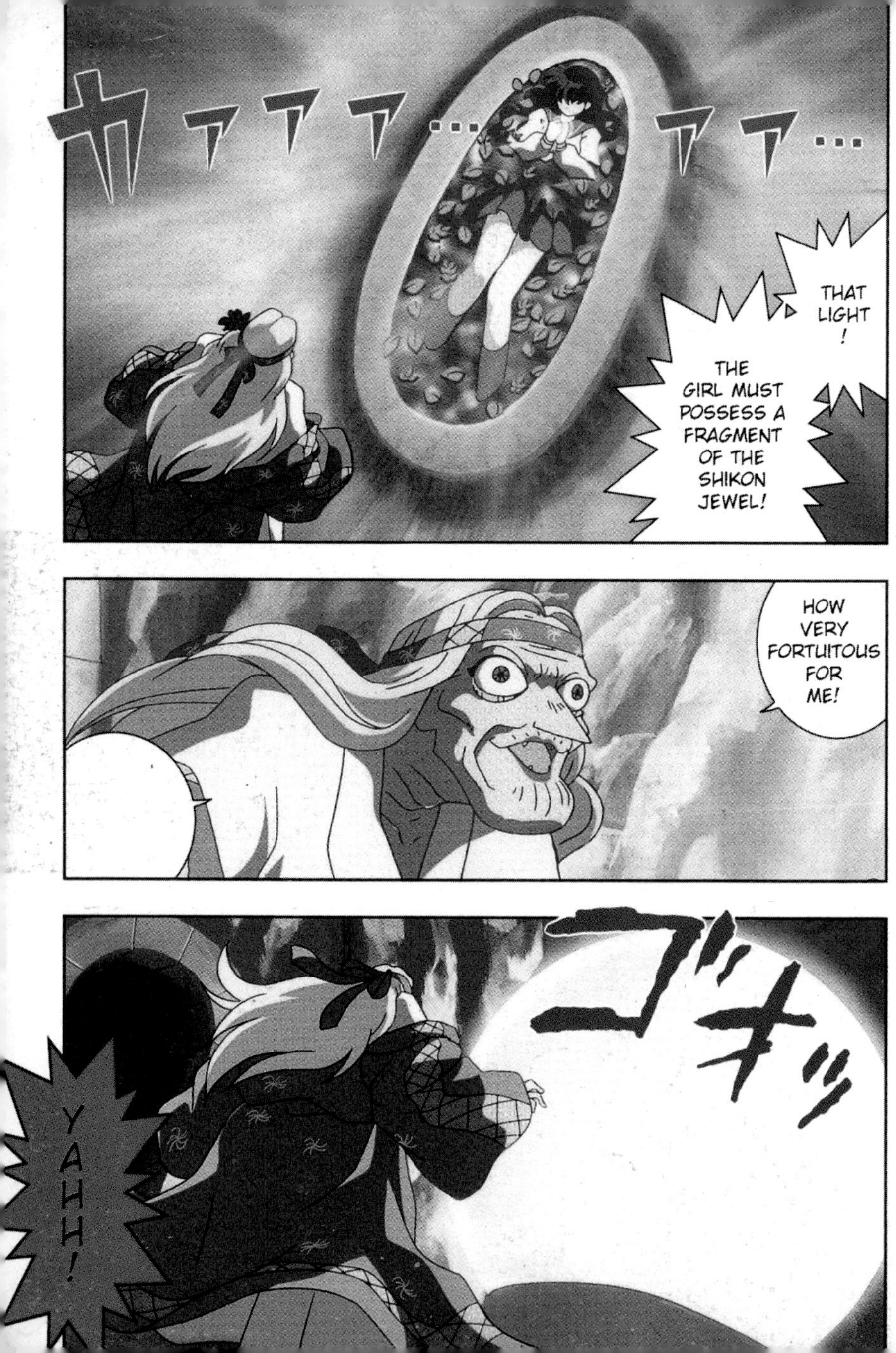
カァアア…アア…
THAT LIGHT!
THE GIRL MUST POSSESS A FRAGMENT OF THE SHIKON JEWEL!
HOW VERY FORTUITOUS FOR ME!
ゴオッ
YAHH!

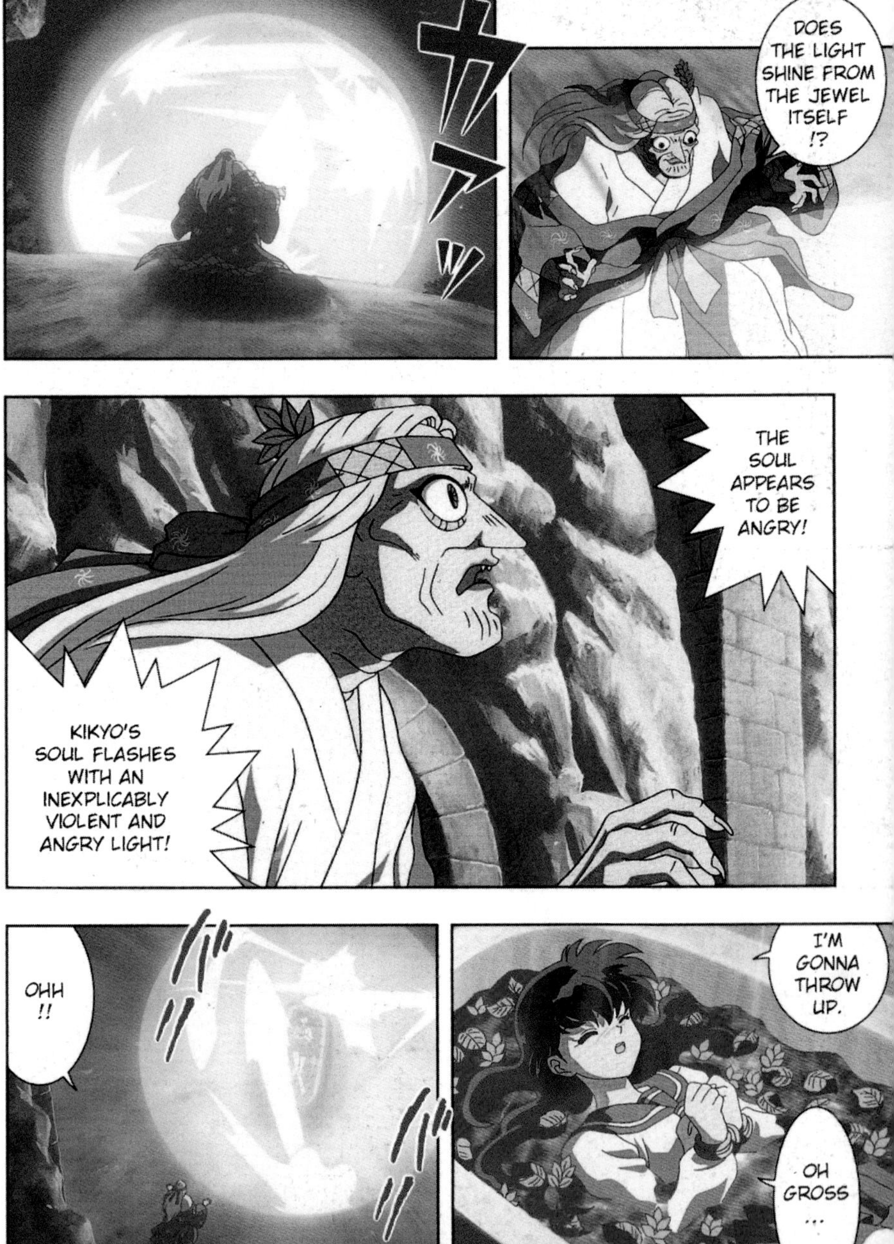
DOES THE LIGHT SHINE FROM THE JEWEL ITSELF !?
カァッ
THE SOUL APPEARS TO BE ANGRY!
KIKYO'S SOUL FLASHES WITH AN INEXPLICABLY VIOLENT AND ANGRY LIGHT!
I'M GONNA THROW UP.
OH GROSS ...
OHH !!

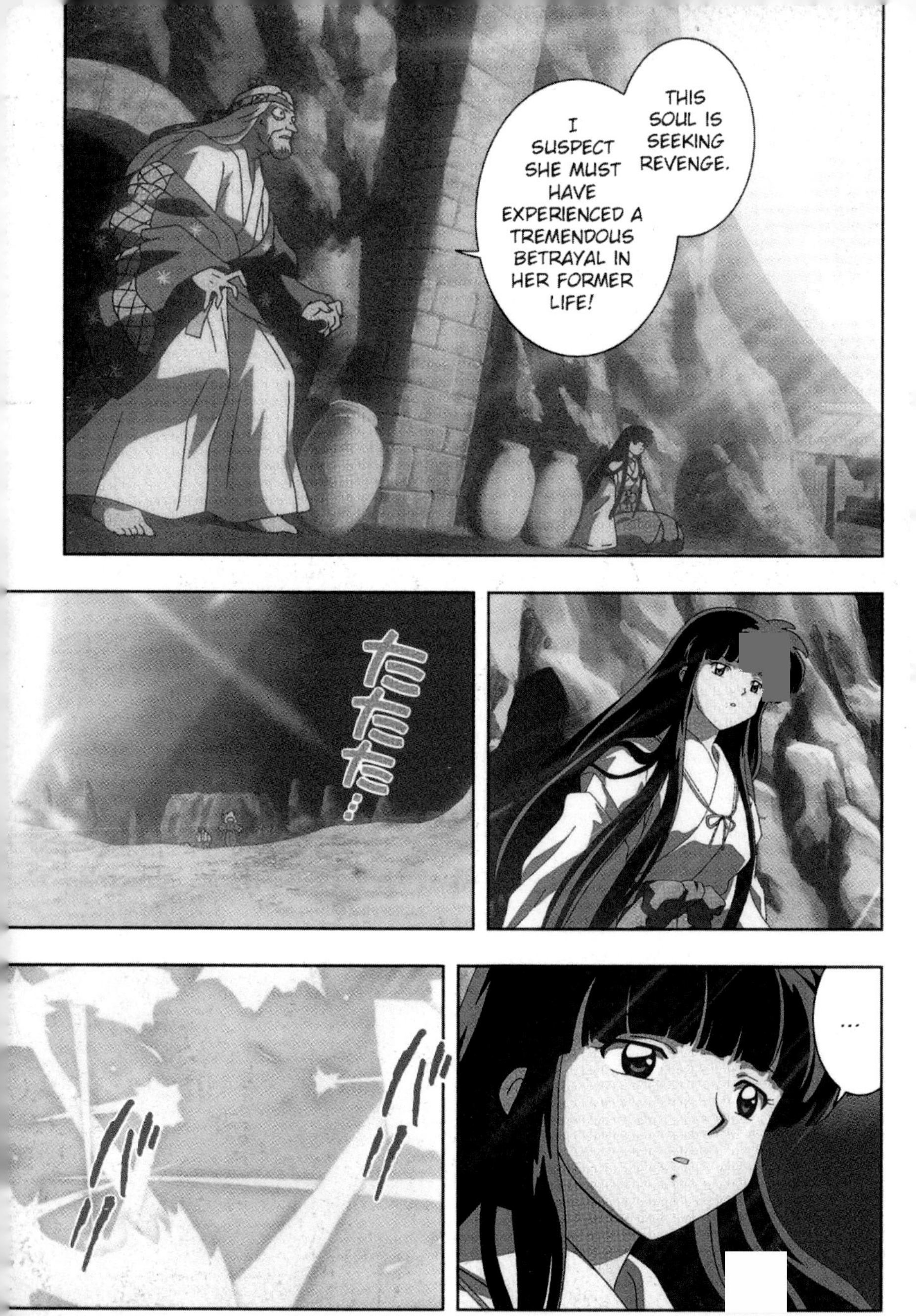
THIS SOUL IS SEEKING REVENGE.
I SUSPECT SHE MUST HAVE EXPERIENCED A TREMENDOUS BETRAYAL IN HER FORMER LIFE!
たたた…
...

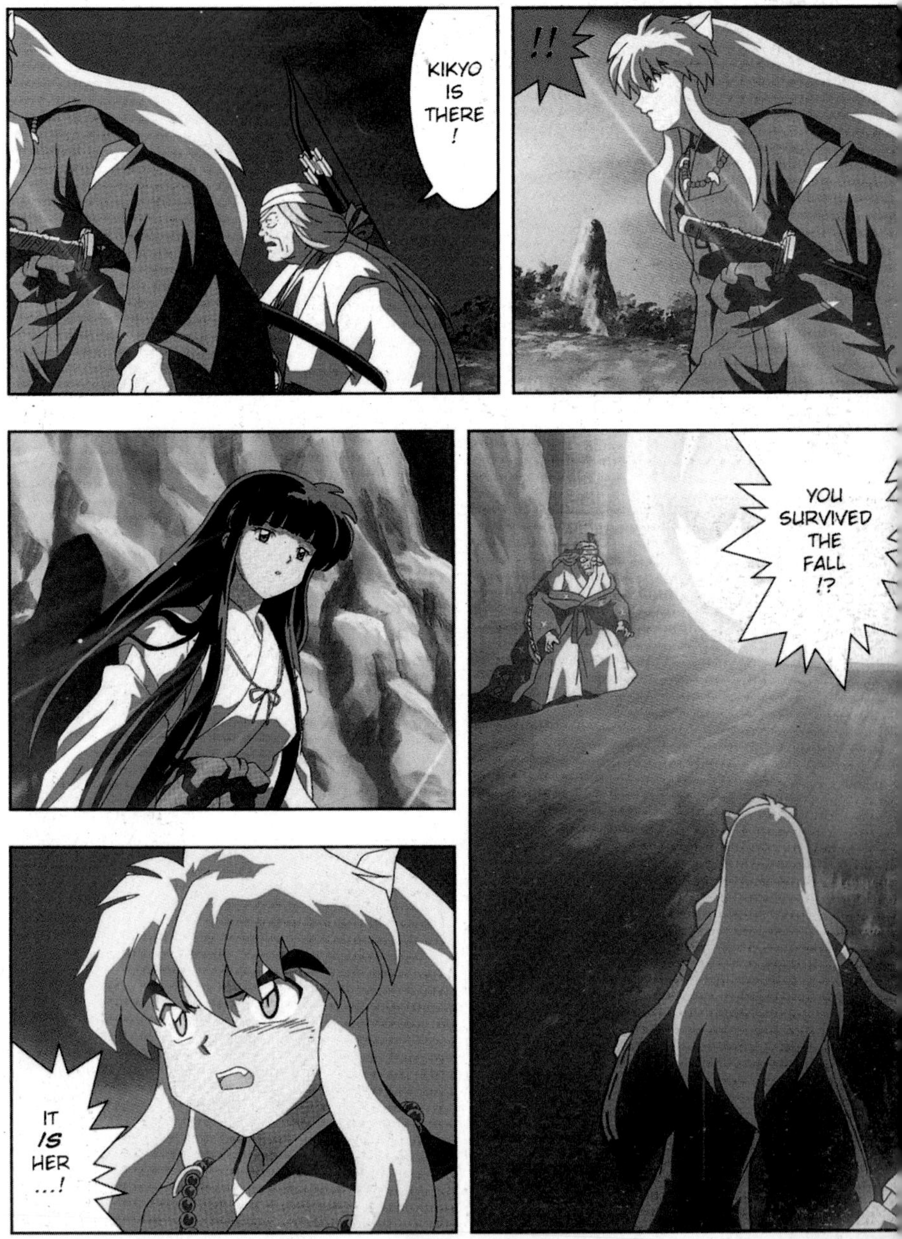
!!
KIKYO IS THERE!
YOU SURVIVED THE FALL!?
IT *IS* HER...!

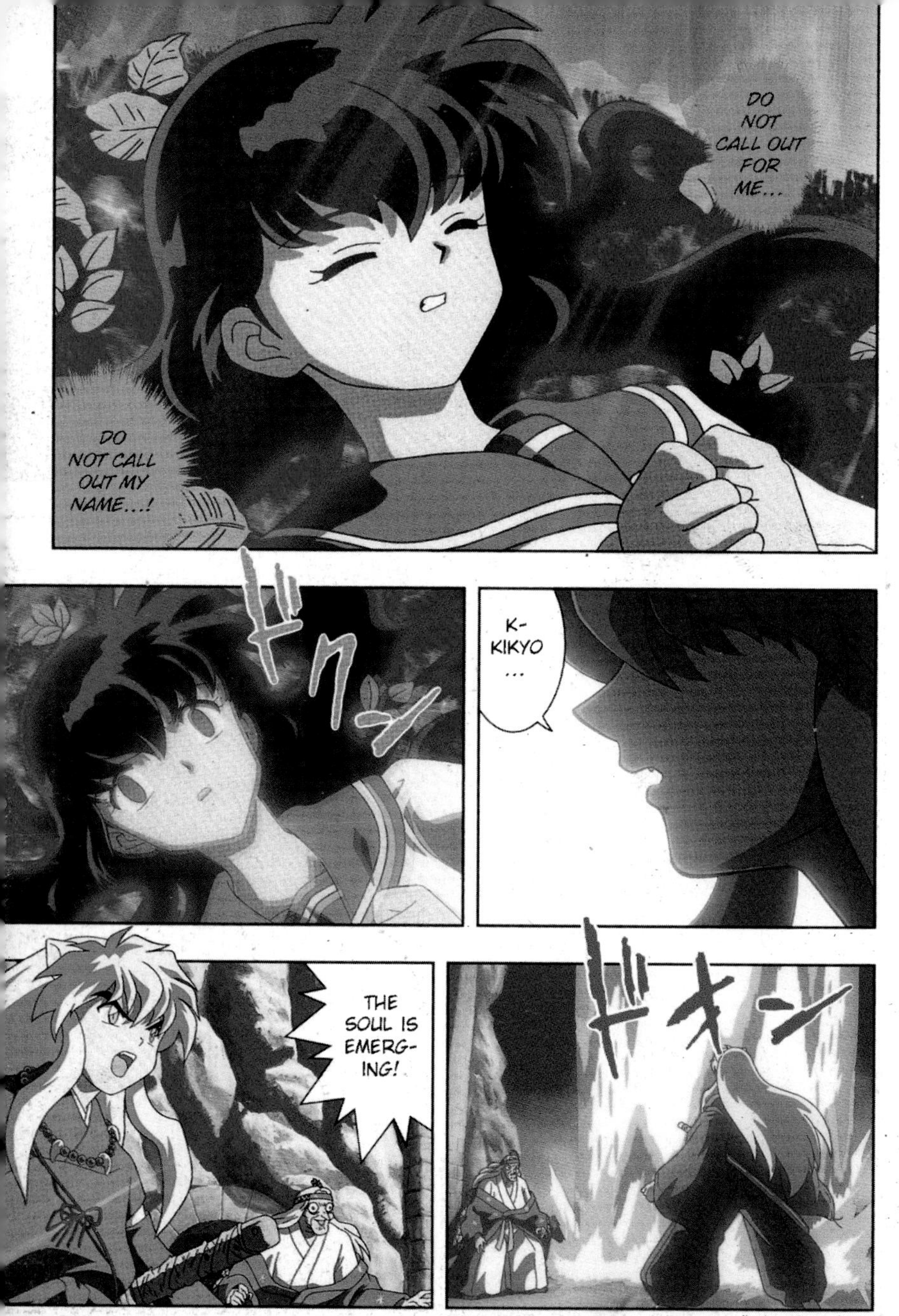
DO NOT CALL OUT FOR ME...
DO NOT CALL OUT MY NAME...!
K-KIKYO ...
ドクン
ドキーン
THE SOUL IS EMERG-ING!

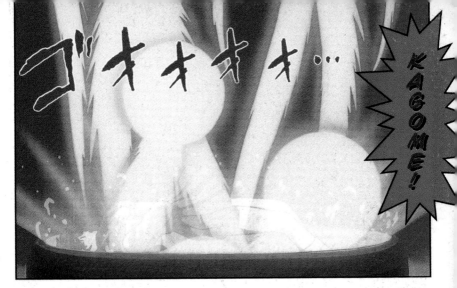

KAGOME!

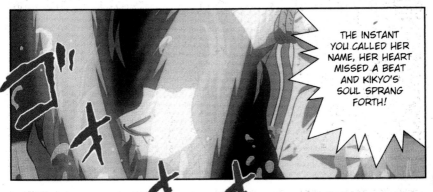

THE INSTANT YOU CALLED HER NAME, HER HEART MISSED A BEAT AND KIKYO'S SOUL SPRANG FORTH!

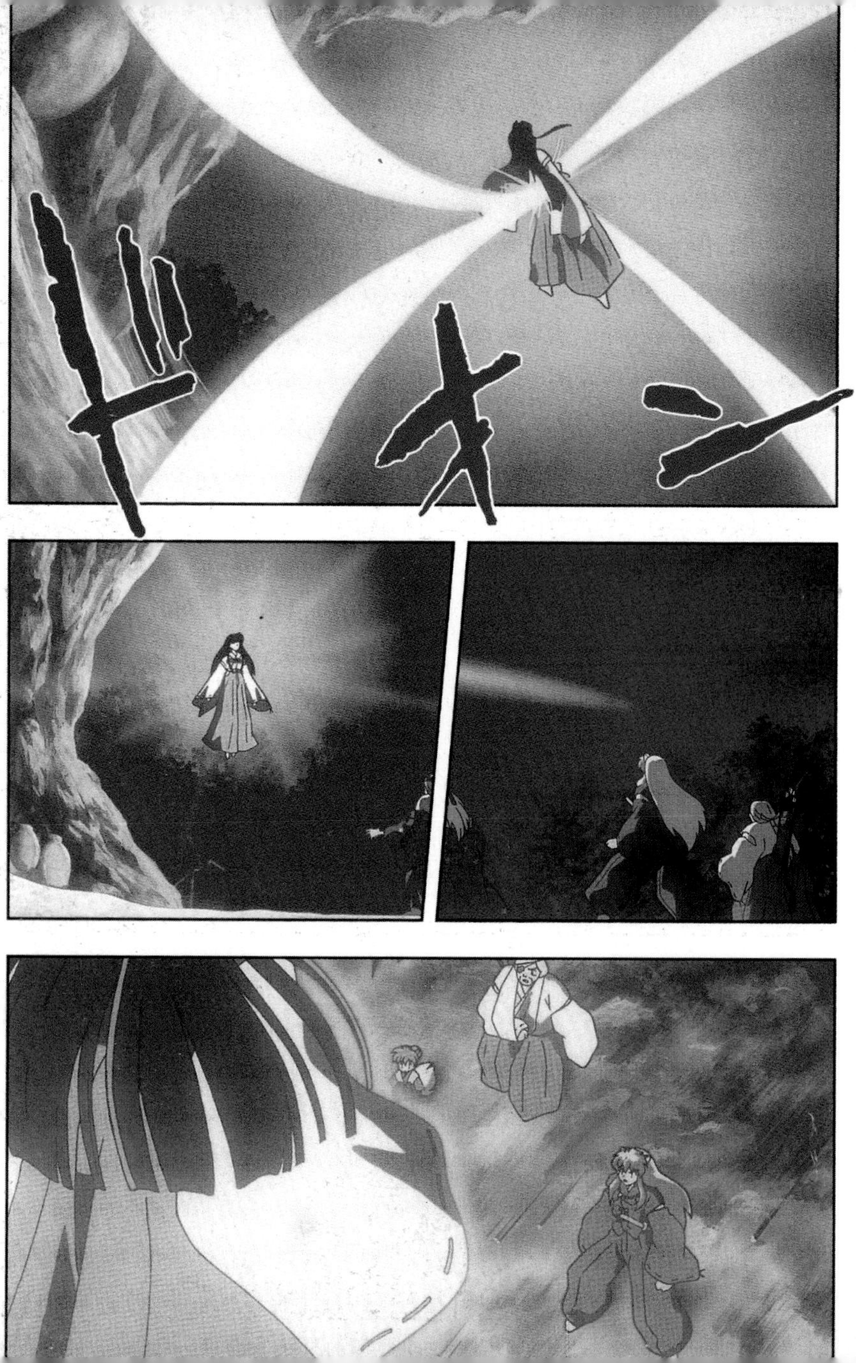
ドオン

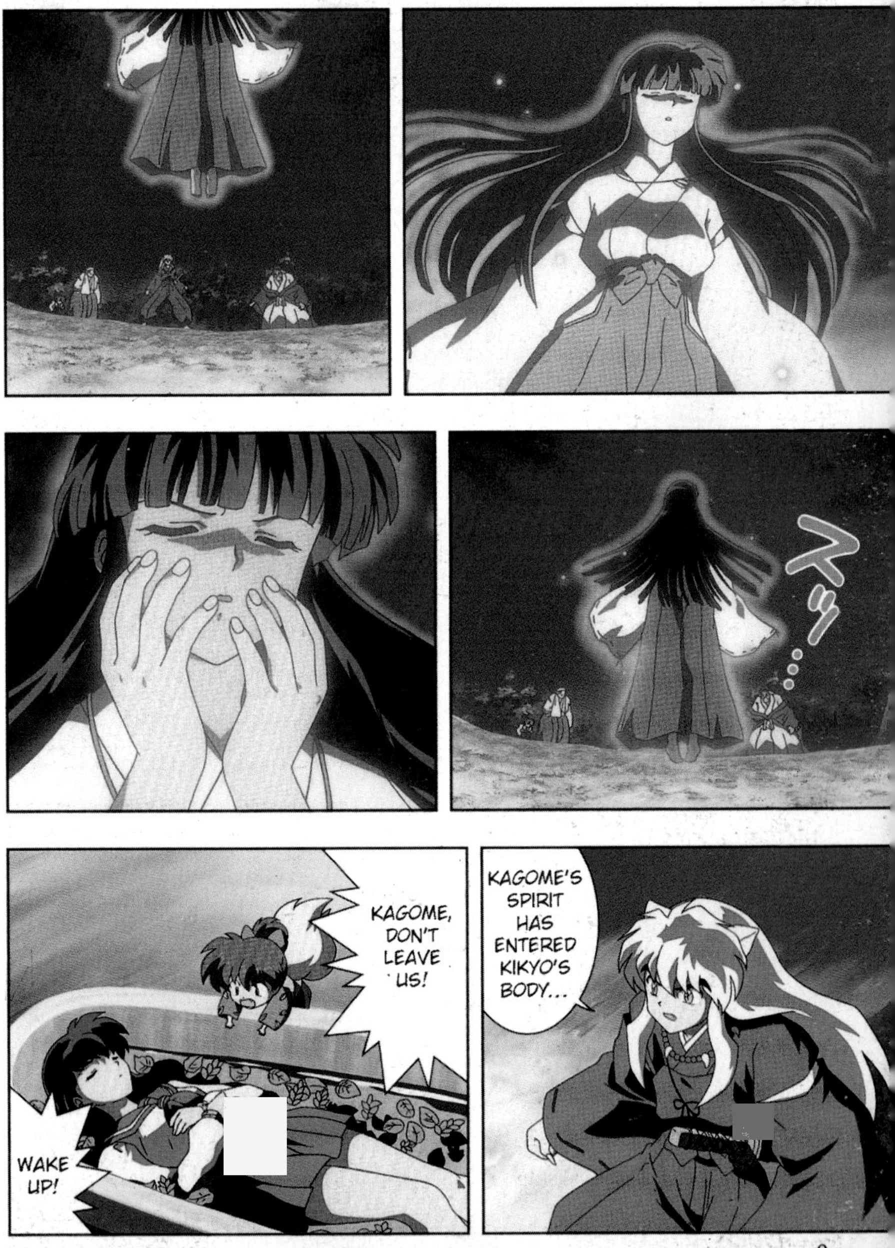
スッ…
KAGOME'S SPIRIT HAS ENTERED KIKYO'S BODY...
KAGOME, DON'T LEAVE US!
WAKE UP!

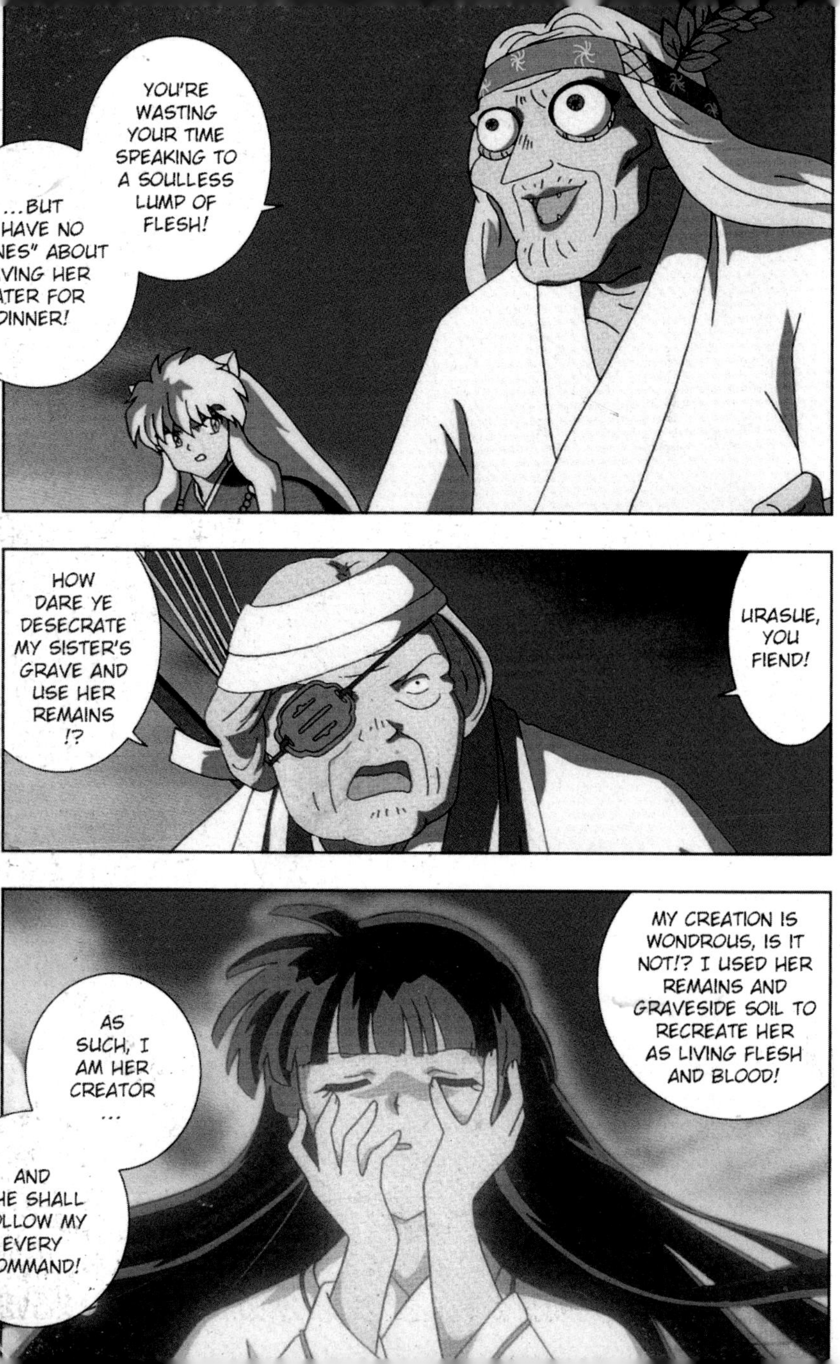
YOU'RE WASTING YOUR TIME SPEAKING TO A SOULLESS LUMP OF FLESH!
...BUT I HAVE NO "BONES" ABOUT HAVING HER LATER FOR DINNER!
URASUE, YOU FIEND!
HOW DARE YE DESECRATE MY SISTER'S GRAVE AND USE HER REMAINS !?
MY CREATION IS WONDROUS, IS IT NOT!? I USED HER REMAINS AND GRAVESIDE SOIL TO RECREATE HER AS LIVING FLESH AND BLOOD!
AS SUCH, I AM HER CREATOR ...
AND SHE SHALL FOLLOW MY EVERY COMMAND!

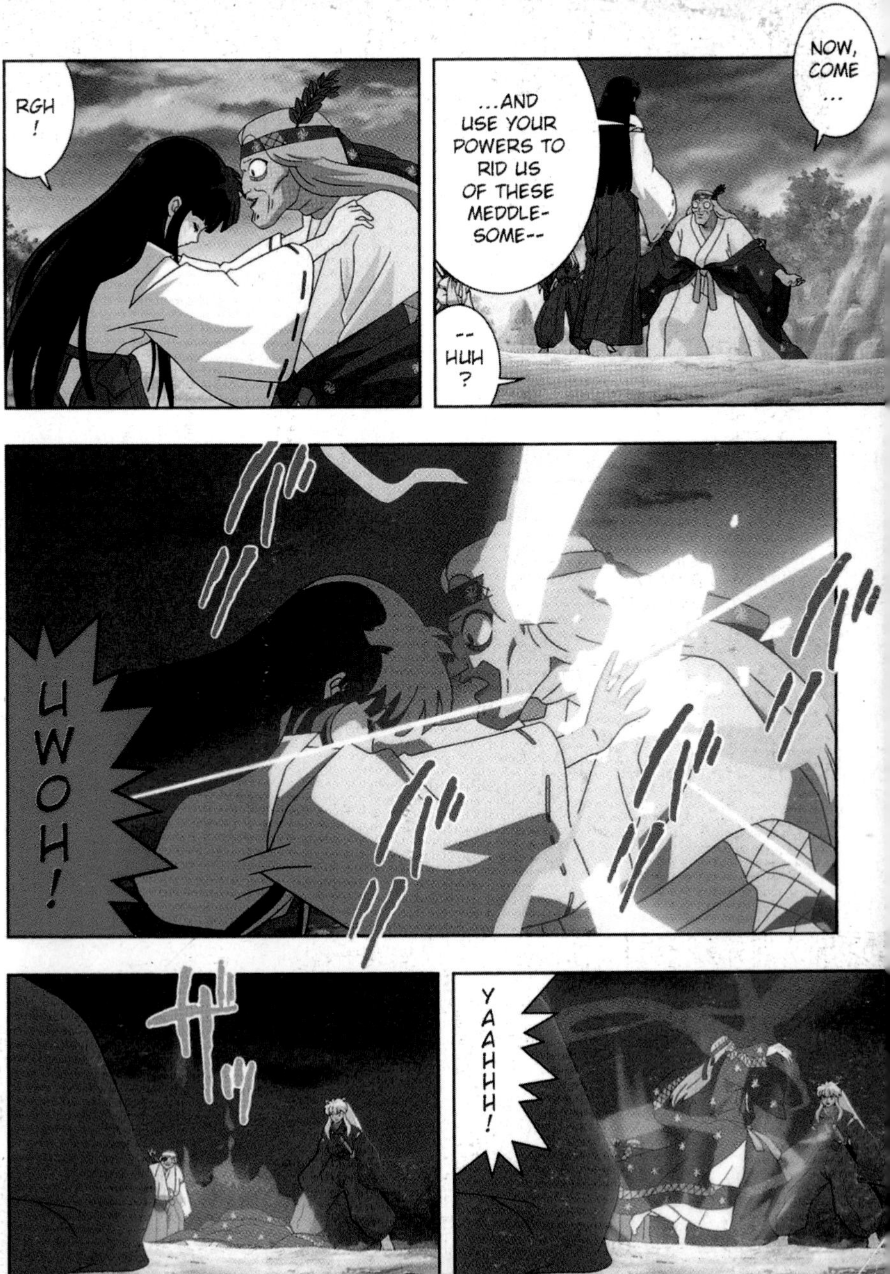
NOW, COME ...
...AND USE YOUR POWERS TO RID US OF THESE MEDDLE-SOME--
--HUH?
RGH!
UWOOH!
YAAHHH!

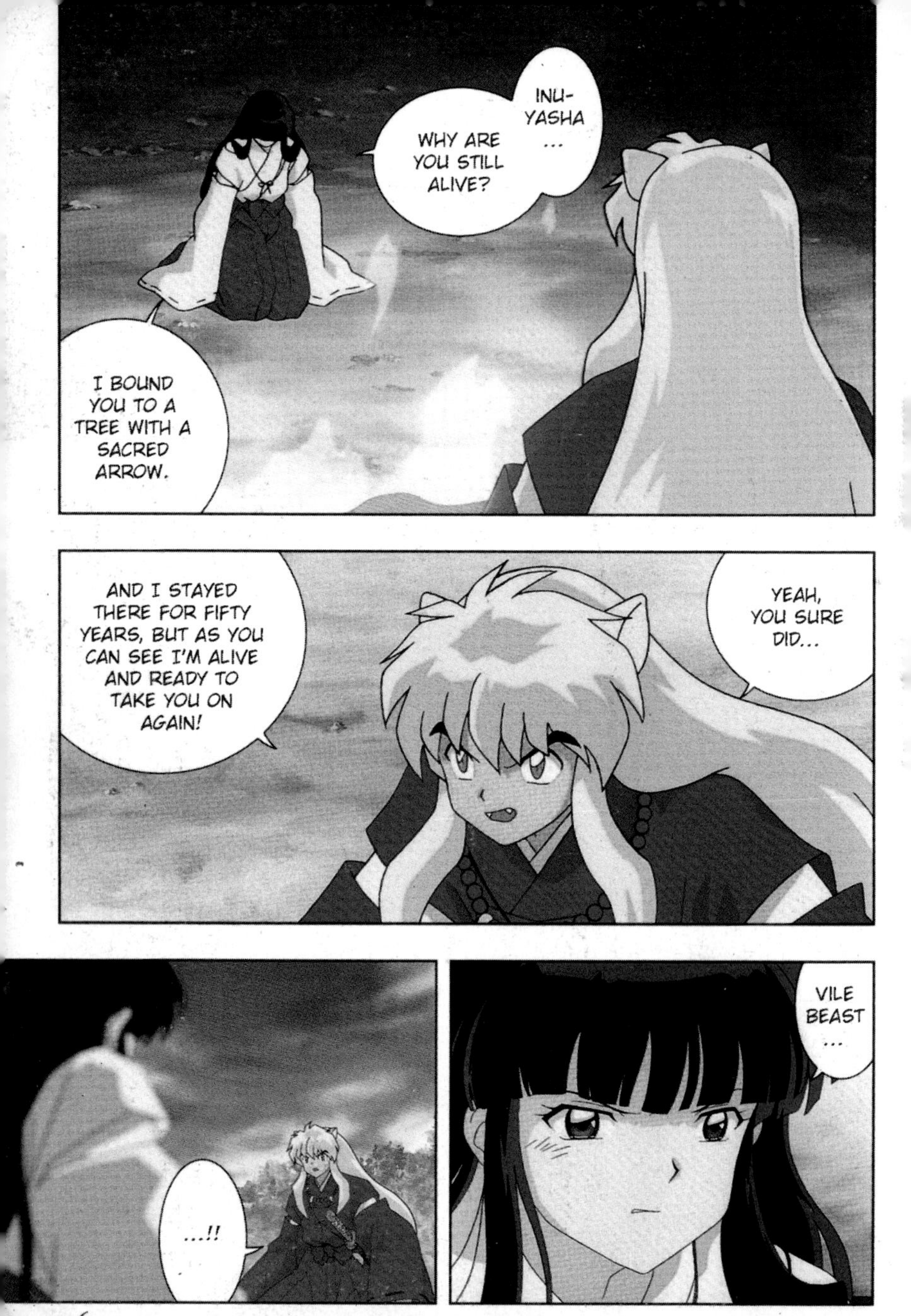
INU-YASHA …
WHY ARE YOU STILL ALIVE?
I BOUND YOU TO A TREE WITH A SACRED ARROW.
YEAH, YOU SURE DID…
AND I STAYED THERE FOR FIFTY YEARS, BUT AS YOU CAN SEE I'M ALIVE AND READY TO TAKE YOU ON AGAIN!
VILE BEAST …
…!!

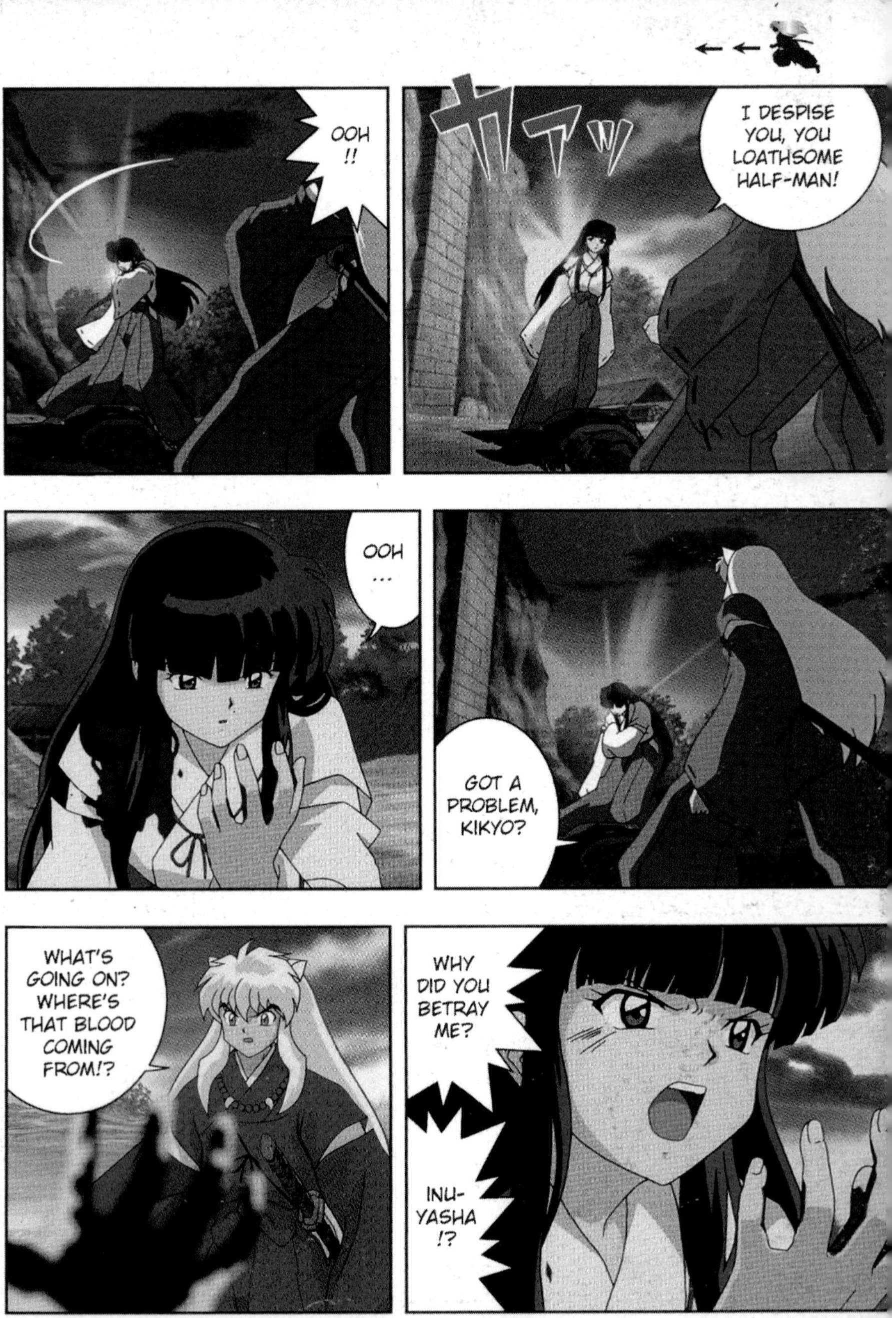
I DESPISE YOU, YOU LOATHSOME HALF-MAN!
OOH !!
GOT A PROBLEM, KIKYO?
OOH ...
WHY DID YOU BETRAY ME?
INU-YASHA !?
WHAT'S GOING ON? WHERE'S THAT BLOOD COMING FROM!?

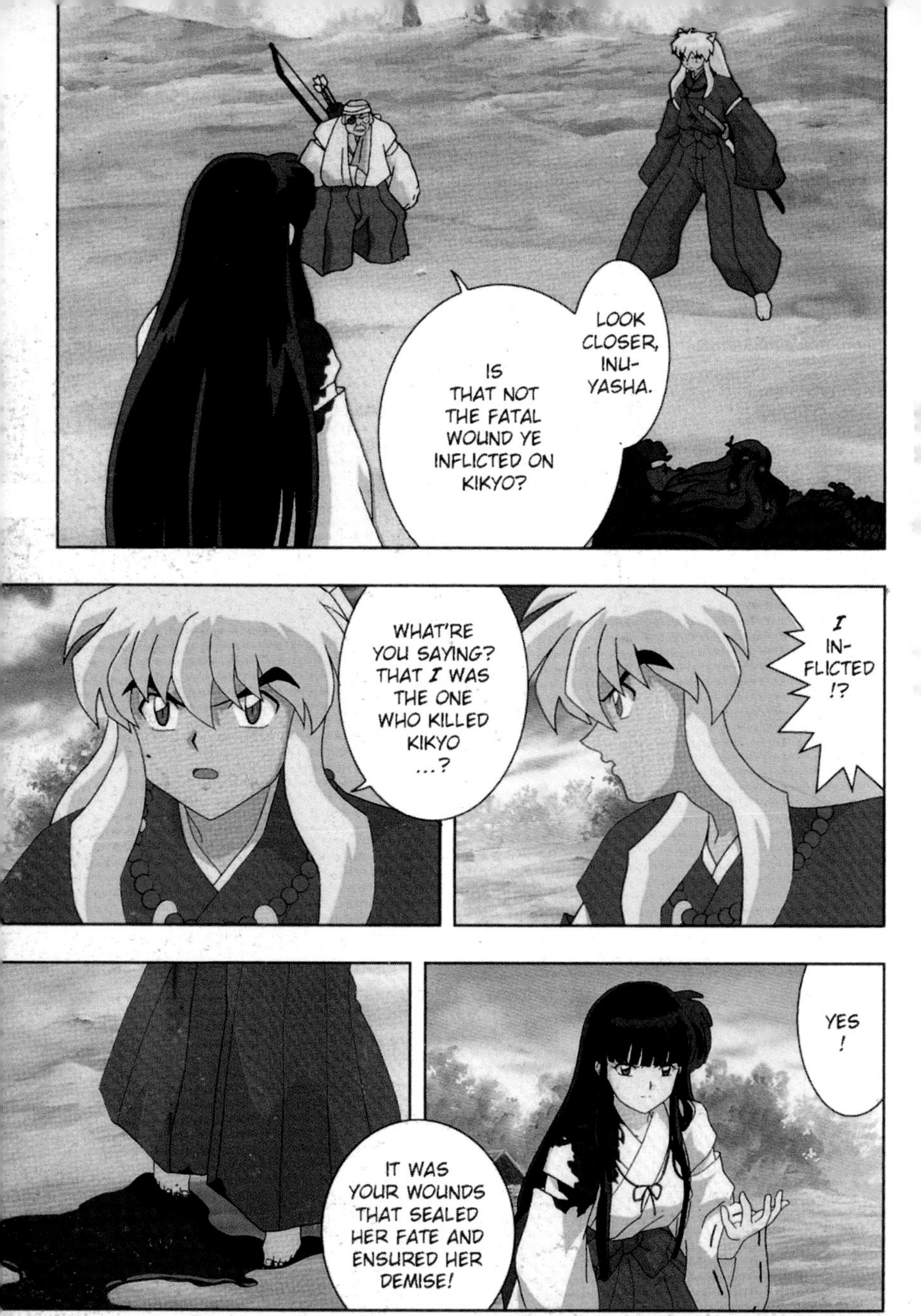
LOOK CLOSER, INU-YASHA.
IS THAT NOT THE FATAL WOUND YE INFLICTED ON KIKYO?
I IN-FLICTED!?
WHAT'RE YOU SAYING? THAT I WAS THE ONE WHO KILLED KIKYO...?
YES!
IT WAS YOUR WOUNDS THAT SEALED HER FATE AND ENSURED HER DEMISE!

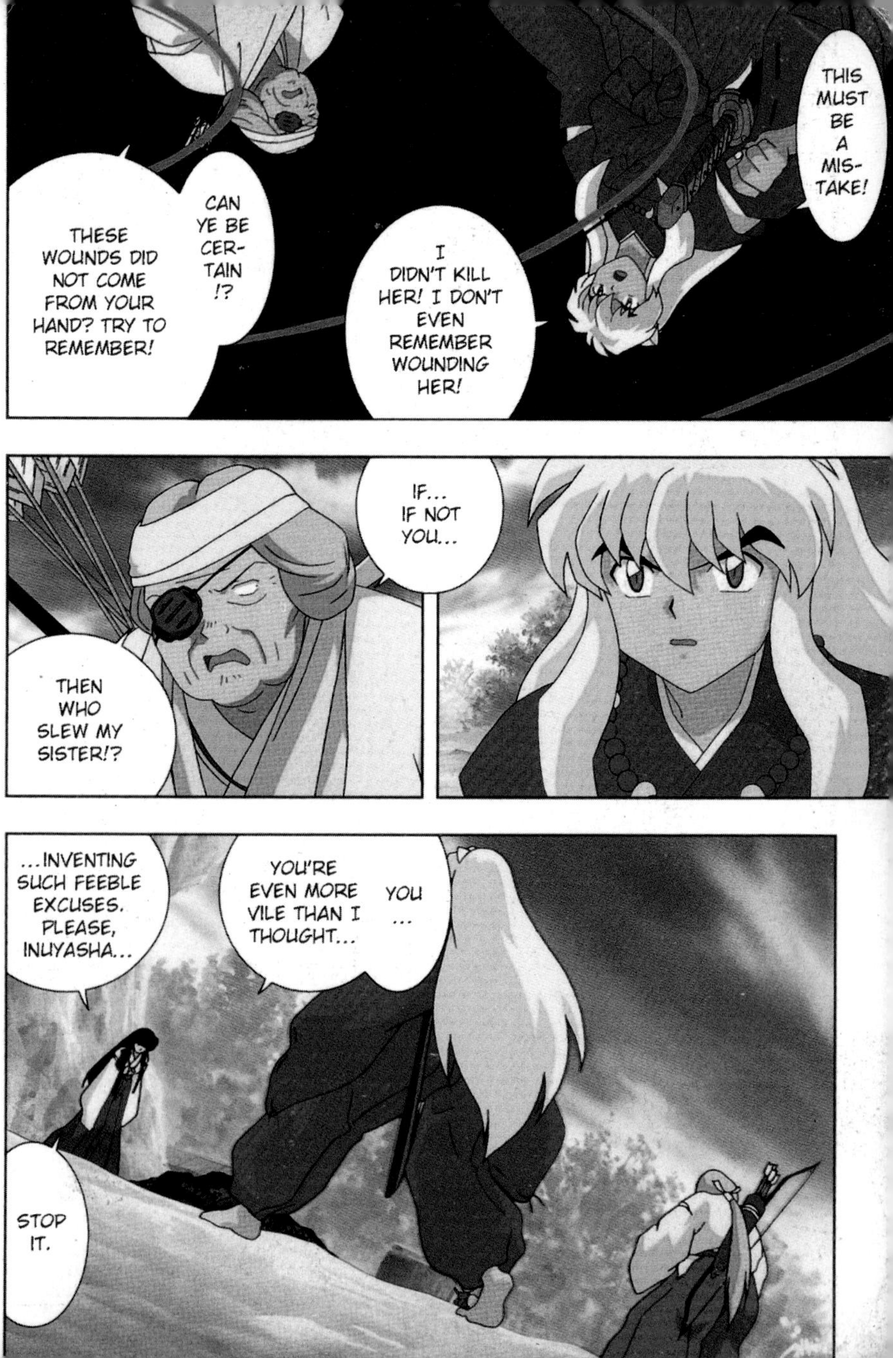
THIS MUST BE A MIS-TAKE!
I DIDN'T KILL HER! I DON'T EVEN REMEMBER WOUNDING HER!
CAN YE BE CER-TAIN !?
THESE WOUNDS DID NOT COME FROM YOUR HAND? TRY TO REMEMBER!
IF... IF NOT YOU...
THEN WHO SLEW MY SISTER!?
YOU ...
YOU'RE EVEN MORE VILE THAN I THOUGHT...
...INVENTING SUCH FEEBLE EXCUSES. PLEASE, INUYASHA...
STOP IT.

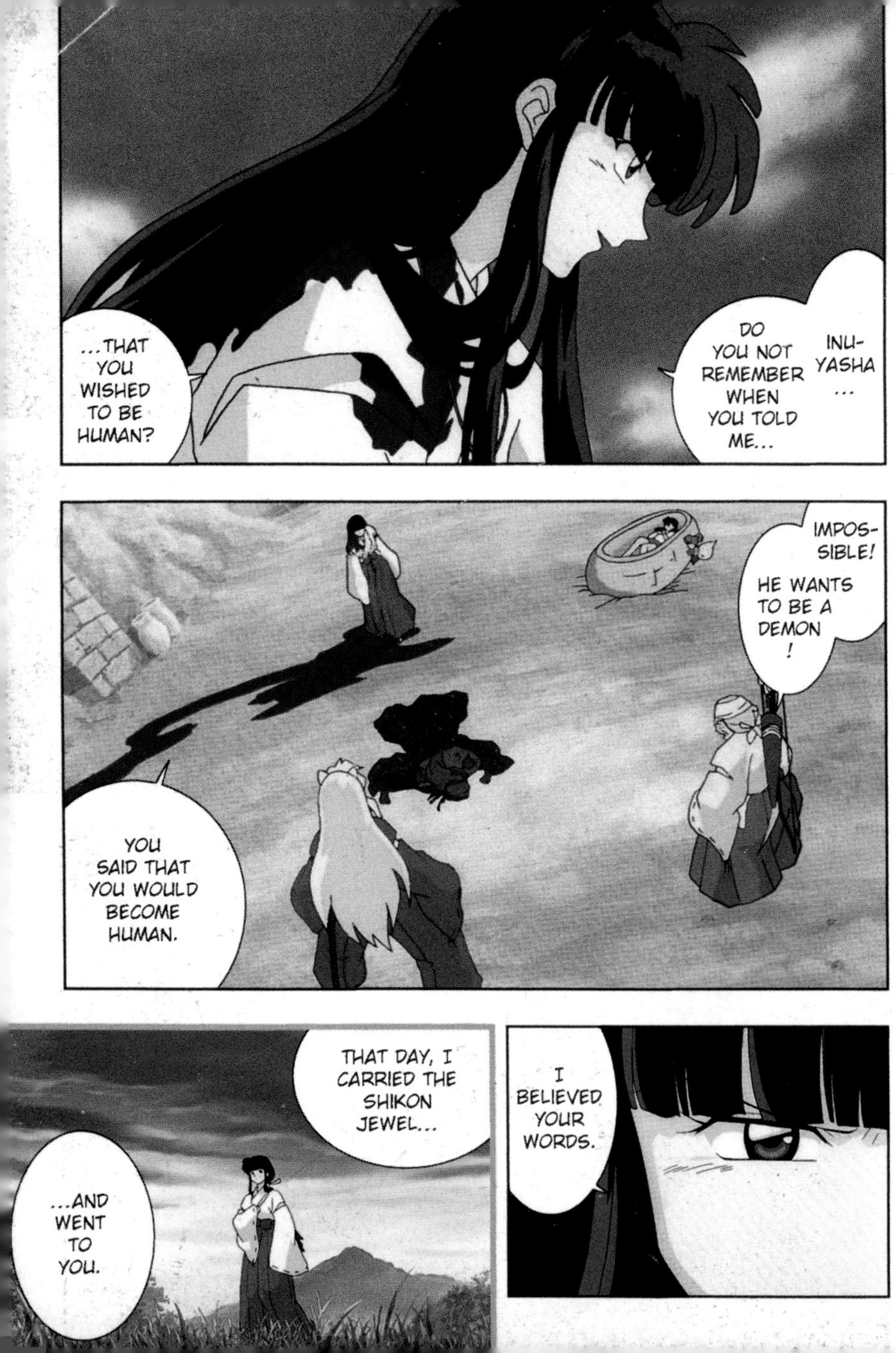
INU-YASHA...
DO YOU NOT REMEMBER WHEN YOU TOLD ME...
...THAT YOU WISHED TO BE HUMAN?
IMPOSSIBLE!
HE WANTS TO BE A DEMON!
YOU SAID THAT YOU WOULD BECOME HUMAN.
I BELIEVED YOUR WORDS.
THAT DAY, I CARRIED THE SHIKON JEWEL...
...AND WENT TO YOU.

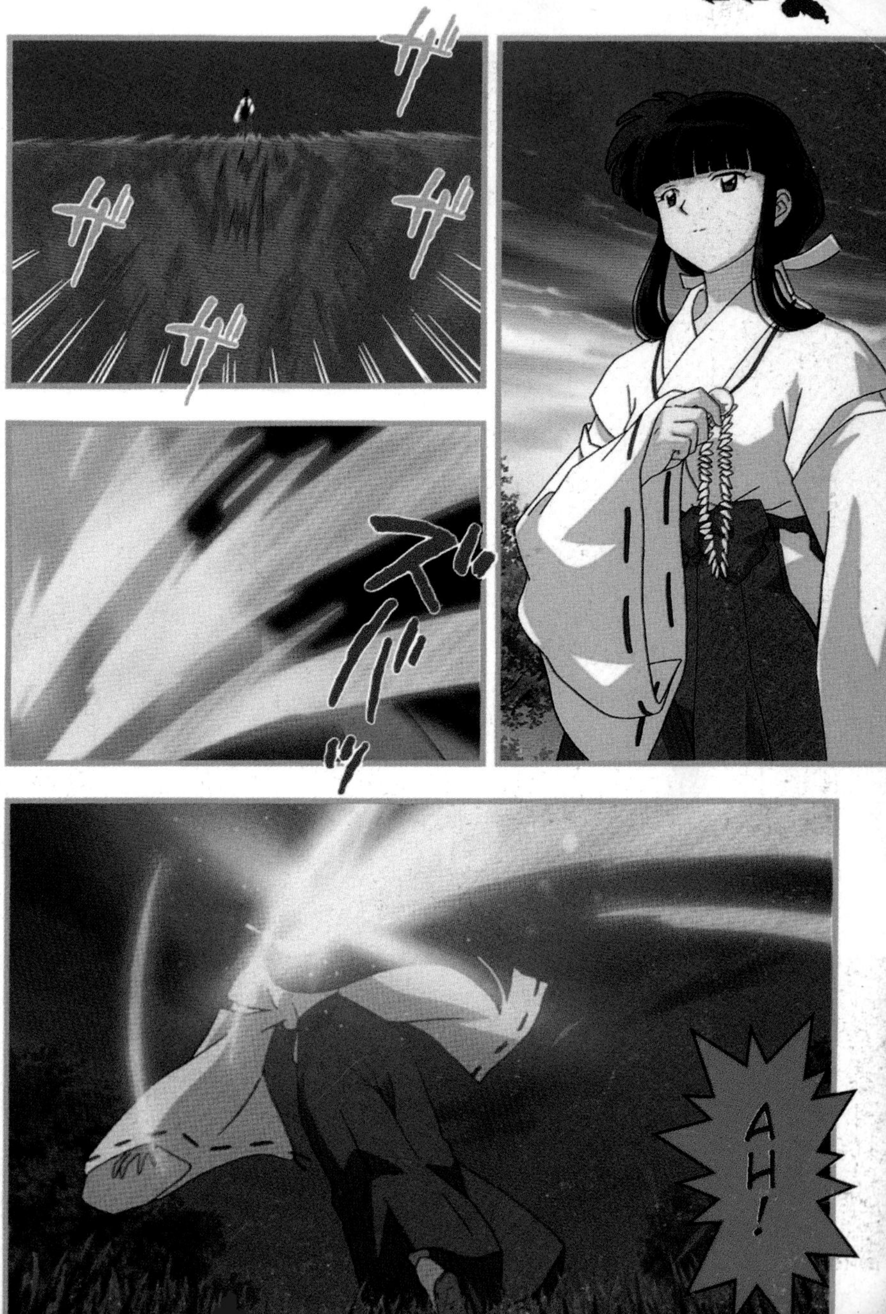
ザ
ザ
ザ
ザ
ズドッ
AH!

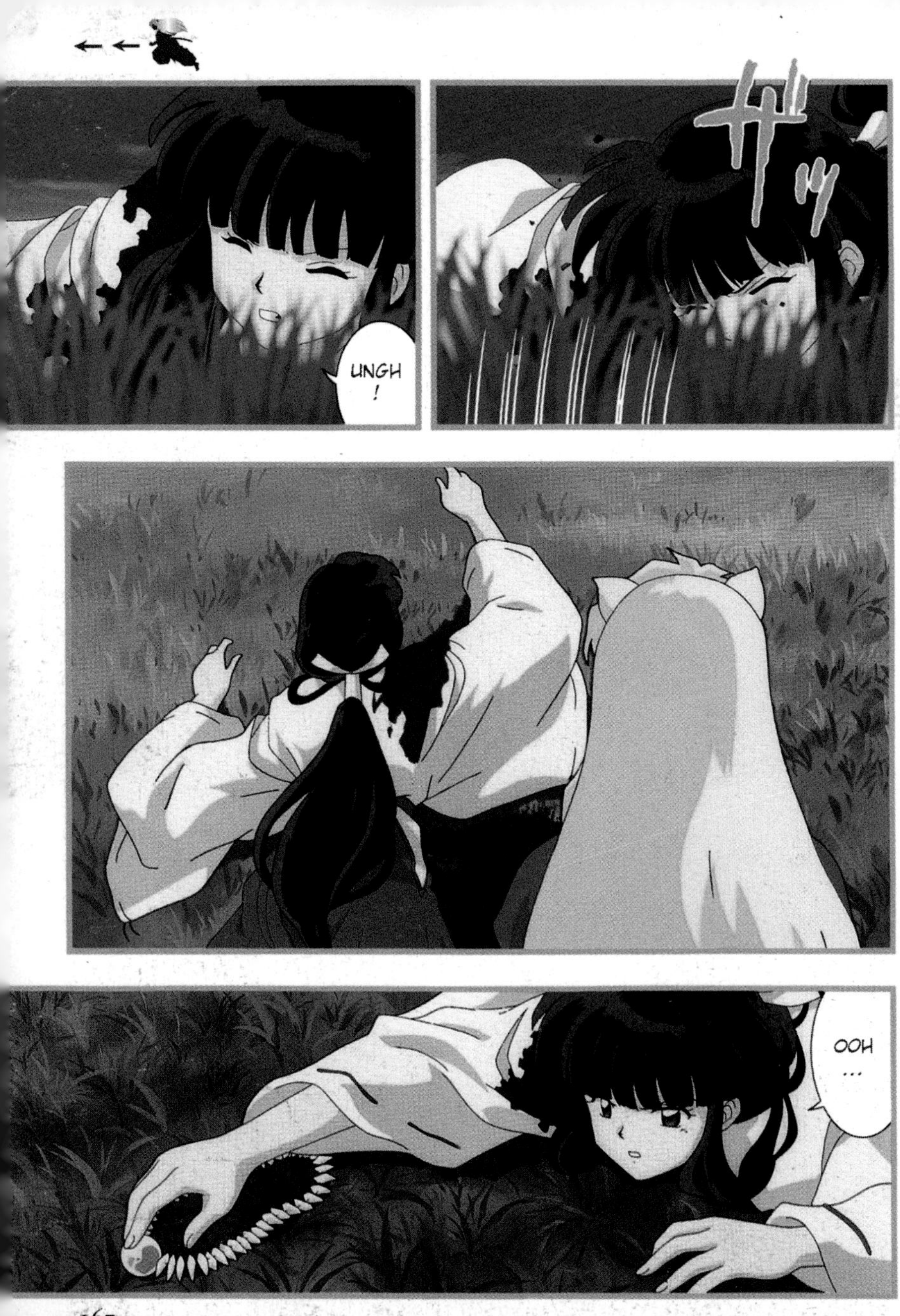
ザッ
UNGH !
OOH ...

FOOL!

I HAVE NO DESIRE WHATSOEVER TO BECOME HUMAN!

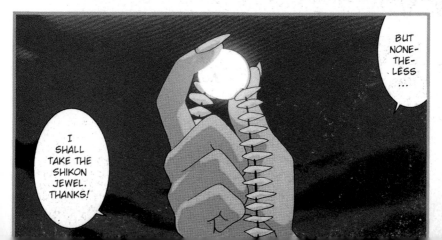

BUT NONE-THE-LESS ...

I SHALL TAKE THE SHIKON JEWEL. THANKS!

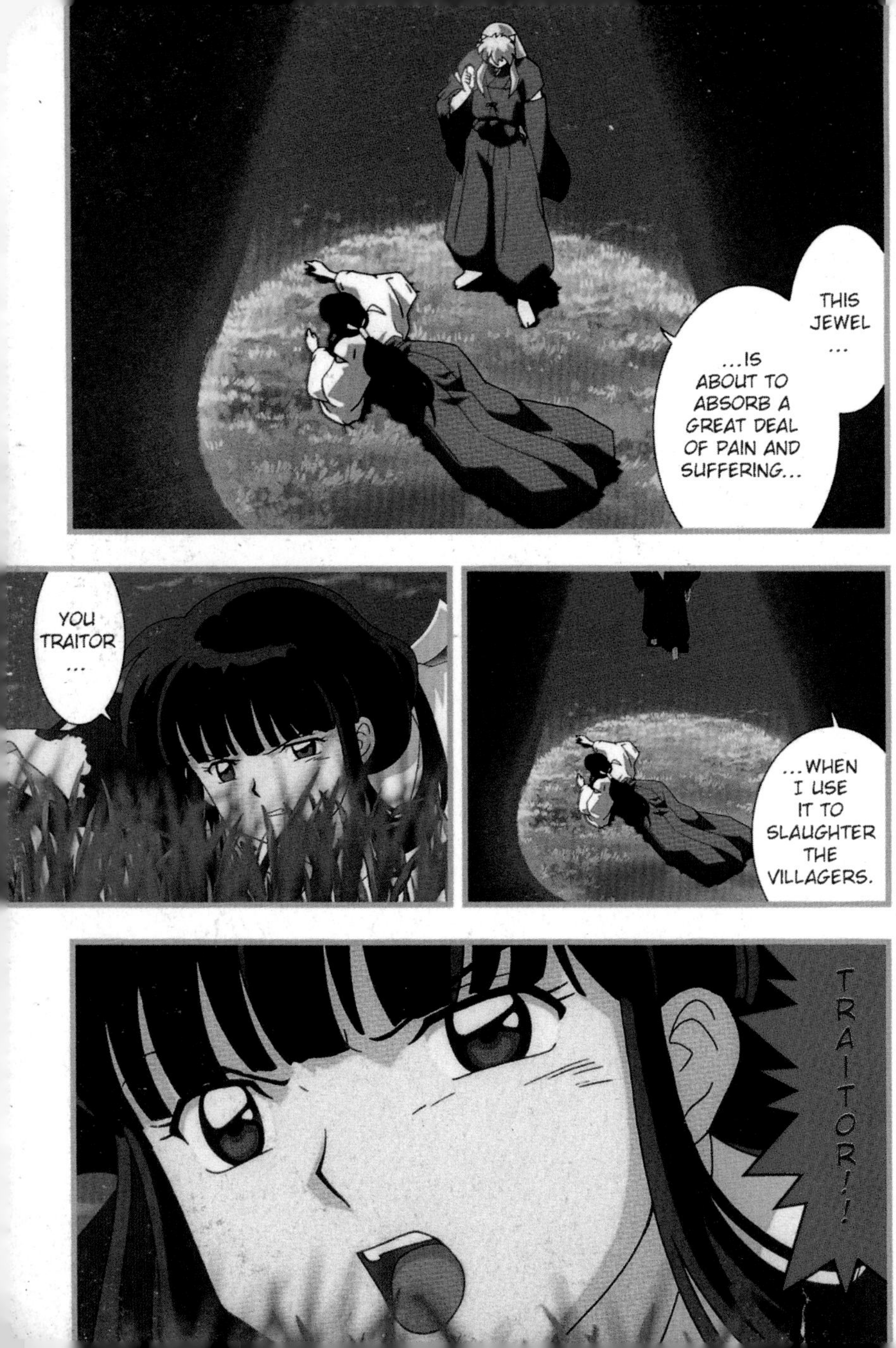
THIS JEWEL ...
...IS ABOUT TO ABSORB A GREAT DEAL OF PAIN AND SUFFERING...
...WHEN I USE IT TO SLAUGHTER THE VILLAGERS.
YOU TRAITOR ...
TRAITOR!!

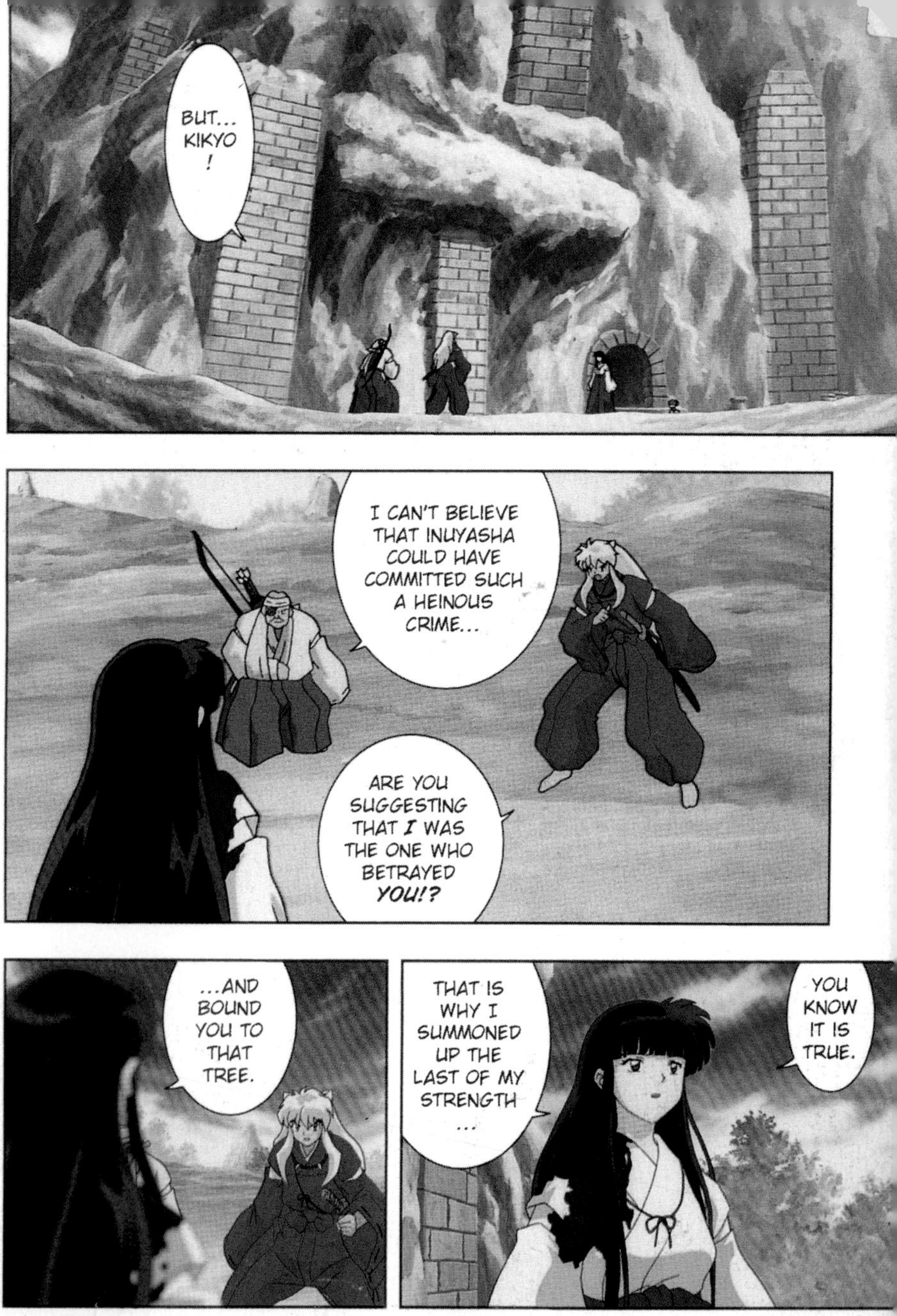
BUT... KIKYO!
I CAN'T BELIEVE THAT INUYASHA COULD HAVE COMMITTED SUCH A HEINOUS CRIME...
ARE YOU SUGGESTING THAT *I* WAS THE ONE WHO BETRAYED ***YOU!?***
YOU KNOW IT IS TRUE.
THAT IS WHY I SUMMONED UP THE LAST OF MY STRENGTH...
...AND BOUND YOU TO THAT TREE.

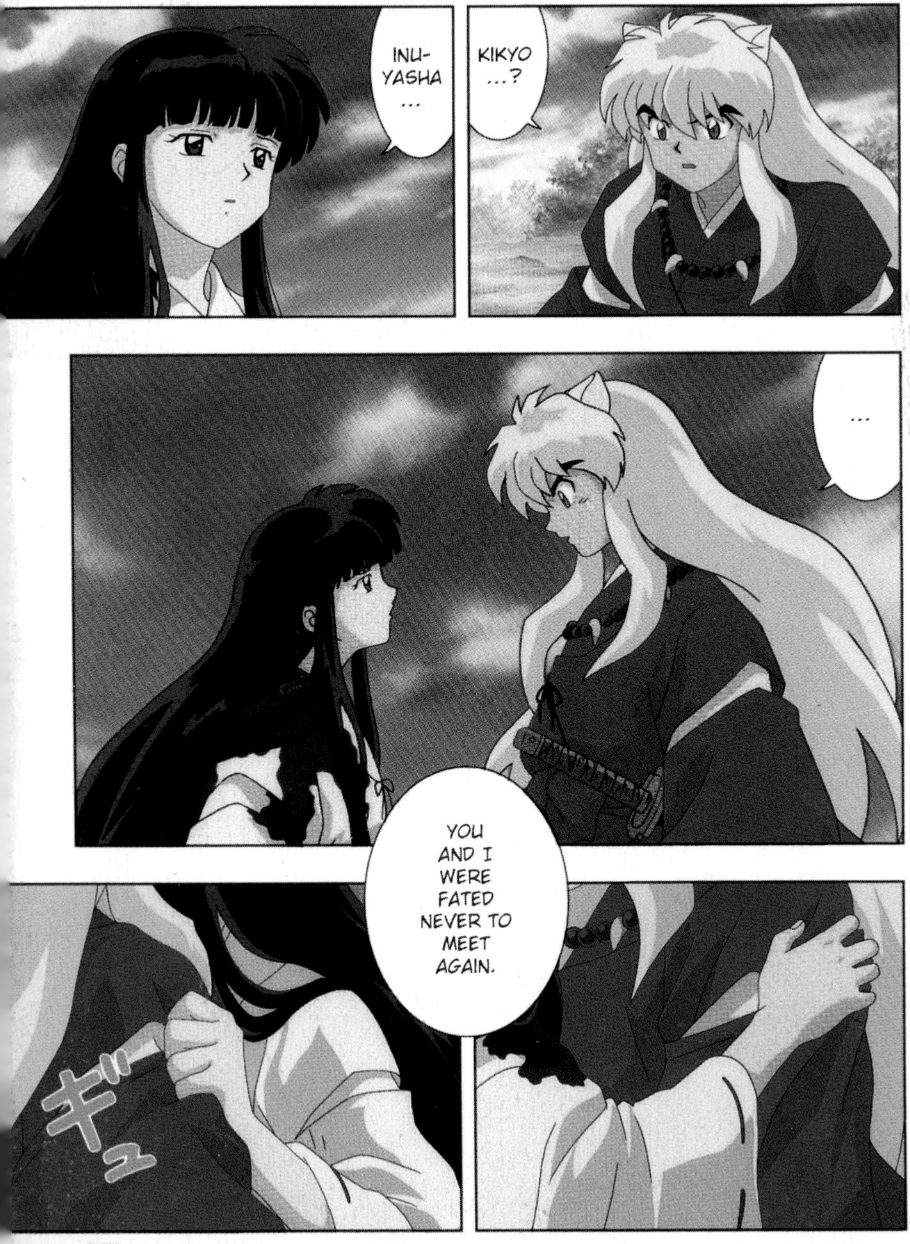
KIKYO ...?
INU-YASHA ...
...
YOU AND I WERE FATED NEVER TO MEET AGAIN.
ギュ

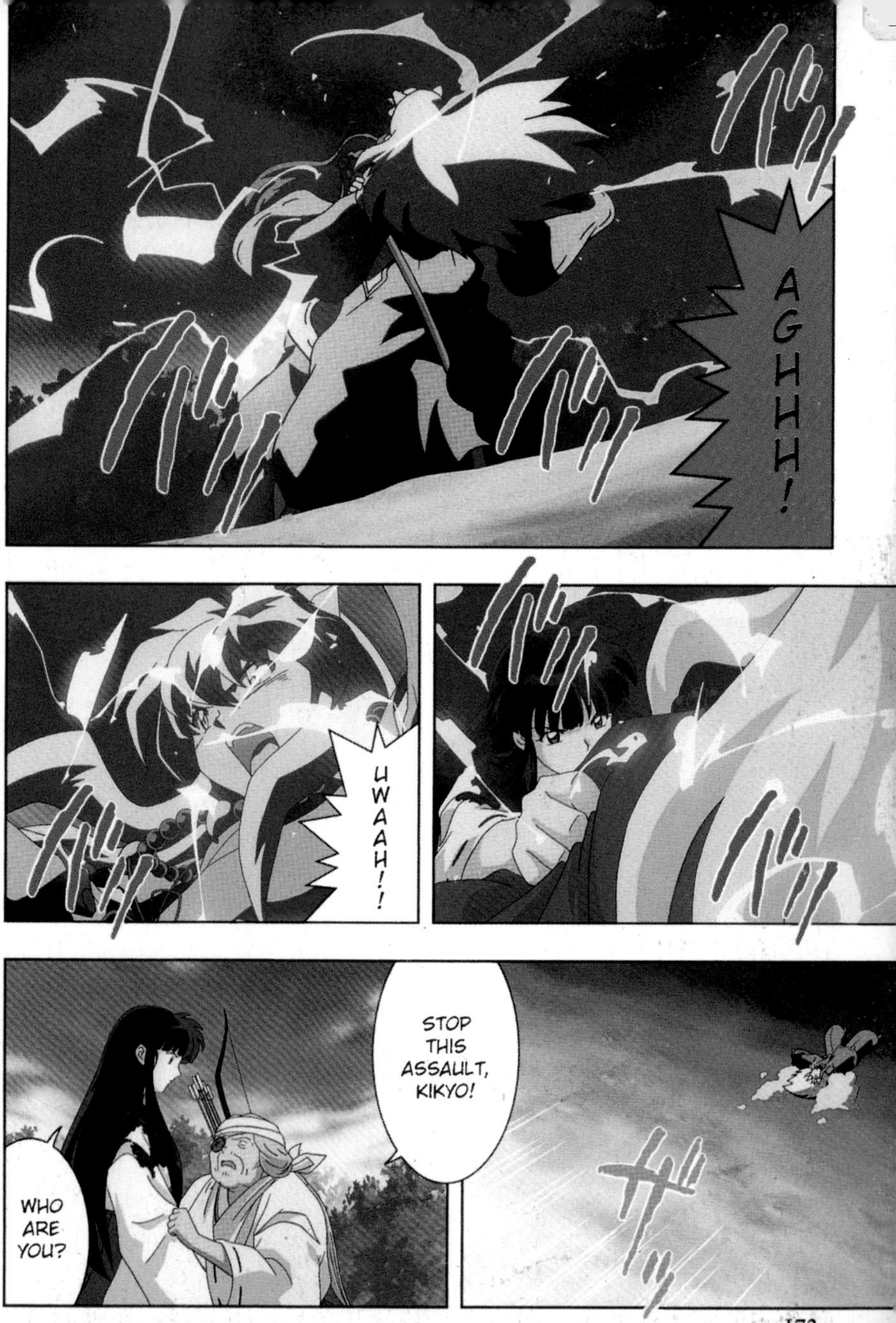
AGHHH!
UWAAAH!!
STOP THIS ASSAULT, KIKYO!
WHO ARE YOU?

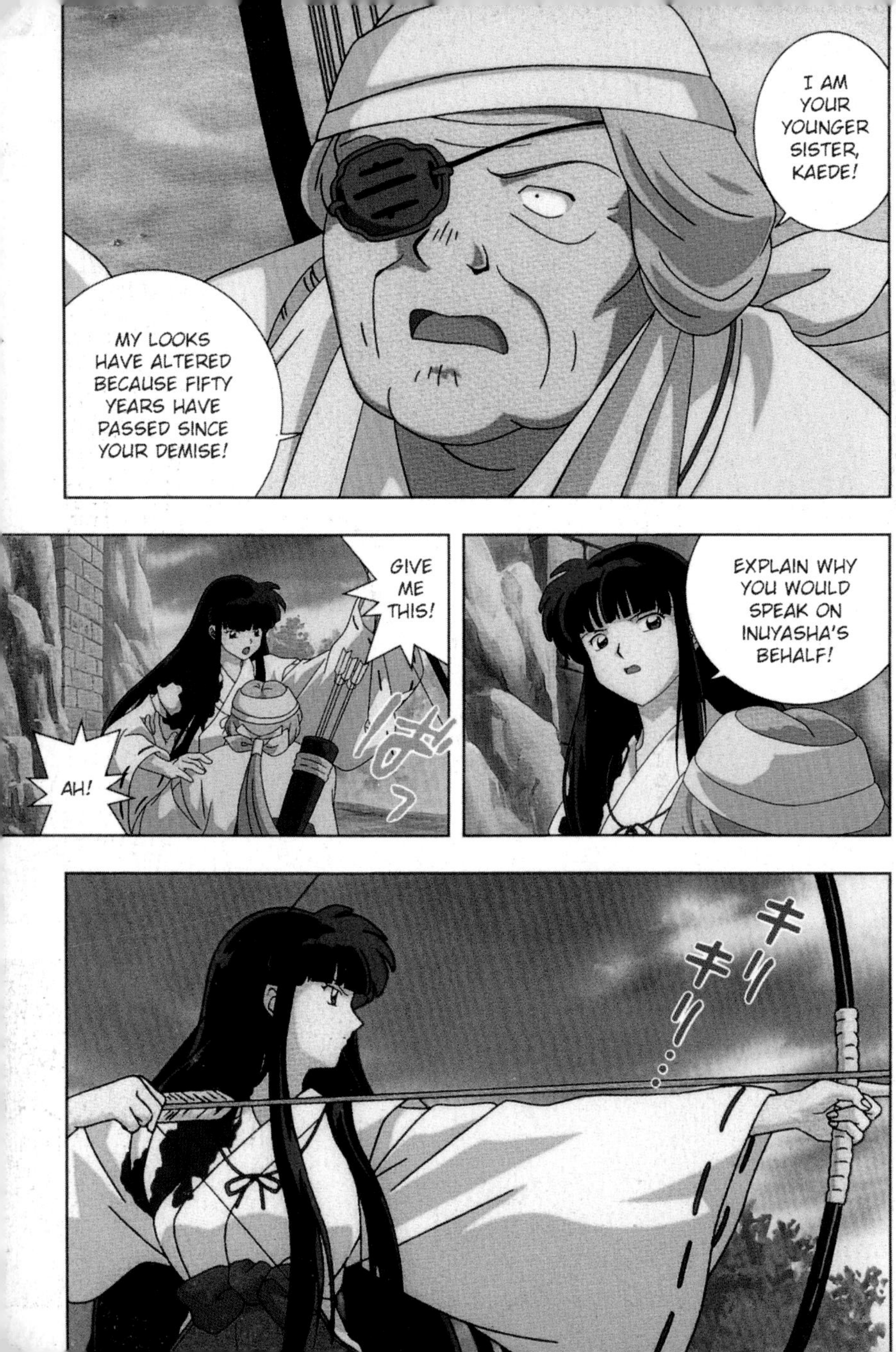
I AM YOUR YOUNGER SISTER, KAEDE!
MY LOOKS HAVE ALTERED BECAUSE FIFTY YEARS HAVE PASSED SINCE YOUR DEMISE!
EXPLAIN WHY YOU WOULD SPEAK ON INUYASHA'S BEHALF!
GIVE ME THIS!
ぱっ
AH!
キリキリ…

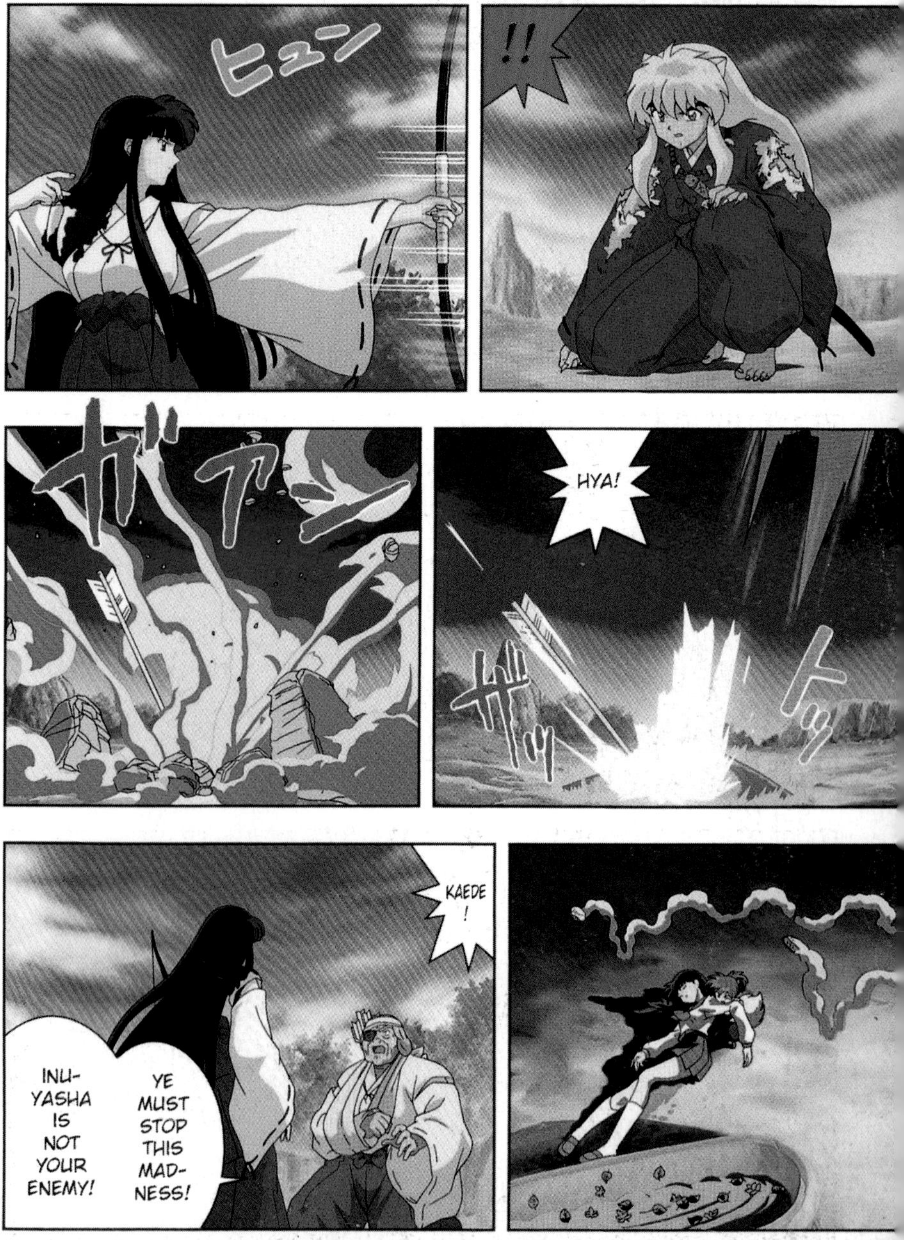
!!
ヒュン
HYA!
ザッ
トッ
ガァーン
KAEDE!
YE MUST STOP THIS MADNESS!
INU-YASHA IS NOT YOUR ENEMY!

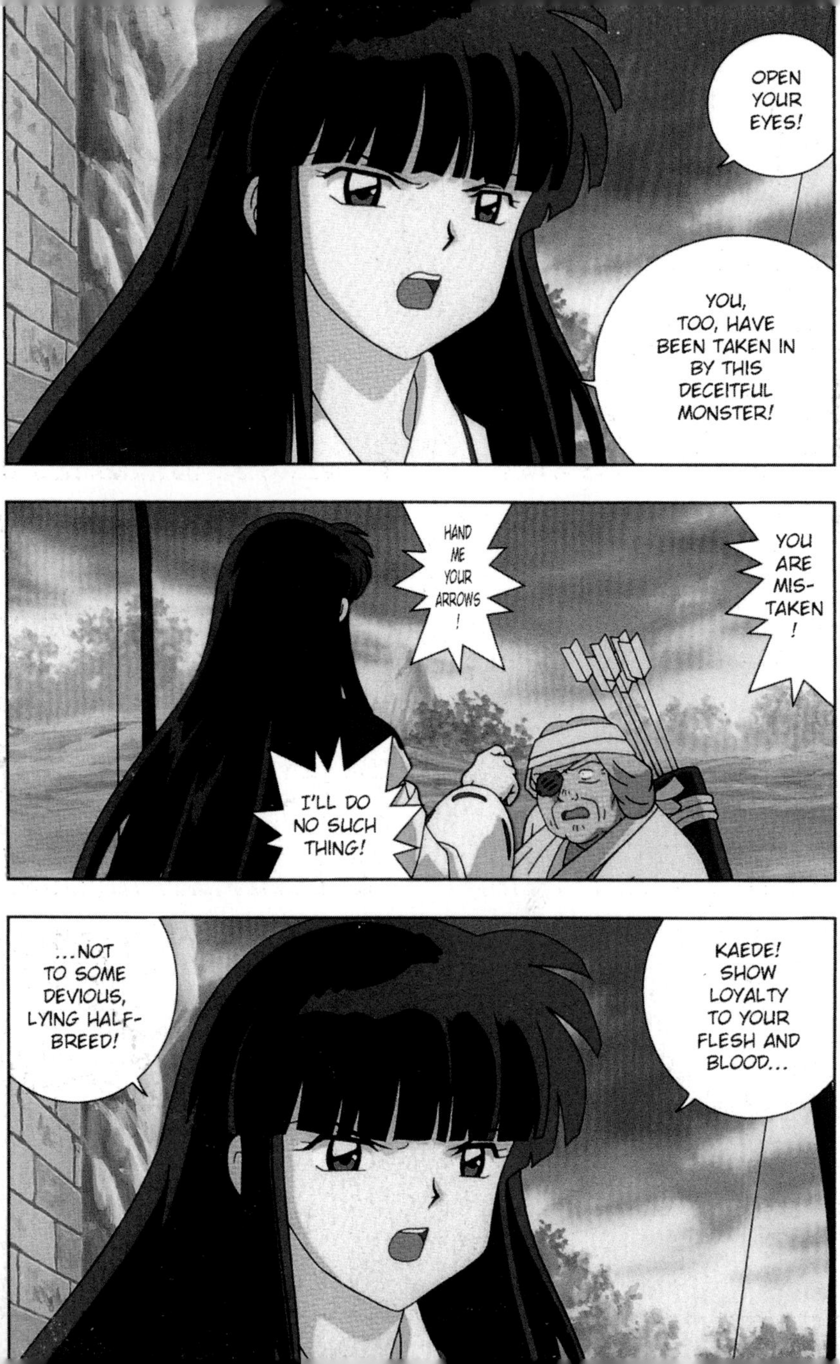
OPEN YOUR EYES!
YOU, TOO, HAVE BEEN TAKEN IN BY THIS DECEITFUL MONSTER!
YOU ARE MIS-TAKEN!
HAND ME YOUR ARROWS!
I'LL DO NO SUCH THING!
KAEDE! SHOW LOYALTY TO YOUR FLESH AND BLOOD...
...NOT TO SOME DEVIOUS, LYING HALF-BREED!

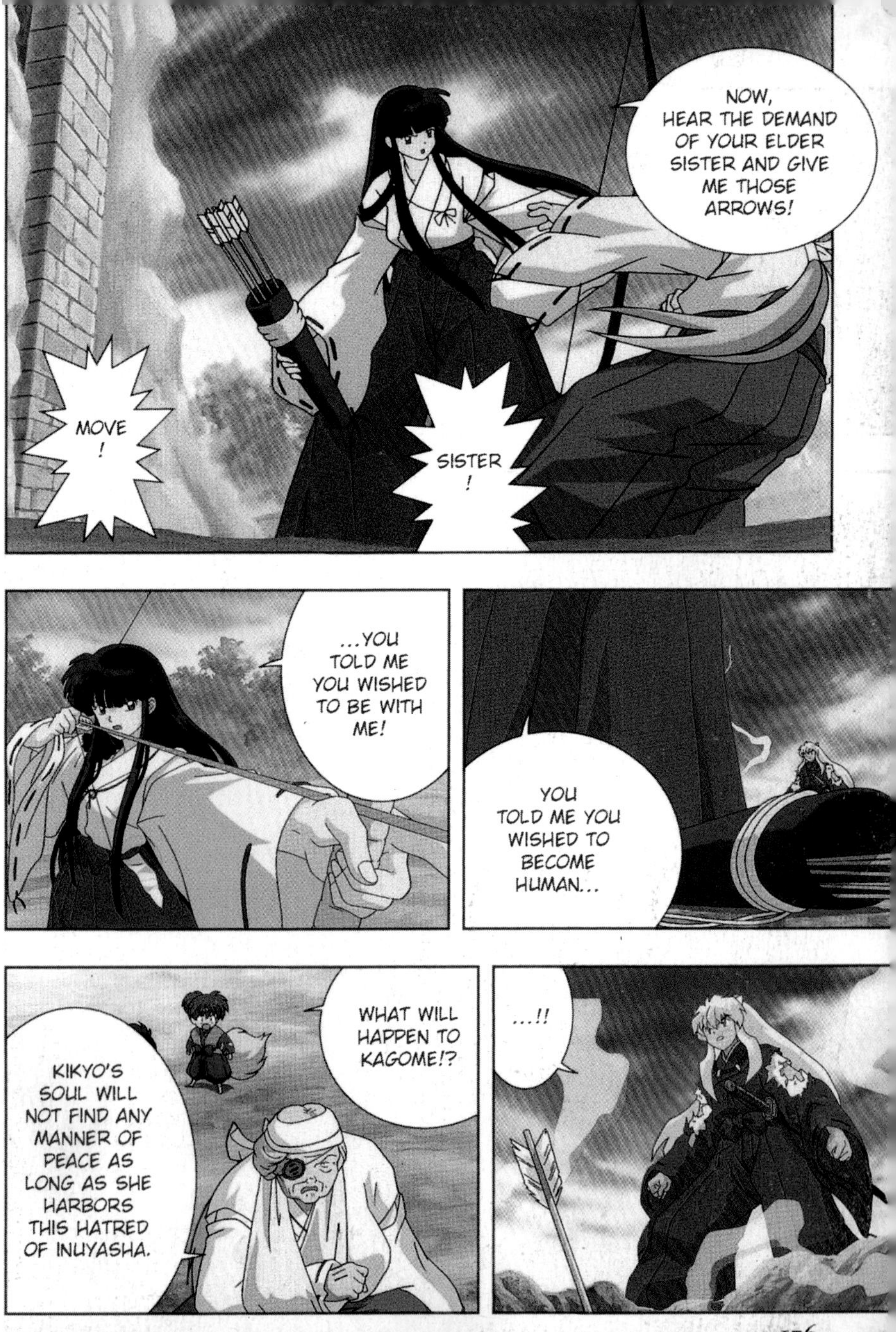
NOW, HEAR THE DEMAND OF YOUR ELDER SISTER AND GIVE ME THOSE ARROWS!
SISTER!
MOVE!
YOU TOLD ME YOU WISHED TO BECOME HUMAN...
...YOU TOLD ME YOU WISHED TO BE WITH ME!
...!!
WHAT WILL HAPPEN TO KAGOME!?
KIKYO'S SOUL WILL NOT FIND ANY MANNER OF PEACE AS LONG AS SHE HARBORS THIS HATRED OF INUYASHA.

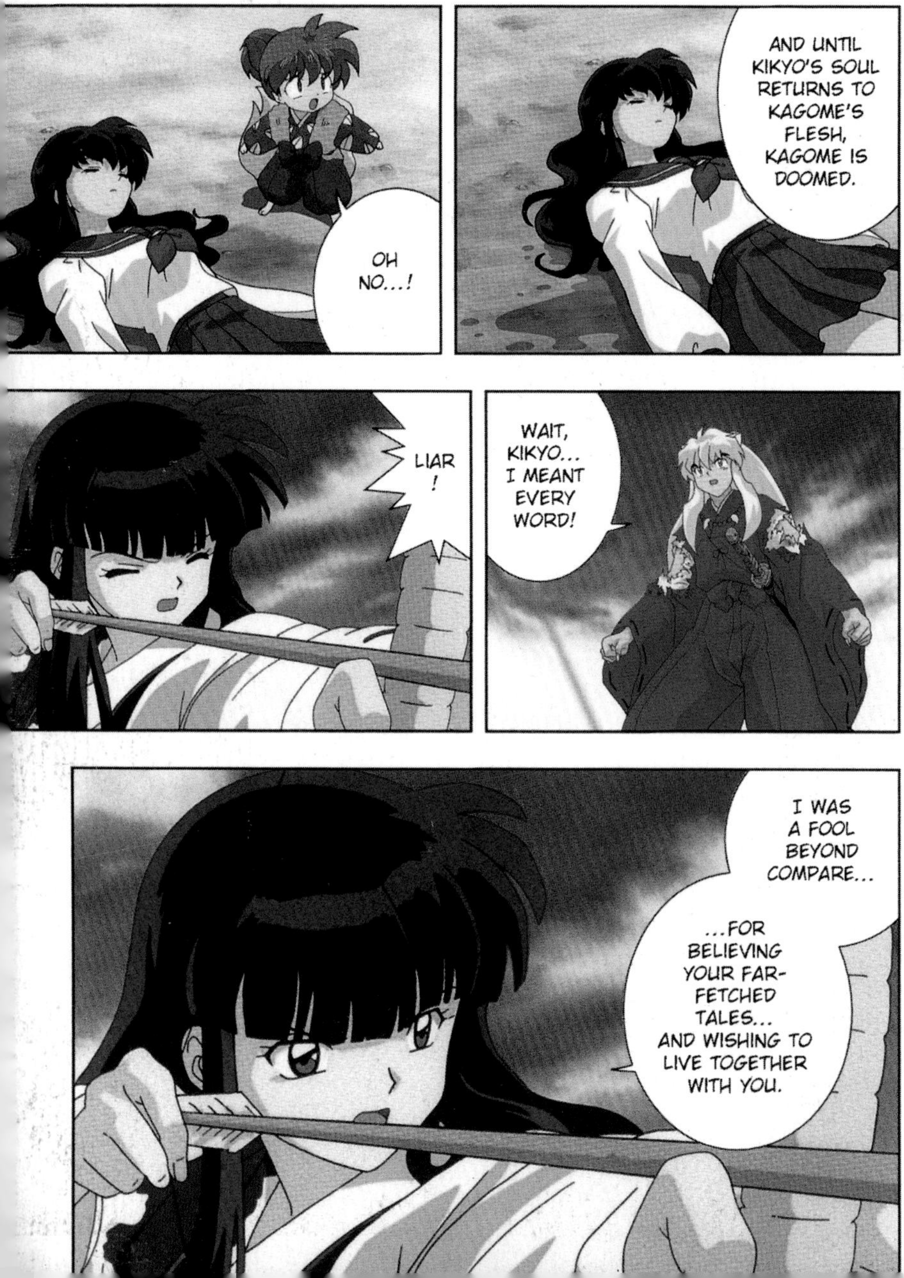
AND UNTIL KIKYO'S SOUL RETURNS TO KAGOME'S FLESH, KAGOME IS DOOMED.
OH NO...!
WAIT, KIKYO... I MEANT EVERY WORD!
LIAR!
I WAS A FOOL BEYOND COMPARE...
...FOR BELIEVING YOUR FAR-FETCHED TALES... AND WISHING TO LIVE TOGETHER WITH YOU.

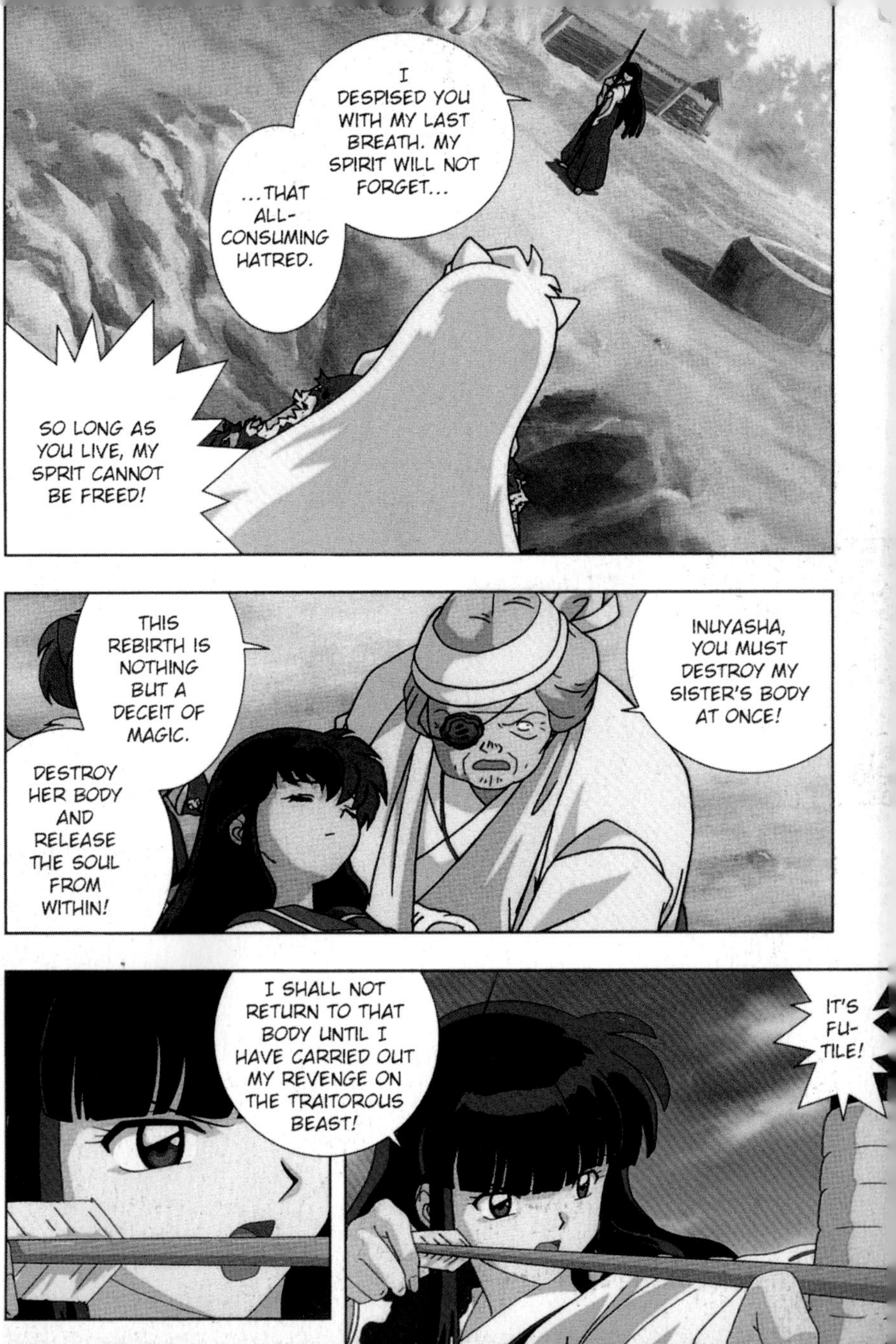
I DESPISED YOU WITH MY LAST BREATH. MY SPIRIT WILL NOT FORGET...
...THAT ALL-CONSUMING HATRED.
SO LONG AS YOU LIVE, MY SPRIT CANNOT BE FREED!
INUYASHA, YOU MUST DESTROY MY SISTER'S BODY AT ONCE!
THIS REBIRTH IS NOTHING BUT A DECEIT OF MAGIC.
DESTROY HER BODY AND RELEASE THE SOUL FROM WITHIN!
IT'S FU-TILE!
I SHALL NOT RETURN TO THAT BODY UNTIL I HAVE CARRIED OUT MY REVENGE ON THE TRAITOROUS BEAST!

INU-YASHA...

YOU ARE THE ONE WHO SHALL DIE!

ギンッ

シュルル...

ばっ

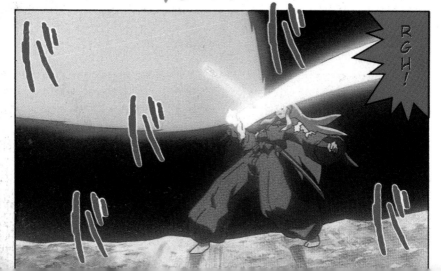

バ

バ

バ

RGH!

バ

バ

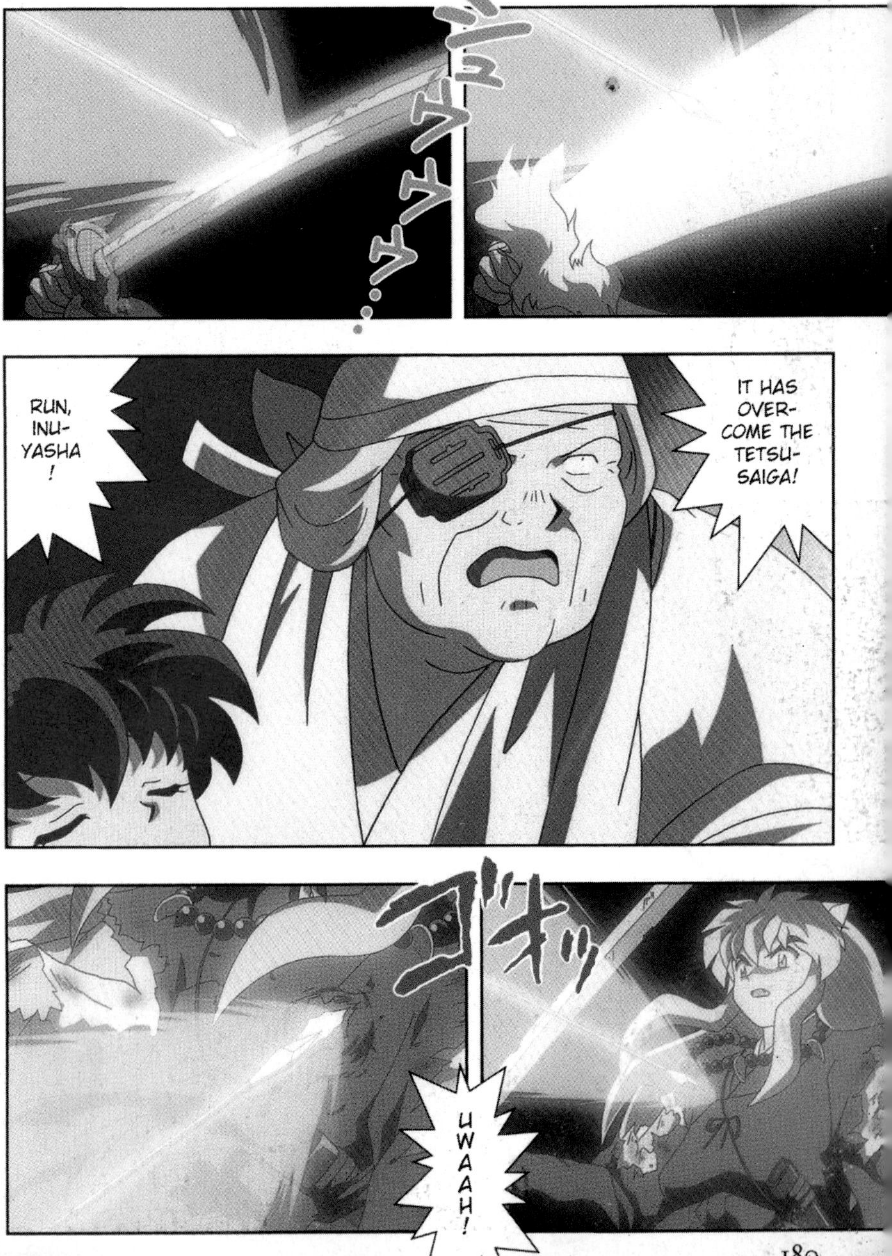
IT HAS OVER-COME THE TETSU-SAIGA!
RUN, INU-YASHA!
ゴキッ
UWAAAH!

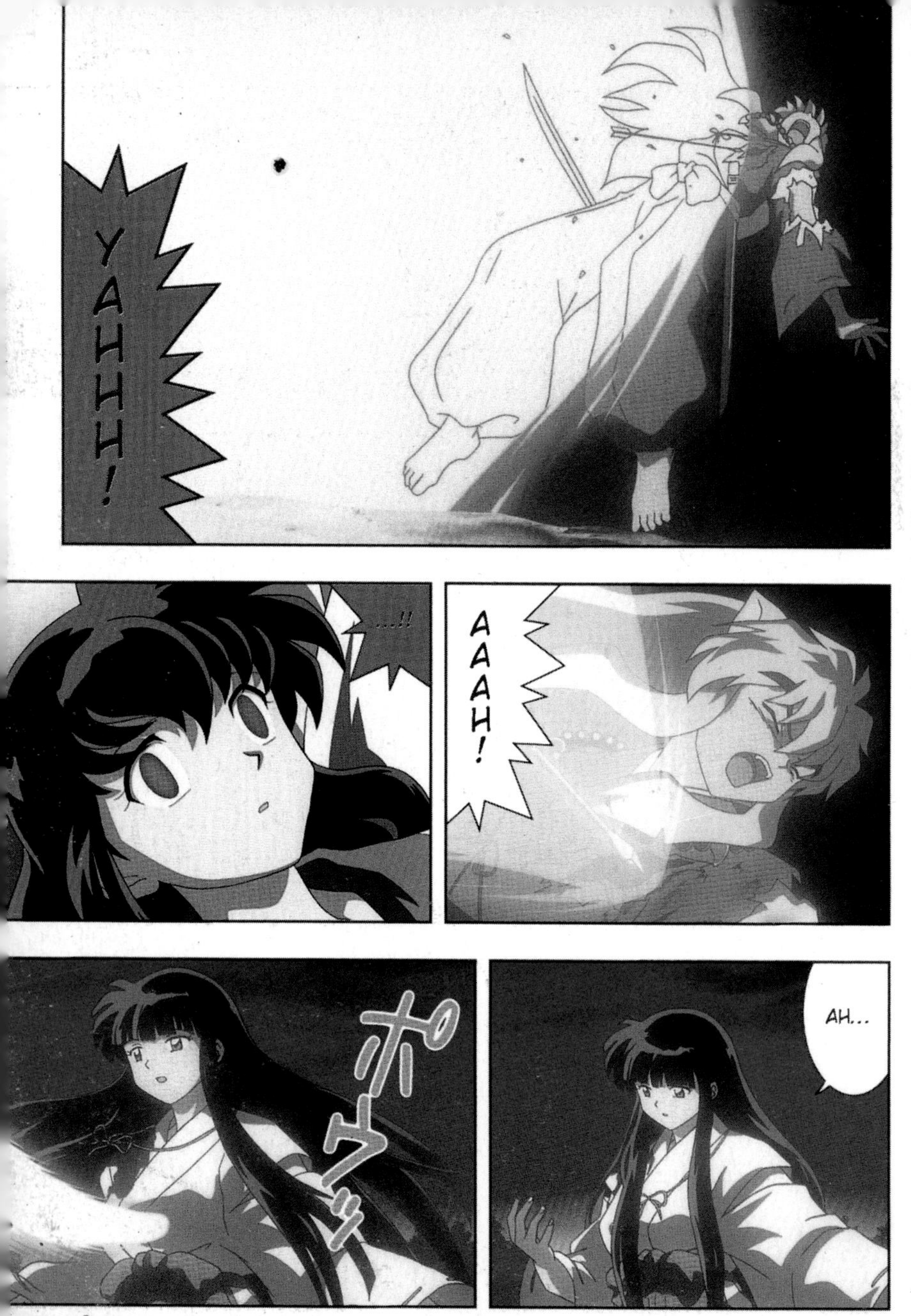
YAHHHH!
AAAAH!
...!!
AH...
ポワッ

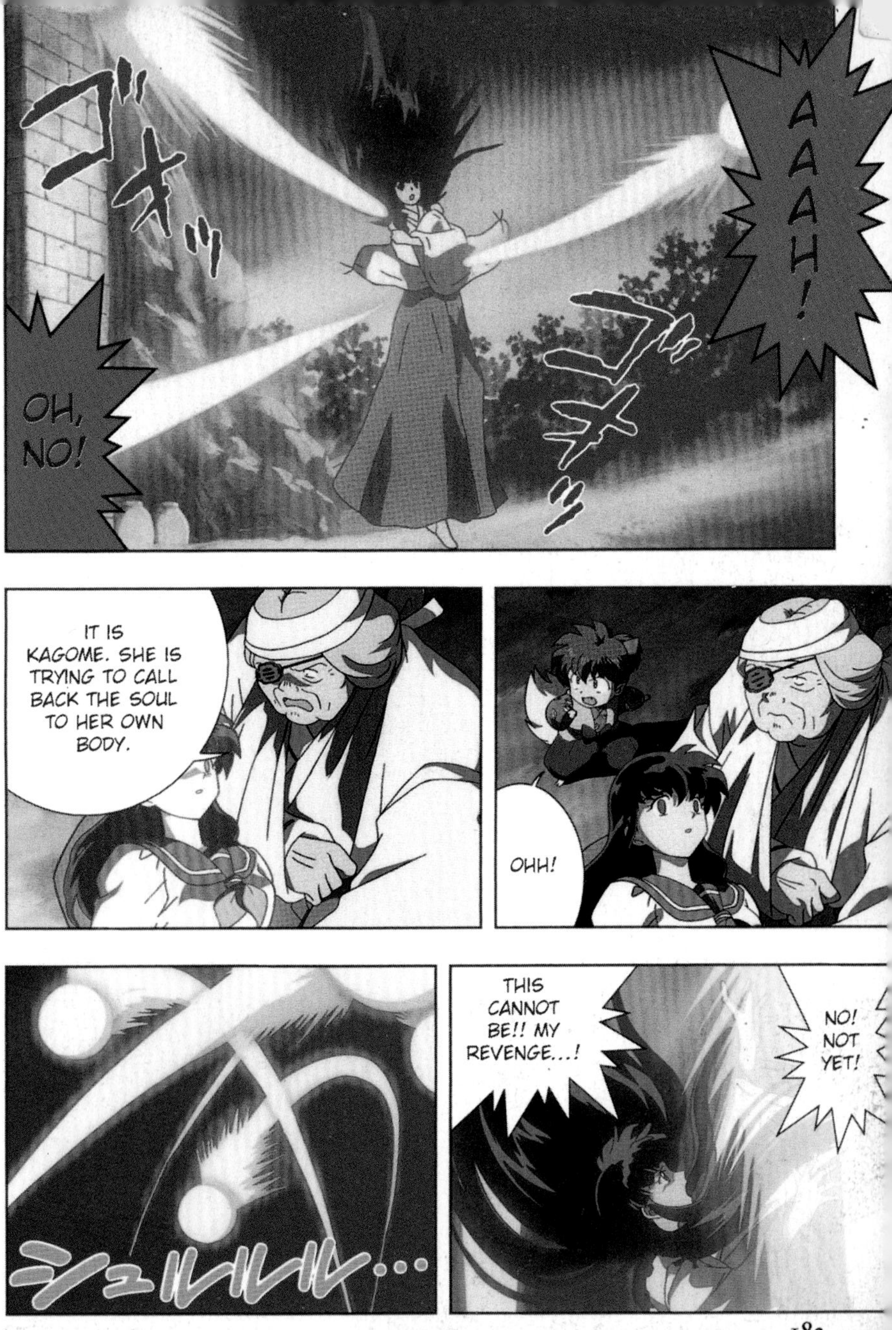
AAAAH!
ゴキッ
ゴキッ
OH, NO!
OHH!
IT IS KAGOME. SHE IS TRYING TO CALL BACK THE SOUL TO HER OWN BODY.
NO! NOT YET!
THIS CANNOT BE!! MY REVENGE...!
シュルルルル...

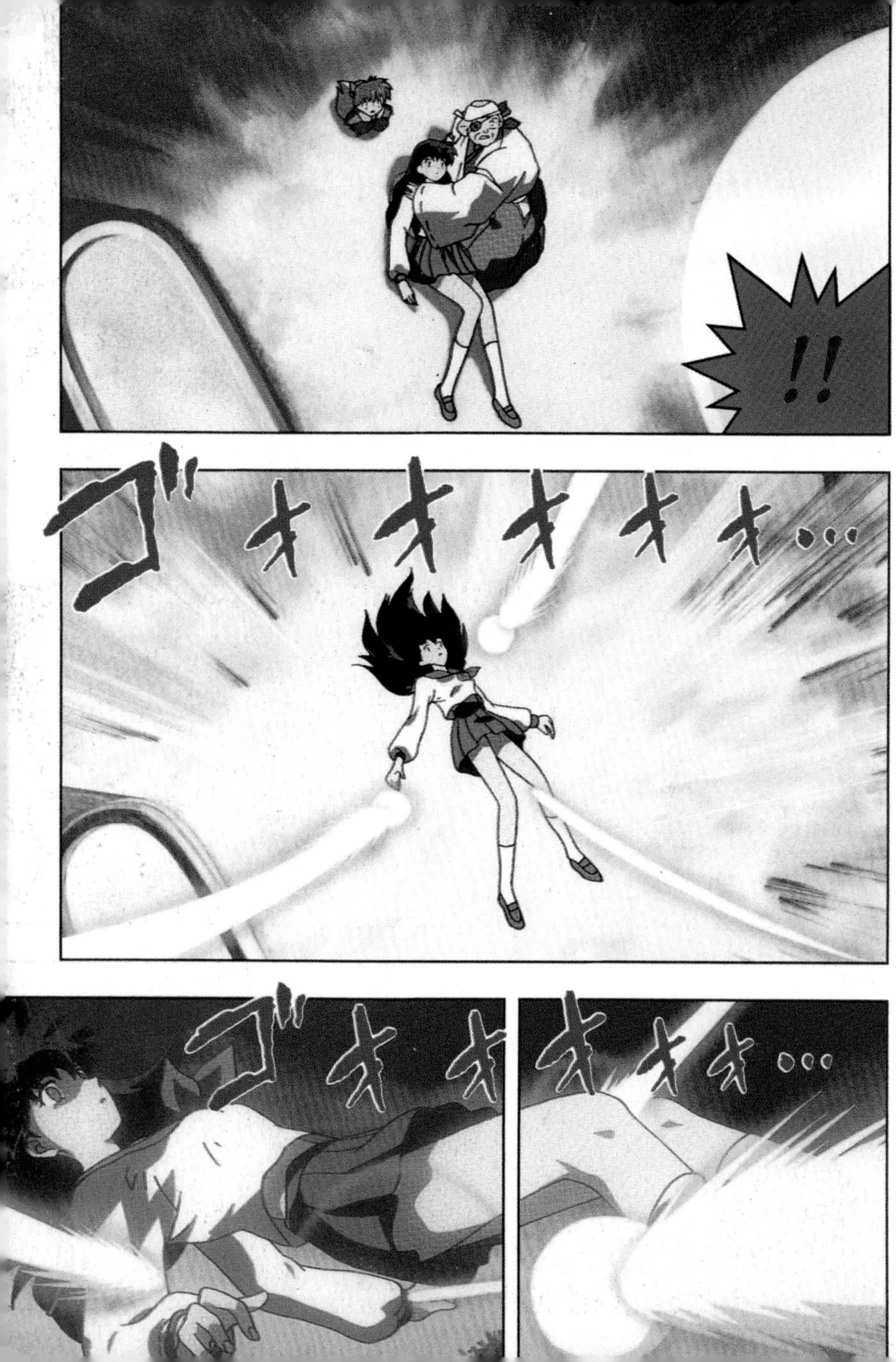
!!
ゴオオオオオ…
ゴオオオオオ…

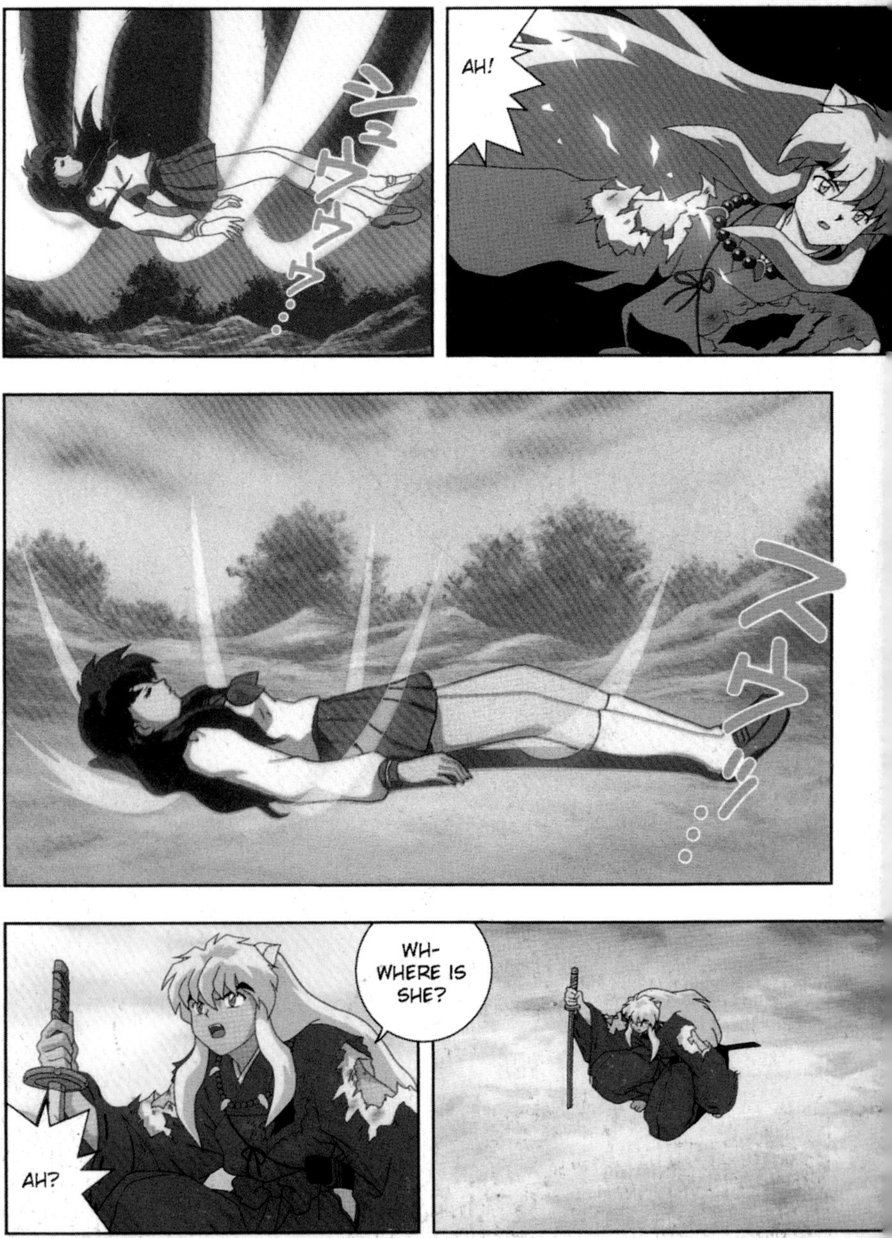
AH!
WH- WHERE IS SHE?
AH?

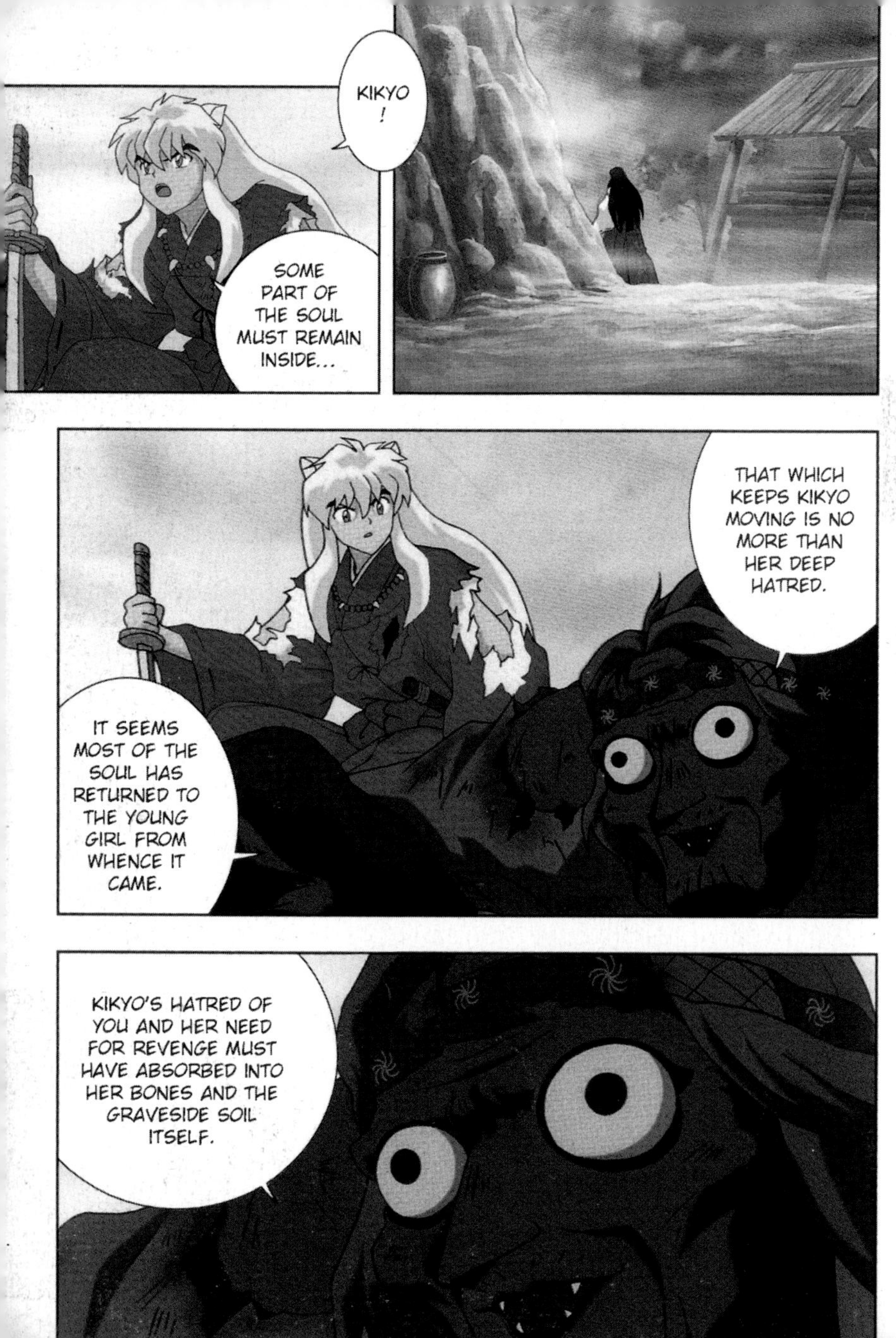
KIKYO !
SOME PART OF THE SOUL MUST REMAIN INSIDE...
THAT WHICH KEEPS KIKYO MOVING IS NO MORE THAN HER DEEP HATRED.
IT SEEMS MOST OF THE SOUL HAS RETURNED TO THE YOUNG GIRL FROM WHENCE IT CAME.
KIKYO'S HATRED OF YOU AND HER NEED FOR REVENGE MUST HAVE ABSORBED INTO HER BONES AND THE GRAVESIDE SOIL ITSELF.

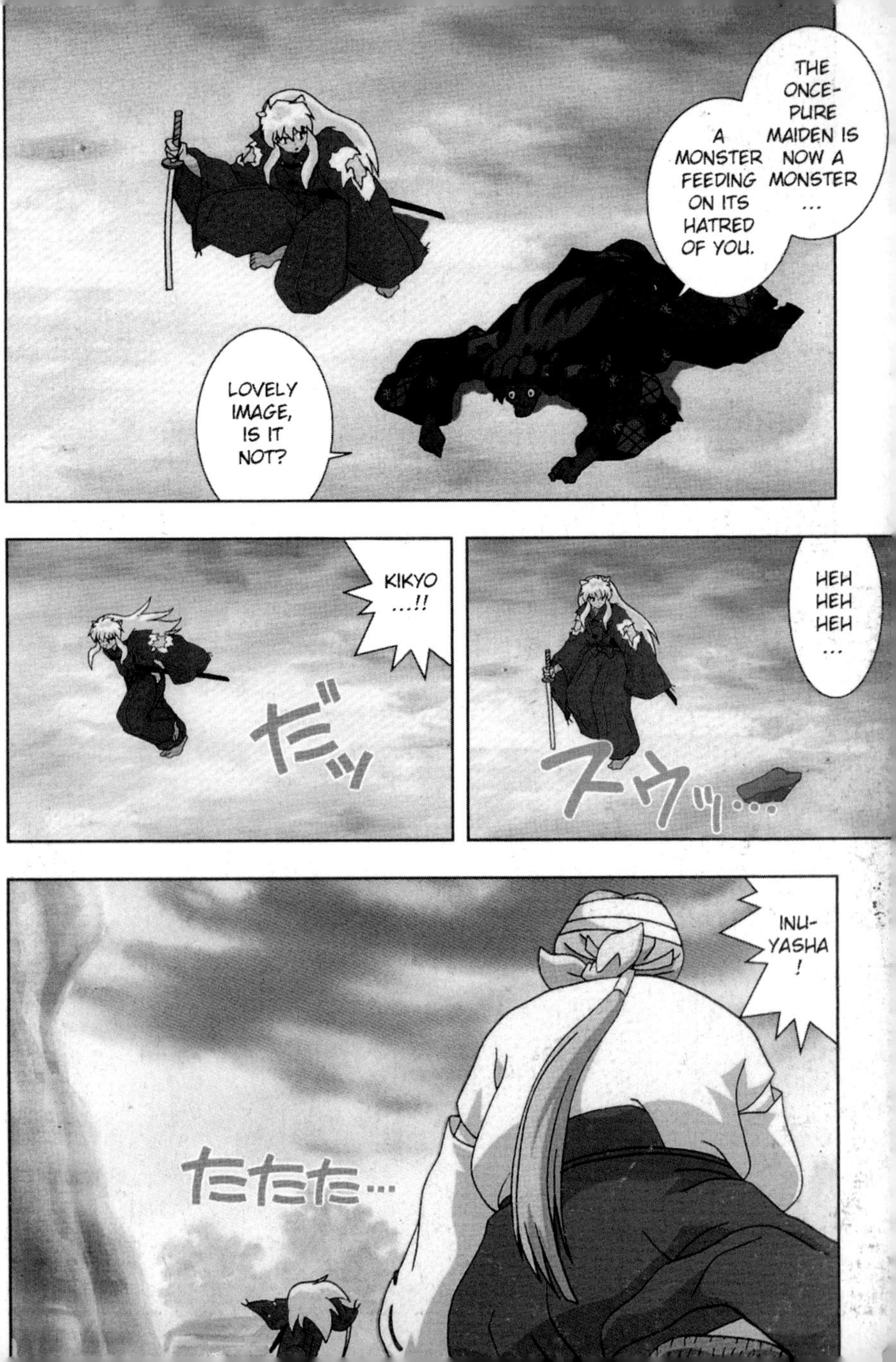
THE ONCE-PURE MAIDEN IS NOW A MONSTER...
A MONSTER FEEDING ON ITS HATRED OF YOU.
LOVELY IMAGE, IS IT NOT?
HEH HEH HEH...
スウッ…
KIKYO...!!
だッ
INU-YASHA!
たたた…

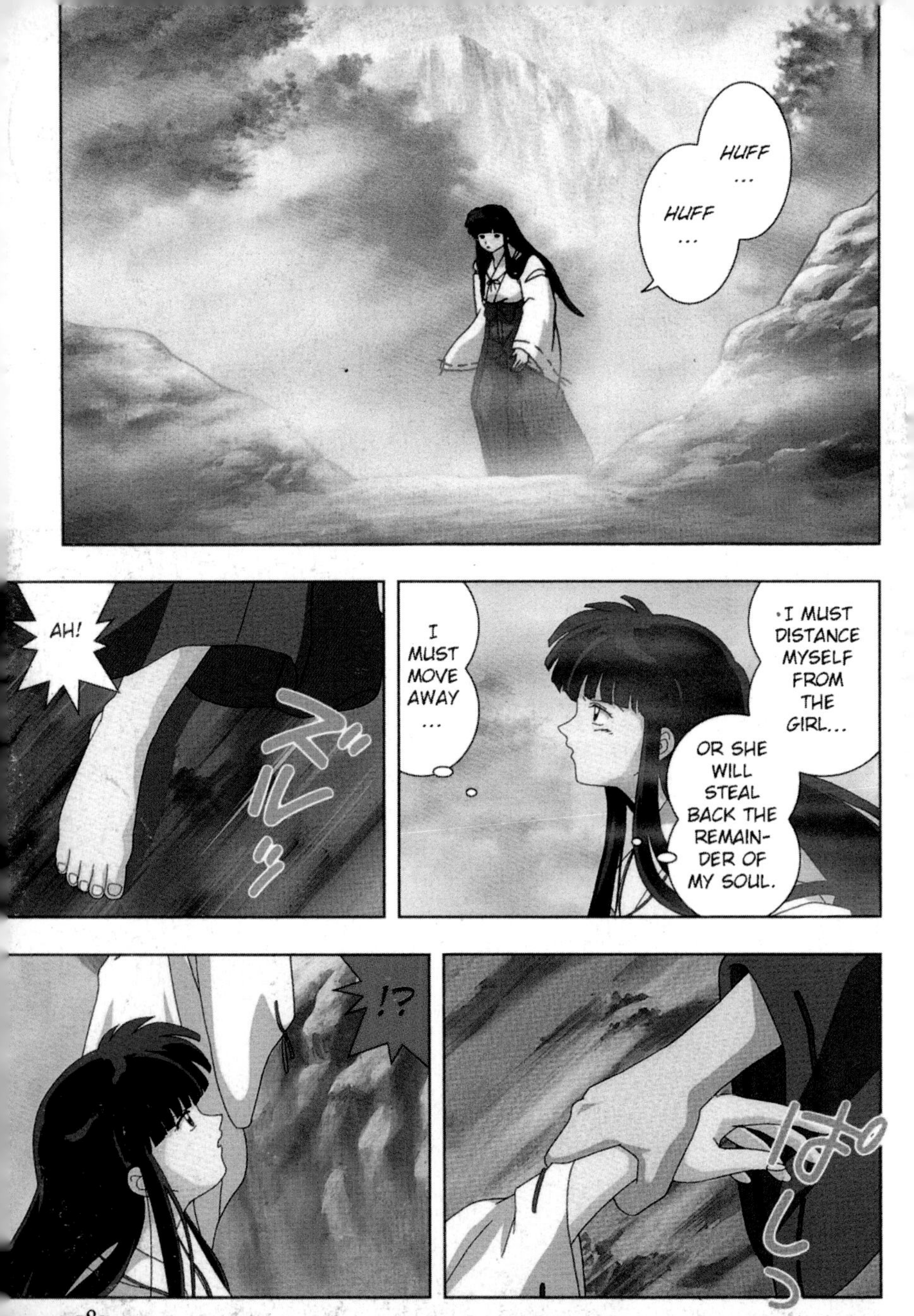
HUFF
...
HUFF
...
I MUST DISTANCE MYSELF FROM THE GIRL...
OR SHE WILL STEAL BACK THE REMAINDER OF MY SOUL.
I MUST MOVE AWAY ...
AH!
ズルッ
はしっ
!?

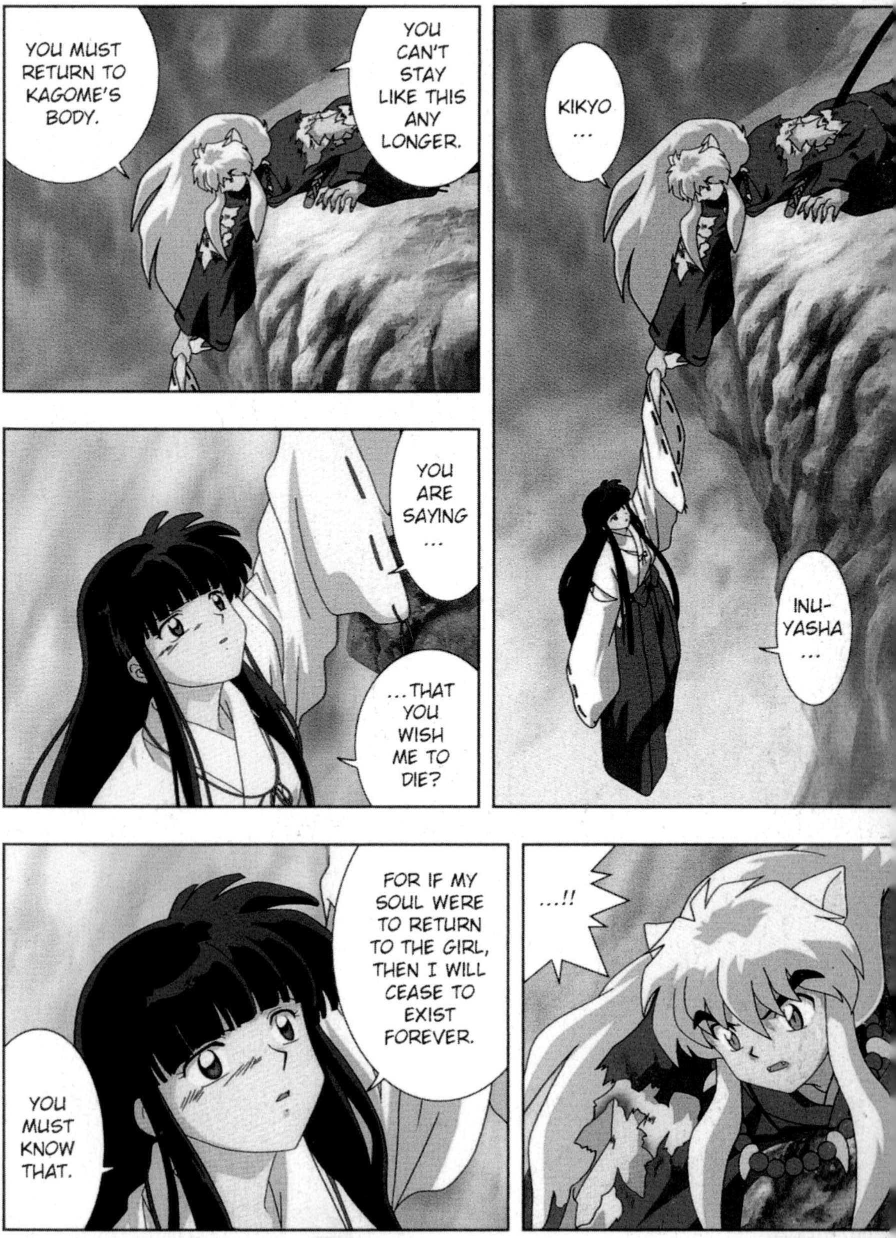
KIKYO ...
INU-YASHA ...
YOU CAN'T STAY LIKE THIS ANY LONGER.
YOU MUST RETURN TO KAGOME'S BODY.
YOU ARE SAYING ...
...THAT YOU WISH ME TO DIE?
...!!
FOR IF MY SOUL WERE TO RETURN TO THE GIRL, THEN I WILL CEASE TO EXIST FOREVER.
YOU MUST KNOW THAT.

IS THAT ...

...WHAT YOU DESIRE, INUYASHA ?

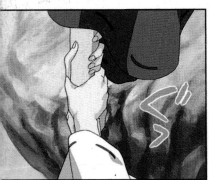

I REFUSE TO DIE ...!

WAH!

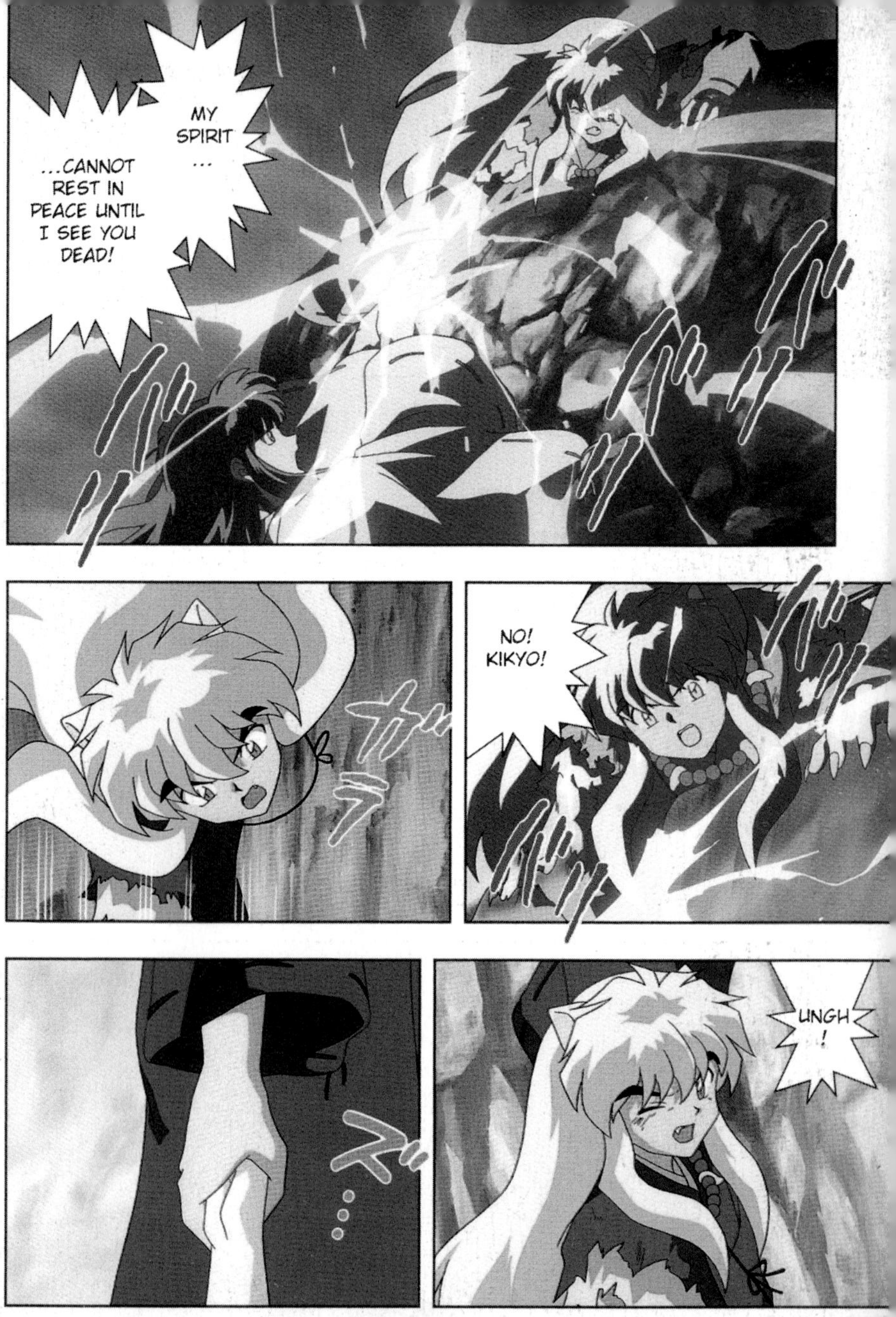
MY SPIRIT ...
...CANNOT REST IN PEACE UNTIL I SEE YOU DEAD!
NO! KIKYO!
UNGH!

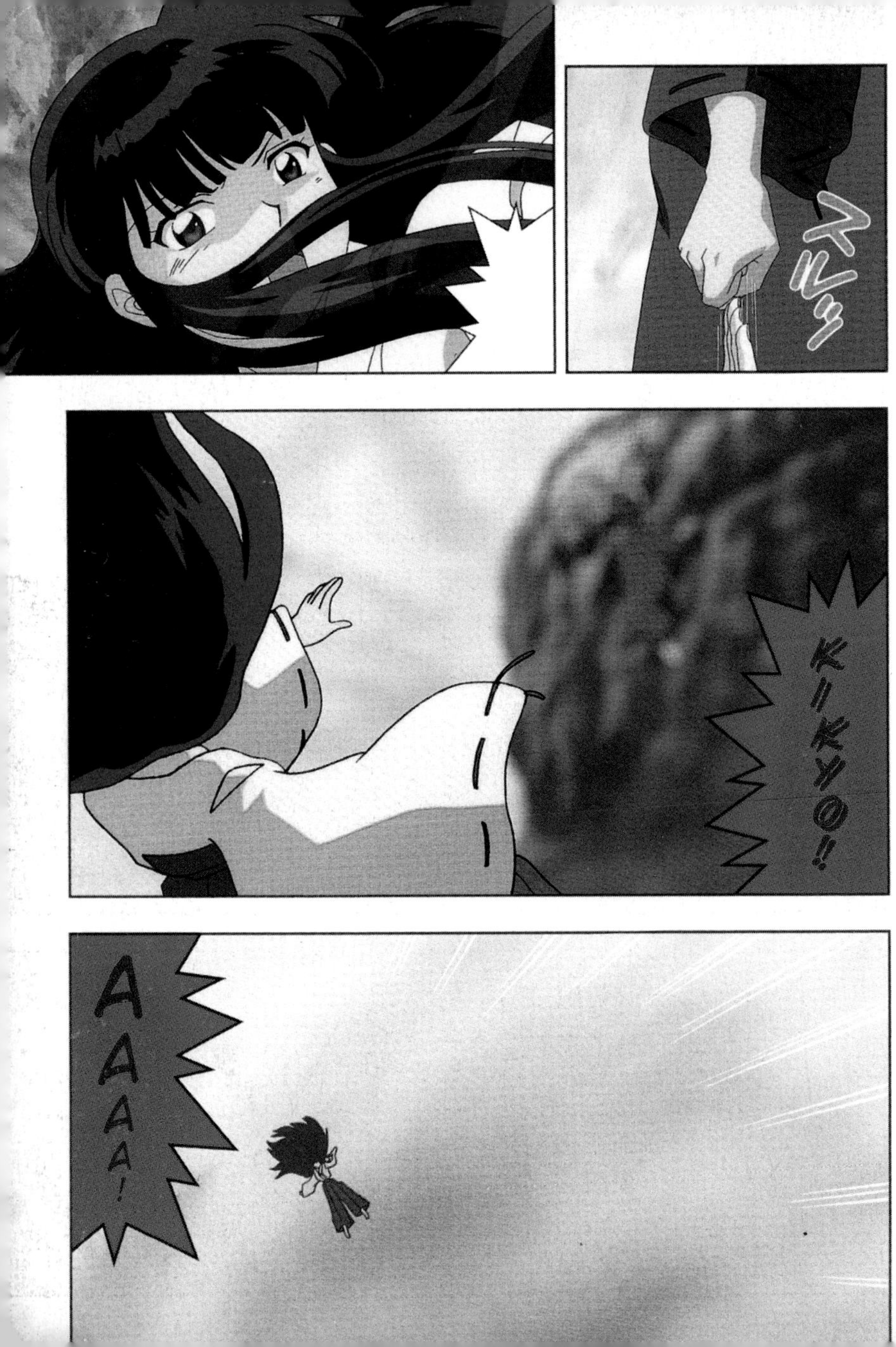
スルッ
KIKYO!!
AAAAA!

WHY DID
IT HAVE TO
COME TO
THIS!?

WHY
...!?

RRGH
!

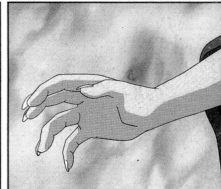

KIKYO HAS
USED HER
SPIRITUAL
POWERS TO
PROTECT THE
SACRED
SHIKON
JEWEL FROM
DEMONS.

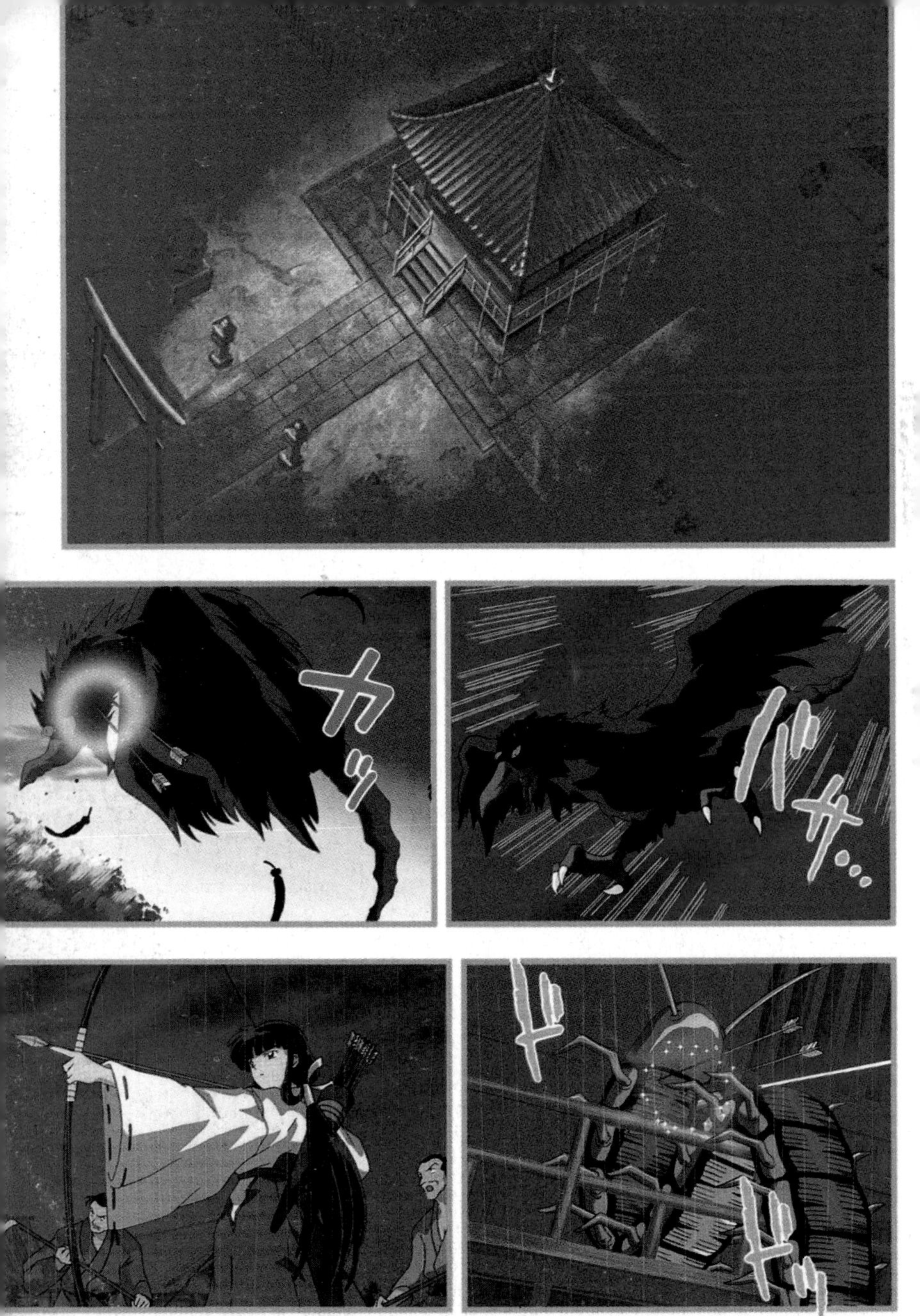
バサ…
カッ
ド
ドドッ

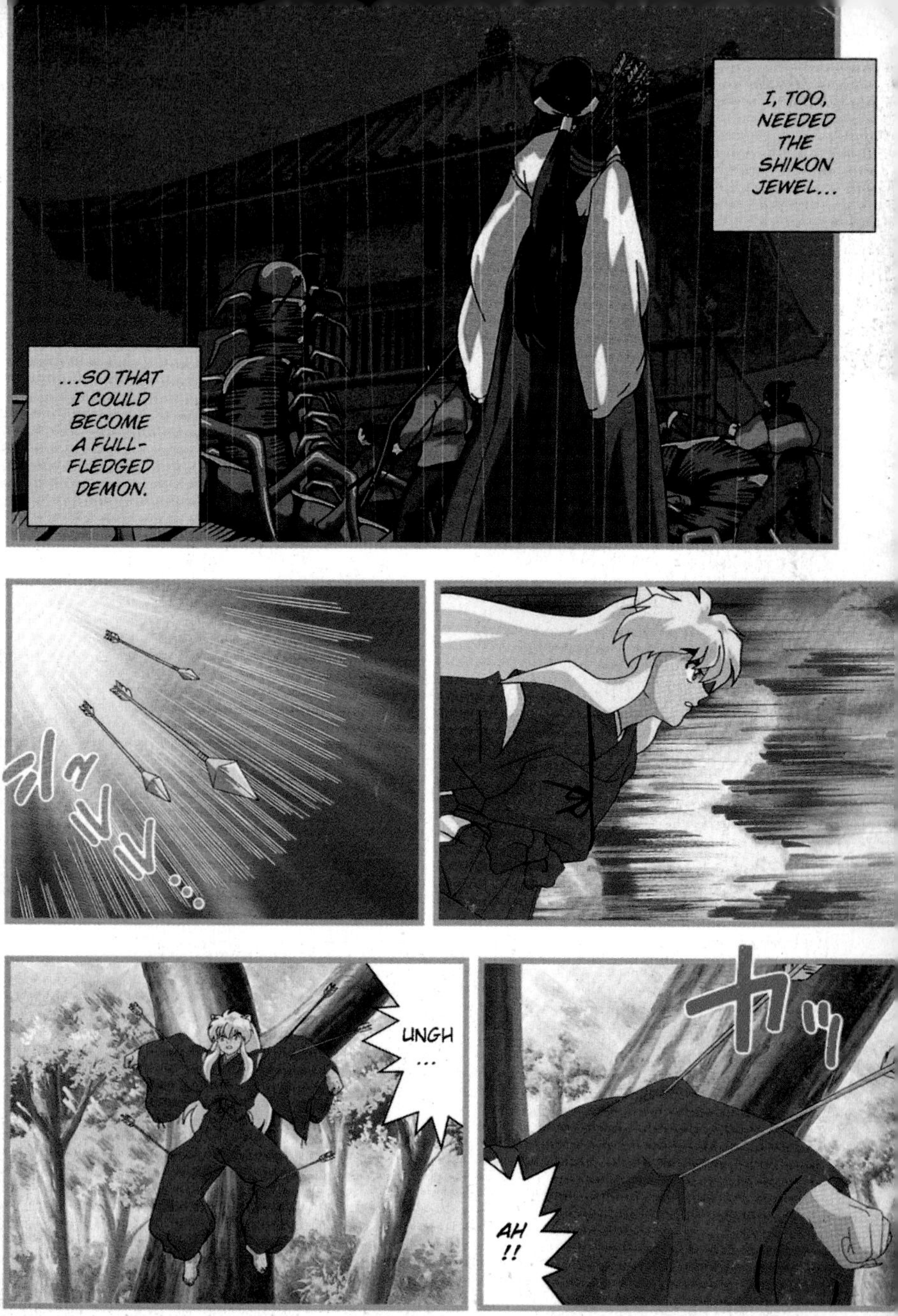
I, TOO, NEEDED THE SHIKON JEWEL...
...SO THAT I COULD BECOME A FULL-FLEDGED DEMON.
カッ
AH !!
UNGH ...

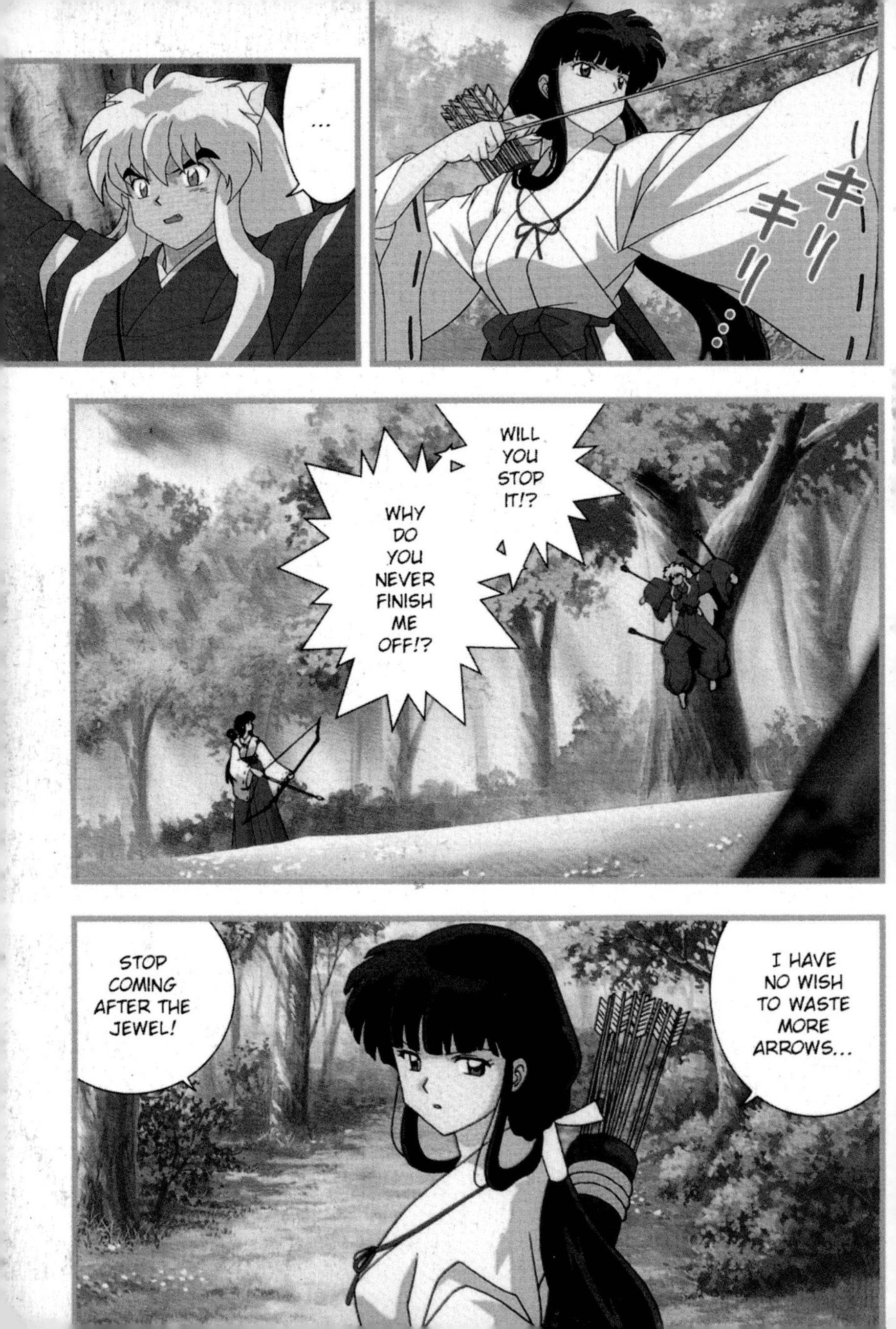
キリキリ
...
WILL YOU STOP IT!?
WHY DO YOU NEVER FINISH ME OFF!?
I HAVE NO WISH TO WASTE MORE ARROWS...
STOP COMING AFTER THE JEWEL!

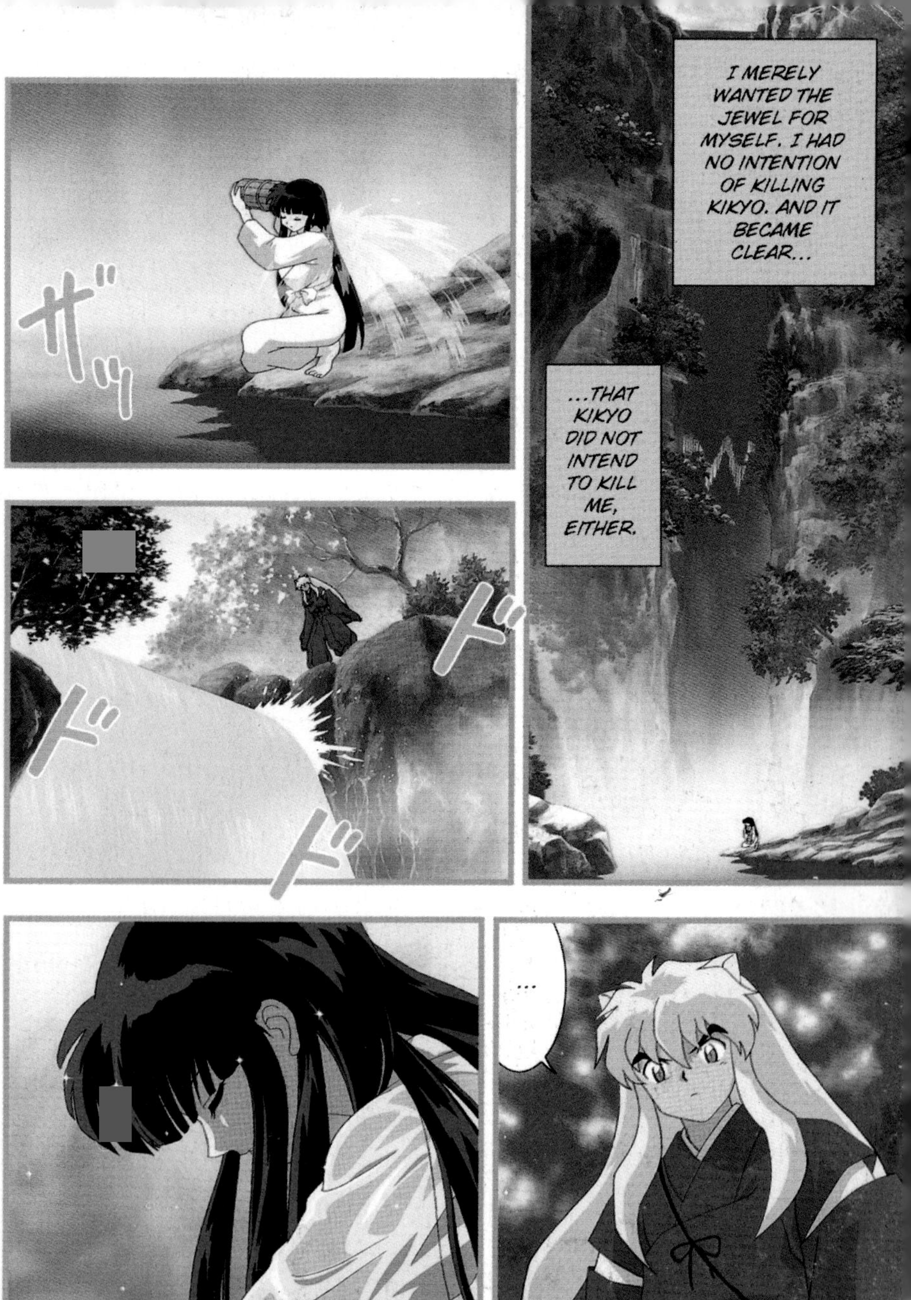
I MERELY WANTED THE JEWEL FOR MYSELF. I HAD NO INTENTION OF KILLING KIKYO. AND IT BECAME CLEAR...
...THAT KIKYO DID NOT INTEND TO KILL ME, EITHER.
ザッ
ドドド
...

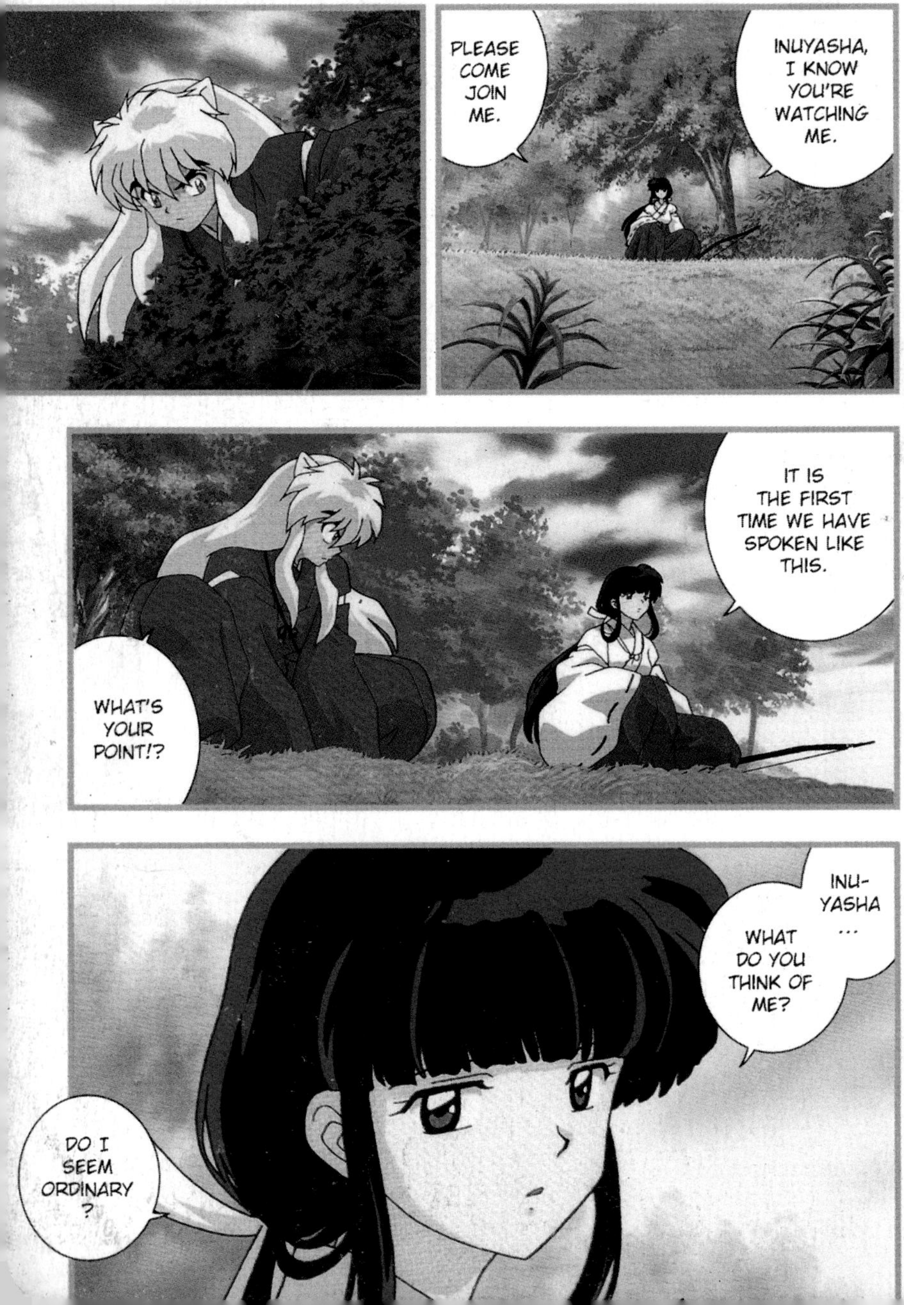
INUYASHA, I KNOW YOU'RE WATCHING ME.
PLEASE COME JOIN ME.
IT IS THE FIRST TIME WE HAVE SPOKEN LIKE THIS.
WHAT'S YOUR POINT!?
INU-YASHA ...
WHAT DO YOU THINK OF ME?
DO I SEEM ORDINARY?

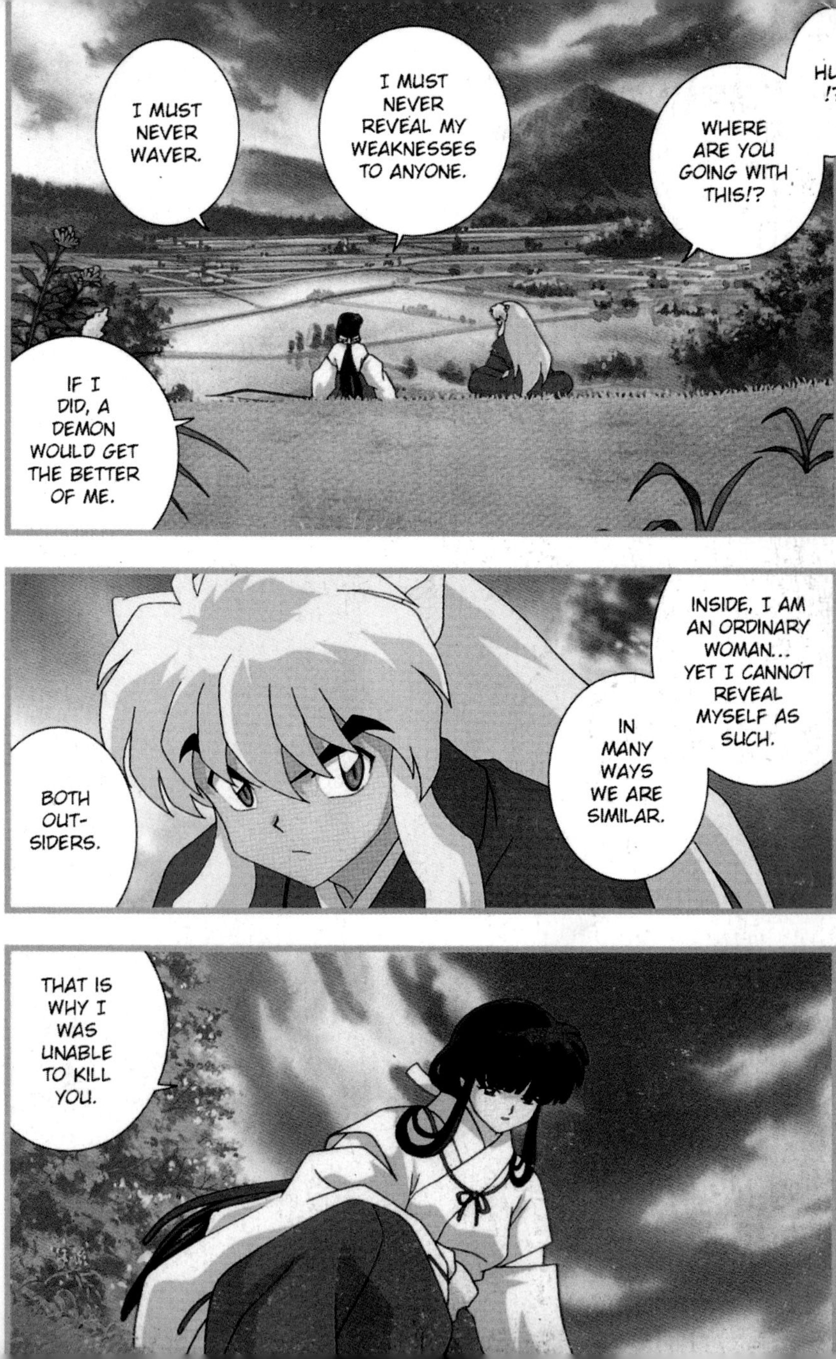
HUH!?
WHERE ARE YOU GOING WITH THIS!?
I MUST NEVER REVEAL MY WEAKNESSES TO ANYONE.
I MUST NEVER WAVER.
IF I DID, A DEMON WOULD GET THE BETTER OF ME.
INSIDE, I AM AN ORDINARY WOMAN... YET I CANNOT REVEAL MYSELF AS SUCH.
IN MANY WAYS WE ARE SIMILAR.
BOTH OUT-SIDERS.
THAT IS WHY I WAS UNABLE TO KILL YOU.

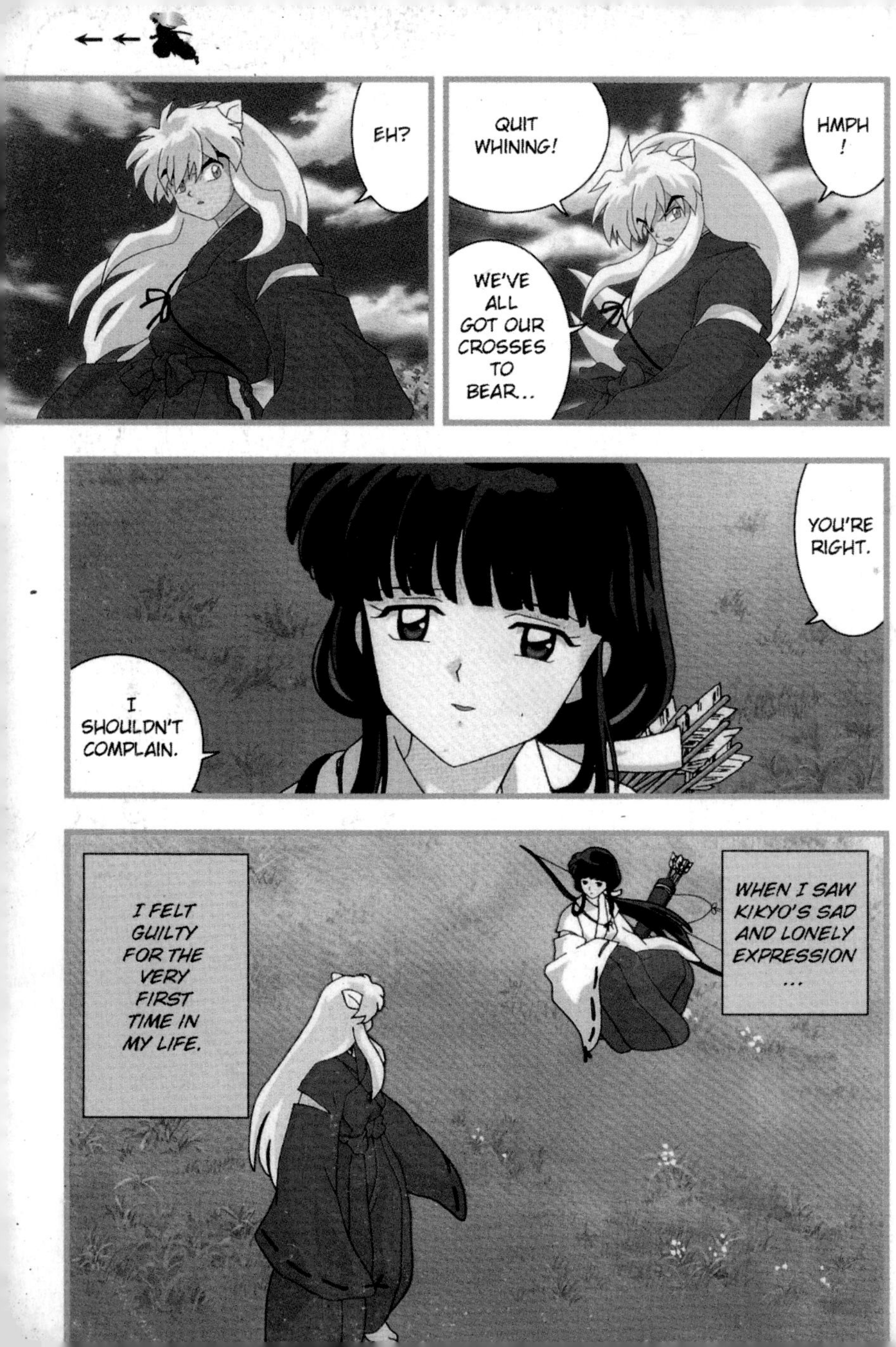
HMPH!
QUIT WHINING!
WE'VE ALL GOT OUR CROSSES TO BEAR..
EH?
YOU'RE RIGHT.
I SHOULDN'T COMPLAIN.
WHEN I SAW KIKYO'S SAD AND LONELY EXPRESSION...
I FELT GUILTY FOR THE VERY FIRST TIME IN MY LIFE.

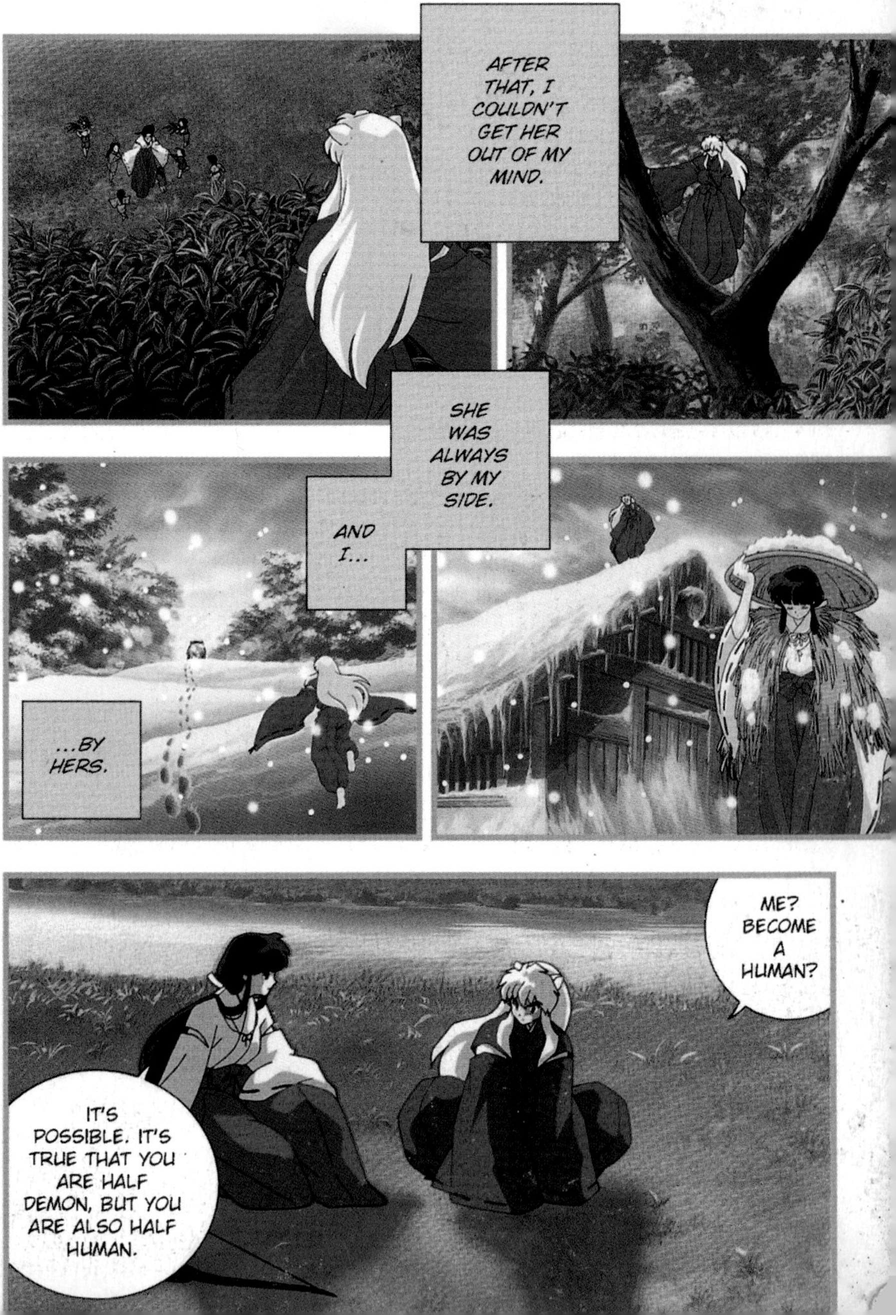
AFTER THAT, I COULDN'T GET HER OUT OF MY MIND.
SHE WAS ALWAYS BY MY SIDE.
AND I...
...BY HERS.
ME? BECOME A HUMAN?
IT'S POSSIBLE. IT'S TRUE THAT YOU ARE HALF DEMON, BUT YOU ARE ALSO HALF HUMAN.

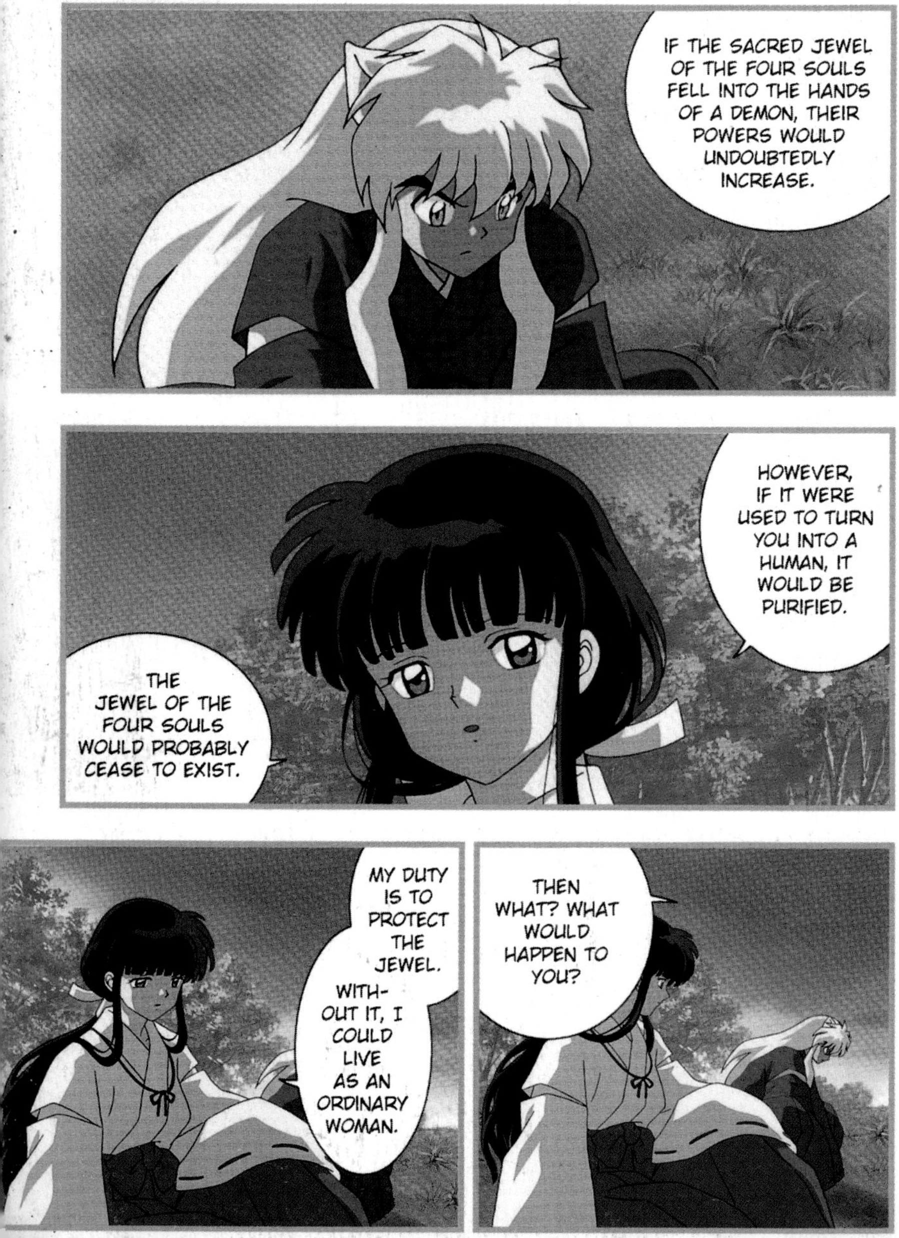
IF THE SACRED JEWEL OF THE FOUR SOULS FELL INTO THE HANDS OF A DEMON, THEIR POWERS WOULD UNDOUBTEDLY INCREASE.
HOWEVER, IF IT WERE USED TO TURN YOU INTO A HUMAN, IT WOULD BE PURIFIED.
THE JEWEL OF THE FOUR SOULS WOULD PROBABLY CEASE TO EXIST.
THEN WHAT? WHAT WOULD HAPPEN TO YOU?
MY DUTY IS TO PROTECT THE JEWEL.
WITH-OUT IT, I COULD LIVE AS AN ORDINARY WOMAN.

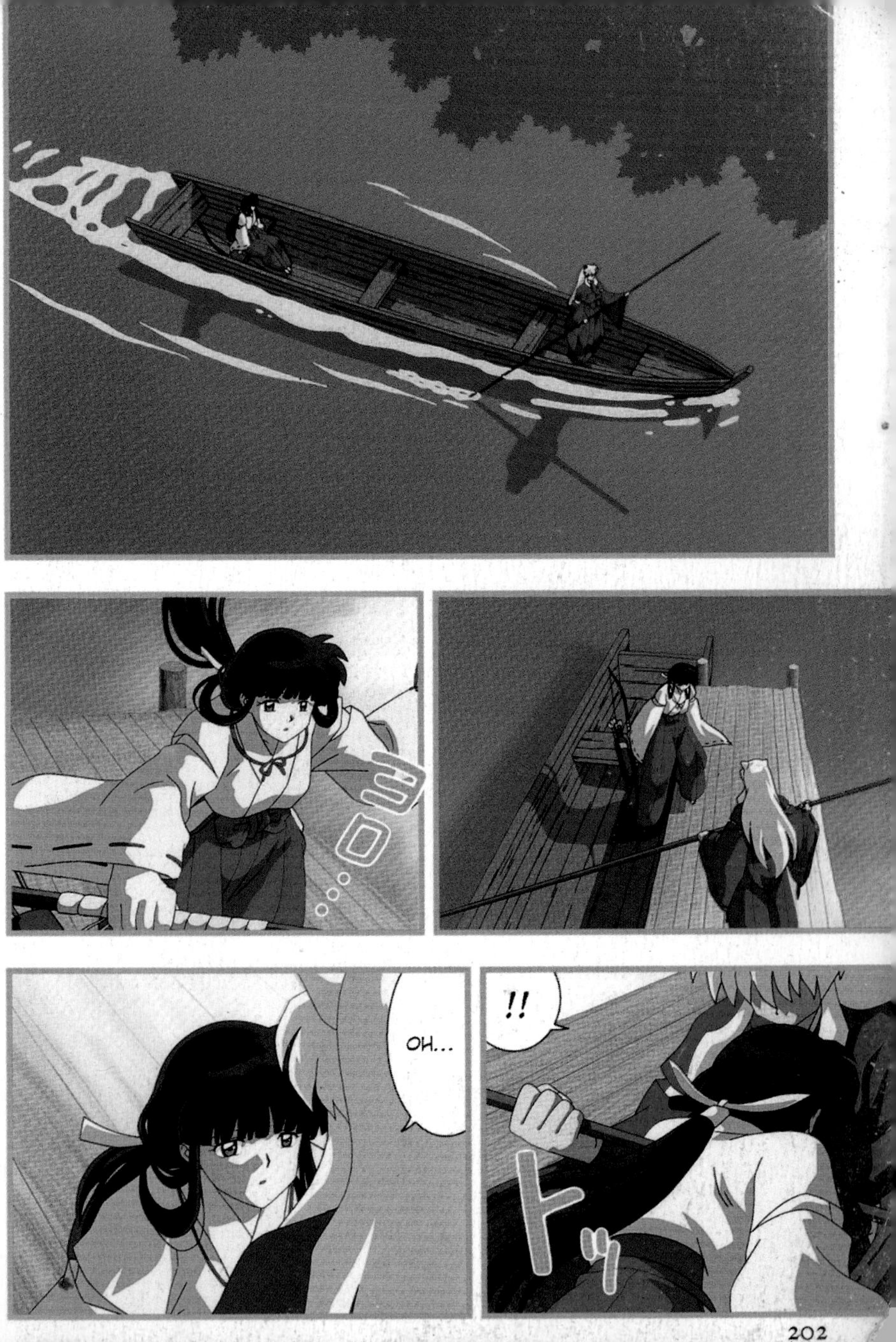
ヨロ
!!
トッ
OH...

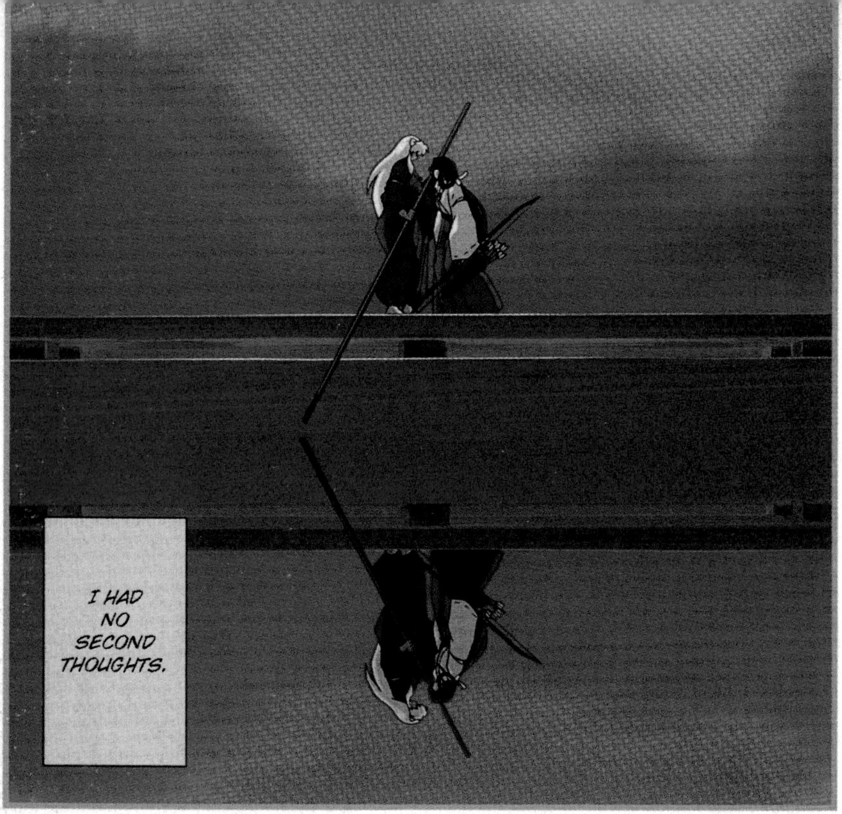
I HAD NO SECOND THOUGHTS.
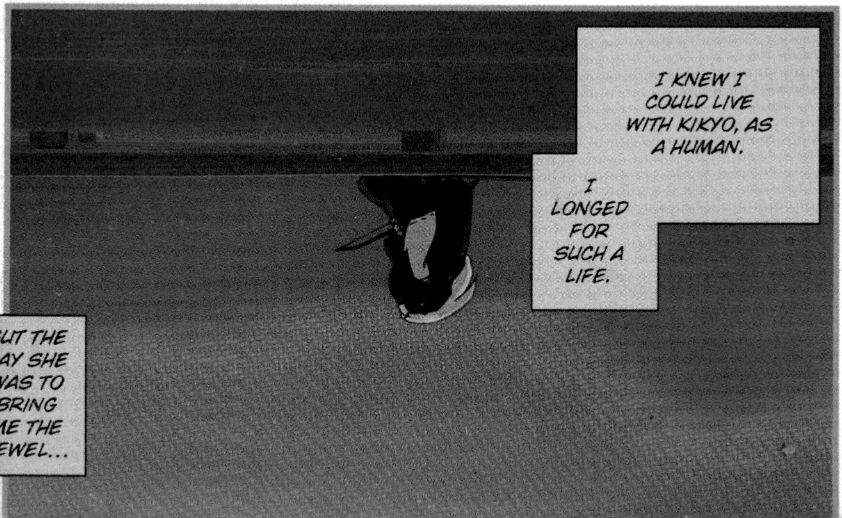
I KNEW I COULD LIVE WITH KIKYO, AS A HUMAN.
I LONGED FOR SUCH A LIFE.
BUT THE DAY SHE WAS TO BRING ME THE JEWEL...

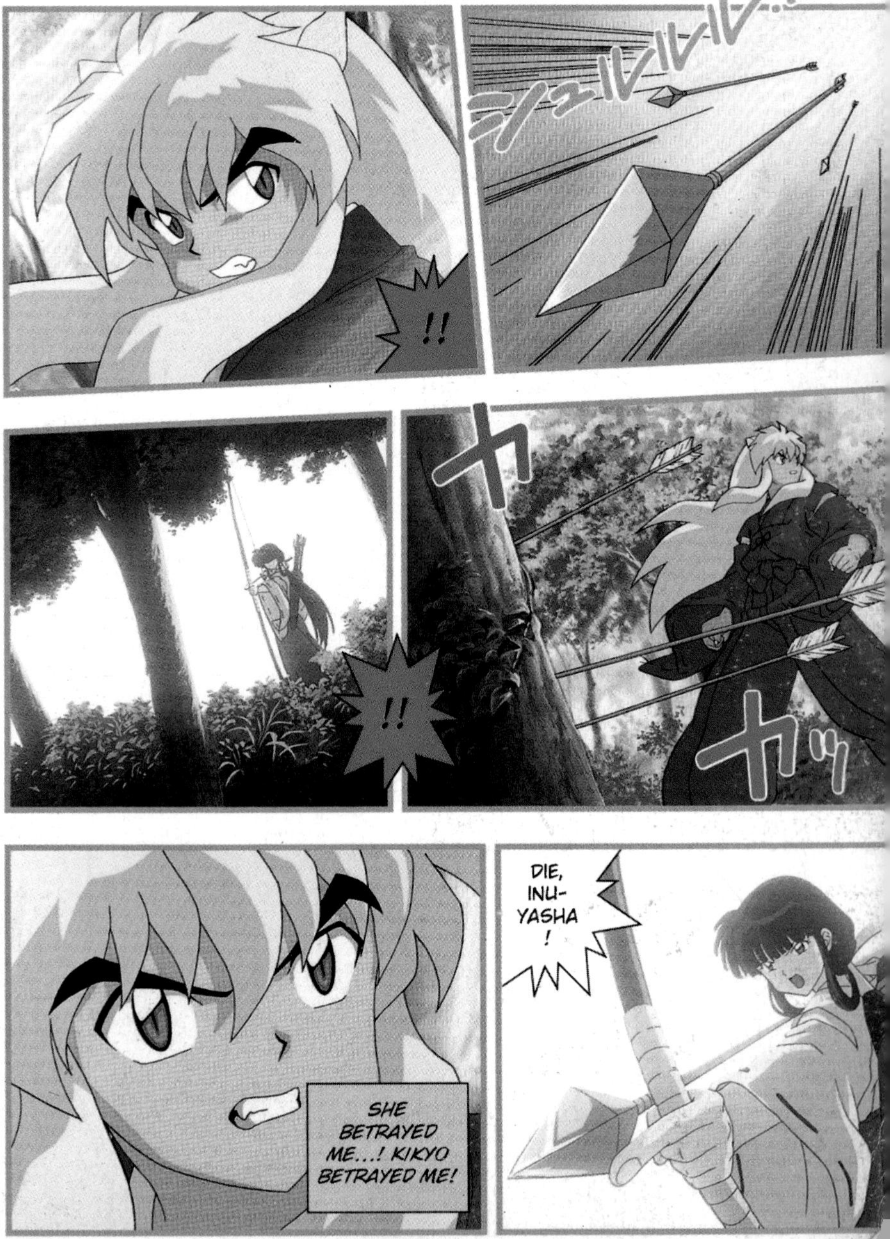
シュルルルル…
!!
カ
カッ
!!
DIE, INU-YASHA!
SHE BETRAYED ME...! KIKYO BETRAYED ME!

172.1 FX: Bari bari bari (crackling of magic)

172.2 FX: Bari bari (crackle crackle)

172.3 FX: Bari (crackle)

172.4 FX: Za (Inuyasha collapses)

173.3 FX: Ba (sudden grab)

173.4 FX: Kiri kiri… (bow and string creaking)

174.2 FX: Hyun (arrow twangs)

174.3 FX: Toh (Inuyasha jumps)

174.3 FX: Za (arrow strikes)

174.4 FX: Gaan (melting)

179.1 FX: Hyu (arrow released from bow)

179.2 FX: Shuru… (arrow flies)

179.3 FX: Ba (arrow heads for Tetsusaiga)

179.4 FX: Gin (arrow hits Tetsusaiga)

179.5 FX: Ba ba ba ba ba (pow pow pow)

180.1/2 FX: Shuuuu… (arrow clashing against Tetsusaiga)

180.4 FX: Goh (arrow moves towards chest)

181.5 FX: Pohh (soul swooshing out of Kikyo)

182.1 FX: Gohh gohh (soul balls swooshing out of Kikyo's body)

182.5 FX: Shurururu… (soul balls whizzing through air)

183.2 FX: Gohhhhhh… (soul balls swoosh down on Kagome)

183.3/4 FX: Gohhhhhh… (soul balls swoosh at Kagome)

184.2 FX: Shuuuu… (soul balls enter Kagome)

184.3 FX: Su… (Kagome sets down)

186.2 FX: Suu… (Urasue dissolves into dust)

186.3 FX: Da (Inuyasha takes off after Kikyo)

186.4 FX: Ta ta ta… (Inuyasha runs)

187.3 FX: Zuru (Kikyo slips)

187.4 FX: Pashi (Inuyasha grabs Kikyo)

189.3 FX: Gu (Inuyasha's grip slips)

189.4 FX: Bari bari bari (magic crackling)

190.1 FX: Bari bari bari (crackling)

190.2 FX: Bari bari (crackling)

190.3 FX: Gara (Inuyasha slowly loses grip)

190.5 FX: Zu… (Inuyasha's grip slips)

191.1 FX: Zuru (Inyasha's grip slips more)

193.2 FX: Basa… (flap of wings)

193.3 FX: Ka! (crow calling)

193.4 FX: Doh doh (arrows thunk into big nasty bug)

194.3 FX: Shururu… (arrows flying)

194.4 FX: Ka (arrow hits)

195.1 FX: Kiri kiri… (bow and arrow creaking)

196.2 FX: Za (water being poured)

196.3 FX: Doh doh doh (sound of water going over waterfall)

202.3 FX: Yoro (Kikyo is unsteady on her feet)

202.4 FX: Toh (Kikyo falls into Inuyasha's chest)

204.1 FX: Shurururu… (arrow flies)

204.3 FX: Ka ka (arrows thunk into tree)

206.2 FX: Doh (Inuyasha drops to his knees)

206.3 FX: Za (Inuyasha does a face plant)

126.3 FX: Ba (strike)

126.4 FX: Dosa (Kikyo falls as Urasue flings her away)

128.4 FX: Pishi pishi (clay cracking)

128.5 FX: Pa—n (clay cracks and breaks off)

130.1 FX: Ta ta ta… (running)

130.2 FX: Zuba (smash)

130.3 FX: Zuba (smash)

130.4 FX: Pari—n (clay breaks)

131.3 FX: Gui (hand squeezing herb)

134.1 FX: Zuba (slices bridge)

134.4 FX: Goh (Urasue flying/leaping)

134.5 FX: Ba (Urasue snatches Kaome in midair)

135.4 FX: Ga (scythe gets close to Kagome's throat)

**Chapter 15:**

**Return of the Tragic Priestess Kikyo**

138.2 FX: Za za za (slipping)

138.3 FX: Goh (tree appears)

138.4 FX: Za (Inuyasha falls in tree)

138.5 FX: Toh (Inuyasha jumps)

139.1 FX: Doh doh doh (Soldiers bouncing off cliff sides)

139.3 FX: Doh (Inuyasha and soldiers land)

140.1 FX: Goh (huge leaf falling)

140.2 FX: Zuuun (leaf lands on Inuyasha)

144.4 FX: Su… (Kikyo's footstep)

148.1 FX: Za (jump)

148.2 FX: Toh te te te… (Shippo scrambling up)

148.3 FX: Suta (Inuyasha lands)

149.2 FX: Za (jump)

149.3 FX: Za Za (jump, jump)

149.5 FX: Ta (Shippo springs)

150.2 FX: Zuru zuru (dragging)

150.4 FX: Kaa (jewel shines)

151.1 FX: Kaaaahh… (jewel shining)

151.3 FX: Gohh (ball of light growing)

152.2 FX: Kaa (light shining from the jewel)

152.5 FX: Bari bari (ever-brighter light from soul)

153.3 FX: Ta ta ta… (running)

153.5 FX: Bari bari (flashing light)

155.3 FX: Dokun (Kagome's heart skips a beat)

155.4 FX: Dohhn (soul emerges)

156.1 FX: Gohhhhh… (soul emerging from Kagome)

156.2-4 FX: Gohhhhhh… (soul still emerging)

156.4 FX: Goh (little comet-like balls whoosh toward Kikyo)

157.1 FX: Dohhn (comet-like soul balls shoot into Kikyo)

158.3 FX: Su… (Kikyo sets down)

160.3 FX: Bari bari bari bari (crackling of magic)

160.5 FX: Za (Urasue slumps down)

162.1 FX: Kaa (painful light begins to glow from Kikyo's shoulder)

166.2 FX: Za za za za (running)

166.3 FX: Zuba (slash)

167.1 FX: Za (Kikyo lands face down in grass)

168.1 FX: Za (Inuyasha steps on Kikyo's hand)

171.5 FX: Gyu (grabbing and squeezing)

80.2 FX: Kiii… (fingernails scraping on metal)

80.3 FX: Kiiiiii… (more nails on metal)

80.4 FX: Shu (arrow whooshes)

80.5 FX: Zuba (Urasue dodges arrow)

81.2 FX: Ba ba ba (scythe slashes 3 times)

81.3 FX: Doh doh doh (little explosions from slashes)

81.4 FX: Dohh (boom of explosion)

82.1 FX: Zuba (scythe slash)

82.4 FX: Zuba (scythe slash)

82.6 FX: Zubo (leaping and landing)

83.2 FX: Gobo (scoops up ash jar)

84.3 FX: Goh (swishy sound as she flies off)

84.4 FX: Shurururu… (whoosh as she flies away)

85.1 FX: Ta ta ta… (running)

85.2 FX: Ta ta ta… (running)

85.4 FX: Shururu… (whoosh of arrow)

85.5 FX: Ka (arrow thunks into Inuyasha)

87.6 FX: Su— su— (soft snores)

89.1 FX: Baki (Kagome slaps Inuyasha)

89.4 FX: Choi choi (Inuyasha's stinging cheek)

90.2 FX: Goh (demon passing in front of moon)

93.4 FX: Pi—hyoro (bird call)

94.4 FX: Goh (demon flying)

94.5 FX: Shurururu… (demons swirling away)

96.2 FX: Dohn (Inuyasha blasts through roof)

97.1 FX: Dohn (explosion)

97.4 FX: Ta (jump)

97.6 FX: Hyun (shoots arrow)

98.1 FX: Shurururu… (arrow flies)

98.3 FX: Ka (Inuyasha is hit by arrow)

98.4 FX: Chari (necklace glints as it falls away)

102.4 FX: Pashi (Inuyasha takes hand and squeezes)

103.4 FX: Don (blow to chest)

104.1 FX: Doki doki (Kagome's heart pounding)

109.2 FX: Su— su— (soft snoring)

110.4 FX: Pashi (Inuyasha squeezes hand)

112.1 FX: Pachi pachi (fire crackling)

116.4 FX: Uru uru… (eyes become twinkly and sad)

117.2 FX: Ta (Inuyasha leaps)

117.3 FX: Toh (Inuyasha lands on bike)

117.6 FX: Shaka shaka (pedaling)

118.3 FX: Zuba (slash)

118.4 FX: Gara gara (rocks fall)

119.4 FX: Harari… (herb drifts down)

119.5 FX: Ka (herb lands)

119.6 FX: Shu shu… (light emanates from mummy-like object)

120.2 FX: Ga (blade thunks into clay)

120.3 FX: Pishi pishi… (clay cracks)

120.4 FX: Gara gara… (cracks open, clay falls away)

121.1 FX: Pa—n (magic sound)

121.2 FX: Yura… (Kikyo gets up)

124.1/2 FX: Gohhhhhh… (magic being cast)

124.4 FX: Gohhh… (more magic being cast)

125.1 FX: Toh (footfalls)

125.2 FX: Fura (Kikyo starting to fall over)

125.4 FX: Dosa (Kikyo hits ground)

48.2 FX: Ga (bares fangs)

49.3 FX: Zuru... (Inuyasha turns his body in the web)

49.5 FX: Ba (webs flying out of mouth)

50.1 FX: Ba ba ba ba (pow pow pow)

52.4 FX: Ka (big ball of light appears)

52.5 FX: Dosa (Kagome and Inuyasha hit the ground)

53.4 FX: Ba (pushes door closed)

53.6 FX: Ga (Tetsusaiga thunks into door)

54.1 FX: Bari bari bari (priest conjures magic strike)

54.2 FX: Shuuuu... (magic flies)

60.2 FX: Su—su— (Inuyasha's soft snores)

60.4/5 FX: Zu zu zu zu zu (thumps on ceiling, ceiling starts to crumble)

61.1 FX: Baki (ceiling starts to buckle)

61.2 FX: Baki (more buckling)

61.3 FX: Zu zu zu (more crumbling)

61.4 FX: Karan (sword falls to floor)

61.5 FX: Doka (ceiling collapses)

62.1 FX: Gara gara (debris falls from ceiling)

62.2 FX: Guoh (hand reaches out)

62.3 FX: Ga (grab)

62.6 FX: Bun (priest tosses Shippo)

63.1 FX: Kira (sparkle)

63.2 FX: Ba (priest snatches them abruptly)

63.3 FX: Dosa (sound of fall)

64.5 FX: Gin (blade glances off spider leg)

65.1 FX: Ga (spider grabs Nazuna)

65.5 FX: Gohh (Nazuna lets go of sword)

65.6 FX: Pashi (Inuyasha catches sword)

66.5 FX: Ba (priest lunges for Inuyasha)

67.4 FX: Dokun (Inuyasha starts to transform)

67.5 FX: Kaaaaa... (continues to transform)

68. 3 FX: Guo (whoosh of spider swinging Inuyasha up to sky to kill him)

68.5 FX: Ba (Inuyasha strikes)

69.2 FX: Shuuu... (blade transforms)

69.5 FX: Ka (sound of big lunge & huge, rending slice)

70.1 FX: Ba Ba (swoosh of slice)

70.2 FX: Dohn (spider blows up)

70.3 FX: Koron (jewel falls on ground)

## Chapter 14:
## Kikyo's Stolen Ashes

74.1 FX: Goh (something flying through air)

74.3 FX: Goh (swooshy flying sound)

75.4 FX: Bohh (demon thingy lands)

76.1 FX: Gohhh... (demon magic)

76.2 FX: Ka (eyes spring open)

76.3 FX: Da (placing arrow in bow)

76.4 FX: Shu (arrow flies)

77.1 FX: Zuba (demon dodges arrow)

77.4 FX: Ta (running)

77.5 FX: Shu ru ru... (arrow flying)

77.6 FX: Ta ta ta... (running)

78.1 FX: Zubah (slice)

78.3 FX: Ta ta ta... (running)

## Glossary of Sound Effects

Each entry includes: the location, indicated by page number and panel number (so 3.1 means page 3, panel number 1); the phonetic romanization of the original Japanese; and our English "translation"—we offer as close an English equivalent as we can.

29.4 FX: Buoh (webs flying)

29.5 FX: Ba (slash)

30.4 FX: Shururuu... (spider spitting webs out)

31.1 FX: Shururuu... (webs being spit out)

40.1 FX: Gasa (rustling in bushes)

42.2 FX: Ba (forcefully holds out sword)

43.2 FX: Goh (shards fall to floor)

43.3 FX: Pari—n (jewel shards scatter)

43.6 FX: Doga (board hits)

44.2 FX: Sa sa (Shippo crawling)

44.3 FX: Doka (priest snatches out at Shippo)

44.4 FX: Gohhh... (sucking up jewel shards)

45.1 FX: Ba (hand snakes out)

45.2 FX: Ga (hand grabs)

45.5 FX: Gui (sound of sticky stuff)

45.6 FX: Ba (Inuyasha throws off hand at throat)

46.1 FX: Shururuu... (web unspooling)

46.2 FX: Doh (impact of web stuff smacking into Inuyasha)

46.3 FX: Doka (smack)

46.4 FX: Gohh (Shippo's magic)

46.5 FX: Ba (swipe)

46.6 FX: Doga (smack that sends Shippo flying)

47.3 FX: Kaa (light)

**Chapter 13:**

**The Mystery of the New Moon and the Black-haired Inuyasha**

6.1 FX: Ki—n ko—n (school bell)

7.2 FX: Doh (sound of smacking into someone)

7.4 FX: Karan (bamboo thing lands on floor)

13.1 FX: Ba (slashes through web)

14.1 FX: Za (demon lunging toward her)

14.3 FX: Za (Inuyasha jumps up)

14.5 FX: Toh (Inuyasha touches down)

15.1 FX: Za (demon withdraws into bushes)

15.6 FX: Zaba (splash)

16.1 FX: Shu— (psssst — spraying)

17.5 FX: Su (Inuyasha abruptly uncrossing his arms and dropping them to his sides)

18.6 FX: Gishi (climbing up vine)

19.1 FX: Buchi (vine snaps)

19.2 FX: Dosa (falls in bushes)

20.3 FX: Ga (smack)

26.3 FX: Za (demon jumps)

27.4 FX: Chari (draws sword)

28.1 FX: Ta ta ta... (running)

29.2 FX: Doga (sword clangs)

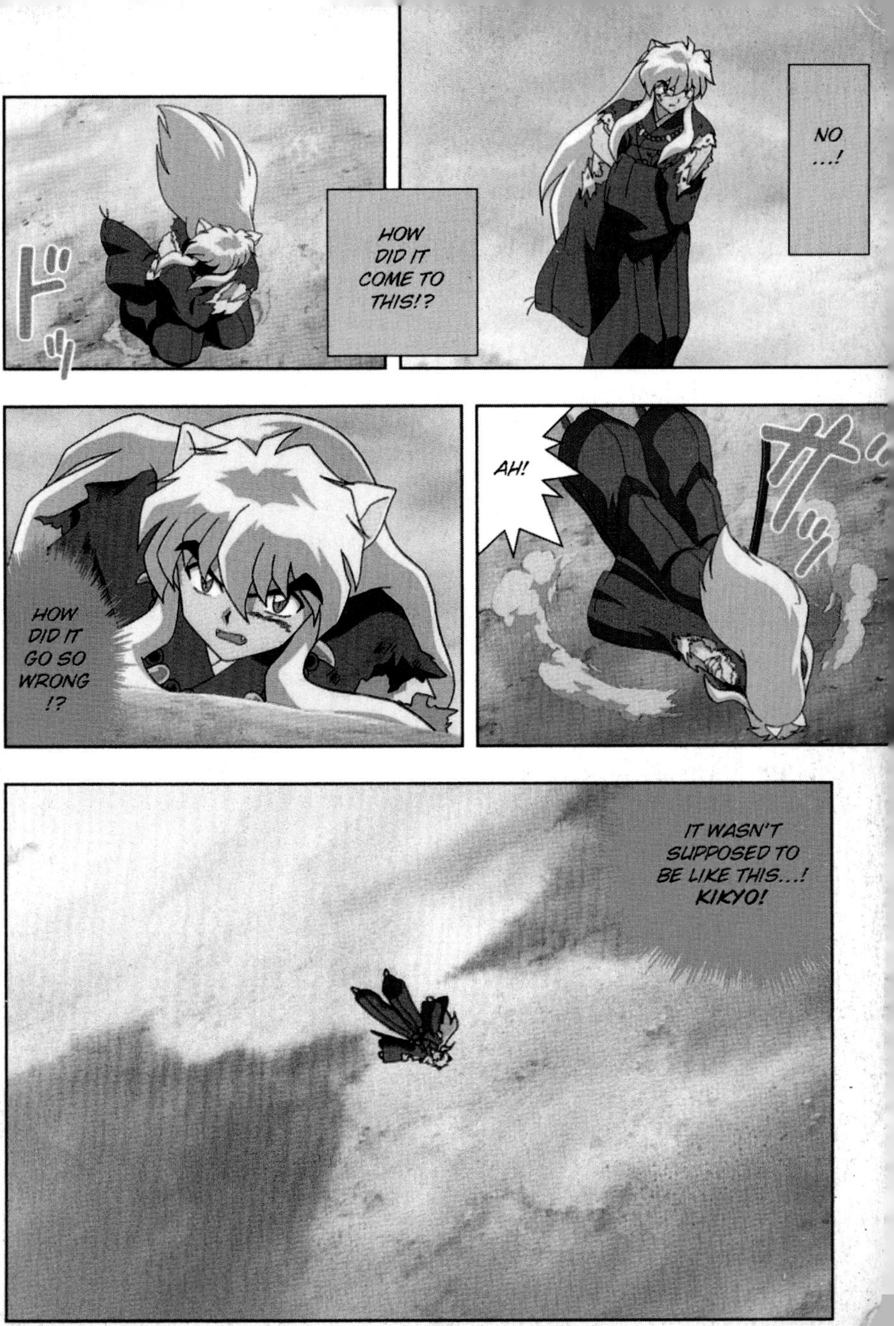
NO ...!
HOW DID IT COME TO THIS!?
ドッ
AH!
HOW DID IT GO SO WRONG !?
IT WASN'T SUPPOSED TO BE LIKE THIS...! KIKYO!

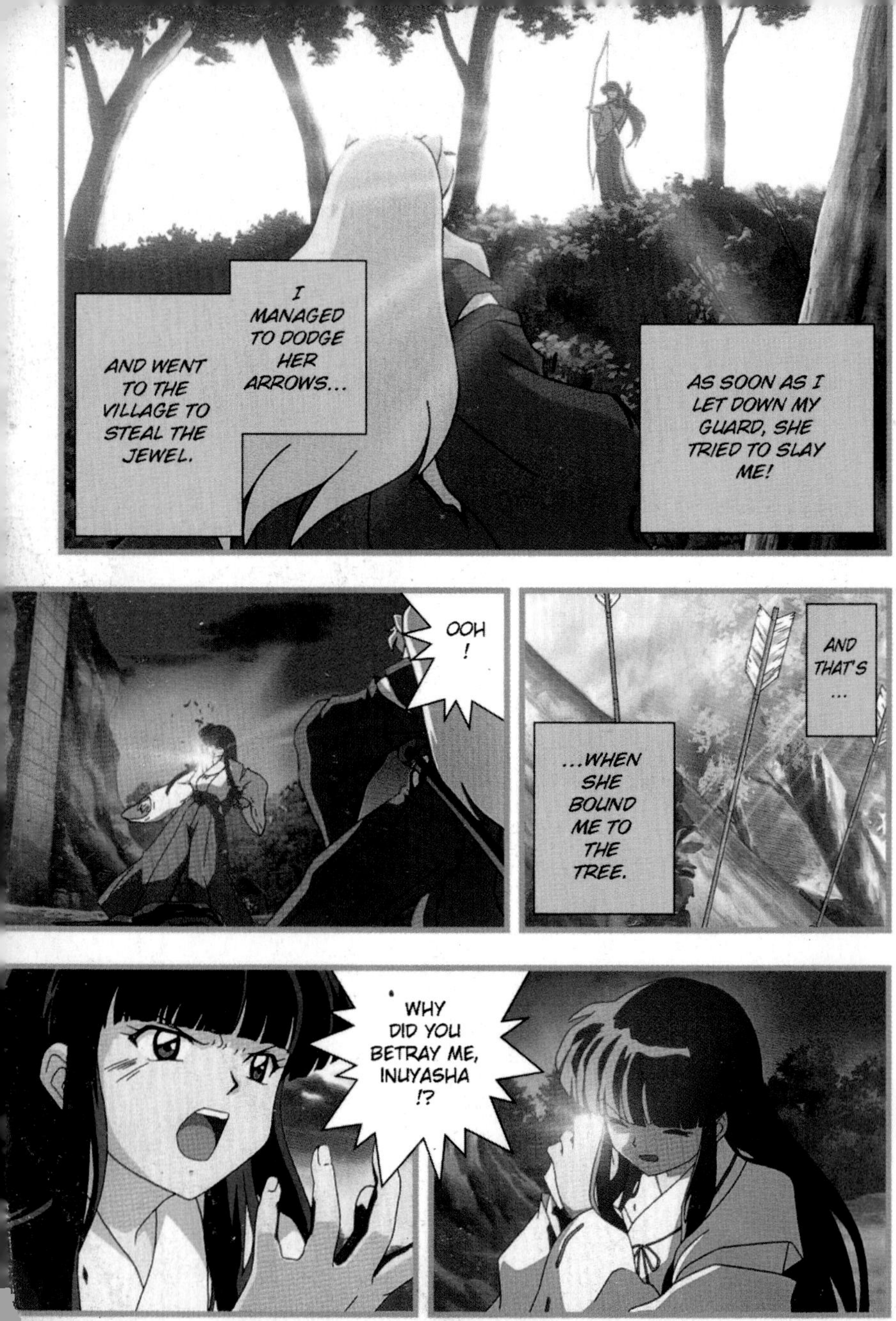
AS SOON AS I LET DOWN MY GUARD, SHE TRIED TO SLAY ME!
I MANAGED TO DODGE HER ARROWS...
AND WENT TO THE VILLAGE TO STEAL THE JEWEL.
AND THAT'S...
...WHEN SHE BOUND ME TO THE TREE.
OOH!
WHY DID YOU BETRAY ME, INUYASHA!?

# Your Favorite Rumiko Takahashi Titles...Now Available From VIZ!

Complete your collection with these Takahashi anime and manga classics!

Get yours today!

www.viz.com